The Economic Theory of Costs

The theory of costs is a cornerstone of economic thinking, and figures crucially in the study of human action and society. From the first day of a principles-level course to the most advanced academic literature, costs play a vital role in virtually all behaviors and economic outcomes. How we make choices, why we trade, and how we build institutions and social orders are all problems that can be explained in light of the costs we face.

This volume explores, develops, and critiques the rich literature on costs, examining some of the many ways cost remains relevant in economic theory and practice. The book especially studies costs from the perspective of the Austrian or "causal-realist" approach to economics. The chapters integrate the history of economic thought with contemporary research, finding valuable crossroads between numerous traditions in economics. They examine the role of costs in theories of choice and opportunity costs; demand and income effects; production and distribution; risk and interest rates; uncertainty and production; monopsony; Post-Keynesianism; transaction costs; socialism and management; and social entrepreneurship.

Together, these papers represent an update and restatement of a central element in the economic way of thinking. Each chapter reveals how the Austrian, causal-realist approach to costs can be used to solve an important problem or debate in economics. These chapters are not only useful for students learning these concepts for the first time: they are also valuable for researchers seeking to understand the unique Austrian perspective and those who want to apply it to new problems.

Matthew McCaffrey is Assistant Professor of Enterprise in the Alliance Manchester Business School, University of Manchester, UK. His research focuses on entrepreneurial decision making, the role of entrepreneurship in social and economic development, and the institutional conditions in which enterprise thrives.

Routledge Frontiers of Political Economy

For a full list of titles in this series please visit www.routledge.com/books/series/SE0345

228 The Social Construction of Rationality
Policy Debates and the Power of Good Reasons
Onno Bouwmeester

229 Varieties of Alternative Economic Systems
Practical Utopias for an Age of Global Crisis and Austerity
Edited by Richard Westra, Robert Albritton and Seongjin Jeong

230 Money as a Social Institution
The Institutional Development of Capitalism
Ann E. Davis

231 Remaking Market Society
A Critique of Social Theory and Political Economy in Neoliberal Times
Antonino Palumbo and Alan Scott

232 Political Economy as Natural Theology
Smith, Malthus and their Followers
Paul Oslington

233 Sharing Economies in Times of Crisis
Practices, Politics and Possibilities
Edited by Anthony Ince and Sarah Marie Hall

234 Philosophy in the Time of Economic Crisis
Pragmatism and Economy
Edited by Kenneth W. Stikkers and Krzysztof Piotr Skowroński

235 Public Policy and the Neo-Weberian State
Edited by Stanisław Mazur and Piotr Kopyciński

236 The Economic Theory of Costs
Foundations and New Directions
Edited by Matthew McCaffrey

The Economic Theory of Costs

Foundations and New Directions

Edited by Matthew McCaffrey

Routledge
Taylor & Francis Group
LONDON AND NEW YORK

First published 2018 by Routledge

2 Park Square, Milton Park, Abingdon, Oxfordshire OX14 4RN
52 Vanderbilt Avenue, New York, NY 10017

Routledge is an imprint of the Taylor & Francis Group, an informa business

First issued in paperback 2019

British Library Cataloguing-in-Publication Data
A catalogue record for this book is available from the British Library

Library of Congress Cataloging-in-Publication Data
A catalog record for this book has been requested

ISBN: 978-1-138-67093-8 (hbk)
ISBN: 978-0-367-32173-4 (pbk)

Typeset in Times New Roman
by Apex CoVantage, LLC

Contents

List of figures vii
List of tables ix
List of contributors xi
Acknowledgements xiii

Introduction: the economic theory of costs in perspective **1**
MATTHEW McCAFFREY

PART 1
Cost and choice 9

1 Contemporary debates on opportunity cost theory and pedagogy **11**
JONATHAN NEWMAN

2 The "income effect" in causal-realist price theory **27**
JOSEPH T. SALERNO

PART 2
The evolution of causal-realist production theory 49

3 From Marshallian partial equilibrium to Austrian general equilibrium: the evolution of Rothbard's production theory **51**
PATRICK NEWMAN

4 *Man, economy, and state*, original chapter 5: producer's activity **73**
MURRAY N. ROTHBARD

PART 3
Risk, uncertainty, and cost 131

5 The myth of the risk premium **133**
JÖRG GUIDO HÜLSMANN

6 Time and the theory of cost **147**
JEFFREY M. HERBENER

PART 4
Causal-realist price theory: debate and synthesis 167

7 Monopsony theory revisited **169**
XAVIER MÉRA

8 Costs and pricing: an Austro-Post-Keynesian synthesis? **191**
MATEUSZ MACHAJ

PART 5
Economic organization, entrepreneurship, and the firm 205

9 Austrian economics and transaction cost economics: notes on a doubtful compatibility **207**
MIHAI-VLADIMIR TOPAN

10 Management is what's wrong with socialism: cost at the expense of value **225**
PER L. BYLUND

11 Economic calculation and the limits of social entrepreneurship **243**
MATTHEW McCAFFREY

Index 265

Figures

2.1	Individual labor supply curve	39
2.2	Individual demand curve for money assets in terms of labor	40
2.3	Reciprocal demand curve for money assets in terms of labor	41
3.1	Market demand curve and the demand curve faced by an individual firm	57
3.2	Optimal production with various constant outlay and product curves	60
3.3	Derivation of a firm's demand curve for a factor of production	61
3.4	Graphical illustration of money revenue and outlay from production of Product P	65
4.1	Graphical illustration of Case (b1)	80
4.2	Graphical illustration of Case (c)	82
4.3	Constant outlay curves with given factor prices	98
4.4	Production of output with various factor combinations	99
4.5	Constant product curves with various factor combinations	100
4.6	Constant outlay and constant product curves	102
4.7	Possible production of output with given constant outlay	102
4.8	Optimal production with various constant outlay and product curves	104
4.9	Possible production of output with constant money outlay	105
4.10	Maximum production of output at various money outlays	106
4.11	Product outlay curve	106
4.12	Total product outlay curve	107
4.13	Graphical illustration of production of Product P for various money outlays	112
4.14	Graphical illustration of money revenue and outlay from production of Product P	112
4.15	Final supply curve of the producer	125
6.1	Short-run costs of production	149
6.2	Marginal unit of output in production	151
6.3	Long-run costs of production	153
6.4	Immediate-run price of a good	154
6.5	Immediate-run price of a good	155

6.6 Immediate-run price of a factor of production 156
6.7 Production costs and the interest rate in the ERE 157
6.8 Production costs with different techniques in the ERE 158
6.9 Falling demand and cost structure in the FSR 159
6.10 Time – sequence and uncertainty 160
6.11 Immediate-run price of a good under uncertainty 161
6.12 Immediate-run price of a factor of production under uncertainty 163
6.13 Production decisions by entrepreneurs under uncertainty 164

Tables

2.1	Individual labor supply schedule	39
2.2	Individual demand for money assets in terms of labor	40
4.1	Jones' money returns	77
4.2	Factor combinations for the production of Good A	78
4.3	Factor combinations and output for the production of Good A	78
4.4	Gross revenue in the production of Good A, Case (a)	79
4.5	Gross revenue in the production of Good A, Case (b1)	79
4.6	Gross revenue in the production of Good A, Case (b2)	79
4.7	Gross revenue in the production of Good A, Case (c)	82
4.8	Extended factor combinations and output for the production of Good A	91
4.9	Factor combinations for constant output	92
4.10	Production costs for constant output	93
4.11	Smith's production decisions for Product P	110
4.12	Smith's money returns for various money outlays	111
4.13	Smith's money returns for various outlays, continued	117
4.14	Smith's money returns for various outlays, total	118
4.15	Smith's money outlays for producing Products P, Q, and R	122
4.16	Maximum net income of Smith for various investment decisions	123
4.17	Smith's money returns for various investment decisions	123
11.1	Types of entrepreneurship by income and organizational method	251

Contributors

Per L. Bylund is Assistant Professor of Entrepreneurship and Records-Johnston Professor of Free Enterprise in the School of Entrepreneurship at Oklahoma State University. He is the author of two books, *The Problem of Production: A New Theory of the Firm* (Routledge, 2016) and *The Seen, the Unseen, and the Unrealized: How Regulations Affect Our Everyday Lives* (Lexington, 2016). His areas of research are entrepreneurship, strategic management, and economic organization.

Jeffrey M. Herbener is Chairman of the Department and Professor of Economics at Grove City College. He serves as Associate Editor of the *Quarterly Journal of Austrian Economics* and is a Senior Fellow of the Ludwig von Mises Institute.

Jörg Guido Hülsmann is Professor of Economics at the University of Angers, a Senior Fellow of the Ludwig von Mises Institute, and a member of the European Academy of Sciences and Arts. He is the author of *Krise der Inflationskultur* (2013), *The Ethics of Money Production* (2008), and five other books. He has also edited *The Theory of Money and Fiduciary Media* (2012) and five other books. His writings have been translated into twenty languages. His current research focuses on the political economy of financial markets, and on monetary theory.

Mateusz Machaj is an Assistant Professor at the Institute of Economic Sciences at the University of Wroclaw, and a Researcher at the Faculty of Social and Economic Studies, Jan Evangelista Purkyně University in Ústí nad Labem.

Xavier Méra holds a PhD in Economics from the University of Angers, France. He is a Teaching and Research Assistant at Université Rennes 2 and an Associated Scholar of the Ludwig von Mises Institute.

Matthew McCaffrey is Assistant Professor of Enterprise in the Alliance Manchester Business School at the University of Manchester. His research focuses on entrepreneurial decision making, the role of entrepreneurship in social and economic development, and the institutional conditions in which enterprise thrives.

Jonathan Newman received his PhD in Economics from Auburn University in 2016. He is a Fellow of the Ludwig von Mises Institute and the Online Course Manager for the Foundation for Economic Education. He currently teaches economics at Auburn University.

Patrick Newman is an Assistant Professor of Economics at Florida Southern College.

Murray N. Rothbard (1926–1995) was a leading economist of the Austrian school and the author of dozens of books and scholarly research articles. His treatise on economic principles, *Man, Economy, and State*, played a major role in the revival of the Austrian tradition in the United States.

Joseph T. Salerno is Professor of Economics at Pace University and Academic Vice President of the Ludwig von Mises Institute. He is the Editor of the *Quarterly Journal of Austrian Economics* and the author of *Money: Sound and Unsound* (2010) as well as of numerous articles in peer-reviewed economics journals and scholarly books.

Mihai-Vladimir Topan is Associate Professor in the Department of International Business and Economics at the Bucharest University of Economic Studies. He is also President of the Ludwig von Mises Institute Romania and Founder of the Academia Privată.

Acknowledgements

Chapter 1: Contemporary debates on opportunity cost theory and pedagogy
Jonathan Newman
I appreciate the discussions with the 2016 Mises Institute Research Fellows on this topic. I would also like to thank Randy Beard, Joseph Salerno, and Michael Stern for discussing opportunity costs and other esoteric economic riddles with me. Matthew McCaffrey is an excellent editor and I thank him for his great advice and his patience. Of course, I take full responsibility for any remaining errors.

Chapter 3: From Marshallian partial equilibrium to Austrian general equilibrium: the evolution of Rothbard's production theory
Patrick Newman
The author would like to thank Peter Boettke, Peter Klein, Matthew McCaffrey, Ennio Piano, Joseph Salerno, and an anonymous referee for helpful comments. In addition, he thanks the Ludwig von Mises Institute for the use of the Murray N. Rothbard archives, as well as Barbara Pickard for archival assistance. Any remaining errors are the author's.

Chapter 5: The myth of the risk premium
Jörg Guido Hülsmann
Comments from Mr Maximilien Lambert and Mr Tom Cleverly are gratefully acknowledged.

Chapter 7: Monopsony theory revisited
Xavier Méra
The author wishes to thank Renaud Fillieule, Guido Hülsmann, Tudor Smirna, and Georges Lane for their comments on an earlier version of this chapter. Any remaining errors are the author's.

Chapter 9: Austrian economics and transaction cost economics: notes on a doubtful compatibility
Mihai-Vladimir Topan
The author would like to thank Radu Muşetescu, with whom he has discussed transaction cost economics *ad nauseam*. Any remaining errors are the author's.

Chapter 11: Economic calculation and the limits of social entrepreneurship
Matthew McCaffrey
The author would like to thank Carmen-Elena Dorobăţ and Patrick Newman for helpful comments on the earlier drafts of this chapter. Any remaining errors are the author's.

Introduction

The economic theory of costs in perspective

Matthew McCaffrey

At first glance, the "economic theory of costs" seems like a mundane topic, even for the dismal science. The term does not call to mind fashionable research trends in economics, nor does it clearly hint at pressing problems in the global economy. In fact, if anything, questions about "the theory of costs" recall the years of "high theory" in the early twentieth century – and rightly so. At that time, economics was still carving out its niche in the social sciences, and therefore welcomed deep and wide-ranging discussion of its fundamental problems. It was thus a very different discipline from the narrowly empirical and formal profession it has become, in which "big" questions, and earlier chapters in the history of thought in general, are mostly irrelevant. However, although they represent a road not taken (or, rather, a road discontinued), the years of high theory are in many ways exemplary. They witnessed many vigorous exchanges of ideas between major economists, debates that laid foundations for modern work that have only partly been exploited.

For reasons that will become clear, many of the vital problems of this era, and of economics in general, can be grouped under the heading "the economic theory of costs." The present book draws together several new and valuable contributions to this literature. Before outlining its contents, however, I would like to explain further what is meant by "the economic theory of costs," as well as clarify how the topic fits within economics in general, and why it is worth studying. Doing so will also help to describe the scope and purpose of the individual chapters, and of the collection as a whole.

Despite appearances, the theory of costs is neither an obscure nor an uninteresting strand of economic research. In fact, it is a cornerstone of economic thinking that can profoundly influence fundamental theory, its countless modern branches and applications, and even other social sciences and management disciplines. Far from being a relic of a forgotten era, then, the study of costs lies at the center of a vibrant and ongoing research agenda in and around all fields of human action and social relations.

The concept of cost has played a prominent role in economics for more than two centuries. Most importantly, in the classical era, costs – specifically, the long-run costs of production – were often given pride of place as the ultimate explanation prices (Klein, 2007, p. 8; Buchanan, 1969, pp. 1–7). They were thus inextricable from any discussion of the essential theorems of economics. Nevertheless, the exact relevance of costs for value and prices was fiercely debated, resulting eventually in the overturn of the classical approach by the marginalist revolution that began in 1871. This sea change in economics thoroughly revised the theory of costs. Today, costs remain inextricable from the theory of value, but for the opposite reason than the one imagined by the classical economists.

The rise of marginalism is mainly associated with the work of Carl Menger, William Stanley Jevons, and Léon Walras. However, it was Menger who most fully realized the potential of the subjective theory of value that lies at the heart of marginalism (Menger, 2007 [1871]). Like his contemporaries, Menger helped revolutionize the theory of cost by explaining that the value of any good is ultimately determined by its marginal utility to consumers. Yet he went a step further in his explanation of the pricing process by showing that costs of production are not an independent cause of value; on the contrary, the prices of the factors of production (which together form the costs of production) are determined by the value consumers assign to the finished goods the factors produce. The subjective valuations of consumers thus stand in a causal relation to the objective prices that appear on real-world markets (Salerno, 1999a).

In elaborating this theory, Menger thus identified two traits of sound economic reasoning: first, it seeks to understand economic phenomena – e.g. prices, wages, and interest rates – *as they appear in the real world*, and second, it investigates *causal* relationships between these phenomena. These characteristics have led some economists to describe Menger's unique approach as "causal-realist." Menger's ideas are usually associated with the geographical Austrian school, but his writings inspired many economists outside the narrow confines of Vienna, including Philip Wicksteed, Lionel Robbins, John Bates Clark, Frank A. Fetter, and Herbert J. Davenport, each of whom contributed to the larger Mengerian, Austrian, causal-realist tradition (Salerno, 1999a, 1999b; Klein, 2008).

Menger's insights into value and price were most notably developed by Eugen von Böhm-Bawerk and Friedrich von Wieser. Wieser is remembered mostly for elaborating the opportunity cost concept, but Böhm-Bawerk also played a formative part in early Austrian research, much of which involved clarifying and defending Menger's subjectivist approach to value theory (e.g. Böhm-Bawerk, 1962a [1891a], 1962b [1894], 2002 [1892]). In particular, Böhm-Bawerk repeatedly debated the role of costs in determining prices, and one of the crowning achievements of early Austrian economics was to show, contra Marshall and the classicals, that all prices are ultimately determined by subjective values, rather than being determined by consumer values on the demand side and costs on the supply side (Böhm-Bawerk, 1962b [1894]). Unlike value, which is a starting point of economic theory, cost is a dependent concept. As Böhm-Bawerk put it,

> The question of the relation of cost to value is properly only a concrete form of a much more general question – the question of the regular relations

> between the values of such goods as in causal interdependence contribute to one and the same utility for our well-being.
>
> (Böhm-Bawerk, 1962a, p. 14)

Nevertheless, costs are connected in various ways to virtually every fundamental concept in economics, including value, choice, utility, exchange, money, profit, loss, and entrepreneurship (cf. for example, Böhm-Bawerk, 1962a, p. 13). Böhm-Bawerk even remarked that in regard to "the interaction of price, value and costs . . . it is in my opinion no exaggeration to state that to understand their connection is to understand a good half of economics" (Böhm-Bawerk, 1959, p. 249).

The present book offers a path toward the understanding to which Böhm-Bawerk alluded. Exploring the theory of costs was instrumental in the early development of Menger's subjective value theory, and it is no less important for contemporary economists who hope to advance Menger's causal-realist approach through their own work. That is the purpose of this collection: to showcase a variety of research strands within the modern Mengerian tradition that relate in some way to the theory of cost. The organization of the topics follows a logical progression, beginning from the fundamental concept of choice – where the idea of cost also begins – and building up to discussions of pricing, production, economic organization, and comparative economic systems.

In Chapter 1, Jonathan Newman surveys a recent controversy over the idea of opportunity cost. Contemporary mainstream economists are divided about the exact meaning of this vital concept, as well as the question of how it should be taught to students. In particular, competing definitions of opportunity costs have sown confusion in both economic research and teaching. Newman explains that this confusion can be resolved by appealing to the thoroughly subjectivist view of opportunity cost developed in the causal-realist tradition. If we recognize that opportunity costs refer to a subjective and ordinal preference ranking, the tension between different views of opportunity cost evaporates. However, some critics close to the Austrian school have disputed whether the idea of opportunity cost is valuable at all. Newman also shows why these views are mistaken, and he defends the continued use of opportunity cost as a foundational concept in economics. Specifically, he argues that criticisms of opportunity cost depend on assuming away the forward-looking nature of action and cost and also on falsely conflating different kinds of choices that actors make.

The concepts of action, preference, and choice lead naturally to a discussion of the formation of individual demand curves. In Chapter 2, Joseph Salerno outlines a causal-realist method for deriving the key principles of demand analysis using the individual's ordinal scale of values. Value scales provide the basis for deriving the law of marginal utility – which requires the assumption of the constancy of money's purchasing power – and in turn allow us to deduce individual demand curves. Unlike mainstream economic theory, the demand curve in causal-realist analysis is a temporal construct that refers to the individual's personal economic situation at the moment of his purchases. This implies that income, as a flow of money, has no direct role in determining the demand curve, which is based solely on the individual's value scale (a ranking of existing stocks of goods *and* money). As a result, movements along the demand curve do not produce income effects, which are a theoretical illusion. However, the causal-realist approach does shed new light on the theory of substitution effects. That is, focusing on value scales reveals that all goods are at least partial substitutes for each other. In fact, substitution is a necessary relationship that prevails among all goods. Finally, Salerno argues that, even without the concept of the income effect, the causal-realist approach still provides an explanation for the existence of a backward-bending labor supply curve.

The causal-realist approach extends beyond the analysis of individual consumer behavior, however. In Chapter 3, Patrick Newman outlines some major differences between the causal-realist and mainstream views of production theory. His discussion relies on a proto-chapter of Murray Rothbard's treatise *Man, Economy, and State*, which appears as Chapter 4 of this book. As Newman explains, Rothbard's early work relied on many conventional mainstream economic assumptions and concepts in order to explain producer's activity, including perfect competition and the isolated firm. Newman compares Rothbard's earlier chapter with his published work in order to chart the evolution of his thinking on these vital economic topics. In particular, he shows that after drafting the original production theory that appears in Chapter 4, Rothbard became increasingly aware of its theoretical shortcomings. He became especially critical of the Marshallian partial-equilibrium analysis he initially embraced. As a result, Rothbard abandoned this analytical apparatus, choosing instead to use the works of earlier writers in the causal-realist tradition to build a highly original "Austrian general equilibrium" production theory that was eventually included in the final version of *Man, Economy, and State*. However, although he eventually took a very different path in his theorizing, Rothbard's proto-chapter – and Newman's comparative study of it – helps tease out several points of contrast between the causal-realist and mainstream views of production, entrepreneurship, and the firm.

To take one example, a truly realist approach to economic theory cannot rely excessively on equilibrium constructs that abstract from the passage of time, and therefore assume away the problems of risk and uncertainty. In Chapter 5, Jörg Guido Hülsmann revisits the theory of risk and questions the current role that risk plays in economics, especially in the theory (and real-world formation) of interest rates. He rejects the view that interest rates can be viewed as the arithmetic sum of several separate, identifiable components. In contrast to this view, he argues that in a free-market setting, all known risks either are accounted for through entrepreneurial judgment, or are irrelevant to acting individuals. As a result, observable interest rates cannot contain a risk premium; instead, differences in prices that appear to reflect compensation for increased risk are actually nothing more than reflections of different subjective evaluations of available investment opportunities.

Importantly, the concept of uncertainty is far more challenging for economic analysis than risk. In Chapter 6, Jeffrey Herbener uses this fact as a starting point for integrating the element of time into causal-realist production theory. Time brings with it the problem of uncertainty, which in turn has a profound influence on the production process. In particular, uncertainty implies that capitalist-entrepreneurs must speculate about the future discounted marginal revenue products of the factors they employ. Their anticipations, and the interaction of the anticipations of all entrepreneurs in the market, cause the costs of production to conform to output prices regardless of the technical relationships that exist in production. The spectrum of quality in entrepreneurial foresight determines the speed and accuracy of this process, and also explains the profits earned by entrepreneurs during the adjustment, profits that are missed by their less-astute competitors.

As explained above, the theory of costs is inextricable from the body of price theory, which in turn provides the basis for analyzing production in both free and hampered market economies. In Chapter 7, Xavier Méra examines the latter case, specifically, the problem of monopsony. Méra explains that although early causal-realist writings hinted at the possibility of monopsony, later writers like Mises and Rothbard largely dismissed the idea as unimportant. The reason is that both older and newer monopsony theories fail to adequately distinguish between monopsonistic and competitive prices. However, Méra argues that in their writings on monopoly the Austrian critics actually laid the foundation for a theory of "monopoly price-gap" in which monopsony and monopoly prices are part of the same phenomenon, namely, the hampered market economy.

Austrians are not alone in their criticisms of the mainstream economic approach to costs. In Chapter 8, Mateusz Machaj surveys some common ground between Austrian and Post-Keynesian theories of price formation. Like Austrians, Post-Keynesians are critical of the conventional view that firms operate in practice by equalizing marginal costs and marginal benefits. A growing body of empirical research suggests that real-world managers do not make decisions according to this rule. Machaj argues that this "business practice" critique is nothing more than an alternate way of expressing how the Austrian theory of "imputation" plays out within the firm. This common ground means that some Post-Keynesian arguments can strengthen Austrian critiques of mainstream price theory.

However, not all strands of economic thought are compatible with the causal-realist approach. Mihai-Vladimir Topan argues in Chapter 9 that the transaction costs paradigm is one such. He examines the transaction costs literature, especially the work of Ronald Coase, in light of the two fields in which it is most successful: the economic analysis of property rights, and the theory of the firm. According to Topan, neither application of transaction costs is successful. The reason is that the concept of transaction costs is both vague and based on a faulty distinction between production and exchange, or between the firm and the market. As a result, transaction costs are at best helpful as heuristic devices in those limited contexts where they can be defined clearly and unambiguously.

Topan's critique of the transaction costs theory of the firm leads logically to the question of economic organization. In this field, causal-realist price theory provides a bridge between the theory of the firm and the study of comparative economic systems. Specifically, Mises's theory of economic calculation can be used to explain the unhampered market economy and the firms within it as well as economic conditions under a system of socialist central planning. Mises's famous critique of socialism showed decisively that without genuine market prices based on private property and the entrepreneurial division of labor, it is impossible for central planners to accurately appraise the costs of their decisions, and therefore to allocate resources to their most urgent uses (Mises, 1990).

In Chapter 10, Per Bylund returns to Mises's argument and elaborates one of its vital distinctions: the difference between entrepreneurs and managers. Entrepreneurs, in their capacity as owners and decision makers, bear the uncertainty of investing in the market in order to create value. Managers, on the other hand, are limited to adjusting the technological conditions of production in order to ensure the physical efficiency of production methods that have already been tried and tested by entrepreneurs. The implication is that although unhampered market economies will tend toward constant improvement in consumer welfare, socialist societies are managerial and lack the ability to revolutionize production in an innovative, entrepreneurial way. Consequently, they will be at best static and at worst – and more likely – will persistently decline in terms of their ability to improve consumer welfare.

The problem of economic calculation also applies outside the extremes of purely for-profit enterprise and socialist central planning: calculation is also a vital lens through which to view alternative forms of economic organization in the market economy. In Chapter 11, Matthew McCaffrey examines one such example: the growing field of social entrepreneurship. Although it attracts major interest in management studies, social entrepreneurship has received scant attention from economists. This chapter resolves this oversight by placing the theory of social entrepreneurship on an economic foundation. McCaffrey outlines the economic meaning of social behavior and shows that conventional market entrepreneurship is deeply social, while at the same time, social ventures are inevitably bound up with some kind of profit motive. This implies that the line between social and conventional entrepreneurship is not as clear as is sometimes thought. Importantly, social enterprises must engage in economic calculation if they want to survive in competitive markets. This means they must rely on external prices for the goods and services they produce, as without them they cannot estimate the social opportunity costs of their decisions.

It is not an accident that this book concludes with discussions of economic calculation; in many ways, Mises's contributions in this field unify and complete the work begun by Menger, Böhm-Bawerk, and many others who attempted to explain the role of costs in individual action and in the social order. The following chapters each attempt to develop a part of the systematic body of economic theory built by these economists over the course of more than a century. By doing so, they show clearly that the theory of costs in the causal-realist tradition is a valuable and indeed a vital theoretical framework for understanding a wide range of economic problems old and new. The tradition established by Menger thus continues to grow and thrive through these and many other published works. However, only a tiny portion of all potentially relevant writings can be discussed in these pages: due to the limitations involved in assembling a collection such as this, and the enormous scope of the theory of cost, some important topics have fallen by the wayside. These include the law of comparative advantage and the theory of externalities, as well as studies of specific works like James Buchanan's *Cost and Choice* (1969) and the many important papers included in his collection *L.S.E. Essays on Cost* (1981 [1973]). These may seem like unforgivable omissions; however, we can satisfy ourselves with the knowledge that these works already receive attention from scholars in and around the Mengerian tradition, and hope that this trend continues.

The chapters included here offer an antidote to some of the worries plaguing mainstream economic thought. The causal-realist approach they embody is especially vital at a time when the economics profession is under attack for its lack of realism and inability to address urgent problems at all levels of the economy, and even to explain them to people outside its ranks. Fortunately, alternative frameworks can and do encourage progress toward addressing each of these criticisms, and their current success in doing so is a cause for optimism. To take only one example, it is notable that in addition to their academic responsibilities, many of the contributors to this book are also founders or leaders of thriving private organizations that take the public teaching of economics as their mission, a task in which mainstream economics has little interest. In any case, it is our hope that this collection will further develop research and teaching in the Austrian, causal-realist tradition, its engagement with other approaches to economics, and its relevance for other disciplines.

Matthew McCaffrey
University of Manchester
May, 2017

References

Böhm-Bawerk, Eugen von. 1959. *Positive Theory of Capital*. Trans. George D. Huncke and Hans F. Sennholz. South Holland, IL: Libertarian Press.

———. 1962a [1891]. "The Austrian Economists." In *Shorter Classics of Böhm-Bawerk*. South Holland, IL: Libertarian Press, pp. 1–24.

———. 1962b [1894]. "The Ultimate Standard of Value." In *Shorter Classics of Böhm-Bawerk*. South Holland, IL: Libertarian Press, pp. 303–370.

———. 2002 [1892]. "Value, Cost, and Marginal Utility." *Quarterly Journal of Austrian Economics* 5 (3): 37–79.

Buchanan, J. M. 1969. *Cost and Choice: An Inquiry in Economic Theory*. Chicago: University of Chicago Press.

———. 1981 [1973]. *L.S.E. Essays on Cost*. New York: New York University Press.

Klein, Peter G. 2007. "Foreword." In *Principles of Economics*. Auburn, AL: Ludwig von Mises Institute, pp. 7–10.

———. 2008. "The Mundane Economics of the Austrian School." *Quarterly Journal of Austrian Economics* 11 (3–4): 165–187.

Menger, Carl. 2007 [1871]. *Principles of Economics*. Auburn, AL: Ludwig von Mises Institute.

Mises, Ludwig von. 1990. *Economic Calculation in the Socialist Commonwealth*. Auburn, AL: Ludwig von Mises Institute.

Salerno, Joseph T. 1999a. "Carl Menger: The Founder of the Austrian School." In *Fifteen Great Austrian Economists*. Ed. Randall G. Holcombe. Auburn, AL: Ludwig von Mises Institute, pp. 71–100.

———. 1999b. "The Place of Mises's Human Action in the Development of Modern Economic Thought." *Quarterly Journal of Austrian Economics* 2 (1): 35–65.

Part 1

Cost and choice

1 Contemporary debates on opportunity cost theory and pedagogy

Jonathan Newman

Introduction

Confusion over the opportunity cost concept came to a head in the economics profession with the publication of Ferraro and Taylor's (2005) finding that only 21.6% of economists could correctly answer an introductory-level question on opportunity cost. Their study was based on a sample of PhD holders and PhD students at an academic conference. The ensuing debate over the definition and exposition of opportunity cost continues even today, including through a special symposium on opportunity cost in the *Journal of Economic Education* (2016).

In the present chapter, we compare the ways the opportunity cost concept is presented in mainstream and Austrian principles textbooks. We then review the lines of argument in the instructive *Journal of Economic Education* symposium, which is taken as representative of broader debate in the economics profession. We show that the causal-realist ordinal and subjective conception of opportunity cost provides the clarity and consistency the symposium participants desire. Moreover, the "value specification" of opportunity cost they reject in favor of a quantity specification is not a true value specification, but another quantity specification. Finally, we address recent debate in Austrian literature on opportunity costs. The aim of these discussions is twofold: (1) to show that the causal-realist theory of opportunity cost does not suffer from the problems now being exposed in the mainstream, and (2) to critique alternative views presented in the mainstream, as well as some eclectic views close to Austrian literature.

Opportunity cost defined

A) Causal-realist theory

The opportunity cost concept is fundamental in economics, and it is one of the first principles taught in introductory-level economics courses. The starting point for the entire edifice of economic theory is human action.

[1] Individuals choose how scarce resources are to be used as means toward the attainment of ends. All action aims at attaining higher-valued ends by forsaking lower-valued ends because the use of means toward one end implies that other

ends must be forgone (Menger, 2007, p. 95). The opportunity cost of any action, then, is the value of the highest-ranked end forgone because of the action.[2] As such, the opportunity cost concept is inseparable from the concepts of value and action. The ordinality and subjectivity of preferences applies to both value and cost. Just as value is appraised in action ex ante, so are costs.

Since value and cost only exist in human action, all costs are opportunity costs.[3] Accountants and economists may refer to different types of costs, like operating costs or transaction costs, but these are only convenient terms for certain kinds of opportunity costs, and they only make sense in view of a proper understanding of opportunity costs. So-called transaction costs, for example, are ends an actor might forgo just to participate in a transaction. Transaction costs are not weighed in a categorically different way in action, because individuals ultimately are exchanging a less desired state of the world for a preferred state of the world. Actors consider everything they deem relevant, including "transaction costs," and finally, a choice is made.

When an actor chooses, he does not simply select one good over others, but one *end* over other ends. More appropriately, when he makes a choice, the actor exchanges one state of the world for another.[4] Rothbard (2009) explains that these states of the world are ranked on the actor's scale of preferences:

> Therefore, *all action involves exchange* – an exchange of one state of affairs, X, for Y, which the actor anticipates will be a more satisfactory one (and therefore higher on his value scale). If his expectation turns out to be correct, the value of Y on his preference scale will be higher than the value of X, and he has made a *net gain* in his state of satisfaction or utility.
>
> (p. 20, emphasis in original)

Each state of the world includes specific consequences that extend beyond the mere immediate and direct satisfaction of consumption, such as "the quenching of thirst." The actor anticipates some of these consequences, and, since each action is forward-looking, anticipates some consequences that only *might* occur. Both the satisfactions and other consequences are bound up in the state of the world he seeks to attain in action. By consuming a beverage, for example, an actor anticipates the removal of thirst, but also forgoes the removal of thirst that could have been achieved by the same beverage consumed later, along with any other use of the beverage. Also, he may accept the possibility that he could spill the drink or that the caffeine in the beverage will make it more difficult for him to sleep that night. These consequences and possibilities, including the possibilities that some of them may occur jointly, are taken into the actor's consideration of the action, and all of them are "wrapped up" in the preferred state of the world at which he aims.

Interestingly, these consequences include, for the actor, knowledge of forgone opportunities. This poses no problem for the logic of action and opportunity costs. If an actor knows that pursuing one end, A, involves the sacrifice of his next-best alternative, B, then he also knows that if he had pursued B, then that too would have involved the sacrifice of A. Put another way, the knowledge of forgone opportunities is applied to each of the actor's options, and therefore such knowledge does not necessarily increase or decrease the psychic profit for the actor in the potential states of the world he may pursue. The same applies to scenarios in which options are added to an actor's choice set. Therefore, it cannot be said that the knowledge of more options necessarily makes an actor worse off, which is one of the criticisms of the opportunity cost concept made by Reisman (1998) and Braun (2014), explored below.

Of course, actors may overlook some consequences. In fact, exchanging states of the world is impossibly complex if *all* consequences are to be considered. As a result, acting man only considers those consequences he deems relevant and important enough to give him pause before he initiates the action and commits to the outcome. Considering an action is also an action because an actor's attention and mental capacity to weigh all the various consequences of an action are limited. He must choose which consequences are relevant and important and forgo dwelling on consequences that are not. In hindsight, the actor may regret that he did not consider a particular consequence, but this is an inevitable fact for finite beings acting under uncertainty. The existence of regret does not pose any trouble for the opportunity cost concept. Regret only exists in hindsight, while opportunity costs are considered by the actor before the action.

B) Examples from textbooks

The above causal-realist view of opportunity costs has been lost in many leading textbooks in favor of a cardinal and objective conception. While a popular criticism of the mainstream approach is that utility is treated in a cardinal and objective way,[5] this is not the direct cause of the confusion over opportunity costs in textbooks. In fact, neoclassical utility functions are not even mentioned in the first pages of principles-level textbooks. Instead, the confusion has a different source, namely, that opportunity costs are presented alongside *production tradeoffs*, and the two terms are used interchangeably. This gives students a muddled understanding of the critical and fundamental concepts of value and opportunity cost. Moreover, this presentation and false conflation are maintained throughout the same textbooks. The result is that, bereft of a correct understanding of opportunity costs, students are ill-equipped to think critically as they learn about a wide range of other important topics, including justifications for government intervention or even Keynesian macroeconomic models.[6]

Consider two examples. In Mankiw (2014, p. 52), the production possibilities of a farmer and a rancher producing meat and potatoes are presented first and then the concept of absolute advantage is introduced and applied. Next, as a stepping stone to the concept of comparative advantage, opportunity costs are introduced:

> Time spent producing potatoes, therefore, takes away from time available for producing meat. When reallocating time between the two goods, Rose and Frank give up units of one good to produce units of the other, thereby moving along the production possibilities frontier. The opportunity cost measures the trade-off between the two goods that each producer faces.
>
> (p. 52)

The natural conclusion students reach is that opportunity costs are a part of the physical relationships of production, and are determined by the producer's technology and available inputs.

Similarly, Krugman and Wells (2009) first introduce the concept of opportunity cost using an example with a student deciding between two college courses (p. 7). Opportunity cost is defined as "what you must give up in order to get an item you want" (p. 7). The definition does not clarify whether the "what" is the actor's forgone satisfaction or a quantity of goods. Indeed, only ten pages later opportunity cost is reintroduced along with production tradeoffs: "the slope of a straight-line production possibility frontier is equal to the opportunity cost" (p. 27). Mankiw's (2014) and Krugman and Wells's (2009) treatments of opportunity costs are typical among popular textbooks. A definition of opportunity cost is offered in the first few pages, where the most fundamental concepts of economics are introduced to get students "thinking like economists." This first definition is typically accompanied by an example of a choice a college student might make. Later, however – often in the very next chapter, in fact – when production possibilities frontiers are introduced, a new definition and application of opportunity cost is introduced as well.[7] The second definition of opportunity cost describes a physical production relationship, and sometimes contradicts the first.[8]

In contrast to the typical mainstream approach, consider two examples from principles textbooks by Austrian authors. Ritenour's (2010) exposition leaves no room for confusion. He presents a section of Helena's value scale, in which flourless chocolate cake is preferred to buttermilk pancakes, which in turn is preferred to orange roughy. Helena must choose how to use her stick of butter, which may be employed in the preparation of any of those three dishes, but only one. She chooses to allocate the butter toward the preparation of flourless chocolate cake, and Helena's forgone enjoyment of the buttermilk pancakes is identified as the opportunity cost of her choice. Ritenour explains:

> Economists refer to this *doing without* as a cost. In fact, they have a special name for it: *opportunity cost*. Opportunity cost is the value of the alternative that must be forgone as the result of choosing to achieve a certain end.
>
> (p. 25, emphasis in original)

In Murphy's (2012) textbook, the opportunity cost concept is presented using Robinson Crusoe as an example:

> The cost of a particular decision is the value that Crusoe places on the most important goal that he *won't* be able to achieve, because of the decision. Economists often drive home the point by using the longer term **opportunity cost**, which they define as *the subjective value placed on the next-best alternative* that must be sacrificed because of a choice.
>
> (p. 61, emphasis in original)

Neither textbook presents opportunity costs alongside production tradeoffs. While Ritenour's example involves Helena producing flourless chocolate cake with butter as an input, it is clear that the opportunity cost is a consequence of her choice, and that her opportunity cost is *not* the physical relationship between the butter and all of Helena's other production possibilities.

Mainstream confusion

A) Ferraro and Taylor spark debate

Confusion in the mainstream led to the embarrassing results of Ferraro and Taylor's (2005) survey, in which only 21.6% of economists could correctly answer a question about opportunity costs from a principles-level textbook. The question was presented as follows:

> You won a free ticket to see an Eric Clapton concert (which has no resale value). Bob Dylan is performing on the same night and is your next-best alternative activity. Tickets to see Dylan cost $40. On any given day, you would be willing to pay up to $50 to see Dylan. Assume there are no other costs of seeing either performer. Based on this information, what is the opportunity cost of seeing Eric Clapton?
> A $0
> B $10
> C $40
> D $50

The correct answer was supposed to be B, $10, though the most popular answer was D, $50. The value of the Dylan concert is taken to be your willingness to pay to see the Dylan concert, $50. However, by going to the Clapton concert, you avoid paying the $40 to see Dylan, and "an avoided benefit is a cost, and an avoided cost is a benefit" (p. 3). Therefore, the $40 avoided cost is subtracted from the $50 willingness to pay to arrive at $10, the opportunity cost of seeing Clapton.

An Austrian economist would have to write in the correct answer because she would not find it among the choices given. With the information given in the question, a preference ranking could be constructed to find the actor's next-best alternative, perhaps like this:

1 Enjoying the Clapton concert, knowing that you will not have to pay for the Clapton concert and that you would miss the Dylan concert, tickets to which are priced at $40
2 Enjoying the Dylan concert, knowing that you will have to pay $40 for a ticket and that you would miss the Clapton concert, the ticket to which was a gift to you
3 $50
4 $40

In this scenario, the ends are bundles of specific consequences in each "state of the world" the actor is considering, including the knowledge of forgone opportunities.

The ends are not simply "the enjoyment of the Clapton concert" and "the enjoyment of the Dylan concert" because the actor attaches to the end that might be attained all the characteristics and consequences he deems relevant. Mises (1998) makes this clear in his famous analogy about the choice between capitalism and socialism: "A man who chooses between drinking a glass of milk and a glass of a solution of potassium cyanide does not choose between two beverages; he chooses between life and death" (p. 676). Therefore, the opportunity cost of seeing Clapton is the actor's subjective value of the counterfactual course of events: the state of the world in which the actor goes to see the Dylan concert.

Ferraro and Taylor's (2005) result sparked debate among economists, including a special symposium in the *Journal of Economic Education* (2016). The symposium features an article by textbook author Michael Parkin (2016a) and commentaries by three critics. Parkin offers his preliminary thoughts on the issue, the three critics respond, and then Parkin responds in turn. Parkin first suggests that there are two ways to present opportunity cost: "a value specification and a quantity specification" (Colander, 2016). In his response to the critics, Parkin concludes that the confusion between the two specifications of opportunity cost is due to two specifications of value. In the end, he unfortunately settles on the "quantity specification," which is in line with the confusing mainstream textbook presentation outlined above, in which opportunity costs and production tradeoffs are presented as the same concept. However, we show below that Parkin's "value specification" is just another quantity specification rather than a version of the more correct causal-realist value specification based on ordinal and subjective preferences.

B) Parkin's "reexamination"

The first question Parkin (2016a) takes on is this: "Is opportunity cost an ambiguous and arbitrary concept or a simple, straightforward, and fruitful one?" (p. 12). Parkin answers the question as follows: "regrettably, opportunity cost is an ambiguous concept, [. . .] because two definitions are in widespread use. One of the definitions is indeed simple, fruitful, and one that students can learn. The other has the potential to be ambiguous" (p. 12). This does not directly answer the question – Parkin appears to be claiming that opportunity cost is ambiguous because there are two versions of opportunity cost, and one of them is ambiguous.[9] Both involve a forgone next-best alternative, but one is "a physical quantity forgone" while the other is "a value forgone" (p. 13). Parkin decides that the two specifications are equivalent in some cases but conflict in others, depending on the problem being solved (p. 12).

To compare the two definitions, Parkin constructs a mathematical model to show that in competitive equilibrium, an opportunity cost in quantity terms is the same in value terms. Parkin uses three ways of measuring value: a marginal rate of substitution, prices, and marginal utilities (as first derivatives of utility functions). This is an important departure from the casual-realist value specification of opportunity cost as a forgone end. The implication is that Parkin is not comparing two meaningfully different definitions of opportunity cost. Both are objective, differentiable quantities – (1) a quantity of means and (2) a willingness to pay, which is a quantity of dollars, or in the case of a MRS, a quantity of the other good. A true value specification would involve two competing ends in relation to each other in an ordinal preference ranking. Nevertheless, Parkin shows how the "two" specifications under scrutiny are equivalent in competitive equilibrium but not in other cases.

Parkin then compares the capabilities of the physical quantity specification and the poorly-defined value specification (measured in dollars) in satisfying various purposes of the opportunity cost concept. For him, the opportunity cost concept should be able to "do" the following: (1) help explain the fundamental economic problem of scarcity, (2) convince students that cost is something more than dollars of expenditure, (3) easily distinguish itself as the *next-best* alternative and not *all* the forgone alternatives, and (4) provide a suitable input in rational choice models.

This exercise is an unfortunate example of a deeper problem in mainstream economics, with roots in Friedmanite positivism: judging economic concepts by their tractability in models (rational choice in this case) and their ability to predict human behavior instead of their truth and logical consistency with the idea of choice. Parkin's faulty view of value and choice notably clouds his view of a value specification's ability to explain the fundamental economic problem:

> Lesson one in the principles course is the insight that scarcity is the source of all economic questions and problems, that faced with scarcity we must make choices, and that in choosing, available alternatives are rejected or forgone. The insight that cost is a forgone alternative can be gained without any notion of value except in the vague sense that wanting something is synonymous with valuing it. The quantity-forgone version of opportunity cost does a good job of deepening this insight. How does the value-forgone version perform in this task? First, it brings an added layer of complexity that obscures the insight. Second, it requires a lengthy detour to define and explain the concept of value. The quantity-forgone version wins on this first purpose of opportunity cost.
>
> (Parkin, 2016a, p. 20)

Although Parkin would like to avoid a "lengthy detour" when teaching the fundamental concept of value, we have shown that, pedagogically, a firm grasp of value should precede the introduction of the opportunity cost concept.

The next purpose of opportunity cost in Parkin's list is that it should help convince students that cost is not simply dollars of expenditure. Since Parkin and the majority of the economics profession express value in dollar terms, Parkin again selects the physical quantity specification as the clearer approach: "The value-forgone version again obscures the insight, and it especially obscures it when value is expressed in dollars rather than other goods willingly forgone" (2016a, p. 20). Here, again, a true value specification of opportunity cost survives Parkin's criticism. In causal-realist value theory, value is never expressed in dollar terms. Opportunity costs are forgone ends, which are immaterial and subjective.

A true value specification would also satisfy Parkin's third purpose of the opportunity cost concept – that it is easily distinguishable as only the next-best alternative and not all the forgone alternatives. He explains that it is sometimes difficult to single out the one forgone alternative and that deciphering the value of that forgone alternative merely adds extra steps to the process. Parkin once again favors the quantity specification: "Figuring out *what* is forgone is the key step and is better not sidetracked by the harder task of figuring out *the value of what* is forgone. Again, the physical quantity version wins" (2016a, p. 21, emphasis in original). It is clear that the extra layer of difficulty added by his value specification derives from the way value is measured and not the fact that it is a value specification per se. For example, given that in causal-realist explanations of value and choice, the ends that are ranked by an actor are often represented in shorthand by the means that the actor would employ to attain those ends, Parkin's "quantity specification" is actually closer to the causal-realist value specification than his own dollar-denominated "value specification." The only difference in this case is an understanding that the physical goods as stated represent ranked ends for the actor.[10]

Parkin's final purpose suggests that opportunity costs should be easily inputted into cost-benefit models. He finds that both the quantity and value specifications are suited for this task, as long as the costs and benefits are denominated in the same way (units of a good, dollars, utils, etc.). He adds that if value is measured in dollars, the quantity specification still wins on the grounds that "it cuts through the veil of money" (2016a, p. 21). While the causal-realist conception of opportunity cost is not tractable in neoclassical rational choice models, the problem may be with the model itself and not with the subjective and ordinal conception of opportunity costs. Here it becomes apparent that the mainstream and Austrian economists work in opposite directions when faced with dilemmas over concepts like opportunity cost. Mainstream economists like Parkin use their models to put a menu of opportunity specification options through trials to see which one performs best. In contrast, Austrian economists, when faced with a similar dilemma, work from the ground up such that any new or revised concepts still comport with the fundamental logic of action and therefore the rest of economic theory.

C) The critics

The first critic, Daniel Arce (2016), generally agrees with Parkin and suggests that economics textbooks simply need more examples of the opportunity cost concept in application. The third critic, Daniel Stone, like Arce, is not critical at all, and even regrets that he began by thinking to doubt such an authority on the issue as Parkin.[11] Only the second critic, Rod O'Donnell (2016), offers meaningful criticism of Parkin's arguments for a quantity specification of opportunity cost.

O'Donnell (2016) arrives at a similar conclusion to the one outlined above regarding textbook treatments of opportunity cost: "In my reading of textbooks, it is not uncommon to find value definitions of OC [Opportunity Cost] followed by physical quantity examples and applications" (p. 27). O'Donnell (2016) also comes close to recognizing that willingness to pay is just another objective, quantity measure: "Benefit is then measured by the maximum amount the agent is willing to give up to get X, so linking benefit to willingness to pay (WTP), an idea aimed at rendering objective that which is subjective" (p. 28). O'Donnell argues that Parkin, by using two- and three-good models, assumes what he needs to prove, especially given that Parkin's three-good models reduce to two-good models because the third good is never an object of choice and so becomes a unit of account for the other two goods. The exercise is therefore fruitless because the opportunity costs in a two-good world are always a quantity of the good not chosen (O'Donnell, 2016, p. 29). Finally, O'Donnell disagrees with each of Parkin's conclusions about the quantity specification's ability to satisfy the various purposes of the opportunity cost concept (O'Donnell, 2016, pp. 29–31). In his reply, Parkin (2016b) attributes the bulk of their disagreements to miscommunication about how value is measured: willingness to pay or market prices. After emphatically declaring for the former ("*Value is willingness to pay*," p. 35, his italics), he doubles down on his original conclusion that the quantity specification of opportunity cost should be adopted by all economists and that "there is no theoretical issue at stake," only "an issue of orderliness in the use of language" (pp. 38–39).

D) Opportunity costs and production tradeoffs

The symposium authors do not mention any problems with presenting opportunity costs along with production tradeoffs as the same fundamental concept. Yet, pedagogically at least, the two should not be introduced together. However, it should be noted that there is a way to appropriately identify opportunity costs in an example involving production possibilities. Consider the classic guns and butter tradeoff. Producing more of one good means less of the other can be produced, and vice versa. Production tradeoffs present a set of options for the actor, such as (A) five guns and zero pounds of butter, (B) four guns and three pounds of butter, (C) three guns and five pounds of butter, etc. One can only claim, "the opportunity cost of three pounds of butter is one gun," with important caveats: (1) referring to the goods chosen and forgone is shorthand for the ends attained by the actor with those goods (in their respective bundles), and (2) the actor must have chosen B, four guns and three pounds of butter, over A, five guns and zero pounds of butter. The actor's preferences must be:

1. B, four guns and three pounds of butter
2. A, five guns and zero pounds of butter
3. C, three guns and five pounds of butter

and not:

1. B, four guns and three pounds of butter
2. C, three guns and five pounds of butter
3. A, five guns and zero pounds of butter

That is, the next highest ranked alternative must be the choice that is consistent with the opportunity cost as stated. Going from A to B, the actor gains three pounds of butter, but loses one gun, and this is consistent with the actor's preferences. To be clear, it would make more sense pedagogically to first present the actor's preferences and his options before identifying opportunity costs. This is not common practice in mainstream textbooks, though, and the caveats are also withheld. Unfortunately, students are left with two separate but falsely conflated ideas.

Critical views in Austrian literature

Other misconceptions about opportunity costs have emerged in literature close to Austrian economics. The most notable example is found in the work of George Reisman (1998). Reisman, along with several of his students, denies what he calls the "opportunity-cost doctrine." He presents multiple scenarios involving missed opportunities for monetary gain to show how allegedly absurd opportunity cost is. Below, we will see that his critique is based on a misunderstanding and misapplication of the concept. We will also cover a scenario offered more recently by Eduard Braun in his book, *Finance Behind the Veil of Money* (2014), which cites Reisman on the same issue. Briefly, the answers to their criticisms are that opportunity costs cannot be identified in hindsight and that opportunity costs may only be identified for one choice at a time.

A) Reisman rejects the "opportunity-cost doctrine"

In his treatise *Capitalism*, Reisman begins his critique of the "opportunity-cost doctrine" by describing the version he is targeting, namely, the one used by Samuelson and Nordhaus (1989):

> An opportunity cost is an imputed cost – a cost which does not actually exist in the sense of an expenditure of money being made, or having been made, but which is treated as though it existed. An opportunity cost is said to exist by virtue of the failure to earn a revenue or income that otherwise might be earned or might have been earned. It represents the absence of a revenue or income, just as imputed income represents the absence of a cost.
>
> (Reisman, 1998, p. 459)

Reisman continues to point out absurdities in using opportunity costs to analyze various hypothetical scenarios in which an actor makes a choice.[12] However, his scenarios are analyzed, and the opportunity costs identified, only in hindsight. Viewing opportunity costs in hindsight is categorically different from weighing opportunity costs before an action is taken. A similar point is made in Howden's (2016b) rejoinder to Braun (2016), as part of their back-and-forth in the *Quarterly Journal of Austrian Economics*. Opportunity costs viewed in hindsight have no bearing on the logic of action – only ex ante opportunity costs matter in economic theory.[13] Of course, hindsight can play a role in an actor's future decision-making, but this simply takes past information as a basis for making a new, forward-looking choice.

We cannot use what could have happened, given knowledge of the course of events and the present state of the world, to describe opportunity costs, else every dollar spent would carry the "opportunity cost" of the winning lottery ticket or the best-performing stock. Yet this is how Reisman treats the opportunity cost concept in his first example, in which the owner of the neighborhood hardware store earns $50,000 in profit over the previous year. A nosy economics textbook author tells him he could have sold the store and earned $15,000 from the invested funds and $45,000 in wages working elsewhere. Reisman says that the "opportunity-cost doctrine" must then say that the hardware store owner, far from earning $50,000, has actually lost $10,000.[14] However, this missed opportunity is only seen in hindsight, and cannot have been the store owner's forward-looking opportunity cost (assuming the store owner only cares about money profit). Even if the store owner knew about the $60,000 opportunity that would have involved him selling his business and still passed on it, there must have been nonmonetary reasons for his choice. The $10,000 difference might be considered his willingness to pay for the state of world in which he retains ownership of the store. Either way, there is not a legitimate way to use the opportunity cost concept to arrive at Reisman's conclusion that the store owner has incurred a loss of $10,000. The costs of production are reckoned by the entrepreneur at the time of his final decision to produce, as factors are committed to the production process.[15] Hindsight may reveal to the entrepreneur that he could have earned more had he sold his inputs, but this information can only be used by the entrepreneur going forward.

The opportunity cost of the hardware store owner's decision to continue his business for another year was the next-best alternative in his mind at the time he made the choice. Afterwards, of course, he may look back and determine whether he made a "good choice" – perhaps it turns out later that what he thought was next-best actually would have been better than the option he chose.[16] And, of course, he can also expand his consideration of the choice beyond the options he thought he had at the time of the decision. This is where the lottery ticket or the great stock pick would come into play. Importantly, though, none of the store owner's reminiscing, new information, or regret changes the opportunity cost *at the time of his choice*. Action is always forward-looking, and so opportunity costs (as they are used and defined in economic theory) may only be identified in the same manner.

Let us consider another one of Reisman's (1998) examples, this time involving changing stock prices:

> Yet another manifestation of the absurdity of this doctrine can be seen if it is applied to the stock market. Imagine that an individual is considering investing a million dollars, and must decide between two stocks, A and B. Both stocks are currently selling at $10 per share. The individual decides on stock A. It goes to $20 per share. In the same period, however, it turns out that

> stock B goes to $30 per share. If one believes the opportunity cost doctrine, this is grounds for leaping from the nearest skyscraper – one has lost a million dollars.
>
> (p. 461)

It should be immediately clear that Reisman has once again incorrectly identified the opportunity cost by viewing the problem in hindsight. The investor may realize after the fact that she could have made more money by investing in B, but this does not change her opportunity costs at the time she made the choice. Reisman takes Samuelson and Nordhaus's (1989) version of opportunity cost as representative of that of all proponents of the opportunity cost concept, and he criticizes it in full. Yet, from the perspective of the causal-realist approach to opportunity costs, this is simply tilting at windmills. The opportunity cost concept on Reisman's chopping block is not the causal-realist subjectivist conception. Rothbard (2009) makes this explicit when he explains that "[opportunity] costs are subjective and cannot be precisely determined by outside observers or be gauged ex post by observing accountants" (p. 341).

B) Braun follows Reisman

Debate over Reisman's controversial position on opportunity costs emerged in the *Quarterly Journal of Austrian Economics* with David Howden's review (2015) of Eduard Braun's book, *Finance Behind the Veil of Money* (2014). Braun maintains Reisman's line of thinking on the opportunity cost concept and, much like Reisman, offers a scenario with the purpose of showing how absurd it is that an actor would suffer more or higher costs when faced with more options. The example involves a hiker who is gifted an apple by a friend. The friend allows the hungry hiker to choose between two identical apples, which, according to Braun, means that choosing one involves incurring the opportunity cost of the other. Thus, the net benefit for the hiker is zero or close to zero, assuming he overcomes the Buridan's ass issue.

Howden (2016a, 2016b) presents valid objections to Braun's argument based on a solution to the Buridan's ass problem (namely, finding the missing alternative) along with the proper application of opportunity cost as a forward-looking concept in action. However, another objection may be raised regarding the hiker's supposed dilemma. Braun presents two choices as one, which prohibits any clear identification of opportunity cost. The two choices are (1) to accept or reject the gift of the apple and (2) to choose one apple of the two for consumption. The hiker clearly benefits by the gift of the apple, even though the giver is not clear about which apple is the gift. We can consider the gift as an apple coupon, redeemable for one apple. The hiker demonstrates a preference for an apple over no apple by accepting his friend's gift. The second choice (which apple to take) is the same type of choice an individual makes whenever he chooses one unit of a homogenous stock – a kind of low-stakes choice the practically everybody makes all the time. I do not toil over which edge of my coffee mug from which to take a sip or what particular M&M happens to fall into my hand when I pour out the bag. Attention is scarce and valuable, so we voluntarily allow some randomness, impulse, and spontaneity to affect which units of a homogeneous stock are selected for consumption and which are saved for later. To the extent that these selections are unconscious, they are outside the realm of economics.

However, to the extent that a unit of an apparently homogeneous stock is consciously chosen over other units, it means that the actor must have noticed some heterogeneity among the units. An actor may consciously choose one unit simply because it is on top of the heap, or nearest to the actor.[17] These characteristics may enter the actor's choice without posing a problem for the fundamental concepts of value, action, and opportunity cost. This is the case even when all the units are perfectly identical from the perspective of an outside observer. In economics, the physical characteristics of any good must first pass through the actor's subjective interpretation and judgement before a choice is made and analyzed, including those characteristics an outside observer may deem negligible or does not notice at all.

Conclusion

Recent literature has brought many misconceptions regarding opportunity costs to light, both in mainstream and Austrian circles. The current debate over the opportunity cost concept in the mainstream is mired in a false choice between two quantity specifications, yet the larger problem is that mainstream principles textbooks present opportunity costs and production tradeoffs as one and the same. Students, teachers, and textbook authors would do well to consider a more intuitive approach to value, choice, and action from the causal-realist Austrian school, such as the one adopted by Ritenour (2010) and Murphy (2012). At the same time, though, George Reisman and others close to the Austrian literature have criticized the opportunity cost concept. Yet it has been shown that their objections do not stand up to scrutiny, though the debate sparked by Reisman and continued by Braun has been a healthy exercise that hopefully will lead to greater clarity for such fundamental concepts in the future.

Notes

1 Mises (1998) provides a complete exposition of the central place of human action in economic theory. See "The Procedure of Economics" (pp. 64–69) for a summary.
2 Mises (1998): "Costs are equal to the value attached to the satisfaction which one must forego in order to attain the end aimed at" (p. 97). Rothbard (2009): " 'Cost' is simply the utility of the next best alternative that must be forgone in any action, and it is therefore part and parcel of utility on the individual's value scale" (p. 136).
3 This conclusion is surprisingly uncontroversial. Consider, for example, Krugman and Wells (2009): "The concept of opportunity cost is crucial to understanding individual choice because, in the end, all costs are opportunity costs" (p. 7).
4 As Mises (1998) explains: "Acting man is eager to substitute a more satisfactory state of affairs for a less satisfactory" (p. 13). This insight is particularly useful in solving apparent conundrums in the logic of action. For example, McCaffrey (2015) uses it to address a separate criticism of causal-realist theory regarding love and gifts: "in the

universal, praxeological sense, it is not material goods that are exchanged, but rather states of the world, as subjectively interpreted by the actor" (p. 213).

5 Rothbard's (1956) "Toward a Reconstruction of Utility and Welfare Economics" is a seminal work in this literature.

6 See Boyes (2014) for an example of how opportunity costs may be applied in a critique of the Keynesian multiplier.

7 For other examples, see Acemoglu, Laibson, and List (2015, pp. 9, 12, 173), Chiang (2017, pp. 9, 36), Coppock and Mateer (2017, pp. 13, 35), Cowen and Tabarrok (2015, pp. 4, 17), Hubbard and O'Brien (2015, pp. 8, 39), Parkin (2015, pp. 9, 33), and Taylor (2007, pp. 5, 12).

8 Consider, for example, the two definitions offered in Chiang (2017): "Opportunity cost measures the *value* of the next best alternative use of your time and money, or what you give up when you make an economic decision" (p. 9, emphasis mine); and "Opportunity cost – The cost paid for one product in terms of the *output* (or consumption) *of another product* that must be forgone" (p. 36, emphasis added).

9 Perhaps he means that *the state of opportunity cost in the economics profession* is ambiguous because there are two commonly used versions of opportunity cost, and that a separate issue concerns whether one of them is ambiguous.

10 Herbener (2011) summarizes the relationship between means and ends in the mind of an actor: "Since attaining the end is the purpose of an action, the value a person attaches to the attainment of the end is primary. A person attaches only derivative value to the means used in action since they are merely aids to the attainment of the end. Means have no value independent of the value a person attaches to the end they help attain. The human mind imputes value to the means according to the aid they render in attaining a valuable end" (p. 14).

11 Stone explains: "I admit it was my instinct to defend the value definition (i.e., my own position, or at least that of my earlier paper), searching for flaws in Parkin's piece and arguments against it. As I read and thought about his article more carefully, however, I realized what should have been obvious right away: Parkin is certainly knowledgeable on this topic, and his arguments are well-founded" (Stone, 2016, p. 32).

12 Some of the scenarios Reisman brings up are quite comical, and intentionally so: "An analogy to this procedure would be the following. One gains ten pounds, but might have gained twenty pounds. This is then taken to mean that one has lost ten pounds. When one's alleged loss of weight cannot be reconciled with the fact that one is now ten pounds too large for one's clothes, one's oversize is explained on the grounds that one's clothes have shrunk the equivalent of twenty pounds" (p. 460).

13 Howden (2016b) suggests that these are two "uses" for the opportunity cost concept, e.g., "The second use of opportunity costs is an ex post facto assessment to determine if the chosen option was the correct one" (p. 184). While I agree with Dr. Howden's claim, for the sake of clarity I hesitate to adopt the same language. Missed opportunities in hindsight are categorically different from forward-looking, anticipated opportunity costs, and only the latter are relevant to economic theory.

14 Reisman (1998), p. 459: "These forgone opportunities or passed-up alternatives, the textbook author then argues, must be counted as costs of the owner's business, just as much as the store's payment for merchandise and the labor of hired help, if its actual profit is to be computed."

15 For more on the entrepreneur's anticipations of the costs of production through the production process, see Jeffrey M. Herbener's (2018) contribution in the present volume.

16 Once again, Rothbard (2009) is indispensable: "It is convenient to distinguish the two vantage points by which an actor judges his action as *ex ante* and *ex post*. *Ex ante* is his position when he must decide on a course of action; *it is the relevant and dominant consideration for human action.* It is the actor considering his alternative courses and the consequences of each. *Ex post* is his recorded observation of the results of his past action. It is the judging of his past actions and their results. *Ex ante*, then, he will

always take the most advantageous course of action, and will always have a psychic profit, with revenue exceeding cost. *Ex post*, he may have profited or lost from a course of action" (p. 277, fourth emphasis added).

17 This is why, in any telling of the Buridan's ass problem, the oases or hay bales are equidistant to the ass.

References

Acemoglu, Daron, David Laibson, and John List. 2015. *Microeconomics*. New York: Pearson Higher Education.

Arce, Daniel G. 2016. "Opportunity Cost and the Intelligence of Economists: A Comment." *The Journal of Economic Education* 47 (1): 23–25.

Boyes, William J. 2014. "The Keynesian Multiplier Concept Ignores Crucial Opportunity Costs." *Quarterly Journal of Austrian Economics* 17 (3): 327–337.

Braun, Eduard. 2014. Finance Behind the Veil of Money: An Essay on the Economics of Capital, Interest and the Financial Market. Liberty.me.

———. 2016. "Reply to Dr. Howden on Opportunity Costs." *Quarterly Journal of Austrian Economics* 19 (2): 173–177.

Chiang, Eric. 2017. *Economics: Principles for a Changing World*. 4th ed. New York: Worth Publishers.

Colander, David. 2016. "Introduction to Symposium on Opportunity Cost." *The Journal of Economic Education* 47 (1): 11.

Coppock, Lee, and Dirk Mateer. 2017. *Principles of Macroeconomics*. 2nd ed. New York: W.W. Norton & Company

Cowen, Tyler, and Alex Tabarrok. 2015. *Modern Principles of Macroeconomics*. 3rd ed. New York: Worth Publishers.

Ferraro, Paul J., and Laura O. Taylor. 2005. "Do Economists Recognize an Opportunity Cost When They See One? A Dismal Performance from the Dismal Science." *Contributions to Economic Analysis & Policy* 4 (1): 1–12.

Herbener, Jeffrey M. (ed.). 2011. *The Pure Time-Preference Theory of Interest*. Auburn, AL: Ludwig von Mises Institute.

———. 2018. "Time and the Theory of Cost." In Matthew McCaffrey, ed., *The Economic Theory of Costs: Foundations and New Directions*. Abingdon, UK: Routledge, pp. 147–166.

Howden, David. 2015. "Review of 'Finance Behind the Veil of Money: An Essay on the Economics of Capital, Interest, and the Financial Market, by Eduard Braun'." *Quarterly Journal of Austrian Economics* 18 (4): 578–583.

———. 2016a. "*Finance Behind the Veil of Money*: Response to Dr. Braun's Comment." *Quarterly Journal of Austrian Economics* 19 (1): 124–128.

———. 2016b. "Finance Behind the Veil of Money: A Rejoinder." Quarterly Journal of Austrian Economics 19 (2): 178–186.

Hubbard, R. Glenn, and Anthony P. O'Brien. 2015. *Macroeconomics*. 5th ed. New York: Pearson Higher Education.

Krugman, Paul, and Robin Wells. 2009. *Macroeconomics*. 2nd ed. New York: Worth Publishers.

Mankiw, N. Gregory. 2014. *Principles of Macroeconomics*. Mason, OH: Cengage Learning.

McCaffrey, Matthew. 2015. "What's Love Got to Do with It? Action, Exchange, and Gifts in Economic Theory." *Quarterly Journal of Austrian Economics* 18 (2): 210–221.

Menger, Carl. 2007 [1871]. *Principles of Economics*. Trans. J. Dingwall and B. F. Hoselitz. Auburn, AL: Ludwig von Mises Institute.

Mises, Ludwig von. 1998 [1949]. *Human Action: Scholar's Edition*. Auburn, AL: Ludwig von Mises Institute.

Murphy, Robert P. 2012. *Lessons for the Young Economist*. Auburn, AL: Ludwig von Mises Institute.

O'Donnell, Rod. 2016. "Complexities in the Examination of Opportunity Cost." *The Journal of Economic Education* 47 (1): 26–31.

Parkin, Michael. 2015. *Economics*. 12th ed. New York: Pearson Higher Education.

———. 2016a. "Opportunity Cost: A Reexamination." *The Journal of Economic Education* 47 (1): 12–22.

———. 2016b. "Opportunity Cost: A Reply." *The Journal of Economic Education* 47 (1): 35–39.

Reisman, George. 1998. *Capitalism: A Treatise on Economics*. Chicago, IL: Jameson Books.

Ritenour, Shawn. 2010. *Foundations of Economics: A Christian View*. Eugene, OR: Wipf and Stock Publishers.

Rothbard, Murray N. 1956. "Toward a Reconstruction of Utility and Welfare Economics." In Mary Sennholz, ed., *On Freedom and Free Enterprise: Essays in Honor of Ludwig von Mises*. Princeton, NJ: D. Van Nostrand, pp. 224–262.

Rothbard, Murray N. 2009. *Man, Economy, and State With Power and Market*. Auburn, AL: Ludwig von Mises Institute.

Samuelson, Paul A., and W. D. Nordhaus. 1989. *Economics*. 13th ed. New York: McGraw-Hill Book Company.

Stone, Daniel F. 2016. "Comments on 'Opportunity Cost: A Reexamination': A Case in Point of No Free Lunch." *The Journal of Economic Education* 47 (1): 32–34.

Taylor, John. 2007. *Principles of Macroeconomics*. 5th ed. Boston, MA: Houghton Mifflin.

2 The "income effect" in causal-realist price theory

Joseph T. Salerno

1 Introduction

The distinction between the substitution and income effects introduced into neoclassical price theory by Hicks (1946) in 1938 has been a fixture in mainstream economics textbooks at least since the early 1950s.

[1] This distinction has been conspicuously absent from the causal-realist tradition in price theory, which is a variant of neoclassical economics that traces back to Carl Menger.[2] The causal-realist analysis of the individual demand curve proceeds exclusively in terms of the elaboration of the law of marginal utility against the background of a strictly ordinal and relative scale of value.

Unfortunately, there has never been an explicit comparison of the causal-realist and mainstream neoclassical approaches to deriving the demand curve. In his treatise, *Human Action*, Mises (1998) never mentioned the Hicksian approach. In a memo written in 1961, Rothbard (Salerno, 2011, p. 14) brushed aside "the alleged division between the 'income effect' and the 'substitution effect,' and the consequent 'Giffen Paradox.'" In his treatise, published a year later, Rothbard (2009, p. 915) gave only a cursory mention of the two effects in a discussion of income taxation. More recently, there has been an awakening of interest in the question of the existence of the income effect in causal-realist price theory. The recent treatments of this topic are widely scattered in time and broadly disparate in depth and focus (Caplan, 1999; Salin, 1996; Gonzalez, 2000; Rajsic, 2010; Hudik, 2011). More important, while of some value, these treatments never achieved resolution of the issue, because they failed to recognize the profound differences that have developed since the 1930s between Mengerian causal-realist price theory and the Marshallian-Walrasian-Hicksian synthesis at the heart of modern neoclassical microeconomics.

In this paper I will argue from an explicitly causal-realist perspective that the income effect is illusory and that the individual demand curve can be fully deduced from the law of marginal utility, which is the logical implication of the existence of individual value scales (Mises, 1998, pp. 94–96, 119–127). In addition, I will attempt to show that the demand curve deduced in this way naturally integrates money into the analysis and explains the determination of the moment-to-moment structure of prices actually paid in real-world transactions. Causal-realist demand analysis is thus able also to provide an integral explanation of the purchasing power of money that does not invoke the (neo)classical dichotomy between real and nominal variables that artificially separates "relative" prices from the "absolute" level of prices.[3]

In section 2, I briefly review the controversy over the nature and assumptions of the Marshallian demand curve that was carried on during the 1950s among neoclassical economists and was never satisfactorily resolved. Section 3 addresses the centrality of ordinal scales of value or preference to demand analysis. In section 4, I argue that, for the causal-realist, the stock of money assets, and not the flow of money income, is the relevant concept for demand theory. The case is made in section 5 that constancy of the purchasing power of money is an indispensable assumption for using the law of marginal utility, which is derived from the ordinal value scale, in deducing the individual demand curve. Section 6 draws a distinction between the "instantaneous" demand curve yielded by causal-realist analysis and the temporally ambiguous conventional demand curve. The nature of the substitution effect in causal-realist demand theory is clarified in section 7. Section 8 presents some concluding remarks on the income effect and the backward-bending supply curve of labor.

2 The neoclassical controversy over the demand curve

The income effect was the central problem in what Leland Yeager (1960) referred to as the "*Methodenstreit* over demand curves." Milton Friedman ([1949] 1970) initiated this controversy in 1949 with his famous article, "The Marshallian Demand Curve," and the debate was carried on sporadically during the 1950s.[4] Friedman challenged the prevailing Hicksian interpretation of the Marshallian demand curve, arguing that: 1. it misrepresented the *ceteris paribus* conditions of Marshall's derivation of the demand curve; and 2. it was less useful for the analysis of practical problems than Marshall's demand curve, properly understood.

In the Hicksian interpretation of the demand curve, the tastes and preferences of the buyers of the good, their money incomes, and the prices of all other goods in the economy are assumed constant. This implies that while money income remains constant for the various points on the demand curve, real income does not. An increase in price, *ceteris paribus*, lowers real income, and a fall in price raises it.

In Friedman's interpretation of the Marshallian demand curve, for which Friedman adduced substantial textual evidence, the following variables are assumed constant: 1. buyers' tastes and preferences; 2. their money incomes; 3. the purchasing power of money; and 4. the prices of all *closely related* goods (substitutes and complements). In this case, Friedman argued, in order to maintain constancy in the purchasing power of money at different prices along the demand curve, the prices of all goods other than the good under consideration and the goods closely related to it – Friedman calls them "unrelated goods" – must vary inversely as price changes along the demand curve. In other words, at each point on the demand curve buyers face a different configuration of prices of the goods unrelated to the good in question. These configurations are conceived to vary in such a way that the purchasing power of money and, therefore, its marginal utility to buyers, remain unchanged along the entire demand curve. Thus, for example, a fall of the price of a good and the accompanying increase in its quantity demanded reflect exclusively the decline of its own marginal utility relative to the marginal utilities of all other goods. The altered price-quantity position on the Friedmanite demand curve is therefore completely unaffected by forces that would increase "real income" by raising the purchasing power and thereby lowering the marginal utility of money with respect to goods in general.

Marshall (1920, p. 62) indeed emphasized the central role played by fixity of the purchasing power of money in his demand analysis:[5]

> If the purchasing power of money rises with regard to some things, and at the same time falls equally with regard to equally important things, its general purchasing power . . . has remained stationary . . . [W]e may throughout the volume neglect possible changes in the general purchasing power of money. Thus the price of anything will be taken as representative of its exchange value relatively to things in general.

Marshall explicitly incorporated these assumptions about money into his statement of the "law of marginal demand price," thus banishing the income effect from his *theoretical* analysis of the demand curve:

> The larger the amount of a thing that a person has the less, other things equal (*i.e.* the purchasing power of money, and the amount of money at his command being equal), will be the price which he will pay for a little more of it: or in other words his marginal demand price for it diminishes.
>
> (Marshall, 1920, p. 95)[6]

Friedman, however, preferred an alternative formulation of the *ceteris paribus* assumptions of the demand curve ([1949] 1970, pp. 51–52), which Marshall himself adopted in the Mathematical Appendix to the *Principles* (1920, pp. 838–858). In this variant, Marshall replaced the assumptions about the constancy of money income and the purchasing power of money with the assumption of a constant real income while additionally assuming a constant *average* of all other prices. To maintain real income unchanged under this set of assumptions implies compensating variations in buyers' money income that offset the income effect of the variation of the price of the good. Friedman opts for this variant of maintaining constant real income because "it is somewhat more convenient mathematically" while "essentially equivalent mathematically" to the constant purchasing power of money/constant money income variant ([1949] 1970, pp. 51–52).

We do not have to probe very deeply into Friedman's methodological rationale for preferring the constant real income demand curve to the Hicksian constant money income demand curve. Suffice it to say that the Friedmanite interpretation of the demand curve reflected his unique brand of positivism. As Yeager perceptively pointed out, for Friedman and the positivists, the income compensated demand curve was an attempt to deal only with "actually or conceptually attainable positions of equilibrium," and to derive "comparative static predictions" about actual price-quantity equilibria that will appear in the market (Yeager, 1960, pp. 53, 58).[7]

James Buchanan put the positivist position on the demand curve starkly:

> In general, demand curves are useful only because they allow some predictions to be made regarding the effects of changes in supply. Hence each point on the demand curve must represent an attainable equilibrium between demand and supply. It is extremely difficult to imagine any other possible use for a demand function.
>
> (Buchanan, 1958, p. 264)

Yeager rejected the positivist view of the demand curve and argued that demand curves are not to be regarded as "objectively existing things" but rather as "a pedagogical device for helping students grasp the inverse price-quantity relation asserted by the Law of Demand" (1960, pp. 63, 64).[8] In addition, Yeager (1960, p. 58) pointed out that the positivist conception of the demand curve precludes consideration of disequilibrium positions and the equilibrating processes that they engender.

3 The individual scale of values and the demand curve

Unlike Friedman, Buchanan, and the Chicago school, the causal-realist rejection of the income effect does not invoke positivist considerations. Indeed, quite the contrary: in formulating the demand curve, the causal-realist approach seeks to illustrate the logical implications of the existence of subjective value scales and the law of marginal utility for price formation. Thus, like Yeager, economists following this approach conceive the demand curve not as a real thing "out there" in the world, but as a hypothetical construct that assists in grasping the reality of the subjective foundations of the pricing process.[9]

What further distinguishes the causal-realist approach from the Hicksian and Friedmanite approaches to the demand curve and to price theory in general is its paramount aim of explaining the determination of *money* prices actually paid on the market. All of the concepts, techniques, and constructs used in causal-realist price theory are shaped by this overriding goal. In a market economy, relative prices are embedded in the structure of money prices, a structure that emerges anew on the market at every moment. Thus, money prices that are actually (or anticipated to be) paid are the prices relevant for the economic calculations of capitalist-entrepreneurs seeking to appraise and erect a complex structure of heterogeneous capital goods. Analyzing a fictional economy without money or where money is neutral is merely a preliminary step – albeit a necessary one – in the development of a realistic theory of price (Mises, 1998, pp. 202–206). Causal-realist price theory thus treats money as an integral part of the valuation process when deriving the demand curve.[10]

The analysis of the demand curve begins with the individual's scale of values or preferences, which is the cause of all economic phenomena in a real and profound sense.[11] Like "choosing" and "preferring," the value scale is part of what we may call the "ordinary language" of action. It is not a psychological category whose existence is established by introspection. Without the concept of a scale of values, it would be impossible to even describe an acting being or speculate meaningfully about the subjective processes that give rise to purposeful behavior.

The scale of values is a strictly personal and ordinal ranking of goods and money that determines and reveals itself in every individual's choices and actions on the market. The interaction of individual value scales thus determines the "equilibrium" prices and quantities exchanged at every instant in all markets. This momentary equilibrium position denotes a state in which all consumers allocate expenditures across goods so that the marginal utility of the last unit of each good purchased just exceeds the marginal utility of the sum of money expended for its price (Wicksteed [1933] 1957, 1: pp. 141–145, 212–233; Rothbard, 2009, pp. 264–267).

Another way of expressing the same situation is to say that the price and quantity exchanged of each good is determined at the intersection of its demand and supply curves. Although the language of demand and supply is more abstract and less precise than that of value scales, it is useful in simplifying and abbreviating the analysis and in highlighting the implications of the operation of the law of marginal utility in the pricing process. This important point has been emphasized by causal-realist price theorists. For example, Böhm-Bawerk (1959, p. 233) wrote that,

> I still find it questionable whether, with its resulting unavoidable suppression of any personal point of view, this method of presentation [by demand and supply curves] is really capable of supplanting and making superfluous a description by running commentary of the determination of price [i.e., in terms of the marginal pairs]. [I]t has been my personal opinion that the running commentary be retained.

Mises also recognized the primacy of the ordinary language of value scales for analyzing the pricing process, explaining that,

> The ultimate source of the determination of prices is the value judgments of the consumers. Prices are the outcome of the valuation preferring *a* to *b* . . . If one says that prices tend toward a point at which total demand equals total supply, one resorts to another mode of expressing the same concatenation of phenomena.
>
> (1998, pp. 329–330)[12]

4 Money income or money stock?

Because it seeks to explain prices as the outcome of a unitary valuation process that includes money, causal-realist price theory holds the following data constant in deriving the individual demand curve: 1. the buyer's value scale; 2. his money balances; 3. all other prices; and 4. the (anticipated) purchasing power of money. "Value scales" are used in preference to the more usual "tastes and preferences" because the former expression is richer and encompasses the utility rankings of money as well as goods, in contrast to the conventional expression that assumes the absence of money or its use purely as an unvalued *numeraire*. Assumed constancy of individual money holdings thus supplants the assumption of constant money income (Hicksian) or real income (Friedmanite). This revision is necessary to adapt the analysis to explain the formation of "realized prices."[13]

At the moment before any set of exchanges is consummated all that objectively exists are given individual stocks of goods and money.[14] These stocks were accumulated by their owners from a series of discrete exchanges in past factor and product markets. The current marginal utilities ascribed to these goods and money balances are *completely* determined by their relative positions on individual value scales. Thus, neither money income nor real income is a direct determinant of the demand curve. Of course, this is not to deny that expectations of future "income" or, more properly, the anticipated pattern of future prices indirectly influence the value rankings and marginal utilities of current stocks of money and goods. But "income" is not an observable and concrete historical outcome of the market process like a money price or the definite quantity of goods for which it is paid. All action takes place in the present moment and all economic action refers to the deployment of existing *stocks* of goods and money according to instantaneously prevailing value scales.

The notion of (net) income as a "flow" is the outcome of the individual entrepreneur's judgment of a recorded sequence of concrete transactions during a definite period of the past; or it may refer to his summary appraisement of quantities of goods or money that will accrue from discrete acts of exchange expected to take place during a relevant future time period. In either case, it is the product of a subjective judgment, because income in economic theory exists on a different plane of abstraction from realized prices and present stocks of goods and money. The concept of a stock of goods or a realized price is a first-order abstraction of an observable phenomenon referring to an objective result of valuation and action. The twin concepts of income and capital are, in contrast, derived abstractions referring to unobservable mental categories used by the actor in calculating the costs and returns of alternative uses of the objective means of action. These categories are employed in the intellectual process of economic calculation to establish a quantitative distinction that enables capitalist-entrepreneurs and factor owners to net out the consumable product from the gross revenues of their productive activities and to thereby maintain intact the capital value of their resources and their level of consumption in the future.[15]

Mises emphasized the crucial conceptual distinction between prices and income thusly:

> A market price is a real historical phenomenon, the quantitative ratio at which at a definite place and at a definite date two individuals exchanged definite quantities of two definite goods. It refers to the special conditions of a concrete act of exchange. It is ultimately determined by the value judgments of the individuals involved . . . *The market does not create or determine incomes. It is not a process of income formation* . . . There is in nature no such thing as a stream of income. Income is a category of action; it is the outcome of careful economizing of scarce factors.[16]
>
> (1998, p. 390; emphases added)

In his comprehensive treatment of price theory in *Man, Economy, and State*, Rothbard repeatedly identified the individual's "money assets" or "money stock" rather than "money income" as the direct co-determinant of the utility rankings of money and goods. Like Mises, Rothbard maintained that a person's current money assets are derived from past market exchanges, "from his and his ancestors' abilities in serving consumers on the market" (Rothbard, 2009, pp. 656–657). He explicitly conceived of money income as derivative of concrete exchanges that feed the reservoir of the directly valued element of money assets: "The . . . distribution of money income (*or rather of money assets*) . . . was the necessary consequence of a market allocation of prices and production" (Rothbard, 2009, p. 623; emphasis added).

Indeed, Rothbard emphatically rejected money income as a determinant of demand. In an evaluation of a textbook on price theory, he critically remarked:

> [W]hat in the world is the justification for the totally illicit leap . . . from talking about marginal utility to talking about a consumer's "money-income." What has happened to the concept of the marginal utility of money? It is completely illegitimate to . . . discuss the utilities of [goods] . . . without even mentioning, or ranking, the marginal utility of the money-price along with them.
>
> (Salerno, 2011, p. 12)

Thus, according to causal realist-theory, an individual always establishes the marginal utility rankings of money and goods, which underlie his demand curves, on the basis of his presently available money stock, not on estimations of past or prospective flows of money income. In sum, according to Rothbard:

> [E]very unit of the money commodity in a man's stock . . . is always being allocated to the three categories of use in accordance with his value scale [i.e., to consumption, saving/investment, and cash balance] . . . [E]ach unit

> will be used for the most useful end not yet achieved. It is in accordance with these principles – the maximization of his psychic income – that each man will allocate his money stock. In accordance with his value scale, each man will judge the respective marginal utilities to be obtained by each monetary unit in each use, and his allocation of money expenditures . . . will be determined by such judgments.
>
> (2009, p. 220)

5 The purchasing power of money and the demand curve

In the causal-realist derivation of the individual demand curve, then, units of various goods and of money are ranked and compared with one another by the individual. But in order to intermingle units of money with units of goods on a unitary value scale and judge their relative utilities, a *pre-existing* purchasing power of money must be assumed. The derivation of the demand curve in causal realist theory therefore necessarily involves reference to the time element, a distinction between "yesterday" and "today." The marginal utilities of goods today are derived directly from the varying importance of the wants they are expected to satisfy today. However, judging the subjective marginal utility of money today necessarily entails knowing yesterday's objective purchasing power of money, that is, the inverse of the structure of money prices in all their particularity. This means that before an individual can formulate his value scale in anticipation of today's exchanges, he must refer back to the purchasing power of money that emerged in the immediately previous round of exchanges. In other words, an individual's value rankings and marginal utilities of goods and money, which are operative in determining today's structure of prices, are based on today's valuations of goods and money. But the valuation of money today must refer back to *yesterday's* purchasing power of money, because it is the only means by which its prospective purchasing power in today's market can be anticipated and its marginal utility set. If money did not have a pre-existing purchasing power – that is, if money never exchanged against goods in the past – market participants would lack the knowledge needed to assign a value ranking to it and, consequently, no one would accept it in exchange for goods today.[17] Every money price therefore always contains a time component.[18]

There is, therefore, no contradiction in assuming that the purchasing power of money is constant *and* that the price of the good whose demand curve is being analyzed is permitted to vary. For the purchasing power of money that is held constant and on the basis of which the individual establishes his demand curve today is the purchasing power of money expected to prevail today, which refers back to yesterday's structure of prices as the starting point for the forecast. As Rothbard summed it up: "[T]oday's purchasing power of the monetary unit is determined by today's marginal utilities of money and goods, expressed in demand schedules, while today's marginal utility of money is directly dependent on yesterday's purchasing power of money" (Rothbard, 2009, p. 315).[19]

6 The illusion of the income effect and the instantaneous demand curve

We now turn to the analysis of the income effect in causal-realist demand theory. As we have argued, the role of the *ceteris paribus* assumption in demand analysis is to permit us to abstract from the complexities of the value scale and to trace out a curve that isolates the relationship between the price and quantity demanded of a single good. This curve illustrates the operation of the law of marginal utility in determining the inverse relationship between price and quantity demanded. As the individual gives away additional units of money (of fixed purchasing power) in exchange for additional units of the good, his "real" money stock declines, causing an ordinal rise in its marginal utility ranking, while his stock of the good increases, producing a fall in its marginal utility.[20] The fall in the marginal utility of the good in relation to money (and to all other goods) as his stock of the good increases and his stock of money declines implies that the demand price of the good will decline and that therefore quantity demanded of the good will increase as its money price declines (Rothbard, 2009, pp. 238–240; Wicksteed [1933] 1957, pp. 468–469).

As argued above, money income plays no part in demand analysis. The shape and position of the demand curve are fully explained by the structure of an individual's value scale, upon which are ranged *existing* stocks of goods and money. An increase in an individual's stock of money or a decrease in his demand for money, *ceteris paribus*, will lower the marginal utility of money and shift the demand curve to the right. A decrease in his stock of money or an increase in his demand for money, *ceteris paribus*, will have the reverse effect. If income, conceived as a "flow" of money (or goods), plays no direct role in the determination of the demand curve, then, strictly speaking, a movement along the demand curve cannot generate an income effect.

The contrast between causal-realist and mainstream demand analysis cuts far deeper, however. Causal-realist analysis distinguishes temporally and logically between cause and effect, in contrast to the timeless nature of the mutual determinism that mars the standard analysis.[21] In the causal-realist view, the relevant curves are the "instantaneous" demand and supply curves that give rise to the prices realized in actual market transactions.[22] These demand curves are derived from the individual's personal economic situation – his value scale, stocks of goods, real money stock, etc. – as it exists at the moment of his impending purchases. But the focus on the present moment does not mean that the influence of the individual's past or future is disregarded. His current stocks of goods and money are the resultant of his whole *history* of market transactions, including his experience of the exchange value of money in his last round of transactions. His scale of values is shaped by these stocks as well as his *expectations* of the prices to be paid and received in his anticipated series of future market exchanges.

The individual demand curve is thus an *ex ante* construct. It is derived from value scales formed on the basis of money prices experienced in the present, which becomes the immediate past once market activities are initiated.[23] Put another way, the demand curve is based on a person's overall economic position and his expectations prevailing in the moment preceding action.[24] If this were not the case, if the demand curve did not refer to a period temporally and logically antecedent to action, it would be impossible for individuals to formulate a coherent value scale, because the purchasing power of money would be unknown and units of money could not be meaningfully ranked against units of goods. The very existence of money prices thus logically implies the absence of an income effect or, more properly, a "purchasing power effect." That is, in causal-realist analysis, the individual's ex ante real money stock cannot vary with movements along the demand curve, because the curve can only be derived based on an already existing and "known" – or rather, definitely anticipated – purchasing power of money.

7 The nature of the substitution effect

Our causal-realist analysis of the income effect has the happy consequence of shedding new light on the nature of the substitution effect. In analyzing the individual value scale, it becomes clear that the substitution effect is an immediate inference from the law of marginal utility. Since the value scale involves a relative or ordinal ranking of all goods and money, all consumer goods are partial substitutes for one another. As Rothbard points out:

> *All* consumer's goods are . . . *partial* substitutes for one another. When a man ranks in his value scale the myriad of goods available and balances the diminishing utilities of each, he is treating them all as partial substitutes for one another. A change in ranking for one good by necessity changes the ranking of all other goods, since all rankings are ordinal and relative.
>
> (2009, p. 282; emphases in original)

Change in the rank-order or the money price of any one good will produce changes in the relative positions of all other goods that will upset the equilibrium among the marginal utilities of goods and their money prices. A reallocation of given money assets among the various lines of consumption expenditure will be required to realign the marginal utilities of all goods with their money prices.

For example, if the price of good A increases along an elastic individual demand curve, the marginal utility of A will fall below the marginal utility of its new money price and also relative to the marginal utilities of the increased quantities of goods B, C, D, etc., which can now be had in exchange for A's higher money price. The more favorable terms on which the alternatives to A can be acquired will also tend to raise their marginal utilities relative to their respective (constant) money prices. Or, in other words, the fact that less of the individual's money stock is spent on good A, *ceteris paribus*, logically implies a decline of the marginal utility of money in relation to substitute goods. The result will be that the individual will readjust the marginal utilities of goods and money by substituting additional units of some or all of these goods for units of good A, shifting his demand curves for these substitutes to the right.

If the individual's demand curve for A is inelastic, then a rise in the price of good A will cause a greater proportion of his money stock to be used to purchase A and less money to be spent on all other goods combined. A's position on the value scale will once again fall relative to its new, higher money price and the law of marginal utility will dictate a restriction in the number of units purchased. However, the increased allocation of money to the purchase of good A will entail a rise of the marginal utility of money relative to some or all non-A goods and the marginal utilities of these substitute goods will decline below their fixed money prices. To re-establish equilibrium in accordance with the law of marginal utility, the individual would reduce his purchases of these goods. In the new equilibrium position: 1. the marginal utility of the stock of each good in his possession would again just exceed the marginal utility of the sum of money representing its price; and 2. expanding the purchase of any good beyond this margin would result in a disequilibrating reversal of the marginal utilities of the good and its money price. In the case of an inelastic demand for good A, the demand curves for substitute goods will thus shift to the left in response to a rise in the price of A.

It is important to note that alterations in marginal utilities that we have been discussing in the last two paragraphs should not be construed as changes in the individual's underlying value scale, which is assumed fixed in demand analysis. Rather, they are expressions of the structure of a given value scale in response to external changes in the market situation, i.e., prices. The configuration of the value scale is necessarily "price dependent" because a change in the external structure of money prices revolutionizes the internal terms on which alternative goods can be substituted for one another.[25] Given that the values of goods are inherently interdependent because they are ranked on a unitary value scale, the law of marginal utility implies that all goods are at least partial substitutes for one another. In contrast to mainstream consumer demand theory, causal-realist analysis treats the concepts of substitutability and complementarity as derived from distinct epistemological bases. Substitution is a necessary and universal relationship among goods that is directly deduced from the existence of value scales, although the degree of substitutability among different goods may be greater or lesser depending on concrete historical circumstances. Complementarity is fundamentally a historically contingent relationship that depends on the concrete structure of individual value scales. Furthermore, complementarity among consumers' goods, where it exists, will always be mixed with the all-pervasive relation of substitutability, and it will only be potentially observable where it is stronger than the substitution effect.[26]

8 The income effect and the backward-bending labor supply curve: a concluding note

It may clarify the argument of this paper to critically analyze the recent controversy among critics and defenders of causal-realist price theory regarding the relationship between the income effect and the backward-bending supply curve of labor. The controversy focused on Rothbard (2009), who, in his treatise *Man, Economy, and State*, ignored the income effect in deriving the demand curve while conceding the possibility of a backward-bending supply curve of labor. Caplan (1999, pp. 828–829) criticizes Rothbard for being inconsistent in banishing the income effect from demand analysis while admitting that a backward bend in the labor supply curve was conceivable. Caplan (1999, p. 829) also notes that Rothbard goes "so far as to mention a substitution and income effect" in discussing the increase in labor supplied in response to an increase in taxation of wages. This does not, however, imply, as Caplan claims, that Rothbard recognizes the existence of a Hicksian income effect and "borrows [it] on an ad hoc basis" (Caplan, 1999, p. 829). First, Rothbard places the terms "income effect" and "substitution effect" in scare quotes in the text (Rothbard, 2009, p. 915).[27] Second, in a later section of his book, Rothbard provides a more elaborate analysis of income taxation and the backward-bending labor supply curve strictly in terms of variations in the marginal utilities of leisure and money assets (Rothbard, 2009, pp. 1164–1165). And, third, as noted above, there is the memo Rothbard (2011) wrote explicitly dismissing "the alleged division between the 'income effect' and the 'substitution effect'" – which he again places in scare quotes.

Salin (1996) presents an immanent critique of the income effect using the Hicksian analytical apparatus. He concludes that "the income effect does not exist as a general phenomenon; it is a mathematical illusion in a badly specified world" (p. 97). The details of Salin's argument do not concern us here. What is important is that in the appendix to his article, he (1996, pp. 104–106) argues for a position Caplan takes for granted, viz., the existence of the income effect is the necessary condition of a backward-bending supply curve. However, since Salin maintains that the income effect is illusory, he concludes that the backward-bending supply curve is impossible.

Gonzalez (2000) explicitly rejects Salin's conclusion and defends Rothbard's position that the backward-bending labor supply curve is compatible with the derivation of the individual demand curve using a purely ordinal value scale and the law of marginal utility. Although his analysis marks a substantive advance of the debate, Gonzalez unfortunately muddies the waters by superfluously importing the terminology, if not the conventional concept, of the income effect into his analysis (Gonzalez, 2000, p. 56). Thus, he concludes, "the possibility of the income effect of a price change is implied by the Misesian pure logic of choice" (Gonzalez, 2000, p. 57). This is particularly jarring in light of Mises's and Rothbard's views on the concept of income discussed above.[28]

The conundrum presented by Rothbard eschewing the income effect in his demand analysis while recognizing the possibility of a backward-bending supply curve was actually neatly resolved once and for all in a brilliant and concise piece of analysis by Lionel Robbins ([1930] 1997) in 1930. Robbins developed his analysis to rebut the arguments of Frank Knight and A.C. Pigou that the law of diminishing marginal utility implied that the quantity of labor supplied always varied inversely to changes in the after-tax wage rate, or, in the words of Robbins

([1930] 1997, p. 81), "that the imposition of a tax will always have the effect of making a man work more, and a rise in his wage rates will always make him work less." Robbins demonstrated that a forward-sloping, as well as a backward-bending, labor supply curve is consistent with the law of diminishing marginal utility.[29] Forty years later, James Buchanan (1971, p. 383) resurrected Robbins's forgotten analysis, which he deems an "essentially correct explanation." Buchanan (1971, p. 383) uses the analysis to demonstrate that the "Hicksian income effect-substitution effect apparatus" was "wholly unnecessary" to derive "the backbending supply curve of labor." Indeed, Buchanan (1971, p. 283) characterizes the view among modern economists that the income effect is necessary to deriving the backward-bending supply curve as "an example of doctrinal retrogression." Robbins's analysis is straightforward, and it can be presented, as it was originally, with the help of a few simple diagrams. While two of the diagrams are similar to the two used by Robbins, I have added a third suggested by Buchanan (1971, p. 383). For clarity of exposition, I have also added tables of hypothetical data, which are used to generate the graphs.

Table 2.1 presents an individual labor supply schedule, which generates the backward-bending supply curve shown in Figure 2.1 as A-B-C. (We ignore for the moment the figure in parentheses.) Between the wage rates of $5 and $20 per

Table 2.1 Individual labor supply schedule

Wage rate	*Quantity of labor*
$/hour	*hours/week*
5.00	25
10.00	40
20.00	50
40.00	30 (20)

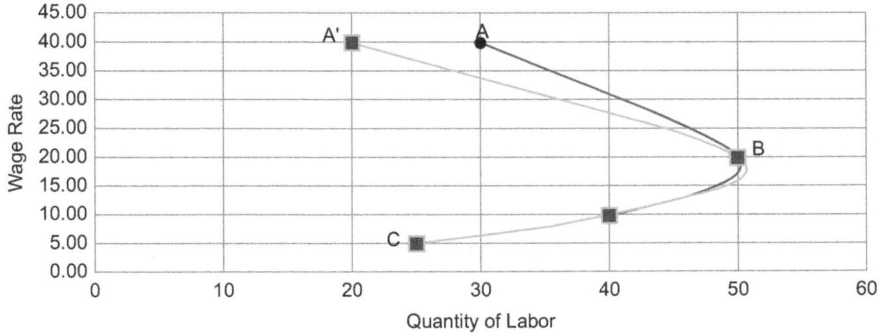

Figure 2.1 Individual labor supply curve

hour, the quantity supplied of labor on a weekly basis varies positively with the wage rate; as the wage rate rises from $20 to $40 per hour, the quantity of labor hours supplied declines and the supply curve bends backwards. Now, as Robbins ([1930] 1997, p. 79n1) demonstrated, this result is easily derived from the law of marginal utility by following Wicksteed and "exhibiting all psychological variables as phenomena of demand." Thus, we portray the laborer as exchanging hours of leisure, which he values and demands as a consumer's good, for real money assets (units of real income in Robbins's example).

In order to transform the supplier of labor hours into a demander of money assets, we translate the labor supply curve into a demand curve for money assets with money on the quantity axis and the reciprocal of the wage rate, that is, labor – or forgone leisure – hours per dollar purchased on the price axis.[30] These results are shown in Table 2.2 and Figure 2.2, where, for example, a wage rate of $20 per hour is equivalent to a labor price of money assets of .05 hours per dollar and the total quantity demanded is equal to $1,000 (= $20/hour x 50 hours). Note that the demand curve for money assets, A-B-C, slopes downward throughout its entire length, despite the fact that it was derived from a backward-bending supply curve. This indicates that as the labor price of money assets falls, *ceteris paribus*, the quantity demanded increases, so that the existence of a backward-bending supply curve does not necessarily contradict the law of marginal utility.

Table 2.2 Individual demand for money assets in terms of labor

Labor price of money, hours/$	*Money assets, $/week*	*Total expenditure of hours on money (column 1 × column 2)*
0.20	125.00	25
0.10	400.00	40
0.05	1,000.00	50
0.025	1,200.00 (800.00)	30 (20)

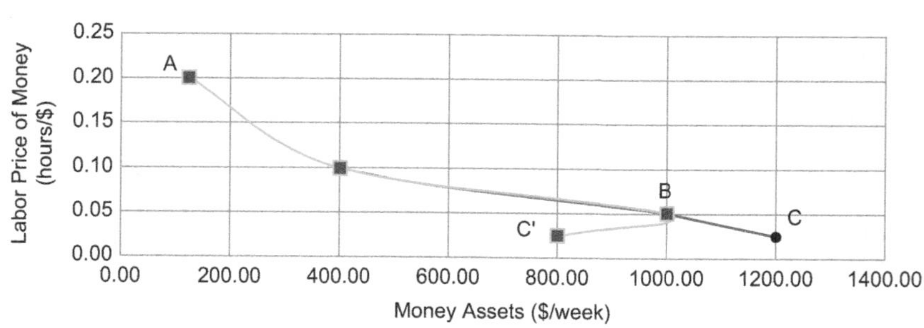

Figure 2.2 Individual demand curve for money assets in terms of labor

In other words, as the "pre-Hicksian" Hicks approvingly summed up Robbins's contribution: "[t]he only natural deduction from the law of diminishing marginal utility is, not that the supply curve of labor must slope downwards [the Knight-Pigou position], but that this demand for income must slope downwards" (Hicks, 1932, p. 98).

To avoid confusion, a few comments on this analytical construction are in order. First, note that the backward-bending segment of the supply curve, A-B in Figure 2.1, corresponds to an inelastic demand for money assets in terms of labor, segment B-C in Figure 2.2. This can be seen from Figure 2.3, which is the graph Robbins derived from the demand curve for money assets by plotting the total expenditure of labor hours for each quantity of money assets purchased as the labor price changes.

A similar "reciprocal demand" or "offer curve," first formulated by Marshall and Edgeworth, is used in international trade theory to show the total exports that a country is willing to expend for each given quantity of total imports as the terms of trade vary.[31] In this case, the "exports" are labor hours and the "imports" are money assets. The reciprocal demand curve is, in effect, a total expenditure curve. As in the case of conventional demand-curve analysis, a decline in total expenditure as price decreases indicates that the associated segment of the demand curve is inelastic. Thus, a backward-bending segment of the labor supply curve implies an absolute value of the elasticity of demand for money assets in terms of labor of less than one.

Second, the law of marginal utility rules out a supply curve that bends back so sharply that it yields a lower quantity of money assets at a higher wage rate. For example, let us substitute a quantity supplied of 20 hours (in parentheses) for 30 hours at a wage rate of $40 per hour in Table 2.1. The labor supply curve in Figure 2.1 changes shape, with the backward-bending segment now represented

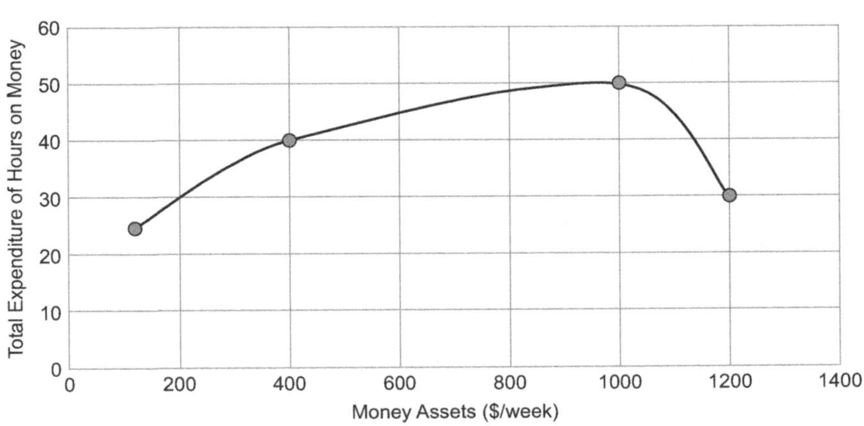

Figure 2.3 Reciprocal demand curve for money assets in terms of labor

by A'-B, which is flatter and more elastic than segment A-B. The total quantity of money demanded now *declines* from $1,000 at a wage rate of $40 per hour to only $800. But this implies that fewer money assets are purchased as their labor price falls from .05 hours/$ to .025 hours/$ and the demand curve for money assets over this range takes on a positive slope, which is B-C'.

This example thus violates the law of marginal utility, which dictates that a lower labor price of money assets must always lead to a greater quantity demanded. For if a laborer responds to an increase in the wage rate by working fewer hours and consuming more leisure, his marginal utility of leisure falls. In order to balance this fall in the marginal utility of leisure, he must allocate his additional resources so that his marginal utility of money also declines, which is inconsistent with a reduction in his quantity demanded of money assets.

Although Rothbard does not cite Robbins's analysis in his own discussion of the backward-bending labor supply curve, he explains the phenomenon in similar terms, referring to the labor price of money income or assets. In his analysis of the income tax, for example, Rothbard writes:

> Income taxation reduces every taxpayer's money income and real income . . . His income from working is more expensive, and leisure cheaper, so that he will tend to work less . . . [M]uch has been made of the fact that every man's marginal utility of money rises as his money assets fall and, therefore, that there may be a rise in the marginal utility of the reduced income obtainable from his current expenditure of labor. It is true, in other words, that the same labor now earns every man less money but this very reduction in money income may also raise the marginal utility of a unit of money to the extent that the marginal utility of his total income will be *raised*, and he will be induced to work *harder* as a result of the income tax. This may very well be true in some cases and there is nothing . . . contrary to economic analysis in such an event.
>
> (2009, pp. 1164–1165; emphases in original)

Rothbard concisely specifies the structure of an individual's value scale that must prevail in order for a change in the wage rate to produce a backward-bending supply curve:

> There will be such a backward supply curve if the marginal utility of money falls rapidly enough and the marginal disutility of leisure forgone rises rapidly enough as units of labor are sold for higher prices in money.
>
> (2009, p. 574n14)

This point can be expressed in terms of our example. At an hourly wage rate of $20, the individual chooses to sacrifice 50 hours of leisure for $1,000. On his underlying value scale, then, the marginal increment of $20 is ranked just above the 50th hour of forgone leisure and, therefore, above infra-marginal hours like the 31st hour. When the wage rate increases to $40 per hour, the individual decides to forgo 30 hours of leisure in exchange for $1,200. The additional earnings of $200 causes the marginal utility of money to fall so rapidly relative to the marginal utility of leisure that at the new equilibrium point on his value scale the previously infra-marginal hours of leisure forgone from the 49th down to 31st that were ranked *below* $20 at the lower wage rate are now ranked *above* $40. This reinforces the point that, although the labor supply curve may bend backwards, its bend cannot be so extreme that a rise in the wage rate yields not only fewer yours of labor but also lower money earnings, since this would result in a rise and not the required rapid decline in the marginal utility of money relative to that of leisure. In technical terms, "the elasticity of individual supply of labor must be either positive or lie between 0 and –1" (Hicks, 1932, n1).

Contrary to Caplan's claim, therefore, Rothbard did not "borrow" the income effect from post-Hicksian neoclassical economics in order to derive the backward-bending labor supply curve, let alone the conventional demand curve. Rather, in ignoring the income effect, Rothbard adopted and consistently applied the causal-realist approach to demand analysis developed in the writings of pre-Hicksian price theorists running back through Mises, Robbins, Wicksteed, Fetter, and Davenport to Böhm-Bawerk and Menger.

Notes

1 See for example Stigler (1952) and Stonier and Hague (1953).

2 The most notable contributors to this tradition include Menger's students Eugen von Böhm-Bawerk and Friedrich von Wieser, as well as prominent Anglo-American economists such as Philip Wicksteed, Lionel Robbins, J. B. Clark, Frank A. Fetter, and Herbert J. Davenport. After World War Two, causal-realist price theory was further elaborated by Ludwig von Mises and, especially, Murray Rothbard. See Salerno (1999).

3 Will E. Mason (1996) demonstrates conclusively that the so-called classical dichotomy was actually an "inversion" of classical monetary theory perpetrated by neoclassical quantity theorists such as Irving Fisher, Alfred Marshall, and Edwin Kemmerer.

4 A comprehensive survey of the debate that also includes a collection of some of the more important contributions can be found in Ekelund et al. (1972). Yeager (1960) provides a critical review of the controversy that emphasizes its methodological aspects.

5 Ekelund et al. (1972, p. 42) argue that Hicks was cognizant of Marshall's assumption of the constant purchasing power of money but viewed it as a "simplifying assumption that was, in rigorous terms, inconsistent with the rest of his formulation."

6 Thus Ekelund et al. (1972, p. 43) conclude: "In the theoretical formulation of the demand curve, Marshall's formulation fits the constant real income classification and the Friedman interpretation appears valid." The authors contend, however, that Marshall dispenses with the assumption of constant purchasing power of money, while retaining that of constant money income in practical applications of the demand curve. In his exhaustive textual analysis of Marshall's derivation and application of the demand curve, Alford (1956) comes to a more or less similar conclusion.

7 Accordingly, Friedman ([1949] 1970, pp. 56, 84–86) interprets the demand curve so as to rule out Giffen goods.

8 At the end of the day, Yeager (1960, p. 63, fn. 32) remains a Hicksian price theorist who accepts that Giffen's Paradox "could conceivably occur" in the real world. Cf. also Yeager (1999).

9 For example, Mises pointed out,

> [W]e do not have any knowledge or experience concerning the shape of such [supply and demand] curves. Always, what we know is only market prices – that is, not the curves but only a point which we interpret as the intersection of two hypothetical curves. The drawing of such curves may prove expedient in visualizing the problems for undergraduates. But for the real tasks of catallactics they are mere byplay.
>
> (Mises, 1998, p. 330)

10 As Mises emphasized:

> Economics is mainly concerned with the analysis of the determination of money prices of goods and services exchanged on the market . . . Catallactics is the analysis of those actions which are conducted on the basis of monetary calculation. Market exchange and monetary calculation are inseparably linked together. A market in which there is direct exchange only is merely an imaginary construction.
>
> (Mises, 1998, p. 235)

11 For example, for Wicksteed ([1933] 1957, p. 36), "The conception of the scale of preferences" is "quite fundamental" and underlies "all investigations" of economic phenomena; and for Rothbard, "[T]he individual's value scale provides the key to the determination of all events on the market" (Rothbard, 2009, p. 379). According to Kirzner: "The fundamental premise the theory of demand (and also market theory in its entirety) is built upon is that *men do not consider all of their desires to be of equal importance* . . . [W]e *rank* these inclinations or desires as either more or less urgent" ([1963] 2011, p. 48; emphases in original).

12 Also, Wicksteed, in the first volume of his treatise, presented exhaustive partial and general equilibrium analyses of price determination using preference scales exclusively. He did not introduce supply and demand curves until the second volume of his work (Wicksteed, [1933] 1957, 1: 126–157, 212–265). And even here, Wicksteed emphasized that these curves present "many problems both of interpretation and construction," are "purely abstract," and are necessarily "isolated" such that a system of such curves cannot be constructed "as to be valid simultaneously" (Wicksteed, [1933] 1957, 2: 439, 474).

13 This felicitous term was coined by Arthur Marget ([1938–42] 1966). According to Marget: "[A] realized price represents the passage of money for an article sold for money . . . [A]ny given realized price is what it is as the result of the conformation and position of the market demand curve and market supply curve prevailing at the moment the price is realized" (Marget [1938–42] 1966, 2: 240).

14 The emphasis on stocks rather than flows in supply and demand analysis is distinctively causal-realist and non-Marshallian. As Creedy notes, it traces back through Wicksteed and Edgeworth to Jevons and Böhm-Bawerk (Creedy, 1991, pp. 690–691). I would also add Menger as a forerunner of this approach.

15 On the meaning and nature of maintaining, accumulating or consuming capital, see Mises (1998, pp. 511–514) and Hayek ([1939] 1975; 1984).

16 As Mises further elaborated:

> The fundamental notion of economic calculation is the notion of capital and its correlative income . . . It is a product of reasoning and its place is in the human mind. It is a mode of looking at the problems of acting, a method of appraising them from the point of view of a definite plan. It determines the course of human action and is, in this sense only, a real factor.
>
> (Mises, 1998, pp. 260, 512)

17 This is the essence of the regression theorem formulated by Mises (1971, pp. 97–123; 1998, pp. 405–413).
18 The historical component of any one particular money price, say, the price of corn today, is not yesterday's price of corn, but the entire structure of prices obtaining on yesterday's market, the reciprocal of which constitutes yesterday's purchasing power of money. See Rothbard (2009, p. 271).
19 In analyzing the individual's scale of preferences, Wicksteed viewed the money price as an "index" of the terms on which alternatives to the good are available, which is tantamount to taking the purchasing power of money as known and constant:

> [W]e will begin by taking for granted . . . the purchasing power of money and the existence of market or current prices as facts . . . [W]e do not know the actual alternatives represented by the price of any one commodity until we know the price of certain other commodities also.
>
> (Wicksteed [1933] 1957, 1: 18, 22)

Davenport also recognized that analysis of the demand curve assumes "an existing system of prices upon goods in general and an established price relation for these goods in terms of money"

(Davenport [1913] 1968, p. 274).

20 All valuations involving money, of course, refer to the real money stock and not to the nominal quantity of money assets (Rothbard, 2009, pp. 774, 916–917, 1166).
21 See the attempt by Patinkin (1965) to explain the purchasing power of money while eschewing temporal, causal analysis in favor of simultaneous mutual determination. For a critique of Patinkin from a causal-realist perspective, see Salerno (2010, pp. 84–87) and Edwards (1985, pp. 59–66).
22 According to Marget ([1938–42] 1966, 2: 235 fn. 31), writing in the late 1930s, the term "instantaneous" was "commonly" used to designate such demand and supply schedules.
23 See the insightful discussion by Rothbard (2009, pp. 279–281) of the *ex ante* nature of valuations, plans, expectations and the formation of individual demand curves.
24 As Marget perceptively stated:

> The essential element . . . is summed up by the statement that the demand schedules of the general Theory of Value are concerned with what has . . . been called "the pre-formation of market prices" . . . [T]he market demand schedules . . . are "*ex ante*" curves representing the *plans* of possible purchasers with respect to the *present* market situation, as that situation is evaluated in the light of his own present economic situation. . . . [S]uch an evaluation and therefore the "plans" based upon it, would take into account (1) the ways in which the purchaser's own present economic position and the general market situation have been affected by past events; and (2) the purchaser's expectations with respect to his own future position and the future market situation.
>
> (Marget [1938–42] 1966, 2: 177–178; emphases in original)

25 On this point see the classic discussion by Wicksteed ([1933] 1957, 1: 18–28).
26 Rothbard presents the clearest and most comprehensive account of the causal-realist approach to substitutable and complementary goods, which highlights the important epistemological distinction between the two kinds of related goods(Rothbard, 2009, pp. 280–288). Mises distinguishes the general praxeological relation of substitution among goods, which he calls the "the general connexity of the prices of all goods and services," from the historically contingent "particular connexities of the prices of a limited number of commodities" (Mises, 1998, p. 389).

27 Interestingly, in an unpublished draft of his article, Caplan (1997) placed quotation marks around the two terms in his own text, but still did not unambiguously indicate that they originally appeared in scare quotes in Rothbard's text.
28 Rajsic (2010) offers a critique of Caplan that purports to derive Hicksian substitution and income effects using Rothbard's ordinal value-scale approach. Needless to say, the attempt, although certainly ingenious, fails. We do not discuss it in the text because it makes no reference to the labor supply curve.
29 It is telling that economists such as Knight, Pigou, and Robbins, who were trained in the analytical techniques of the pre-Hicksian era, had no problem grasping that a backward-bending supply curve did not violate the law of marginal utility.
30 Steeped as he was in Austro-Wicksteedian theory, Robbins evidently did not think it necessary to draw the labor supply curve and perform this transformation, but immediately began his analysis with the demand curve for "income in terms of effort." This is the omission that Buchanan (1971, p. 79) regretted.
31 On the development of reciprocal demand analysis from Mill to Marshall and Marshall's formulation of the offer curve, see Allen (1965, pp. 11–27) and Wu ([1939] 2007, pp. 163–175). For the derivation and use of the offer curve in modern trade theory, see, for example, Thompson (1993, pp. 142–160).

References

Alford, R. F. G. 1956. "Marshall's Demand Curve." *Economica* 23 (89): 23–48.

Allen, W. B. (ed.). 1965. *International Trade Theory: Hume to Ohlin.* New York: Random House.

Böhm-Bawerk, E. V. 1959. *Capital and Interest*, Vol. II: *Positive Theory of Capital.* Trans. George D. Huncke. South Holland, IL: Libertarian Press.

Buchanan, J. M. 1958. "*Ceteris Paribus*: Some Notes on Methodology." *Southern Economic Journal* 24 (3): 259–270.

———. 1971. "The Backbending Supply Curve of Labor: An Example of Doctrinal Retrogression?" *History of Political Economy* 3 (2): 383–390.

Caplan, B. 1997. "Why I Am Not an Austrian Economist," http://econfaculty.gmu.edu/bcaplan/whyaust.htm, retrieved April 1 2017.

———. 1999. "The Austrian Search for Realistic Foundations." *Southern Economic Journal* 65 (4): 823–838.

Creedy, J. 1991. "The Role of Stocks in Supply and Demand: Wicksteed's Problem." *Oxford Economic Papers* 43 (4): 689–701.

Davenport, H. J. 1968 [1913]. *The Economics of Enterprise.* New York: Augustus M. Kelley.

Edwards, J. R. 1985. The Economist of the Country: Ludwig von Mises in the History of Monetary Thought. New York: Carlton Press.

Ekelund, R. B., E. G. Furubotn, and W. P. Gramm. 1972. "Demand Theory in Marshall's Tradition." In R. B. Ekelund, E. G. Furubotn, and W. P. Gramm, eds., *The Evolution of Modern Demand Theory: A Collection of Essays.* Lexington, MA: D.C. Heath and Company, pp. 39–53.

Friedman, M. 1954. "The Marshallian Demand Curve: A Reply." *Journal of Political Economy* 62 (3): 261–266.

———. 1970 [1949]. "The Marshallian Demand Curve." In M. Friedman, ed., *Essays in Positive Economics.* Chicago: University of Chicago Press, pp. 47–99.

Gonzalez, R. 2000. "Misesian Economics and the Response to a Price Change." *Quarterly Journal of Austrian Economics* 3 (1): 55–58.

Hayek, F. A. 1975 [1939]. "The Maintenance of Capital." In Friedrich August Hayek, ed., *Profits, Interest and Investment and Other Essays on the Theory of Industrial Fluctuations*. Clifton, NJ: Augustus M. Kelley, pp. 83–134.

———. 1984. "Capital Consumption." In Roy McCloughry, ed., *Money, Capital and Fluctuations: Early Essays*. Chicago: University of Chicago Press, pp. 136–158.

Hicks, J. R. 1932. *The Theory of Wages*. New York: Palgrave Macmillan.

———. 1946. *Value and Capital: An Inquiry Into Some Fundamental Principles of Economic Theory*. London: Oxford University Press.

Hudik, M. 2011. "Rothbardian Demand: A Critique." *Review of Austrian Economics* 24 (3): 311–318.

Kirzner, I. M. 2011 [1963]. *Market Theory and the Price System*. Ed. P. J. Boettke and F. Sautet. Indianapolis, IN: Liberty Fund.

Klein, P. G. 2008. "The Mundane Economics of the Austrian School." *Quarterly Journal of Austrian Economics* 11 (3–4): 165–187.

Marget, A. W. 1966 [1938–1942]. *The Theory of Prices: A Re-Examination of the Central Problems of Monetary Theory*. 2 vols. New York: August M. Kelley.

Marshall, A. 1920. *The Principles of Economics: An Introductory Volume*. 8th ed. London: Macmillan and Co., Limited.

Mason, W. E. 1996. *Classical Versus Neoclassical Monetary Theories: The Roots, Ruts, and Resilience of Monetarism – and Keynesianism*. Ed. W. N. Butos. Boston: Kluwer Academic Publishers.

Mises, L. V. 1971. *The Theory of Money and Credit*. Trans. H. E. Batson. 2nd ed. Irvington-on-Hudson, NY: Foundation for Economic Education.

Mises, L. V. 1998. *Human Action: A Treatise on Economics*. 2nd Scholar's ed. Auburn, AL: Ludwig von Mises Institute.

Patinkin, D. 1965. *Money, Interest, and Prices: An Integration of Monetary and Value Theory*. 2nd ed. New York: Harper & Row.

Rajsic, P. April 8, 2010. "Did Rothbard 'Borrow' the Income and Substitution Effects?" *Mises Daily Articles*. https://mises.org/library/did-rothbard-borrow-income-and-substitution-effects, retrieved March 15, 2017.

Robbins, L. 1997 [1930]. "On the Elasticity of Demand for Income in Terms of Effort." In S. Howson, ed., *Economic Science and Political Economy: Selected Articles*. New York: New York University Press, pp. 79–84.

Rothbard, M. N. 2009. *Man, Economy and State: A Treatise on Economic Principles With Power and Market: Government and the Economy*. 2nd Scholar's ed. Auburn, AL: Ludwig von Mises Institute.

Salerno, J. T. 1999. "The Place of Mises's Human Action in the Development of Modern Economic Thought." *Quarterly Journal of Austrian Economics* 2 (1): 35–65.

———. 2010. "Ludwig von Mises's Monetary Theory in Light of Modern Monetary Thought." In J. T. Salerno, *Money, Sound and Unsound*. Auburn, AL: Ludwig von Mises Institute, pp. 61–114.

———. 2011. "Varieties of Austrian Price Theories: Rothbard Reviews Kirzner." *Libertarian Papers* 3: 1–23.

Salin, P. 1996. "The Myth of the Income Effect." *The Review of Austrian Economics* 9 (1): 95–106.

Stigler, G. J. 1952. *The Theory of Price*. 2nd ed. New York: Palgrave Macmillan.

Stonier, A. W., and D. C. Hague. 1953. *A Textbook of Economic Theory*. New York: Longmans Green and Co.

Thompson, Henry. 1993. *International Economics: A Microeconomic Approach*. White Plains, NY: Longman.

Wicksteed, P. H. 1957 [1933]. *The Common Sense of Political Economy and Selected Papers and Reviews on Economic Theory*. 2 vols. Ed. L. Robbins. London: Routledge and Kegan Paul.

Wu, C.-Y. 2007 [1939]. *An Outline of International Price Theories*. Auburn, AL: Ludwig von Mises Institute.

Yeager, L. 1960. "*Methodenstreit* Over Demand Curves." *Journal of Political Economy* 68 (1): 53–64.

———. 1999. "Should Austrians Scorn General-Equilibrium Theory?" *Review of Austrian Economics* 11 (1): 19–30.

Part 2

The evolution of causal-realist production theory

3 From Marshallian partial equilibrium to Austrian general equilibrium

The evolution of Rothbard's production theory

Patrick Newman

> [C]oncentration on a single firm and the reaction of its owner is not the appropriate route to the theory of production; on the contrary, it is likely to be misleading. . . . In the current literature, this preoccupation with the single firm rather than with the interrelatedness of firms in the economy has led to the erection of a vastly complicated and largely valueless edifice of production theory
>
> (Rothbard, 2009 [1962], p. 455)

I Introduction

Murray Rothbard's *Man, Economy, and State* (2009 [1962]) is a landmark book in Austrian economics. In the tradition of earlier writers, especially Ludwig von Mises (2008 [1949]), it is written in the form of a treatise that derives the general body of economic theorems from the ground up, starting with isolated individual action, moving on to various forms of interpersonal exchange, and ending with government intervention. When developing this economic organon Rothbard synthesized the ideas of many economists working in the Austrian tradition, including Carl Menger, Eugen von Böhm-Bawerk, Frank Fetter, Phillip H. Wicksteed, Ludwig von Mises, and F. A Hayek. The Austrian, or "causal-realist," approach adopted by these writers concentrates on issues such as real-world price formation, entrepreneurship and the market process, and the relationship between time and the production structure. It uses the praxeological method, deduction grounded in the fact that humans behave purposively, along with a series of realistic empirical assumptions, such as that there exist a variety of natural resources and that humans value leisure as a consumer good (Salerno, 2009, pp. xxxii–xxxiii).

One of Rothbard's monumental contributions in this book was the construction of a systematic production theory that integrated various strands of thought developed by earlier writers working in the same tradition, including theories of capital and interest, the structure of production, rent and factor pricing, and entrepreneurship (Salerno, 2009, p. xxvi). One especially notable achievement of Rothbard's was his integration of the Mises-Fetter pure time preference theory of interest with the Hayek-Wicksell structure of production analysis (Salerno, 2009, p. xxvii; Rothbard, 2009 [1962], p. lvii). In general, his production theory integrated all of the interrelations of the production structure and set out to actually explain the formation of output and input prices throughout the economy. This synthesized Austrian production theory is different from the more well-known Marshallian partial equilibrium approach. The latter is best represented in modern economics by Chicago production theory, which was mainly developed by George Stigler and Milton Friedman, who each built on the works of Alfred Marshall and Frank Knight (Salerno, 2011, pp. 1–2). This theory analyzes equilibrium production decisions from the viewpoint of an isolated firm with given input and output prices.[1]

In contrast, Austrian production theory is the halfway house, or middle ground, between excessive microeconomic analysis – the Marshallian partial equilibrium view that concentrates on a single firm facing fixed prices – and excessive macroeconomic analysis, exemplified by the Keynesian aggregative approach that hermetically seals off sectors of the economy from each other. The Austrian theory shows that a change in any sector of the economy must always impart its influence through repercussions in the structure of prices and production in other sectors. This Austrian general equilibrium is starkly different from Walrasian general equilibrium for three important reasons. The first is that it is dynamic, not static, because it emphasizes the importance of uncertainty and change and reveals the equilibrating processes between equilibrium states that are driven by profit-seeking capitalist-entrepreneurs. The second is that it recognizes the intertemporal heterogeneous capital structure. The third is that it expresses its theorems using verbal logic rather than non-causal, mutually determined mathematical equations (Rothbard, 2009 [1962], p. 361; 2008 [1963], pp. 65–66). At the beginning of his treatise, Rothbard explained these distinctions as follows:

> One "radical" feature of our analysis of production is a complete break with the currently fashionable "short-run" theory of the firm, substituting for this a general theory of marginal value productivity and capitalization. *It is a "general equilibrium" analysis in the dynamic Austrian sense, and not in the static, currently popular Walrasian sense.*
>
> (Rothbard, 2009 [1962], p. lvii; emphasis added)[2]

However, many readers of Rothbard's are unaware that the original drafts of his treatise contained a production theory grounded in Marshallian partial equilibrium theory, and that only after writing extensively did Rothbard realize much of it was untenable. Only in a 1990 interview did Rothbard briefly mention the lost chapter, stating that "I took Chapter 5 out of *Man, Economy, and State*, which included the usual cost-curve analysis. I wrote the whole chapter before I realized that the approach I was taking was nonsense. So I started over" (Rothbard, 1990). Tentatively titled "Chapter 5: Producer's Activity" (2018 [1953]), the manuscript was recently reconstructed by the present author from the materials available in the Rothbard archives at the Ludwig von Mises Institute. Among other things, what is particularly interesting is that Rothbard constructed the chapter from the point of view of an individual firm, and based the analysis on four points about which he later changed his mind: the distinction between a free-market, competitive price and a monopoly price; the model of perfect competition and the price taker assumption for output prices; using the price taker assumption for input prices and the isoquant-isocost framework to derive factor demand curves; and using the isolated firm as a unit of analysis to understand optimal production and investment decisions.

The competitive-monopoly price distinction is inappropriate for analyzing free market situations because it arbitrarily assumes that a certain price is competitive and a higher price that increases revenue is monopolistic. Both prices still are market prices that are consonant with consumer wants, especially when one realizes the restriction of output that increases revenue releases factors of production that can be used elsewhere. The price taker assumption in perfect competition is unrealistic because every firm contributes to the total market supply and commands some influence on its output price. As a result, all firms are price searchers and engage in so-called imperfect competition, and the traditional efficiency benchmark of perfect competition is a poor standard because it is impossible to attain. The factor demand curve derived from the isoquant-isocost framework does not actually explain the formation of the input price it sets out to explain, nor does it show the causal influence of the output price on the input price. Lastly, the correct unit of analysis for understanding optimal production and investment in a firm is not that of the manager of a firm, but of the capitalist-entrepreneurs who invest in the firm. This is because, unlike the manager of a firm, capitalist-entrepreneurs can invest in multiple firms. The most important implication of this is that, as opposed to a static general equilibrium where all investment returns are equal, in a dynamic world of multiple investment opportunities for capitalist-entrepreneurs with varying degrees of profitability, profit may not be maximized in a given firm where marginal revenue equals marginal cost (MR = MC).

This paper traces the evolution of Rothbard's thinking on these issues. It is important to realize that this is not an arcane exercise in the history of economic thought, as juxtaposing Rothbard's divergent production theories highlights important differences and shows the weaknesses of modern Marshallian partial equilibrium production theory using Austrian general equilibrium theory. This reinforces the view of Klein (2010b [2008], p. 149) that the "mundane economics" of the Austrian school is distinct from the neoclassical paradigm.

The rest of the paper is outlined as follows: Section II provides a brief history of Rothbard (2018 [1953]) and his changing ideas on production theory; Section III juxtaposes Rothbard's analyses of monopoly prices and perfect competition; Section IV compares Rothbard's analyses of the derivation of factor demand curves; Section V discusses the profit maximizing output level of a firm in a dynamic world, and Section VI concludes.

II A historical overview of Rothbard's production theory

In the fall of 1949, the Volker Fund asked Rothbard to write a "college-style" economics textbook modeled after Mises's *Human Action* (1949). After Mises reviewed and approved a sample chapter on money, Rothbard began working on the project. What was originally supposed to be a principles-level textbook, however, developed into an advanced economic treatise that would occupy a large part of Rothbard's intellectual efforts in the 1950s, eventually becoming *Man, Economy, and State*.[3] The order in which he initially wrote the textbook mirrored the structure of his later treatise. By April 1953 he had written rough drafts of what can be considered Chapters 1–4 of *Man, Economy, and State* (Stromberg, 2004, pp. xxvi–xli).

Following this, Rothbard moved on to writing a large chapter on production theory, tentatively titled "Chapter 5: Producer's Activity" (2018 [1953]). Its main focus was the production decisions of an individual firm and an analysis of input and output pricing. It also contained a competitive-versus-monopoly price framework which included perfect competition. When discussing the production decision of a firm, he derived constant outlay (isocost) and constant product (isoquant) schedules as well as rates of constant outlay and constant product substitution in order to show that the cost-minimizing level of output is where these two rates are equal. Rothbard also developed a theory of the optimal investment decision of the producer.

One important feature of the chapter is that it lacks a Misesian or Austrian "feel." As the original plan was for Rothbard to write a textbook version of Mises (1949), this is surprising and puts a unique perspective on the chapter. His first chapters had followed Mises and earlier Austrians more closely, as they directly dealt with topics on which those writers concentrated. For instance, the first chapter tried to clarify Mises's analysis of the fundamental laws of praxeology, i.e., the means-end relationship and the laws of marginal utility, time preference, and returns (Stromberg, 2004, p. xxxii). His other chapters, particularly those on exchange and pricing, built significantly on writers other than Mises, not because their views were different, but because Mises had assumed his audience already knew the material, and as a result had not covered supply and demand analytics in depth (Stromberg, 2004, p. xxxv). For example, on the topic of basic price analytics, Mises simply assumed his readers understood the "marginal pairs" framework, and briefly cited Böhm-Bawerk (1959 [1889], pp. 207–256) for those who wanted more information (Mises, 1949, pp. 202, 324). Aside from citing Fetter on time preference – a point on which Rothbard planned to elaborate in a later chapter – and Mises and others on monopoly price theory, for the bulk of his chapter Rothbard utilized the standard tools of price theory, relying in particular on Stigler (1947 [1946]) and Weiler (1952). This is interesting because Rothbard (2009 [1962]) would later use these works as models for criticism of contemporary production theory. His initial use of these writers, and not Mises, most likely stems from the fact that Mises did not talk about the topic Rothbard wanted to discuss, namely, the optimal production decisions of an individual firm.

Ultimately, Rothbard decided that his approach was totally in error (for reasons to be described in later sections), and as a result proceeded to completely rewrite his production theory. In particular, he realized he would have to forge a new path into areas that Mises did not explicitly develop, and in some cases – such as the competitive-versus-monopoly price distinction – correct his views. This decision was mainly responsible for his proposal in February 1954 to switch from writing a textbook based on Mises (1949) to a full-blown economic treatise. Writes Rothbard:

> The original concept of this project . . . was as a step-by-step, spelled-out version of Mises's *Human Action*. However, as I have been proceeding, the necessary elaborations on the sometimes sparse framework of Mises has led inevitably to new and original presentations. Now that I have been proceeding to the theory of production where the whole cost-curve situation has to be faced, Mises is not much of a guide in this area. It is an area which encompasses a large part of present-day textbooks, and therefore must be met, in one way or another. Mises, in his treatise, deals only tangentially with the problem[4] and really with good reason, but a more detailed treatise, or one that attempts to be a textbook, must tackle this issue. After much thought about the problem, and many false writing starts, I have come to the conclusion that the whole complex of cost curves . . . and the whole emphasis on the size of firm, cost curves to plant, etc. . . . is all erroneous speculation on technological irrelevancies . . . [T]his whole line of approach [is] now glorified in the texts as the "theory of the firm" . . . [T]he first draft of Chapter 5 . . . is now being completely rewritten to omit "the theory of the firm" . . . [It] has become evident from my work on the book, that the result cannot be a textbook of general principles in the traditional sense.
>
> (Rothbard, 1954, pp. 1–2; Stromberg, 2004, pp. xli–xliv)

By July 1955, Rothbard decided to split his work on production into multiple chapters, what are now Chapters 5–10 of Rothbard (2009 [1962]) (Stromberg, 2004, p. liv). Major work on the book apparently stopped around 1956, and by 1959 Rothbard had completed it (Stromberg, 2004, p. lxiii). As explained below, Rothbard's revised production theory did not suffer from the pitfalls of the partial equilibrium firm analysis of his early work. We now turn to a discussion of the evolutions of Rothbard's thought on some of these critical matters.

III The competitive-monopoly price and perfect-imperfect competition

The original marginalist framework used to analyze the pricing decisions of firms was the distinction between a competitive and a monopoly price. If a firm is able to restrict output and raise price above the competitive market price such that revenue increases (i.e., the demand curve is inelastic above the competitive price), it is said to attain a monopoly price. This competitive-monopoly price distinction was not used exclusively by neoclassical economists but also by prominent Austrians such as Mises, Menger, Fetter, and von Wieser (Rothbard, 2009 [1962], p. 672). Kirzner (2013 [1973], pp. 15–18, 70–107) provides the most recent defense and elaboration of Mises's views. During the Monopolistic Competition Revolution in the 1930s, this approach was superseded by the familiar perfect-imperfect competition framework (Salerno, 2004; Rothbard, 2009 [1962], p. 720). Modern economics now analyzes markets as situations in which firms engage in either perfect or imperfect competition. Under perfect competition, the individual firm is so small relative to the total market that it has no influence on the price of its product and takes the market price as "given," i.e., it can increase or decrease its output without changing the price. There are no barriers to entry, all firms in the given market produce a homogenous product, and all firms in the market have perfect knowledge (Stigler, 1946, p. 21).[5] Under imperfect competition, the firm has an influence on the price of its product, and when it increases or decreases its output, the price must change.[6] The important assumption for Rothbard (2018 [1953]) was the inability of the producer to influence the output price.

Rothbard's earlier production theory employed both frameworks in a hybrid fashion. In the first two sections of Chapter 5, titled "Section 1: The Demand for a Firm's Product" and "Section 2: Competitive Price and Monopoly Price," he discusses the various production possibilities a firm can use to make Good A, and explains the scenario under different pricing situations. Rothbard presents possible combinations of inputs X and Y that can produce varying amounts of Good A at a constant cost, assuming the prices of X and Y are fixed (Rothbard, 2018 [1953], pp. 77–79). He then analyzes the firm's output decision in various pricing scenarios (a), (b), and (c) for Good A. In (a), the firm's individual demand curve is horizontal, or perfectly elastic, as opposed to sloping downward as in (b) and (c). In (b) and (c), the firm faces downward-sloping demand curves, but in (b) the point of maximum output from a given amount of money invested in the factors is the point of maximum revenue, while in (c) the point of maximum revenue is no longer at maximum output, i.e., the demand curve is inelastic above the point of maximum output. It therefore pays for the firm in (c) to restrict output relative to its counterfactual production level under more competitive conditions (Rothbard, 2018 [1953], pp. 79–83). Rothbard argues that a competitive price will result in both (a), which is traditionally described as perfect competition, and (b). However, in case (c) a monopoly price will result (Rothbard, 2018 [1953], pp. 83–84).

Rothbard grudgingly adopts the terms "competitive price" and "monopoly price," noting that their use in economics is unfortunate and misleading, but also that they "must be used for traditional reasons" (Rothbard, 2018 [1953], pp. 84, 88). Much of the analysis in Section 2, on monopoly prices and monopoly, are later reproduced as whole paragraphs in Rothbard (2009 [1962]), "Chapter 10: Monopoly and Competition." For example, Rothbard notes that monopoly was originally defined as a grant of state privilege to produce a good or service, that defining a monopolist as the producer of a single good is a poor definition, and that there is a built-in tendency for cartels to break down. He even notes that a monopoly price does not defy the wishes of consumers and is not immune from competition, since all goods compete for consumers' money. Exchanges are still voluntary because the consumers still voluntarily form their demand curves (Rothbard, 2018 [1953], pp. 88–90). Importantly, Rothbard pins the unfortunate monopoly-competitive price distinction on Marshallian partial equilibrium theory, writing that, "the terminology is the result of an old neoclassical preoccupation with single 'industries'" (Rothbard, 2018 [1953], p. 88).

Rothbard later scrapped the entire competitive-monopoly price distinction and trenchantly critiqued it (Rothbard, 2009 [1962], pp. 672–704). He wrote that on the free market the entire distinction is spurious because it is impossible to define a competitive price. There is no way to look at the demand curve a firm faces and decide which is a competitive price and which is a monopoly price (Rothbard, 2009 [1962], p. 689). In order to show that a firm obtains a monopoly price by restricting output along an inelastic demand curve to increase revenue, one has to assume the original price was a competitive price. Yet this assumption is completely arbitrary because a competitive price cannot be identified, since in both cases the firm is trying to produce at the most profitable level of output. Rothbard notes that there is no way to distinguish the monopoly price situation from a situation in which the capitalist-entrepreneur has overestimated the demand for a given stock of a good and realizes he can earn more by producing less. Moreover, this analysis of a "restriction of production" is spurious in general once it is realized that decreased production releases factors of production that can be used elsewhere in the economy. Those factors will go to more profitable uses that better satisfy consumer wants (Rothbard, 2009 [1962], pp. 638, 690). Even the requirement that the demand curve be inelastic above the competitive price is arbitrary. As Méra (2010, pp. 51–55; 2015) points out, the demand curve can be elastic above the competitive price and yet net revenue still increase because costs of production fall by even more. The competitive-monopoly price distinction that tries to show a violation of consumer sovereignty is a misleading partial equilibrium framework that narrowly concentrates on one market instead of looking at the entire economy.[7]

What of case (a), a situation of perfect competition where the demand curve is perfectly elastic? Rothbard seems to use it only grudgingly and even contradicts himself at times when defending its applicability. He describes the perfectly competitive case (a) as a situation where, regardless of how much the firm produces, "the market-supply curve will not be affected sufficiently to lower the price" (Rothbard, 2018 [1953], pp. 78–79, 81–84). One could extend Rothbard's logic to the traditional neoclassical juxtaposition of the firm's perfectly elastic demand curve and the industry's downward-sloping demand curve (Stigler, 1946, p. 91). Figure 3.1 depicts this distinction:

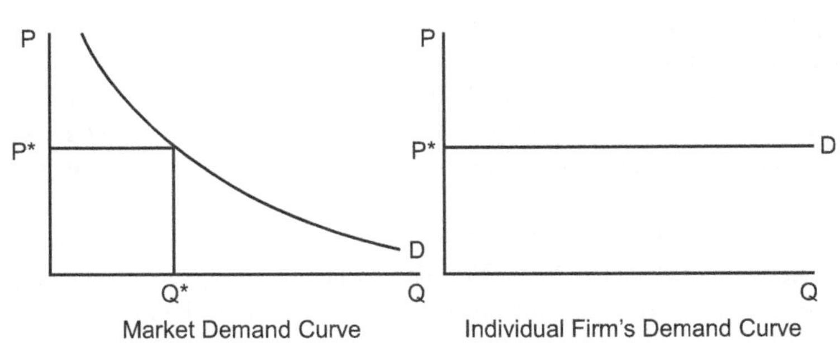

Figure 3.1 Market demand curve and the demand curve faced by an individual firm

This comparison highlights the fact that the firm's marginal contribution to output is "so" small it cannot affect the price. Only large enough increases in supply can accomplish that. Rothbard writes that even in case (a), with a change in output, there has to be "some effect" on the supply curve that will "tend to affect the price," but that the overall change would be "too small to alter the point of intersection" (Rothbard, 2018 [1953], p. 79). When he later explains that the market supply is always affected, he states that, "It may well be, of course, that, within the relevant range, the action of the firm is not large enough in relation to the product as a whole, to change the market-price" (Rothbard, 2018 [1953], p. 111).

Rothbard's defense of the model is confusing. How is it possible that every change in supply must tend to affect the price, but in some scenarios, when the change is small enough, price does not change? Either every change influences prices, even in extremely small ways, or some marginal amounts of supply have no impact on prices. Basic economic analysis shows that Rothbard's original logic is correct: every nonzero change in supply must change the market price. Total market supply is the sum of the individual supplies produced by the firms; an increase in the output of one must increase the supply and lower the price.

The error derives from approximating a very small number as zero. For example, Stigler uses the example of a market with 10,000 sellers, where each produces an equal quantity. If one firm increases its sales by 100 percent, then the total quantity increases by 0.0001 percent, an amount so imperceptible that it can be treated as zero (Stigler, 1946, pp. 91–92). But 0.0001 percent is not equal to 0 percent. Stigler (1957, p. 8) recognizes this and writes that only when there are an infinitely large number of firms does every firm have zero influence on price and a perfectly elastic demand curve. Otherwise, every firm has an (albeit extremely small) nonzero influence on price and faces a downward sloping demand curve. However, he also maintains that as the number of firms increase, the market approximates perfect competition.[8] Yet infinity is not a real number and can never be "reached," so it is impossible for a firm to have no influence on price. Furthermore, approximating a very small number as zero carries enormous implications that drastically change how the market is analyzed. Every firm, no matter how small, must have an influence on supply: the perfectly elastic demand curve is impossible.[9]

The constant price assumption does seem plausible when taken from the real world perspective of an individual firm with many competitors. The firm, when entering the market, "looks around" at the going market price for a given homogenous product. It uses this as an estimate and appraisement of the future selling price of its product. It may in fact sell all its stock at the ruling price. But this does not mean that the demand curve is horizontal; all it means is that the demand curve shifted slightly outward to accommodate the increased supply, or that some producers now have a surplus of unsold goods (which means not all of the supply was sold at the market price). If all else could be held equal in the real world when the producer sells his additional supply, then the price would have to fall (Armentano, 1999 [1982], p. 23). The isolated firm approach is completely unhelpful and misleading when analyzing the formation of the output price. Only when one understands this and abstracts from the firm to look at the market as a whole is the fallaciousness of the approach revealed. Even though the output price is determined by the industry supply and demand curves, each individual firm within the industry confronts a downward-sloping demand curve that gives it some influence over price. Rothbard later realized this point and as a result concluded that the perfectly elastic demand curve was a deceptive illusion and "utterly fallacious" (2009 [1962], pp. 721–722).

In addition to his critique of the competitive-monopoly price distinction, Rothbard's argument that the perfectly competitive framework is invalid because it is impossible for a firm not to have any influence on its output price is a unique criticism in the Austrian tradition. The most well-known Austrian work in this field is Hayek (2009 [1946]), which does not attack the price-taker assumption, but rather the assumption of perfect knowledge. Hayek emphasizes that competition is not an end state but rather a dynamic process involving entrepreneurship and uncertainty. The capitalist-entrepreneur is not given the relevant knowledge, such as the demand curve, but instead must estimate and discover it in the market. Similar Austrian criticisms include Ludwig Lachmann (1977 [1954]) and Israel Kirzner (2011 [1963], pp. 312–315; 1973, pp. 71–74, 90–95).[10] Real world competition is not an optimization problem with given demand and cost curves, but rather requires uncertainty-bearing capitalist-entrepreneurs trying to estimate consumer wants and allocate resources using economic calculation, i.e., through profit and loss accounting (Mises, 1949, pp. 349–354). This is not to say that Rothbard disagreed with this argument. In fact, he embraced and emphasized it in his analysis.[11] He simply added additional arguments regarding competitive prices and perfect competition.

Once we realize that every firm's demand curve slopes downward, no matter how slightly, it becomes clear that all firms engage in imperfect competition, and the differences between them are of degree, not of kind. In this case, the degree refers to the relative slope of the demand curve, while a difference of kind would be between a downward-sloping demand curve and an impossible horizontally sloping one. Yet there is no difference between the kind of demand curve faced by the small wheat farm and the one faced by the Hershey Chocolate Company, as both are downward-sloping (Rothbard, 2009 [1962], pp. 721–722). This carries important implications for some neoclassical efficiency analyses of competition. It is sometimes held that imperfect competition is less efficient than perfection competition because the former's most profitable level of output is exists only where MR = MC and not where P = MC. However, firms with downward-sloping demand curves are not necessarily "inefficient," nor do they "restrict output" or necessarily "misallocate resources," because the efficiency benchmark of perfect competition to which they are compared is an impossible standard that cannot obtain in the real world. All firms face a downward sloping demand curve of some kind and are imperfect, and therefore do not produce where P = MC (Armentano, 1982, pp. 22–25).

The contrast between Rothbard (2018 [1953]) and Rothbard (2009 [1962]) on competitive and monopoly prices and perfect competition is stark. In the former, the concepts are used to analyze actual markets in the unhampered economy. In the latter, in addition to emphasizing the older Mises-Hayek position that competition is a rivalrous process that involves efficient entrepreneurs earning profits and inefficient entrepreneurs sustaining losses, Rothbard emphasized that there are no differences in kind between various firms and their output prices. Every price is a market price based on entrepreneurs' estimations of the wants of consumers. Every firm exercises some influence on its output price and cannot take it as given.

IV The factor demand curve and the causal influence of output prices

Like fixed output prices, fixed input prices are a tool used in much of neoclassical production theory. For example, they are prevalent in isocosts, cost curves, and perfect competition in factor markets. Rothbard (2018 [1953]) frequently employed this assumption, but later realized it was highly misleading and discarded it in exchange for a framework that explained the formation of input prices without taking them as given. This section surveys Rothbard's analysis of isoquants and isocosts in preparation for tracing out factor demand curves, and compares it with his later derivation of the factor demand curve, as well as his remarks on the causal influence of output prices on input prices.

After finishing Section 2 with a discussion of the competitive-versus-monopoly price distinction and some possible definitions of monopoly, Rothbard returns to the individual production decisions of a firm in "Section 3: The Product and Outlay Schedules of the Firm." Aside from unique terminology, which will not be used here for ease of exposition, the section provides a fairly familiar exercise in production theory. Rothbard derives isoquants and isocosts, and shows that the slope of the isoquant is the marginal rate of technical substitution, and the slope of the isocost is the ratio of the fixed prices, and that the cost minimizing combination of factor inputs for a given level of output is where the slopes of the isoquant and isocost are equal (Rothbard, 2018 [1953], p. 96). Later, in a subsection, Rothbard engages in a mathematical and graphical formulation of the above exposition, and concludes with the figure seen in Figure 3.2:

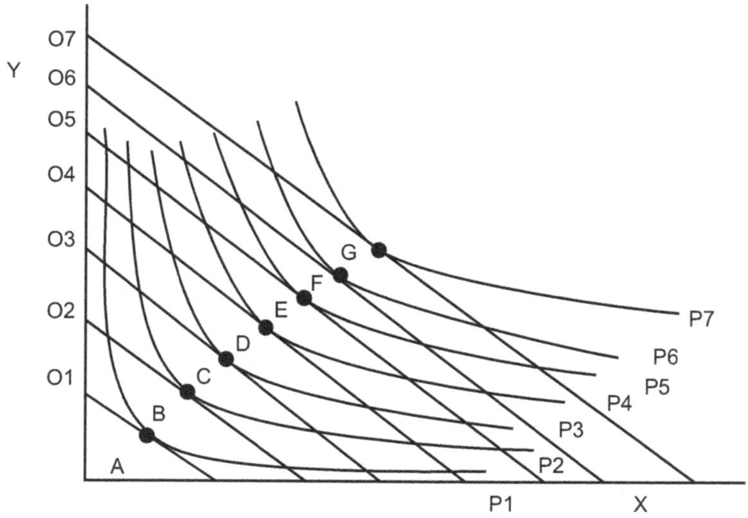

Figure 3.2 Optimal production with various constant outlay and product curves

P1, P2 . . . P7 are the firm's isoquants for given levels of production, while O1, O2 . . . O7 are the firm's isocosts for given levels of expenditure based on the fixed input prices for X and Y. A, B . . . G represent the cost minimizing combinations of factor inputs for each level of output.

Aside from illustrating a firm's optimal production decisions, Rothbard seems to undertake this analysis in order to draw out a firm's demand curve for a factor, analysis which apparently was to take place in another chapter that appears not to have been written. Rothbard initially writes that the isoquant-isocost apparatus is "essential to an analysis of the prices of factors of production" and describes it as one that "will be handy in later analyses of the pricing of factors of production" (Rothbard, 2018 [1953], pp. 96, 103). The demand curve Rothbard appears to have wanted to derive would have been taken from Weiler (1952, pp. 154–161).[12] The modern analysis based on this approach, described in Benjamin, Gunderson, and Riddell (2002, pp. 147–153),[13] incorporates both scale and substitution effects, which are similar to the familiar income and substitution effects in consumer demand curves, and is shown in Figure 3.3:

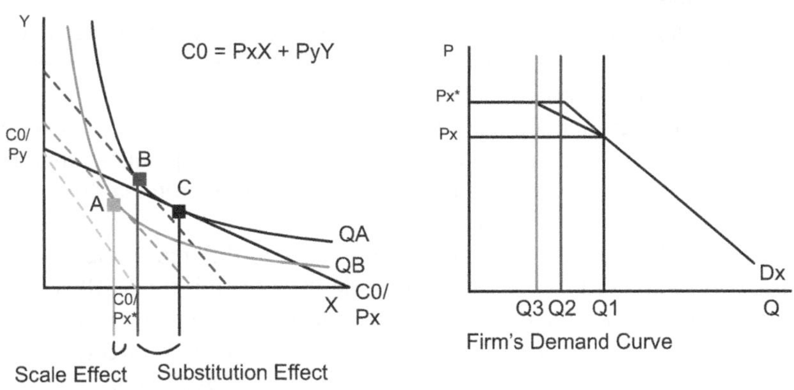

Figure 3.3 Derivation of a firm's demand curve for a factor of production

At prices Px and Py, the firm originally demands Q1 of X. To show the downward sloping nature of a factor demand curve with the isoquant/isocost approach, let the price of factor X rise relative to the price of factor Y from Px to Px*. This pivots the isocost inward to reflect the higher price of factor X, which is then shifted rightwards until it is tangent with the original isoquant at a new cost minimizing combination B, and as a result, the firm demands only Q2 of X. The difference between Q2 and Q1 is the substitution effect. There is also a scale effect that occurs because the increase in the relative price of X increases the firm's marginal costs, which causes it to produce at a lower level of output and raise its price. Thus, the firm's new isocost shifts leftward from where it was tangent with the original isoquant to a point where it is tangent to the new profit-maximizing isoquant. The cost minimizing combination is now at A and the firm demands only Q3 of X. The difference between Q3 and Q2 is the scale effect. Overall, at the higher price, the firm demands less of factor X and more of factor Y, and so its demand curve for factor X slopes downwards (Benjamin, Gunderson, and Riddell, 2002, pp. 147–153).

It is important to realize that this process takes place from the perspective of an individual firm facing given input prices. Nowhere does Rothbard explain how this given input price was originally determined, or why it changed. Furthermore, there is no recognition of the fact that input prices are imputed from output prices. In fact, in this framework, the analysis implies the reverse. A rise in the price (for some reason) of input X leads to a decrease in the production of the output and a rise in its price. Rothbard realized the weaknesses of this approach and argued that "the chief error is that of basing a causal explanation of factor pricing on the *assumption of given factor prices*" (Rothbard, 2009 [1962], pp. 454–455; emphasis in original).

For Rothbard, the correct method of deriving a demand curve for a factor of production is through marginal productivity analysis that does not assume the price of the factor is already given. Moreover, this procedure does not start from the perspective of a firm but rather from the general demand for the factor and its interrelations. In the Austrian static general equilibrium known as the Evenly Rotating Economy (ERE), the price of any given factor is its discounted marginal revenue product (DMRP). It must be noted that there is an important yet neglected difference between Austrian "Böhm-Bawerkian" input price theory and the neoclassical "Knightian" input price theory. Namely, for the Austrians, a factor price is equal to its DMRP and not simply its MRP, because the capitalist-entrepreneur, due to time preference, receives an interest return on his investment from supplying present goods in return for future goods.

To be fair, the MRP in these approaches refers to different things. The neoclassical view argues that the factors are paid their MRP if the MRP is taken to be the revenue from selling the immediate semi-finished product. However, this semi-finished product does not mean anything to the capitalist-entrepreneur; what he cares about is selling the *future* product for expected *future* money. And since future money is discounted due to time preference, he will only supply to factors in the present a smaller amount of present money. This difference is interest (Block, 1990; Rothbard, 2009 [1962], pp. 504–507; 2011a [1987], pp. 265–266). The Austrian approach thus emphasizes the importance of time and futurity in production, as opposed to the Knightian view. The Knightian view is present in the works of Stigler and contemporary price theorists, and is traceable to the works of Clark, Marshall, and Walras. It neglects the temporal structure of production analysis involving heterogeneous capital goods, and as a result its capital theory is seriously deficient (Huerta de Soto, 2006 [1998], pp. 512–522).

This DMRP is the marginal physical product (MPP) of a factor times the marginal revenue earned from its employment discounted by the pure rate of interest. The DMRP of a factor in its general uses (among different production processes and in a single production process) is decreasing as its supply increases because both the MPP and the output price fall as output increases. The DMRP of a factor in a particular process is the point where the total stock of the factor intersects the general DMRP curve, and, through the entrepreneurial process, the price of the factor is brought into alignment with its marginal use (Rothbard, 2009 [1962], pp. 456–476). If the prices of a given factor are unequal, then entrepreneurs shift factors from lower-priced lines of production into higher-priced ones to try to earn profits, thereby bidding up the price of the factor in the former and lowering it in the latter until the uniform DMRP is established.

The prices of the factors of production are ultimately determined by the output prices of the goods they produce. The causal formation of prices is as follows: anticipated future output prices determine present input prices, or the costs of production, not the reverse. This is Böhm-Bawerk's (1889 [1959], pp. 248–256; 1962 [1894]) "Law of Costs" that Rothbard emphasized in his analysis of the firm (Rothbard, 2009 [1962], pp. 361, 588–589). The fixed input prices a firm sees are not costs determined beyond its control. They are the prevailing prices of factors based on other capitalist-entrepreneurs' estimations of their marginal uses elsewhere as determined by consumer demand. In short, these prices reflect the opportunity cost of using the factors in other lines of production. By entering into this factor market, the firm directly influences the formation of the new prices by bidding them up, which would increase them if other intervening processes did not occur during the interim. This is similar to the firm's influence on its output price – the output price appears given, but in reality, by producing for the market the firm is directly contributing to the formation of the price and does exert an influence. As opposed to the original factor pricing theory that Rothbard planned to write, his revised theory is one that explains the formation of the factor price without assuming it is given, and clearly shows the causal influence of output prices on input prices (Rothbard, 2009 [1962], p. 476).

The above factor demand curve derivation is similar to the derivation of the short-run demand curve for a factor where marginal productivity analysis is also used (Stigler, 1946, pp. 175–178). This is opposed to the long-run demand curve for a factor, which is the isoquant-isocost method critiqued above. The short run refers to a period where some factors are fixed and cannot be changed, while in the long run all factors are variable. While Rothbard and Stigler's approaches are largely similar for the short-run curve compared to the long-run demand curve, there are important differences. Aside from the fact that the factor in Rothbard's analysis earns its DMRP while in Stigler's it earns its MRP, the main difference is that Stigler's analysis begins from the vantage point of a firm facing a given input price (as determined in the general market). The firm then hires the factor along its diminishing MRP schedule until the MRP is equal to the price of the input, because that is the point where its MR = MC. It is true that in the ERE, the firm will produce where MR = MC, as any other output level will lead to negative profits (as opposed to the point at which MR = MC, where the firm will earn zero). However, as will be explained below, in the dynamic world, the profit-maximizing level of output for the capitalist-entrepreneur investing in the firm is generally where the firm's MR is greater than its MC. When applied to a non-general equilibrium world, however, this factor demand curve derivation is incorrect, as the firm's MR and MC convergence does not always occur.

V The capitalist-entrepreneur and the optimal level of investment in a firm

This section is framed differently from the prior two because it presents an important critique of the Marshallian partial equilibrium firm theorizing, a critique that Rothbard (2018 [1953]) describes but does not fully emphasize in Rothbard (2009 [1962]), and only briefly mentions in other writings.

In the final elongated section that the present author pieced together,[14] tentatively titled "Section 4: The Output and Investment Decision of the Producer," Rothbard strives to develop an optimal theory of investment of the capitalist-entrepreneur. The implication of this analysis is that in the dynamic world where there is a mélange of firms with varying degrees of profitability for their capitalist-entrepreneur investors, there can be no theory of optimal investment formulated for a single firm in isolation. This implies that a given firm's optimal production may not be where its MR = MC. This momentous realization undoubtedly contributed to Rothbard's later decision to discard the isolated firm analysis and completely rewrite his production theory.

Although in many ways Rothbard (2018 [1953]) is quite similar to traditional neoclassical production theory, one major difference between the two is that the "producer" Rothbard concentrates on is a capitalist-entrepreneur investing his own money, while the neoclassical producer is a propertyless manager who can borrow an unlimited amount of money at a given interest rate and *only invests in the given firm*. When analyzing the firm, Rothbard views the capitalist-entrepreneur as the controlling factor who earns an interest rate of return on his money invested, while the manager is a hired factor of production whose income is a money cost. The capitalist-entrepreneur can also earn a profit when his total rate of return is greater than the interest return (Rothbard, 2009 [1962], p. 510). In the neoclassical framework, the entrepreneur is considered to be a propertyless manager and the controlling factor in the firm who pays an interest return on money borrowed from capitalists, which is counted as a cost of production. The manager still earns a management wage, which is also counted as a cost of production, but also can earn a profit, which is the difference between his total revenue and the principal and interest payments on his borrowed money. The former has been explicitly called the "Austro-Wicksellian" theory of the firm, which views interest as revenue, as opposed to the neoclassical theory, which views it as a cost (Gabor and Pearce, 1958, pp. 537–539; Moroney, 1972, p. 339; Salerno, 2009, p. xliii).

This difference is present even in the beginning of Rothbard's chapter. In Section 1, before discussing the various production decisions and possible demand situations a single-product firm might face, Rothbard briefly looks at the optimal investment decision of a representative capitalist-entrepreneur who can invest in multiple lines of production. The capitalist-entrepreneur has a given stock of money that he can spend on consumption, investment, or keep in his cash balances. He will only invest if the rate of return is greater than or equal to his rate of time preference, the specific premium on present money over future money that represents the minimum return the capitalist-entrepreneur requires in order to invest. For a given amount of money invested, the capitalist-entrepreneur will choose the line of production that maximizes his expected monetary return (Rothbard, 2018 [1953], pp. 75–77). Rothbard then postpones further analysis of the investment theory, and for the rest of Section 1 through Section 3 turns to analyzing competitive prices, monopoly prices, perfect competition, and the isoquant-isocost apparatus that shows the cost minimizing level of output. This is described above in Sections III and IV of the present chapter. After this analysis, Rothbard then returns to investigating investment decisions in the final section of his chapter.

In Section 4, Rothbard considers a capitalist-entrepreneur who has chosen to invest in a given firm that produces Product P. Rothbard describes various amounts of expenditure, or total costs, which lead to various total revenues the capitalist-entrepreneur can earn by investing in the given firm. For ease of exposition, Figure 3.4 depicts Rothbard's (2018 [1953], p. 112) results with the familiar continuous and nicely shaped curves rather than jagged lines and discrete points:

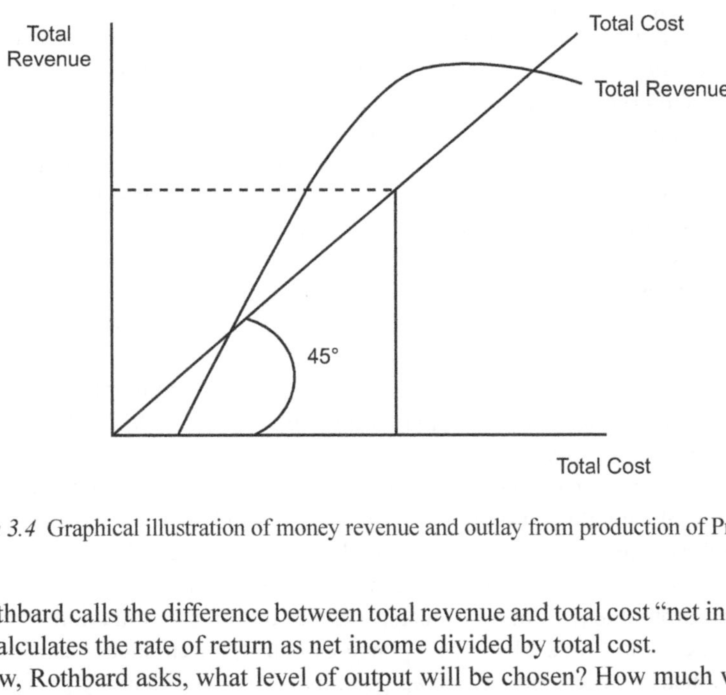

Figure 3.4 Graphical illustration of money revenue and outlay from production of Product P

Rothbard calls the difference between total revenue and total cost "net income," and calculates the rate of return as net income divided by total cost.

Now, Rothbard asks, what level of output will be chosen? How much will the capitalist-entrepreneur invest in the given firm, and, consequently, how much Product P output will the firm produce? What is the optimal level of output? The traditional answer is that the optimal level of investment and output is where net money income is maximized, i.e., the greatest distance between total revenue and total cost. In familiar terminology, using continuous curves, this is the point where MR = MC. As explained above, the usual perspective taken is that of the propertyless manager, with a fixed interest return to the investing capitalist included in the cost curve. To maximize his profit amount, the manager of the firm should borrow from the capitalist-entrepreneurs at a given interest rate and invest until MR = MC.

However, the crucial problem with this analysis is that it neglects the question of whether or not the capitalist-entrepreneurs can invest their money in other firms that earn higher than the rate of return earnable in this firm. The output level that maximizes the firm's profit may not be the output level where the capitalist-entrepreneurs who invest in the firm maximize their profits. This is because capitalist-entrepreneurs are not restricted solely to investing in a given firm but can also invest in others where they could potentially earn a higher rate of return on their marginal money invested. The rate of return that can be earned always varies, because in the real world there is uncertainty and, consequently, profits and losses. Only in a static general equilibrium devoid of uncertainty are all rates of return uniform (and equal to the interest rate). The problem does not go away if we postulate that the given firm can produce multiple products, since the unit of analysis is still "a firm" rather than the capitalist-entrepreneurs who can invest among multiple firms producing multiple products. To maximize their total profits, capitalist-entrepreneurs may spend only a certain amount of money in one firm such that it produces where its MR > MC because they can invest in other firms to increase their total profits more than they could if they were to solely invest in the original firm up to the point where its MR = MC. As a result, one cannot look at a firm in isolation in the partial equilibrium approach and figure out how much will be produced or invested in it (Gabor and Pearce, 1952, 1958; Rothbard, 1961, pp. 7–8, 18; Rothbard, 1993; Klein, 2010c [1999], pp. 38–39; Klein and Foss, 2012, p. 238). Although Rothbard (2018 [1953]) does not frame the problem in terms of MR and MC, this is clearly what he is getting at, as he trenchantly writes that "there is no precise theory of the determination of the investment in, and output of, the firm" (Rothbard, 2018 [1953], p. 114).

To clarify, this is not to say that in an isolated firm the maximization of profit for the manager does not occur at an output level where its MR = MC: *Given a total revenue and total cost curve for the firm that includes interest payments, the optimum is clearly where MR = MC*. What it does say is that from the vantage point of capitalist-entrepreneurs who supply funds to the firm, and once the range of investment opportunities is broadened beyond the individual firm to the entire production structure, in a dynamic world where lines of production earn different profitable (i.e., above interest) rates of return, profit maximization may occur where the firm's MR > MC, since capitalist-entrepreneurs can invest in other industries where they can reap potentially greater economic profits. Only in the ERE, where all profits are wiped out and all lines of production earn the same uniform interest return will the optimal level of output be at the point where the firm's MR = MC. This is because the capitalists cannot invest their funds in another firm to earn a higher-than-normal rate, as such opportunities do not exist (Rothbard, 2009 [1962], pp. 600, 695, 734–736). At such an output level, since profit is zero, total revenue will be equal to total cost, assuming the capitalists' interest return is included as an opportunity cost. At any other output level, there will be negative profits. In order for the firm to exist in general equilibrium, it must not earn negative profits, so it will have to produce where its MR = MC. The problem appears when the economy is out of general equilibrium, and not all lines of production earn the same uniform interest return. Now the production of a firm may not be where its MR = MC, since the capitalist-entrepreneurs who invest their money in it can invest in other, more remunerative firms. The Austrian general equilibrium approach stresses this dynamic world because it is the dynamic world in which we live and that consequently we try to understand. On this entire issue, we find much on which to agree with Gabor and Pearce (1952, 1958), whose articles – which heavily influenced Rothbard – emphasize this important distinction between the Austrian and neoclassical approaches with regards to optimal production in a given firm in disequilibrium. It is worth quoting them in full:

> [T]here is much to suggest that a great deal has been lost by the failure to produce a more adequate synthesis of all that is best in the work of both the Austrian and the neoclassical schools. In the first place, the fact that two theories of profit lead to the same general equilibrium is not sufficient to make them the same theory. *The route by which equilibrium is attained is often as important as the equilibrium itself.* We have shown elsewhere [Gabor and Pearce, 1952] that, if general equilibrium has not been attained, and the fact that an investment is being contemplated in any industry implies that it has not, then the two theories of profit, the [Austro]-Wicksellian and the neoclassical, lead to different conclusions
>
> (Gabor and Pearce, 1958, pp. 538–539; emphasis added).

Instead of trying to look at the optimal level of investment in and output of a compartmentalized firm, Rothbard argues that the correct approach is to develop an optimal theory of investment of the capitalist-entrepreneurs who face a gamut of various firms in which they can invest (Rothbard, 2018 [1953], pp. 114–115). This is what Rothbard seeks to do throughout the rest of Section 4. Rothbard stresses that a theory of optimal investment decisions needs to focus not only on maximizing the rate of return on a given amount of money invested, but on weighing the rate of return with the capitalist-entrepreneur's rate of time preference. Rothbard calls this the Law of Investment Decision (Rothbard, 2018 [1953], p. 121). The capitalist-entrepreneur will invest his own money *in general* up to the last discrete point where the average and marginal rate of return are greater than or equal to his average and marginal rate of time preference. *In each individual firm*, the capitalist-entrepreneur invests up to the last discrete point where his marginal rate of return in that firm is greater than or equal to the marginal rate of return of investing that money elsewhere (Rothbard, 2018 [1953], pp. 120–124).

Rothbard's revised production theory (2009 [1962]) unfortunately does not explicitly mention any Law of Investment Decision for the capitalist-entrepreneur. However, it does start with an analysis of time preference, interest rates, and the important function of the capitalist who invests in a temporal structure of production in the ERE (Rothbard, 2009 [1962], pp. 319–451). The ERE is essential because, in Rothbard's presentation, it is the point toward which the economy always tends, and would reach if the data remained constant. It is necessary in order to isolate the differences between profit and loss, on the one hand, and interest on the other. In addition, the ERE is indispensable for deducing economic theorems, as it allows the economist to mentally hold constant all changes in the data except one in order to isolate the effects of that change. However, Rothbard extended the edifice in order to describe the *processes to the ERE*, the processes that describe the dynamic world in which we live. Capitalist-entrepreneurs take center stage by investing in various profitable firms with different periods of production and by engaging in a rivalrous process of efficient competition with each other that consequently distributes scarce resources according to the intertemporal preferences of consumers. In the end, Rothbard substituted an Austrian general equilibrium for a Marshallian partial equilibrium framework.

VI Conclusion

This paper provides a comparison of Rothbard's earlier production framework with his final system. The earlier theory was closer to the Marshallian partial equilibrium theory. It analyzed production from the perspective of an isolated firm and employed many standard tools such as the competitive-monopoly price distinction, perfect competition theory, the isoquant-isocost framework used to derive factor demand curves, and the isolated firm. Rothbard's later revised theory, and in some cases parts of his earlier theory, criticized these tools.

It is shown that Rothbard argued that the competitive-monopoly price distinction is inappropriate for analyzing free market situations because it arbitrarily assumes the existence of a competitive and a monopoly price. In addition, all firms are price searchers that exercise some influence on their output price and consequently engage in "imperfect" competition. Thus, the traditional efficiency benchmark of perfect competition is a poor standard because it is impossible to attain in the real world. The factor demand curve derived from the isoquant-isocost framework does not show that expected output prices determine input prices, and assumes the input price it tries to explain. Finally, and most importantly, in order to understand optimal production in a firm, the correct perspective is not that of the borrowing manager in the isolated firm who seeks to maximize his profit, but rather that of the capitalist-entrepreneurs who supply money for the firm while seeking to maximize the rate of return on their total capital invested. This is because – unlike the manager – the capitalist-entrepreneur can invest in multiple firms, which means that in a dynamic world, he may not maximize his profit in a given firm up to the point where its MR = MC.

Ultimately, the evolution of Rothbard's production theory leads from the Marshallian partial equilibrium approach to the Austrian general equilibrium approach. This is because Rothbard shows the causal influence of input and output prices and actually explains their formation, and his mature theory does not analyze production from a single isolated firm that can treat prices as fixed in a static world, but rather from the decisions of competing profit-seeking capitalist-entrepreneurs who invest in the entire production structure in a changing world.

Notes

1 In this paper, the "Chicago theory of the firm" refers to the "black box" production function view, where the firm is given a set of underlying data and chooses its output level through mathematical optimization (Klein, 2010a [1996], pp. 3–4; Foss and Klein, 2012, pp. 136–137). It does not refer to Coasean theories that analyze the reasons for the existence, organization, and limits of the firm. With regard to the latter, Rothbard was heavily influenced by Coase and was one of the first economists to incorporate the Coasean framework into his own research (Klein, 2010a, pp. 3–4).

2 Mark Blaug has similarly contrasted what he calls Austrian "total equilibrium analysis" with both Marshallian partial equilibrium and Walrasian general equilibrium analysis (Blaug, 1990, pp. 185–186).

3 Mises asked Rothbard on several occasions throughout this period to present some of the chapters at his New York University seminar (Hülsmann, 2007, pp. 936, 939).

4 Rothbard is most likely referring to Mises (1949, pp. 336–347).

5 The price assumption also applies to input prices, which are treated in the next section.

6 Imperfect competition can still occur with no barriers to entry and perfect knowledge.

7 This is not to deny, as Rothbard emphasized, that the distinction is unimportant when a government intervention allows the firm to restrict output and attain a monopoly price. Here, the element of coercion has tampered with the voluntary actions of consumers, and now the restriction exists in defiance of their choices. For the consequences of factor pricing under such conditions, see Méra (2010).

8 See also Hirschleifer et al. (2007, p. 165), who argue along similar lines: "While [perfect competition is] never literally true, this may approximate reality if the firm produces only a small fraction of the output in its industry."

9 For more, see Keen (2011, pp. 76–77, 85–90, 95), who presents a critique very similar to Rothbard's (2009 [1962]), although from a more mathematical perspective.

10 Kirzner notes that Mises thought the model was confusing and unrealistic, and intentionally avoided discussing it (Kirzner, 2001, pp. 100–101).

11 While agreeing with Kirzner's dynamic critique of the model, Rothbard did criticize Kirzner's use of the perfectly elastic demand curve (Kirzner, 1963 [2011], pp. 98–99; Rothbard, 2011b [1961], pp. 14–15). See Mises (1949, pp. 356–357) for his limited remarks on perfect and imperfect competition.

12 Rothbard (2018 [1953]) cited Weiler (1952, pp. 147ff) in his discussion of factor ratios and production coefficients, and Weiler (1952, pp. 141–161) was also cited later in Rothbard (2009 [1962], pp. 589–590), in his critique of cost curves. The above citation is to a Weiler chapter devoted entirely to the analysis of the demand for the factors of production. Although Rothbard also cited Stigler (1946) in both places, his demand curve is derived differently and is discussed below. For an explanation similar to Weiler, see Hicks (1979 [1946], pp. 89–98). Kirzner (1963 [2011], pp. 194, 215–216) also describes this approach.

13 See also McGraw (2002) for another exposition of this factor demand curve.

14 See the editor's Foreword to Rothbard (2018 [1953], p. 73).

References

Armentano, Dominick T. 1999 [1982]. *Antitrust and Monopoly: Anatomy of a Policy Failure*. Oakland, CA: The Independent Institute.

Benjamin, Dwayne, Morley Gunderson, and W. Craig Riddell. 2002. *Labor Market Economics*. Canada: McGraw-Hill Ryerson Ltd.

Blaug, Mark. 1990. "Comment on O'Brien's 'Lionel Robbins and the Austrian Connection.'" In Bruce J. Caldwell, ed., *Carl Menger and His Legacy in Economics*. Durham, NC: Duke University Press.

Block, Walter. 1990. "The DMVP-MVP Controversy: A Note." *Review of Austrian Economics* 4: 199–207.

Böhm-Bawerk, Eugen von. 1959 [1889]. *Capital and Interest*. South Holland, IL: Libertarian Press.

———. 1962 [1894]. "The Ultimate Standard of Value." In Eugen von Böhm-Bawerk, ed., *Shorter Classics of Böhm-Bawerk*. South Holland, IL: Libertarian Press.

Foss, Nicolai, and Peter Klein. 2012. *Organizing Entrepreneurial Judgment: A New Approach to the Firm*. New York: Cambridge University Press.

Gabor, Andre, and I. F. Pearce. 1952. "A New Approach to the Theory of the Firm." *Oxford Economic Papers* 4 (3): 252–265.

———. 1958. "The Place of Money Capital in the Theory of Production." *Quarterly Journal of Economics* 72 (4): 537–557.

Hayek, Friedrich August. 2009 [1946]. "The Meaning of Competition." In *Individualism and Economic Order*. Auburn, AL: Ludwig von Mises Institute.

Hicks, John R. 1979 [1946]. *Value and Capital*. 2nd ed. Oxford: Oxford University Press.

Hirschleifer, Jack, Amihai Glazer, and David Hirschleifer. 2007. *Price Theory and Applications: Decisions, Markets, and Information*. New York: Cambridge University Press.

Huerta de Soto, Jesús. 2006 [1998]. *Money, Bank Credit, and Economic Cycles*. Auburn, AL: Ludwig von Mises Institute, 2006.

Hülsmann, J. Guido. 2007. *Mises: The Last Knight of Liberalism*. Auburn, AL: Ludwig von Mises Institute.

Keen, Steve. 2011. *Debunking Economics*. New York: Palgrave Macmillan.

Kirzner, Israel. 2001. *Ludwig von Mises*. Wilmington, De: ISI Books.

———. 2011 [1963]. *Market Theory and the Price System*. Indianapolis, IN: Liberty Fund.

———. 2013 [1973]. *Competition and Entrepreneurship*. Indianapolis, IN: Liberty Fund.

Klein, Peter G. 2010a. "Economic Calculation and the Limits of Organization." In *The Capitalist and the Entrepreneur*. Auburn, AL: Ludwig von Mises Institute.

———. 2010b. "The Mundane Economics of the Austrian School." In Peter G. Klein, ed. *The Capitalist and the Entrepreneur*. Auburn, AL: Ludwig von Mises Institute.

———. 2010c. "Entrepreneurship and Corporate Governance." In Peter G. Klein, *The Capitalist and The Entrepreneur*. Auburn, AL: Ludwig von Mises Institute.

Lachmann, Ludwig. 1977 [1954]. "Some Notes on Economic Thought, 1933–1953." In Ludwig Lachmann, ed., *Capital, Expectations, and the Market Process*. Menlo Park, CA: Institute for Humane Studies.

McGraw Hill. 2002. "Chapter Notes." McGraw Hill Online Learning Center. http://highered.mheducation.com/sites/0070891540/student_view0/chapter5/chapter_notes.html.

Méra, Xavier. 2010. "Factor Prices Under Monopoly." *Quarterly Journal of Austrian Economics* 13 (1): 48–70.

———. 2015. "A Note on the Limits to Monopoly Pricing." In Per Bylund and David Howden, eds., *The Next Generation of Austrian Economics*. Auburn, AL: Ludwig von Mises Institute.

Mises, Ludwig von. 2008 [1949]. *Human Action*. Auburn, AL: Ludwig von Mises Institute.

Moroney, John R. 1972. "The Current State of Money and Production Theory." *American Economic Review* 62 (1/2): 335–343.

Rothbard, Murray N. February 1954. Letter to R. Cornuelle, "Textbook or Treatise?"

———. 1990. "The Science of Liberty: An Interview With Murray N. Rothbard." *The Austrian Economics Newsletter* (Summer), pp. 1–5.

———. 2008 [1963]. *America's Great Depression*. Auburn, AL: Ludwig von Mises Institute.

———. 2009 [1962]. *Man, Economy, and State with Power and Market*. Auburn, AL: Ludwig von Mises Institute.

———. 2010c [1993]. "Letter to Sandra K. Johnson." From Peter G. Klein, 1999. "Entrepreneurship and Corporate Governance." In Peter G. Klein, ed., *The Capitalist and The Entrepreneur*. Auburn, AL: Ludwig von Mises Institute.

———. 2011a [1987]. "Breaking Out of the Walrasian Box: Schumpeter and Hansen." In Murray N. Rothbard, ed., *Economic Controversies*. Auburn, AL: Ludwig von Mises Institute.

———. 2011b [1961]. "Comments on Israel M. Kirzner's MS." *Libertarian Papers* 3 (25): 7–23.

———. 2018 [1953]. "Chapter 5: Producer's Activity." In Matthew McCaffrey, ed. *The Economic Theory of Costs: Foundations and New Directions*. Abingdon, UK: Routledge, pp. 73–130.

Salerno, Joseph T. 2004. "Menger's Theory of Monopoly Price in the Years of High Theory: The Contribution of Vernon A. Mund." *Managerial Finance* 30 (2): 72–92.

———. 2009. "Introduction to the Second Edition." In Murray N. Rothbard, ed., *Man, Economy, and State With Power and Market*. Auburn, AL: Ludwig von Mises Institute.

———. 2011. "Varieties of Austrian Price Theory: Rothbard Reviews Kirzner." *Libertarian Papers* 3 (25): 1–6.

Stigler, George. 1947 [1946]. *The Theory of Price*. New York: Palgrave Macmillan.

———. 1957. "Perfect Competition, Historically Contemplated." *Journal of Political Economy* 65 (1): 1–17.

Stromberg, Joseph. 2004. "Introduction to Man, Economy, and State with Power and Market." In Murray N. Rothbard, ed., *Man, Economy, and State with Power and Market*. Auburn, AL: Ludwig von Mises Institute.

Weiler, Emanuel T. 1952. *The Economic System*. New York: Palgrave Macmillan.

4 *Man, economy, and state,* original chapter 5*

Producer's activity

Murray N. Rothbard
(Edited by Patrick Newman)

Editor's foreword

The following manuscript is an unpublished chapter of Murray N. Rothbard's *Man, Economy, and State* (hereafter, MES) (2009 [1962]). As the tentative title, "Chapter 5: Producer's Activity," indicates, it was meant to be the fifth chapter of the book and the first on production theory. In it, Rothbard discusses the optimal production and investment decision of the producer, and uses familiar analytical tools such as perfect competition, the isoquant-isocost framework, and the competitive-versus-monopoly price distinction. This chapter was drafted when Rothbard still planned to write a textbook version of Ludwig von Mises's *Human Action* (1999 [1949]), before he decided to write a full blown treatise. Rothbard's decision to change course was heavily influenced by his concurrent decision to abandon this chapter and rewrite his production theory, as he thought that the new material would be unsuitable for an introductory textbook. In particular, the above-mentioned analytical tools were all subjected to trenchant criticism by Rothbard in his final production theory.

The chapter is meant to serve as a companion to Newman (2018), a concurrent paper written by the present author to discuss the evolution of Rothbard's approach to production theory and its implications for modern theory. However, this chapter is also a valuable resource for scholars interested in Rothbard and Austrian economics, as well as for historians of production theory in their own research projects.

The chapter was found and reorganized by the present writer in the Murray N. Rothbard archives at the Ludwig von Mises Institute in Auburn, Alabama. Over the years, Rothbard saved many of his draft pages for MES on various topics, including both those that would eventually appear in the book and those that would not. Rothbard did not neatly organize his draft pages, so many of the pages that could be found next to each other in the archive boxes concerned completely different topics. Fortunately, Rothbard did number his pages, so the present writer was able to reconstruct the chapter by sifting through the archive boxes and linking up pages based on their pagination and also on the practical matter of whether the sentences ran from one page to the next. The document that follows pieces together as much as possible the missing chapter based on the available surviving resources.

The chapter is in a rough stage, as Rothbard appears to have written only one draft before deciding to revise his production theory and remove the chapter from his planned work. However, it is written very clearly and is easy to understand, so in terms of editing the paragraphs, for the most part I have only had to make a few grammatical and stylistic changes regarding his numerical examples. In some cases, exclusively in the last section, I had to add a few words and sentences in order to clarify Rothbard's argument. The largest of such additions occur toward the end of the chapter, where several of Rothbard's draft pages could not be found. Consequently, I had to fill in the gap with some summary transitional sentences, and in one case, a paragraph detailing what I believe Rothbard would have discussed in these pages, based on some references contained later in the chapter. All additions I have made are in brackets, and the reader will see that I have faithfully written only what can be inferred from the rest of the chapter, and in a style consistent with it. In addition, I have provided information in endnotes (prefaced with *Editor's endnote*) about various references Rothbard makes to either previously written or planned chapters of MES.

I have also had to make some minor changes to the structure of the chapter. The three sections I located were sections 1, 2, and 4, and there was a missing third section of the chapter that I could not find. Furthermore, Section 4 included all of the material that is now Section 3, which made it quite large and unwieldy. Therefore, I have split Section 4 into two parts based on their respective topics and given Section 3 an appropriate title so that there are now four well-organized parts that smoothly flow from one to the next.

In the first section, titled "The Demand for a Firm's Product," Rothbard concentrates on the production function of an individual producer for a given good. With fixed prices for inputs, Rothbard investigates the optimal production choices in situations where the firm either has or does not have an influence on the output price. In Section 2, "Competitive Price and Monopoly Price," Rothbard introduces the terms "perfect competition," "competitive price," and "monopoly price," and defines a monopolist as someone who receives a grant of state privilege. In Section 3, titled by the present author "The Product and Outlay Schedules of the Firm," Rothbard returns to the firm's production decisions and analyzes factor ratios and production coefficients. Rothbard derives constant cost (isocost) and constant product (isoquant) schedules as well as rates of constant outlay and constant product substitution. Rothbard shows that the cost minimizing level of output is the point at which these two rates are equal. In a subsection, he presents a mathematical and graphical formulation of the above theories and briefly mentions their relation to the determination of factor pricing. Rothbard finishes the chapter with Section 4, titled "The Output and Investment Decisions of the Producer," by constructing "The Law of Investment Decision" using the concepts of rates of net income, marginal, and average rates of return. Rothbard argues that the investor will not produce at the outlay where either his profit amount or percentage rate of return is maximized, but rather up to the last outlay where the average and marginal rates of return are greater than or equal to his average and marginal rates of time preference. This theory may be useful for those scholars interested in an Austrian "Theory of Investment," as it is a portfolio theory of how the capitalist-entrepreneur allocates his money across various enterprises. This is linked with a brief criticism of firm analysis, which undoubtedly influenced Rothbard to drop the chapter and revise his production theory.

In conclusion, this chapter will be a fertile source for both historians of thought and contemporary theorists interested in Austrian economics and production theory.

– Patrick Newman

Section 1: the demand for a firm's product

We have seen that the money prices of goods on the market are set at the intersection of the demand and supply curves. Setting aside the relatively simple problem of the market for old stock, the market price and quantity exchanged are determined by the intersection of the market supply curves of the producers, and the demand curve. We have seen above that the stock thrown on the market in any given period is largely determined by *previous* anticipations of market conditions in this period. This notion has been presented in terms of the "final supply curve" of producers. In other words, if the selling price of a certain line of washing machines is expected to be 20 ounces of gold next September, how many washing machines will Smith begin to invest in *now* so that the final product will emerge next September? We have described this final supply in terms of the *present* price calling forth a *present* investment for a *future* production; strictly, of course, it is the *expected future price* that calls forth investment now for future production. All present production is necessarily the result of such previous anticipation.[1]

Thus, all producers' activity – the central nexus of the economy – is based on certain anticipations of future selling prices. We have analyzed above the determinants of market price for consumer goods, durable and nondurable, and now we must analyze the "final supply curve," and the process of producers' activity. Consumers' goods, the end of human activity, must be produced by producers, and the overwhelming number of *exchangeable* goods must be produced through the monetary exchange process outlined in Chapter III.[2] Therefore, analysis of producer activity is vital; not only will it provide the final clue to the analysis of consumer goods' prices – through discussing the determination of the size of the stock thrown on the market – it is also the key to the analysis of the determination of the money prices of factors of production. All other goods but consumer goods are factors, and all of these are demanded and bought solely by producers. It is producers that purchase with money, capital goods, land, and labor, and it is producers that use other factors to produce the capital goods. It is only through a more detailed analysis of producer activity, therefore, that the prices of factors can be explained.

To analyze the actions of a producer let us take a hypothetical case, Mr. Jones. Jones, like all others, must decide on the allocation of his money assets to investment expenditures, consumption expenditures, and to his cash balance. Let us postpone discussion of changes in cash balance to a later chapter on the demand for money and its utility.[3] Jones must allocate his expenses between consumption and investment expenditure. The motive that impels him to spend money on present consumption is the gratification of his desires through present consumption. What is the motive that impels him to *save* a certain amount of money by restricting his possible consumption, and invest that money in expenditure on various factors of production? This motive must be the expectation of *greater* money income in the future. We have already seen that every man prefers a satisfaction of a desire earlier than later, and therefore that a given amount of present money is always preferred to the same amount of money in the future.[4] At any given point, he will have a certain rate of time preference, a rate by which he will prefer *present money* to the *present prospect of money at some date in the future*.[5] We have seen that the more he allocates to investment, the greater will be the marginal utility forgone of present consumption, and the less will be the marginal utility of each additional future ounce of money income.[6]

"Investment opportunities" for a greater supply of future consumer goods are always open to man, because investment in capital goods adds to the capital structure, and increases future product of consumer goods. On the other hand, man must satisfy his present needs first. Thus, men must always balance their prospect of future gain as against their rate of time preference for present as against future satisfactions. The primary activity in deciding whether or not to be a producer is the weighing of the anticipated future gain against the person's rate of time preference. In the words of Professor Fetter, "The different time-periods, present and future, and their different economic situations are brought into comparison . . . by conscious choice between the thing actually present and the future good more or less clearly pictured in the imagination."[7]

We must postpone detailed consideration of time preference and its effects to later chapters of this work.[8] Here it suffices to point out that each individual has his own rate of time preference, expressed as a percentage premium of present over future goods, and that the more he saves at any time, the greater his subjective premium will tend to be.

Let us suppose now that Jones is considering whether or not to invest 1000 ounces of gold, or spend this money in consumption. Let us say his rate of time preference for these 1000 ounces is 6% per annum. In other words, if he anticipates a return on this investment of 6% or less for the following year (assuming for simplicity that only one year is taken into account), he will not make the investment. Thus, in deciding on productive investment or not, his minimum return for the year will be an anticipated 1060 ounces. If he anticipates this or less, "it will not pay for him" to make the investment.[9]

Now Jones surveys the prevailing conditions, and estimates that he has available four different lines of investment. For the sake of simplicity, we will now assume that all of these lines are in the production of consumer goods (since we have not yet explained the determination of any capital goods prices), and we will also assume that the *period of production* for each of these processes is exactly one year. This period of production, as explained in Chapter I, is the length of time from the beginning of the action – the investment – to the reaping of the final product.[10] It should be clear that it is a simple task to make the necessary adjustments in calculation if one or other of the processes takes more or less time to complete. The four lines of investment open to Jones he estimates will net him, in the year to be considered, net money returns of 10%, 8%, 7%, and 5% respectively.[11] In other words, with an investment in factors of 1000 ounces now and in the near future, Jones will be able to reap the following returns for lines of investment A, B, C, and D, as illustrated in Table 4.1:

Table 4.1 Jones' money returns

Line	*Gross money return*	*Net return*	*% of net return on investment*
A	1100	100	10%
B	1080	80	8%
C	1070	70	7%
D	1050	50	5%

It is clear that Jones will not invest in line D in any case, since his rate of time preference is *6%*, and he would prefer to spend his 1000 ounces on consumption now rather than make the investment. If all of his prospects were like D or worse, he would make no investment at all. In this case, it is clear that he will invest the 1000 ounces in line A, where the greatest percentage net money return is to be found. Here, we must remember the qualification that he will only choose such a course if other psychic factors are neutral. Thus, if he has a special fondness for the production of Good B, or a special hostility toward the production of Good A, the 8% money return may be worth more to him on his value scale than the 10% return to be made in Good A. Noting this qualification, however, it will be convenient for us to set it aside, and assume that psychic factors are neutral in our example, in which case the investor will always choose the greatest prospects for money return.

We must now investigate the line of production more closely. Suppose that we confine our attention to the line of production that produces Good A. Jones is eager to maximize the percentage return from his investment. What are the factors that will determine the size of his return? These factors are: a) the money prices of the factors purchased, b) the selling price of his product, and c) the physical productivity of the factors in their transformation into the product. It is obvious that, other things being equal, the *lower* the prices he must pay for the factors, the greater will be his return; the *higher* the price of his product, the greater his return; and the *greater* his physical productivity, the greater his return. Let us assume for the moment that the prices of the factors are given. Jones also discovers that there is available to him a range of technical possibilities in the production of the particular good. For the sake of simplicity, let us suppose that only two factors,

X and Y, are required in the production of Good A. The money price of X and the money price of Y are fixed on the market – say it is 4 ounces per unit of X, and 10 ounces per unit of Y. Jones knows (or believes) that there are several possible proportions of X and Y that he can buy with his 1000 ounces in order to produce Good A. These may be the following:

Table 4.2 Factor combinations for the production of Good A

1)	40X plus 84Y
2)	50X plus 80Y
3)	60X plus 76Y

With prices at 4 and 10, these combinations will all add up to expenditures of 1000 ounces. As Table 4.2 depicts, in the first combination, Jones spends 160 ounces on X and 840 on Y; in the second, he spends 200 ounces on X and 800 ounces on Y, etc. Now the question arises: which combination does Jones choose to adopt? First, this depends on the physical productivity of each combination. This physical productivity is the effect of the production *recipe*, a recipe which is known to the producer in making his decision. The relationship between physical input and product is sometimes known as the "production function."[12] Let us say that the above combinations of input would yield the following products:

Table 4.3 Factor combinations and output for the production of Good A

	Combinations of input	*Resulting product*
1)	40X plus 84Y	96 units
2)	50X plus 80Y	100 units
3)	60X plus 76Y	110 units

It would certainly seem that Jones will pick that combination which will yield him the *maximum physical output*. In this case, it would be Combination 3, by which we can produce 110 units from 1000 ounces' worth of factors. There is one qualification to this course of action, however, and that would be if his increase in units produced would so lower the market price of the product as to *decrease* his gross revenue from the sale of the produced stock. In other words, suppose as Case (a), that the price of his product will be 10 ounces per unit, and that he correctly estimates it as such. Furthermore, suppose that regardless which production process he chooses, the market price will continue to be 10 ounces. In other words, whether he chooses to produce 100 or 110 or 96, etc. units, the market supply curve will not be affected sufficiently to lower the price. In this case, the gross revenue from the various combinations will be as shown in Table 4.4:

Table 4.4 Gross revenue in the production of Good A, Case (a)

	Combinations of input	*Resulting product*	*Price of product*	*Cross revenue*
1)	40X plus 84Y	96 units	10 oz./unit	960 oz.
2)	50X plus 80Y	100 units	10 oz./unit	1000 oz.
3)	60X plus 76Y	110 units	10 oz./unit	1100 oz.

Jones will choose Combination 3, yielding the largest gross revenue and hence the largest net revenue with a given investment (1000 oz.) and the largest percentage net revenue on the investment. It is evident that, regardless of the number of alternative combinations available, where the price is constant, the combination chosen will be the one that maximizes the physical product from a given amount of money invested in factors.

Now suppose Case (b), where Jones' production is important enough in the market supply of his product so that a change from one combination to another *does* affect the market price at which the product will be sold.[13] Within the range of choice of combinations, a larger output will increase the market supply curve enough to lower the price of the product. It is evident that this is the usual rule on the market. Strictly, indeed, even in Case (a) there must have been *some* effect on the market supply curve from the change in output, however small, and this minute change will tend to affect the price. In Case (a), however, the change was too small to alter the point of intersection. In Case (b), the price is affected by the change in quantity, but not so much as to lower the gross revenue with an increased output. Thus, a typical situation might be that shown in Table 4.5:

Table 4.5 Gross revenue in the production of Good A, Case (b1)

	Combinations of input	*Resulting product*	*Price of product*	*Gross revenue*
1)	40X plus 84Y	96 units	10.5 oz./unit	1008 oz.
2)	50X plus 80Y	100 units	10.4 oz./unit	1040 oz.
3)	60X plus 76Y	110 units	10.0 oz./unit	1100 oz.

In this case, the increase in product and supply of the producer lowered the market price, but not in any case enough to lower revenue. Strictly, this condition only need prevail, in Case (b), *at and above the point of maximum output*. Thus, it would have been possible for the price, at a supply of 96 units, to have been 11 ounces per unit, and the gross revenue therefore to have been 1056 ounces. Table 4.6 depicts this situation:

Table 4.6 Gross revenue in the production of Good A, Case (b2)

	Combinations of input	*Resulting product*	*Price or product*	*Gross revenue*
1)	40X plus 84Y	96 units	11.0 oz./unit	1056 oz.
2)	50X plus 80Y	100 units	10.4 oz./unit	1040 oz.
3)	60X plus 76Y	110 units	10.0 oz./unit	1100 oz.

Here, it is true that as the supply increases from 96 to 100 units, the configuration of the demand curve and the market price is such that the revenue is lowered. However, the important consideration is that *the point of maximum output is also the point of maximum revenue*. Should Jones shift to another than the maximum combination in order to restrict the product, the higher price will not be sufficient to compensate for the loss of revenue. In both Case (b1) and Case (b2), the producer will choose the point of maximum output, which will also be the point of maximum revenue.

This data can be translated into terms of the *demand curve to the individual producer*. The individual producer, after all, is not concerned with what the market demand curve will turn out to be – he is concerned what the price will be for his particular product. He must ask himself the question: if I produce so many units, what will the selling price be; if I produce so many more units, what will be the effect on the selling price? In other words, he in effect is estimating what price the buyers will pay for different possible supplies of *his particular product. This analysis applies whether or not the producer is one of hundreds producing the same product, or whether he is the only one producing that good.* In any case, he must estimate at what price he will be able to sell his product to the buyers.

For Case (b1) above, the *demand curve to the individual producer* can be constructed as seen in Figure 4.1:

	SUPPLY OF PRODUCER	PRICE OF PRODUCT
1)	96 units	10.5 oz./unit
2)	100 units	10.4 oz./unit
3)	110 units	10.0 oz./unit

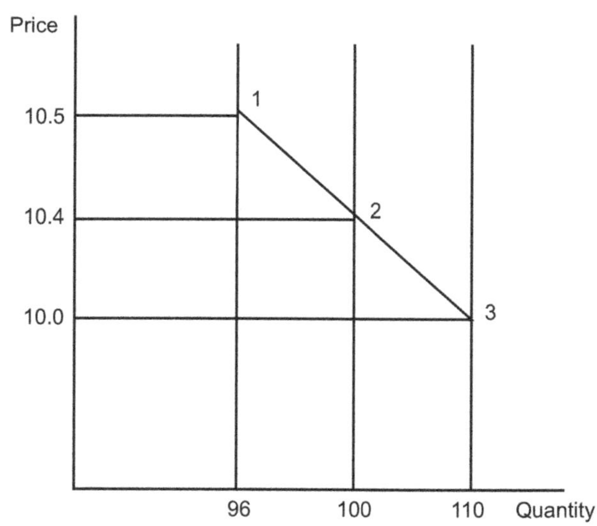

Figure 4.1 Graphical illustration of Case (b1)

When the supply of Jones is 96, the market price will be 10.5 – in other words, consumers will be prepared to demand 96 of Jones' units at a price of 10.5. This gives Jones one of the points, 1, on the *demand curve for Jones' product*. The price and supply at 10.4 and 100 respectively, and the various other items on the schedule, yield the other points on this demand curve (such as 2 and 3). These points are drawn together in one line for convenience. The schedule above also tells Jones how much of his product will be demanded at any particular price. Thus, it is clear that the producer knows that if he produces 96 units, they will be sold for 10.5, and 100 units will be sold for 10.4, etc. He *also* knows that, regardless of the size of his stock, if he sets the price for his product at 10.5 he will be able to sell only 96 units; if he sets the price at 10.4 he will be able to sell 100 units, etc. Thus, the supply and estimated market price yield him an estimate of a true *demand curve for his individual product*. Not only will he know that a supply of 110 units will provide him with the maximum revenue, he will also know that, once the 110 units are produced, *it will not pay for him to destroy or withhold some units in order to raise the price on the remainder*. Thus, with this type of demand curve for his own individual product, it is to his interest to produce his maximum physical product, and not to deliberately restrict or withhold his product to obtain a higher price. Even if he can obtain a higher price, restriction will not compensate him in revenue for the lesser quantity sold.

This property of the demand curve for the individual producer, determining whether decreased production will raise or lower revenue, is called its *elasticity*. We remember from Chapter II that a demand curve is termed "elastic" over any given range if the total outlay of the sale will be greater at a lower than at a higher price.[14] In the money economy, this means that a demand curve is *elastic* between a range of two prices *if the amount of money spent at the lower price is greater than the amount of money spent at the higher price*. In the case of the *demand curve to the individual producer*, the money outlay by the consumers constitutes his gross money revenue at that price. Thus, in Case (b1), the gross revenue obtained by the producer at a price of 10.5 and supply of 96 is 1008 ounces; at a price of 10.4 and supply of 100 units is 1040 ounces, etc. What we are concerned with in this problem is the elasticity of the demand curve for the individual producer at and above the point of maximum output. We compare the revenue at that point with the revenue at possible lower outputs. In the case of (b1), the gross revenue at the point of maximum output – the price of 10.0 – *is greater than* any revenue that could be obtained from restricting Jones' production to sell at a higher price. Thus, Jones will sell at a point of maximum output when the demand curve for his particular output is *elastic* at and above that point.

What of Case (b2)? Here, the demand curve for Jones' product is inelastic, if we compare the price of 10.4 and supply of 100 and the price of 11.0 and the supply of 96. *Between these two points on the curve, the demand is inelastic, and it would be more profitable for Jones to restrict his production from 100 to 96 in order to take advantage of the greater money revenue. However, this is irrelevant for Jones' action, because the demand curve is still elastic relative to the point of maximum output*. The point of maximum output yields the point of maximum revenue, and hence with respect to this point, the demand curve for Jones' product is elastic throughout its range. The choice will still be Combination 3, the supply of Jones will still be 110 units, and the market price will still be 10.0.

If Jones were in the situation of Case (a), the analysis would be even simpler. It is obvious that if the price were 10 regardless of Jones' product in the relevant range, the demand curve for his product is completely elastic, and it would always pay for him to be at his most productive, and produce the maximum physical output with a given monetary investment on factors. In this case, too, the producer strives for maximum physical productivity, and maximum output coincides with maximum revenue.

Another conceivable case is Case (c), where the demand curve for the individual producer is inelastic at the point of maximum output. Suppose, for example, that the following conditions obtained:

Table 4.7 Gross revenue in the production of Good A, Case (c)

	Combinations of input	*Resulting product*	*Price of product*	*Cross revenue*
1)	40X plus 84 Y	96 units	11.6 oz./unit	1114 oz.
2)	50X plus 80Y	100 units	11.5 oz./unit	1150 oz.
3)	60X plus 76Y	110 units	10.0 oz./unit	1100 oz.

Or, diagramming the data in Table 4.7, as Figure 4.2 shows, in the form of the individual demand curve:

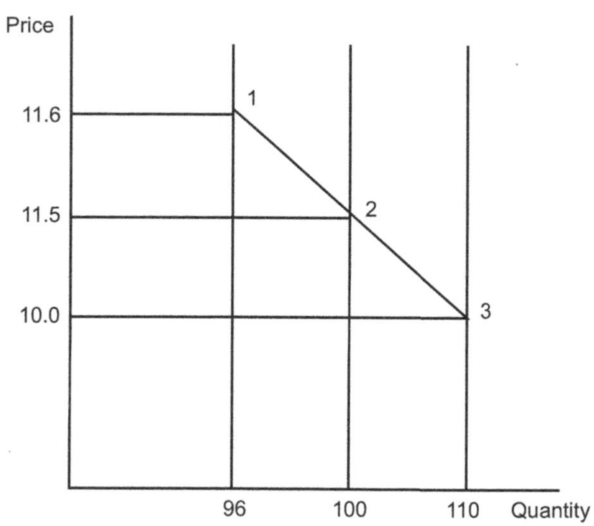

Figure 4.2 Graphical illustration of Case (c)

With this sort of demand curve facing him, it pays the producer best to supply to the market 100 units instead of the 110 units which he could supply. With a price of 11.5 per unit instead of 10.0, the result is a larger gross revenue of 1150, and a net revenue of 150 instead of 100.

Jones can restrict his production in either of two ways, and it does not matter which course he takes. He may use the less productive combination of factors, Combination 2 instead of Combination 3, thus reducing his physical productivity; or, he may produce the maximum amount (Combination 3) and destroy the difference (the 10 units). Economically, it doesn't matter which course he takes, since the result is to supply less for the market than he could have done with the purchased factors.

We see that when a demand curve confronting the individual producer is inelastic as in Case (c), there are two major points of differentiation from the Cases (a, b1, and b2), where this curve is elastic. First, in the other cases, physical productivity (output on a given investment in factors) is at a maximum, and all of this output is supplied on the market. In Case (c), there is a restriction of productivity by the producer to obtain greater revenue. Secondly, the final market price is always lower in the other cases, other things being equal. The effect of the action in Case (c) is *always to raise the price to the buyer*. The effect of the restrictive action is always to raise the price of the individual firm's product *higher* than it would have been at the point of maximum supply and output.

Section 2: competitive price and monopoly price

When the market price of a firm's product is arrived at as in Cases (a) and (b) above, this is termed *the competitive price*; when it is arrived at as in Case (c), through the restriction of production and supply, the resulting price is termed *the monopoly price*.[15] The monopoly price can only be attained in the case of a demand curve inelastic to the producer, and is the result of a restrictive cut back from maximum productivity; it is always higher than the competitive price would have been. *How much* higher the monopoly price is, *how much* production is restricted, depends of course on the conditions of each particular case. Evidently, the more inelastic the demand curve for the individual producer, the higher, relatively, will be the monopoly price.[16, 17]

Many writers have assumed that "competitive price" only refers to such conditions as Case (a), where the action of the individual producer has no effect on price. Such a rare condition is dubbed "perfect" or "pure" competition. More common situations like Case (b), where the action of the individual producer does affect the price, are termed, invidiously, "monopolistic" or "imperfect" competition, and it is assumed that this "monopolistic competitive" price is higher, and the quantity less, than would have obtained under "pure" competition.[18] We have seen that this contention is completely fallacious. If the demand curve for the individual producer is elastic at the competitive price, so that this point yields maximum revenue, the product will sell at the competitive price regardless of the fact that the action of the individual producer may have a strong influence on the market price. Thus, we see that there is *not* a large range of possible prices with the competitive price at the bottom, and monopoly price at the top, and a variety of "monopolistically competitive" prices that could be set in between. *There is only the competitive price and the monopoly price.*

Whichever price is set, whether competitive or monopoly price, the determination of the price takes place in the way we have analyzed above, via the supply and demand schedules. The difference comes through the determination of the quantity of stock produced. Under competitive price the producer estimates what his selling price will be, or rather, what price he will be able to sell his stock for, and produces the maximum stock that he can from his investment. But if the demand curve to the producer is inelastic at that price, he can restrict his production somewhat, produce less stock, and increase his monetary revenue. The market price which will obtain as a result of such restriction is the monopoly price.

The extra revenue which the producer obtains from the monopoly price as compared to his revenue at the competitive price is a *monopoly gain*, and this concept, along with further details of the monopoly question, will be studied further in a later section.[19]

It is most unfortunate that traditional terminology in economics makes it necessary to use such terms as "competitive price" and "monopoly price." The terms are highly misleading and can lead to serious errors in analysis, and they are highly charged emotionally – they are "loaded terms" to most people. "Competition" is usually regarded as fine and praiseworthy, while "monopoly" is somehow sinister and tyrannical. There was good reason for the sinister attachments to the word "monopoly" in the public mind. The original meaning of monopoly was *a grant of special privilege by the State* to a person or group of persons to produce a good to the exclusion of other producers. As the great jurist Lord Coke defined monopoly:

> A monopoly is an institution or allowance by the king, by his grant, commission, or otherwise . . . to any person or persons, bodies politic or corporate, for the *sole* buying, selling, making, working, or using of anything, whereby any person or persons, bodies politic or corporate, are sought to be restrained of any freedom or liberty that they had before, or hindered in their lawful trade.[20]

The original meaning of monopoly therefore was a grant or exclusive trade in some area, conferred by the State to the hindering of the "lawful trade" of other would-be traders, or "competitors," in the same field. Such monopoly grants were historically important in the Western world, and it is not surprising that, with the growth of the spirit of liberty and of the libertarian movement, monopolies became more and more odious.[21, 22]

Many present day writers have changed the original meaning of the word "monopoly," and the result is an unwarranted transference of this acquired hostility toward entirely different conditions. Some define "monopoly" as any producer who is alone in the production and sale of any particular product, or "monopolistic" as the exertion of any perceptible influence over the market price. These conditions are far removed from privileged grants of monopoly. On such definitions, any individual producer of a good that the consumers regard as unique, and differentiate from other goods, is a "monopolist." Ford has a monopoly over the sale of Ford cars; John Williams, lawyer, has a monopoly over the sale of the legal services of John Williams, etc. In this interpretation, every seller of an individualized commodity is a "monopolist."

Labels for concepts are basically immaterial, the main requirement being that the original meaning continue in force to avoid confusion and error. In view of its historic origins, and emotional connotations, such a use of the term "monopolist" is highly inexpedient, and should be rejected. Similarly, to classify *trademarks* and *brand names* for individual products as grants of monopoly is an illegitimate use of the term. For the government to protect any individual in the use of his own trademark is identical with protection against Jack Smith calling himself "John Williams" and selling his own legal services in the guise of forgery. In other words, it is equivalent to the governmental function of defending an individual's freely obtained property against violence and fraudulent theft.[23] Each individual, in a free economy, has the right to his own self, to *his own name*, and to the exclusive use of his own property. He is no more a "monopolist" over his own name, than he is over his own will or his own property. The governmental function of defense of person and property, so vital to the existence of a free economy and a voluntary society, necessarily involves the defense of each person's particular name or trademark against the fraud of forgery. It is absurd to use the term "monopoly" or "monopolistic" with respect to the consumers' differentiation of various individual's products and services. If the consumers consider Williams' and Smith's legal services as different in quality and therefore as different goods, then they are different goods. To allow Smith to pass himself off as Williams, because of the latter's greater reputation for quality, is to permit violation of each person's ownership over his name and product.

To define "monopolist" as the exclusive seller of any given product is thus highly inexpedient. We shall employ the original definition of monopoly as a grant of special privilege by the State, confining a field of trade of produce to one individual or group, to the exclusion of others who would be eligible to enter such production in a purely free economy.[24] We shall define that voluntary society where there are no grants of monopoly privilege as a society of *free competition*, i.e., one where anyone may enter any field of production that he desired (so long as he does not usurp the name of another individual). His *ability* to do so in any case depends of course on the capital he can invest or borrow, and on his entrepreneurial ability in forecasting future conditions, but this of course is his *own* responsibility. He is *free* to compete, not only when he has the ability to do so, but generally when there are no coercive restrictions preventing him from doing so.

It should be clear by this time that there is a great distinction between the concept of "monopoly" and of "monopoly price," and hence the misfortune of the same word applying to different concepts. The two are entirely different. The monopolist, in our sense, may or may not be able to achieve a monopoly price. The demand curve for his product may be elastic, or there may not be even any consumer demand for his product at all, in which case he could make no net return in producing the good. Thus, the State may grant Hiram Jones an exclusive monopoly privilege for the manufacture of kerosene lamps, but if so few people wish to buy these lamps as to make the production unprofitable, the monopolist is not able to achieve a monopoly price or a monopoly gain. On the other hand, the production may be profitable, but the demand curve elastic, so that the monopolist does not restrict production and sells at what would have been the competitive price. Similarly, the "monopolist" in the faulty sense of a single seller of any product, may not be able to achieve a monopoly price for his sale. A lawyer will probably not be able to gain more revenue by restricting his hours of legal service in order to raise the market price; a producer of a particular brand of breakfast cereal may not be able to make gains by restricting his production in order to raise the price and earn a monopoly gain.

Thus, it is perfectly possible for a "monopolist," either in the sense of a privileged seller or as the sole seller of an individualized commodity, not to be in the position of charging a monopoly price for his product. The result depends on the demand curve for his individual product. On the other hand, it is possible to be able to charge a monopoly price without being a "monopolist" in either of the two senses. Thus, let us suppose that there are several sellers of the same product, and that therefore there is no monopoly. For each of the producers, the demand curve for his individual product is elastic at the competitive price, and therefore there is no way to achieve an extra monopoly gain by restricting production and raising price. On the other hand, the demand curve for the product as a whole, the total market demand curve, might be decidedly inelastic at the market price. In such a case, there might well be a tendency for the various producers to get together and decide production and price policy as if they were one firm only. If they could make such an agreement, they could act as one firm, and the market demand curve would then be identical with the demand curve for that "firm," and the inelasticity would permit a general restriction of production and a rise to a monopoly price. Such an agreement by many producers to act as one firm in the market is known as a *cartel*. A cartel arrangement can permit numerous firms to act as "monopolists" in the sense of sellers of an individualized commodity.

There are many stumbling blocks in the paths of firms attempting to form such a cartel, however. Although the demand for the whole product may be inelastic, the demand for each firm will be elastic. Therefore, each firm will agree that the total product and sale should be restricted in order to raise the price, but each producer will be reluctant to restrict *his own* product and sales. For if the other firms restrict their sales, each firm can gain considerably by expanding his own and taking advantage of the higher price. Hence, it is necessary for each cartel member to agree on a certain quota of the aggregate product and sales, and restrict himself to that quota. It is quite clear that the difficulties to the establishment, and the maintenance, of such a cartel are well-nigh insuperable. In the first place, there is likely to be a great deal of bickering about the assignment of quotas since each firm will try to acquire a larger quota. Whichever basis quotas are assigned are arbitrary, and will always be subject to challenge. As Professor Benham states:

> Firms which have produced a relatively large share of output in the past will demand the same share in the future. Firms which are expanding – owing, for

> example, to an unusually efficient management – will demand a larger share than they obtained in the past. Firms with a greater "capacity" for producing, as measured by the size of their . . . plant will demand a correspondingly greater share.

Particularly likely to be restive under a cartel system are the more efficient producers, those who are making larger profits, and who are eager to expand their business. These firms will be eager to take advantage of the elastic demand curve to their own sales, and to test their own mettle against the less efficient firms protected by the assured cartel's quota. It is obvious that the cartel, increasingly as it persists, tends to protect the sales and earnings of the *inefficient* as compared to the more efficient competitors.

As Benham puts it:

> The successful maintenance of a combination, once it is formed, is threatened both from within and without. Conditions will change as time goes on, and will make it difficult for the combination to retain the adherence or "loyalty" of some of its members. Some firms will find that consumers demand more of their particular products than before and will resent having to pass on orders (in excess of their quota) to be executed by other members of the combination. Again, some firms will outstrip others in taking advantage of the progress of technical knowledge, and will conclude that they have more to gain by expanding their sales at lower prices than by continuing their membership of the combination. If the demand for the products of the industry falls considerably, the proportion of "unused capacity" will increase, and this will strengthen the desire of some firms to break away and make fuller use of their plants, thus increasing their receipts, by selling at lower prices.[25]

The ever present temptation to each producer, particularly a venturesome and efficient one, is to defy the cartel, either secretly or openly, and expand his own sales. The great instability of the cartel stems from the fact that once the firm steps out of line, the others must do so as well. For with A, B, C, etc. restricting their output to maintain the monopoly price, if competitor D expands his output, and cuts the price slightly, he tends to take a great deal of business away from the other producers. Even if price is not affected a great deal, D's expansion earns revenues while the others must limit theirs.[26] The result is a speedy breakup of the cartel and a return to competitive pricing and output conditions.

Just as great a menace to the existence of a cartel is the threat of outside competition from newcomers. As a matter of fact, the greater the success of the cartel in maintaining its internal cohesion, and earning monopoly gains which are apportioned to the members, the greater will be the temptation for new firms to enter the field. These new firms, unhampered by cartel agreements, can expand their production and sales to take business away from the cartel, and may cut the price of the product as well. This factor is a powerful one in causing the dissolution of the cartel agreements. As a result of these factors, it is not an exaggeration to state that almost no cartel agreement, unaided by special privileges from governments, has been able to survive more than a very short period of time.[27] The type of State privilege is varied, and will be dealt with in the chapters on State intervention and the Hampered Market.[28] One such measure is compulsory cartelization, another is the imposition of artificial restrictions in the freedom of entry of potential competitors into the field.

Another important factor tending to prevent the rise of cartels is that, in a free economy, an agreement to form a cartel *is not enforceable* in the courts. In other words, if Jones signs an agreement to join a cartel and only process 10% of the output of certain other firms, he may violate the agreement at any time without suffering governmental penalties, such as payment of damages of compulsion to abide by the contract. This is due to the particular scope which governmental enforcement of contracts has in a free economy. It was seen in Chapter II that the governmental agency, in a voluntary society, enforces contracts, not simply because they are contracts or promises *per se*, but because they represent *unfinished exchanges of property*.

Suppose, however, that a monopoly price has been established on the free market, either by an individual firm or by a remarkably stable cartel. Are the consequences necessarily sinister, as has often been assumed? In the first place, it must be realized again that the term "monopoly price," used in contrast to "competitive price," is really a misnomer, although the terms must be used for traditional reasons. The monopoly seller or sellers are not immune from, or beyond the pale, of competition. Quite the contrary. The terminology is the result of an old neoclassical preoccupation with single "industries." Every monopoly seller competes with every other seller for the money of the consumer. Every consumer allocates his money expenditure among all the available uses, and therefore this fundamental competition obtains between all sellers of all the goods and services. Producers compete for wide groups of laborers of various types, of lands and capital goods. Thus, Ford does not only compete with General Motors; it competes with the sellers of washing machines, of television sets, of houses, of caviar, of concert music, etc. Everyone on the free market is a mutual competitor. Thus, the monopoly seller who obtains a monopoly price is not beyond competition. He does not dictate to the consumer or anyone else.

But even if the monopoly seller is subject to competition, isn't the consumer worse off when a monopoly price and restricted production obtains? Can we not say that there is a loss of consumer welfare in a monopoly price situation? Isn't this an important exception of the harmony of interests that prevails on the voluntary market? To answer these questions, let us recall the exchange situations detailed in Chapter II.[29] Jackson and Smith are in isolated exchange, the former has a horse and the latter has fish, and they bargain to make an exchange. Let's say the agreed upon terms of exchange are 90 barrels of fish for the horse. Now, critics could charge that Jackson is worse off than he would have been if the price had been set at 95 or higher, while Smith is worse off than he would have been if the agreed price were less than 90. Such charges, however, miss the point of the analysis. The point is that both voluntarily agreed on the price, that both believed that there were no better alternatives available. The same is true for every price in every exchange, regardless of the number of exchanges. The purchase or the sale of the unit of the good at the agreed upon price is considered the best possible alternative action by each party. Thus each is the best off, has the highest welfare, that he can obtain, consistent with the maximum welfare of everyone else. Smith could force Jackson at the point of a weapon to make the exchange for 80 or 70 or 60 or no fish at all. But in that case, it is obvious that the use of coercion has made Jackson worse off, and that Jackson is being exploited by Smith. Furthermore, this action brings up all the problems of violence and an exploitative society, which have been mentioned previously and will be discussed fully in later parts of this book.[30] Within the framework of a voluntary society, the market price is the best price that either the seller or the buyer can get, and therefore comparing the welfare of either one with some impossible ideal is vain. In the same way, buyers and sellers on the market are "included" or "excluded" from exchange by their own voluntary action in accordance with their value scales.

But what of the case of a monopoly price? When it is set in the framework of the free market, again all parties to the exchange benefit. A coerced lower price or greater product could only exploit the sellers for the immediate benefit of the buyers. Monopoly pricing, on the other hand, is not the exploitation of the consumers, because the payment is voluntary. This conclusion is confirmed by a closer look at the inelastic demand curve, which must obtain in all cases of monopoly price. Thus, suppose that a firm's maximum productivity would yield a product of 100 units at the competitive price of 10 ounces. Its inelastic demand curve is such that a stock of 50 units raises the market price to 30 ounces, the monopoly price. In the former case, the firm's revenue is 1000 ounces from its investment; in the latter case, it is 1500 ounces. This means that consumers have *voluntarily* paid more money for the product in the monopoly price situation. How can it be deduced from this that the consumers are worse off under a monopoly price? After all, the inelasticity of the demand curve is not fixed in Heaven; it is the result of the voluntary action of the consumers in paying more money for the product at a monopoly price. If the consumers really felt that they were worse off than they could be because of the monopoly price, they could, individually or jointly, *boycott* the product and refuse to buy at the higher price. Such action, would, of course, render the demand curve for the good elastic, and force the firm or the cartel to increase its output and lower the price to the competitive one. The money withheld in the boycott could be added to cash balances, spent on the products of competitors, or used to invest in a competitor to a cartel. There is therefore never any need to worry about the situation of the consumers in a free market. The shape of their demand curve, and therefore the final market price, is purely the result of their own voluntary action.

It should be clear from the above discussion that there is nothing particularly reprehensible, or frustrating of consumer freedom, in the establishment of a "monopoly price" or in a cartel action. A cartel action, if it is a voluntary one, cannot injure freedom of competition or, if is profitable, cannot injure consumers. On the contrary, they are, as are all other actions on the free market, perfectly consonant with a free society, with individual self-sovereignty, and the earning of money through serving consumers.

As Benjamin R. Tucker brilliantly concluded in dealing with the problem of cartels and competition:

> That the right to cooperate is as unquestionable as the right to compete; the right to compete involves the right to refrain from competition; cooperation is often a method of competition, and competition is always, in the larger view, a method of cooperation . . . each is a legitimate, orderly, non-invasive exercise of the individual will under the social law of equal liberty.
>
> Viewed in the light of these irrefutable propositions, the trust, then, like every other industrial combination endeavoring to do collectively nothing but what each member of the combination might fully endeavor to do individually, is, *per se*, an unimpeachable institution. To assail or control or deny this form of cooperation on the ground that it is itself a denial of competition is an absurdity. It is an absurdity, because it proves too much. *The trust is a denial of competition in no other sense than that in which competition itself is a denial of competition.* (Italics ours.) The trust denies competition only by producing and selling more cheaply than those outside of the trust can produce and sell; but in that sense every successful individual competitor also denies competition. . . . The fact is that there is one denial of competition which is the right of all, and that there is another denial of competition which is the right of none. All of us, whether out of a trust or in it, have a right to deny competition by competing, but none of us, whether in a trust or out of it, have a right to deny competition by arbitrary decree, by interference with voluntary effort, by forcible suppression of initiative.[31]

This is not to say, of course, that joint co-operation or combination is necessarily "better than" competition among firms. We simply conclude that the relative extent of areas within or between firms on the free market will be precisely that proportion most conducive to the well-being of consumers and producers alike. This is the same as saying that the size of a firm will tend to be established at the level most serviceable to the consumers.[32]

Section 3: the product and outlay schedules of the firm

Let us now return to the activity of the firm and its *production function*. We will assume now that the firm is competitive, and produces for a competitive price, so that its situation either fits Cases (a) or (b) above. In the production schedule drawn up for Jones shown in Table 4.3, the ratios between the quantities of the factors differ for the various technical alternatives available. Thus, 50X combined with 80Y produces 100 units of product, and 60X combined with 76Y produces 110 units. The ratios between the quantities of factors: 50/80, 60/76, etc. may vary considerably. The list of technological alternatives varies according to the specific "engineering" data of the product in question. In very rare cases, there might be cases where only one ratio, or one set of "production coefficients," is permissible. In such cases, for example, the product could only be produced with a combination of 5X to 8Y, in that ratio. In almost all cases, however, it is possible to vary the ratios of the factors. Thus, some might assume that the factor ratios in a firm producing, say, chemical dyes are inalterably fixed by the chemical formula of the dyes. This is a complete misconception of the problem, however. The point is that the variations can take place among the number of workers, the number of vats, the amount of land, management, etc., that will be used. The greater the development of the economy, the advance of technological knowledge, and the amount and variety of factors, the greater the opportunity for variability of factor ratios. It is doubtful, indeed, if there are any instances of production where the factor ratios are absolutely fixed.[33]

In Jones' case, given the factor prices, and the production functions available, it is clear that he will choose the combination 60X plus 76Y in order to attain the maximum output, and hence maximum revenue, from the original investment. In order to analyze more fully the problem of production combinations, the firms' production, and factor prices, we will assume a far greater range of production alternatives by extending Table 4.3. Suppose, for example, that with the price of Factor X at 4 ounces per unit, and the price of Factor Y at 10 ounces per unit, 1000 ounces will purchase the following alternative combinations of factors yielding the listed quantities of product:

Table 4.8 Extended factor combinations and output for the production of Good A

Price of X equal 4 oz. per unit	*Price of Y equal 10 oz. per unit*
1000 ounces worth of alternative combinations	*Units of product*
40X plus 84Y	96
45X plus 82Y	97
50X plus 80Y	100
55X plus 78Y	105
60X plus 76Y	110
65X plus 74Y	107
70X plus 72Y	105
75X plus 70Y	100
80X plus 68Y	96

These are the technological alternatives that can be accomplished with 1000 ounces' worth of factors. The maximum productivity is still at 60X plus 76Y, and this will still be chosen.

Now, simply from the given factor prices, we can deduce the *rate of outlay substitution*, i.e., the rate at which one factor must be subtracted to compensate for the addition of another factor, so as to have a *constant outlay* (in this case, 1000 ounces). In the present case, 2 fewer units of Y have to be compensated by 5 additional units of X in order to arrive at the "constant outlay combination" of

1000 ounces. For example, starting from the first line, we know that 40 times 4 equals 160; 84 times 100 equals 840, and the sum equals 1000. If we add 5 units of X and subtract 2 units of Y to move to the second line, we know that 45 times 4 equals 180, 82 units of Y times 10 will give 820, to sum to 1000. It will be seen below algebraically below that the *rate of outlay substitution of one factor for another is equal to the ratio of the prices of the two factors*. Therefore, the rate of substitution of factor X for factor Y is 2/5, while the ratio of the money price of X to the money price of Y is 4/10, or 2/5. This ratio of 2/5 obtains regardless of what constant outlay is in view; whether it is 500 ounces or 700 or 1800 ounces.

As yet, we have not progressed far beyond the conclusion that Jones will produce at the (60X; 76Y) combination. However, this line of approach permits further insight into the activity of the firm, and the interplay of technological and financial factors. Let us now shift the focus of attention and consider this type of question: assuming for the moment that Jones wishes to produce, say, 105 units; what are the alternative combinations of factors which can produce them? The answer is a purely technological one, and in accordance with the technological knowledge available, Jones can draw up a list of alternative physical combinations that would yield this result. *So far*, in this sort of problem, no financial or monetary considerations have yet entered. We already know that 105 units can be produced by the combinations: (55X and 78Y) and (70X and 72Y). Let us say that the following, shown in Table 4.9, are the combinations of the two factors that will yield 105 units of product:

Table 4.9 Factor combinations for constant output

Combinations of producing 105 units of product	*Chances in factors*	
	Plus X	*Minus Y*
40X plus 100Y	–	–
45X plus 90Y	5	10
50X plus 84Y	5	6
55X plus 78Y	5	6
60X plus 75Y	5	3
65X plus 73Y	5	2
70X plus 72Y	5	1
75X plus 71Y	5	1

It is obvious that in investigating any *constant product* combinations, an addition in the amount of one factor must be offset by a decrease in the quantity of the other for the final product to be the same.[34] This can be deduced from the mere fact of these factors as instruments of production. It is *also* deducible from the very fact of the existence of factors. As more and more of one factor is added, and another factor is diminished, the added quantities must compensate less and less for losses in the other factor. Conversely, the more a factor is diminished, the greater will be the need to compensate by adding to another factor, to produce the same product. This is called the *imperfect substitutability of factors*. This imperfect substitutability is deducible from the very existence of human action. The very fact that consumer goods are scarce implies that factors of production are scarce, and the very fact that there *are* factors implies that there is more than one factor, since if there were only one factor it would be a consumer good and not a producers' good. The very fact that there is more than one factor, in turn, implies that the different factors are *not* perfectly substitutable for each other; otherwise, they would not be separate factors at all. The common example of such imperfect substitutability is that if labor were perfectly substitutable for land on a farm, constant production could be insured with a constantly diminishing area simply by adding to the number of workers, so that 100,000 workers in the space of a thimbleful of land could produce as much wheat as 100 workers on a hundred acres of land. The imperfect substitutability, however, applies to *all* factors of production in all cases, and not just to labor and land.

We may define the *marginal rate of production substitution* of one factor for another as the ratio of the amount of the second factor that can be diminished as a result of an increase in the first factor in order to yield a constant product. It is clear that the marginal rate is *diminishing* as the factor continues to be added. When the combinations change from (40X; 100Y) to (45X; 90Y), the marginal rate of substitution of X for Y is 10/5, equal to 2; but later on in the proceedings, when the combination changes from (65X; 73Y) to (70X; 72Y) the marginal rate of substitution is 1/5. What the actual rates are depend on the specific technological data, but economics does tell us that the *marginal rates of product substitution diminish.*

Suppose that Jones decided to produce 105 units of product; he could affect the production in each of the above different ways. Which alternative would he choose? Obviously, he could choose the alternative that involved the least expense in money, and that would depend on the prices of the factors. *Technologically*, he would have no way to choose between the various combinations, because technologically all of them are equally effective. It is only the existence of factor money prices that permits the producer to choose among these combinations. With the original factor prices of 4 ounces of gold per unit for X, and 10 ounces for Y, the necessary money expenses he would incur for the production of 105 units of product would be as follows:

Table 4.10 Production costs for constant output

Combinations producing 105 units of product	
Price of X equal 4 oz. per unit	*Price of Y equal 10 oz. per unit*
Combinations	*Money outlay necessary*
40X plus 100Y	1160 ounces
45X plus 90Y	1080
50X plus 84Y	1040
55X plus 78Y	1000
60X plus 75Y	990
65X plus 73Y	990
70X plus 73Y	1000
75X plus 71Y	1010

In this particular example, Jones will choose either (60X; 75Y) or (65X; 73Y) either of which minimizes his required money outlay at 990 ounces. Given the amount of production at 105 units, the *minimum outlay combination of factors* will be the one chosen.

Some writers discuss the activity of the firm as if this were the most appropriate manner of analysis, as if a quantity of product is arbitrarily set, and the producer looks for the minimum outlay combination of factors to produce it. In reality, however, it is clear that the beginning point is the decision to invest a certain amount of money in factors, and the attempt to choose a combination so as to maximize the productivity of the factors, as we have seen above. The present analysis is subsidiary and supplementary to the previous one, but it is useful to revealing the relationship between technological and monetary elements.

Reverting back to the 1000 ounces' worth of combinations depicted in Table 4.8 we saw that Jones chose that combination which maximized production for 1000 ounces, at 110 units of product (60X and 76Y). We shall now demonstrate that this combination is also the minimum outlay combination of all the factor combinations that could produce 110 units of product. The demonstration of this truth is simple. In the first place, we may rule out those combinations which require less of *each* factor, such as (55X; 74Y). We have seen above that obviously wasteful combinations are discarded immediately; therefore, if (60X; 76Y) are *required* to produce 110 units, there could not be another constant product combination with less of each factor that could also produce 110 units. This follows from the very nature of scarce goods and scarce factors. Therefore, the possible combination which might be able to produce 110 units for less outlay would have to be a constant product combination schedule such as listed above in Table 4.10 for 105 units, with more of one factor compensating for the subtraction of another. Now suppose that this supposed minimum outlay combination for 110 units has a quantity of X of more than 60, and a quantity of X of less than 76. But to be cheaper, the combination would have to have less of one factor – given the other – than the combination on the 1000-ounce constant outlay schedule. But for each addition of X (X is assumed for convenience to only change in blocks of 5 units, but this does not alter the fundamental result), the constant outlay combination produces *fewer* units of product: 107, 105, 100, etc. In order to be cheaper for any given X, the units of Y would have to be even fewer; and it is manifestly impossible for such a combination to produce as much as these amounts, let alone 110 units. Symmetrically, the same is true for combinations with less X and more Y. For constant outlay, each of the possible alternative combinations produces less than 110 units; to be cheaper than each of these, any other combination could only produce still less, and could not produce 110 units.

It is therefore universally true that the maximum product combination for any given outlay of money is also the minimum outlay combination for that particular physical product.

Thus, we see that, on the free market, each firm, in maximizing the product that can be produced from any given outlay, is also engaged in reducing the money outlay required for each product. Given the prices of the factors, there is only one way to increase his money income from the investment: to find a factor combination that will be the most productive of physical product, and that, in consequence, will be the cheapest method of producing that amount. This analysis enables us to see clearly the different roles played in production by technological and by economic considerations. Technological considerations yield knowledge of the various series of constant product schedules that would be available. At any given product that could possibly be considered, the prospective producer could command a series of tabulations that would yield him the production functions and combinations that could produce it. This would be the contribution of technology. But this knowledge by itself would tell the entrepreneur next to nothing about the crucial questions in the whole problem of producers' activity: should he enter the business at all? How much should he invest? Which of the alternative constant product combinations should he choose? The answers to these vital questions can only be provided by *economic*, by *financial*, as opposed to *technological*, considerations. Specifically, it is the establishment of money on the market which enables the businessman to make these decisions in a rational and intelligible manner. The prospective producer will invest in that line of business, in that particular firm, which will maximize his expected money income, over any period of time that he chooses. This rule, as we have explained before, is modified when psychic nonmonetary matters intervene, thus obeying the general, universal rule that in *all* action the actor maximizes his expected psychic income. Setting aside cases of conflict between money and psychic income, which have already been noted, investors drive to maximize their money income. They will enter that line of business which promises the greatest return on their investment, they will invest in accordance with their expected return balanced by their time preference, and they will produce that combination which requires the least monetary expenditure for the particular product. And to accomplish this they will sell their products for as much as they can – which we have seen will quickly tend to be the competitive market price; will try to buy their factors for as little as they can – which we will see below will be the competitive price; and will try to increase the physical productivity which can be obtained from any given set of factors, i.e., increase their *productive efficiency* to the utmost. But it is clear that none of these decisions could be made if the investor did not have the various price data and estimates to guide him in his choices. And it is only because the money commodity has become the general medium of exchange that such markets, and such price and income comparisons and estimates, are possible.[35] And these price and income calculations and estimates are most emphatically *money* estimates; they can in no way be reduced to, or considered equivalent to, barter.

We have already demonstrated that the maximum product combination for any given outlay of money is also the minimum outlay combination for that particular physical product. It is therefore also true that every minimum outlay combination is the maximum product for that outlay. Let us then take the case of an investor with 990 ounces of gold to invest. His maximum product combination will produce 105 units, at either the combination (65X; 73Y) or (70X; 72Y), which are also the minimum outlay combinations for 105 units. We may see above the behavior of the rate of product substitution as the number of units of factors change; the rate of product substitution of X for Y changes from 2, to 6/5, to 3/5, etc. We notice that the minimum outlay combination is reached at the approximate point where the rate of product substitution is equal to 2/5; i.e. is equal to the rate of outlay substitution, which, given the prices, is constant throughout at 2/5. If the rate of product substitution is appreciably less than or more than the rate of outlay substitution, it will pay for the producer to shift to other alternatives until the two rates are approximately equal.

Thus, there is a tendency for the firm to produce at such a rate and such a way that the *rate of product substitution between factors is equal to the rate of outlay substitution between them*. And, since as we have seen, the rate of outlay substitution always equals the ratio of the prices of the factors, the firm will always tend to produce *so that the rate of product substitution between the factors equals the ratio of their money prices*.[36]

In the particular case of Jones, he will tend to produce in such a way that the rate of substitution between the two factors is 2/5.

Actually, this analysis does not help us in the specific determination of the productive combination that will be chosen: this will always be given by the requirement of maximum product per outlay (which will be the minimum outlay for that product). On the contrary, the two ratios will not by any means always be equal, because the range of production alternatives available may not be sufficient. If there are only a few production alternatives, then there cannot be the small steps which are necessary to allow equality of rates, or meaningful discussion of such rates. Thus, if only two combinations can produce 105 units of product: namely, (45X; 90Y), and (65X; 73Y), Jones will choose the minimum outlay combination, but the "rate of product substitution" between such distant combinations will be 17/20. However, the rate will still be the nearest approach possible to 2/5, and in that sense, we may still say that the tendency will be to approach that rate. The value of the concepts of rate of substitution will fully emerge as essential to an analysis of the prices of factors of production, and, specifically, the demand schedules for the producers for these factors.

The product and outlay schedules of the firm-mathematical analysis

At this point, it is now time to turn to an algebraic and geometric presentation of the above analysis for two factors.

The definition of a constant outlay schedule is that the total sum of money expended be constant, whatever that sum may be. In other words, for two factors, the sum of the amount of money spent on factor X plus the sum of the amount spent on factor Y is always equal. The amount of money spent on each factor, in turn, is always equal to the price of that factor times the total quantity of the factor that is purchased. Thus, if the price is 10 ounces per unit, and 5 units are bought, the total sum of money expended is 50 ounces. Therefore, for a constant outlay schedule, if px is the money-price of factor X; py is the money-price of factor Y, a is the number of units of X bought at any given point; b is the number of units of Y bought at any given point; and k is any constant sum of money outlay; then:

$$apx + bpy = k \qquad (1)$$

This equation defines any given point on any constant outlay curve for two factors. Now, suppose that we wish to move from this point to any other point on the constant outlay curve. The amount of X then becomes *a+m*, while the amount of Y, which diminishes in compensation, becomes *b-n*. At this point then:

$$(a + m)px + (b - n)py = k \qquad (2)$$

Now, we may multiply out in equation *(2)*, and substitute from equation *(1)*. Then:

$$apx + mpx + bpy - npy = k$$
$$apx + mpx + bpy - npy = apx + bpy$$
$$mpx - npy = 0$$
$$mpx = npy$$
$$n/m = px/py \qquad (3)$$

This gives us proof of the statement in the text that the *rate of outlay substitution between two factors is equal to the ratio of the prices of the factors*. As X increases, the ratio of the decline in Y due to the increase in X needed to maintain the same total cost is equal to the ratio of the prices of X to Y.

Returning to equation *(1)*, let us solve for *b*, the quantity of Y at any given point:

$$bpy = k - apx$$
$$b = (k - apx)/py$$
$$b = k/py - a(px/py) \qquad (4)$$

Now, let us solve equation *(1)* for those points where *a* is equal to zero, i.e., there are zero quantities of X. Then:

$$0 + bpy = k$$
$$b = k/py \qquad (5)$$

This value of *b*, at the point where *a* equals zero, may be termed *b0*.

Now, we may substitute (*5*) into (*4*), and the equation becomes:

$$b = b0 - a(px/py) \qquad (6)$$

Now, we can see that equation *(6)* is directly applicable to the case of Jones' 1000 ounces. *b* refers to the values of Y at each point, and therefore may be written as Y. Similarly, *a* refers to the values of X and can be written as X. The ratio of *px/py* is equal to 4/10 or 2/5. *b0* is the value of Y when X is zero; it is equal to the constant outlay (1000) divided by the price of Y (10) – this equals 100.

Therefore, for Jones' condition of 1000 ounces and the given prices of the factors:

$$Y = 100 - (2/5)X \qquad (7)$$

This is Jones' constant outlay curve for 1000 ounces.

All constant outlay curves for two factors have the shape of a straight line. The slope of the line is negative, and is the ratio of the prices of the two factors, which is also equal to the rate of outlay substitution between them. When X is zero (even though such a choice will never arise in practice), Y is equal to the constant outlay sum divided by the price of X; and when Y is zero, it is easily seen that the value of X is the constant outlay divided by the price of Y.

This algebraic analysis enables us to establish a whole series of constant outlay curves for different values of k for different constant outlays. Whatever the constant outlay, the curve can be determined: it again will be of the same slope as the other curves, while the difference will be in its position. Thus, say the constant outlay is 800 ounces of gold. In this equation, when X is zero, Y will be equal to 800/10, or 80. When Y is zero, X will be equal to 800/4, or 200. And the constant outlay curve for 800 will connect the two points.

In this way, we can establish a whole *family* of constant outlay curves. All that is needed is the knowledge of the prices of the two factors, which are assumed to be given; and then for each possible constant outlay, the combinations of the factors can be determined. Some of the members of the family of constant outlay curves in Jones' case are as in Figure 4.3:

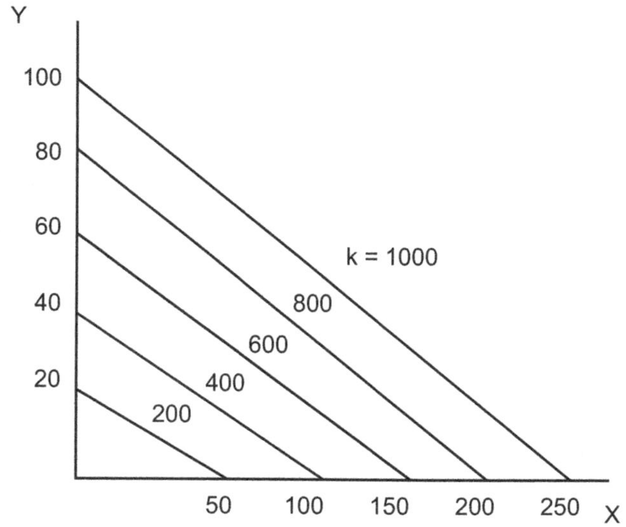

Figure 4.3 Constant outlay curves with given factor prices

Now, it is important to realize that the prices of the factors are the sole determinants of the family of constant outlay curves. These prices are always approaching uniformity on the market. Therefore, the constant outlay curves are not only applicable to Jones; *the very same ones are applicable to all producers who use these two factors*. Thus, the given set of constant outlay curves and the given rates of outlay substitution are the same for all the firms producing with these factors, not just for one firm alone. At any one time, then, the family of constant outlay curves for any two factors is the same for all producers on the market. This family of constant outlay curves is a series of regular, similarly sloped lines, easily determined by anyone once the prices are given, and the same for all producers.

The *production function*, on the other hand, is *not* a given data to all producers. The production function is the estimate of the maximum quantity that could be produced from each combination of factors. Although this is technological rather than catallactic knowledge, it by no means follows that it is "given" to all prospective producers. This knowledge is not simply of engineering formulae; it involves numerous minute details of individual skills, correctness of estimates, judgment of materials and location, etc.[37] It is far more likely that each individual's production function differs than that it is the same, even with the same product and the same factors. As we will see below, this likelihood is made a certainty when there are many more than two factors of production, and when, as is almost always the case, some of these factors are unique (*specific*), in some ways to the individual firm. Production functions, therefore, are irregular and differ from one producer to another. Furthermore, they are not "objectively" given; they are only estimates in men's minds.

What is the shape of the production function? Some might be of fixed proportions, i.e., only one combination of factors can produce each possible quantity of output. We have seen in the text that this is practically never the case, but if it were, a diagram would be as follows: the quantity of one factor on the horizontal axis (say X), and the quantity of the other factor on the vertical axis (say Y):

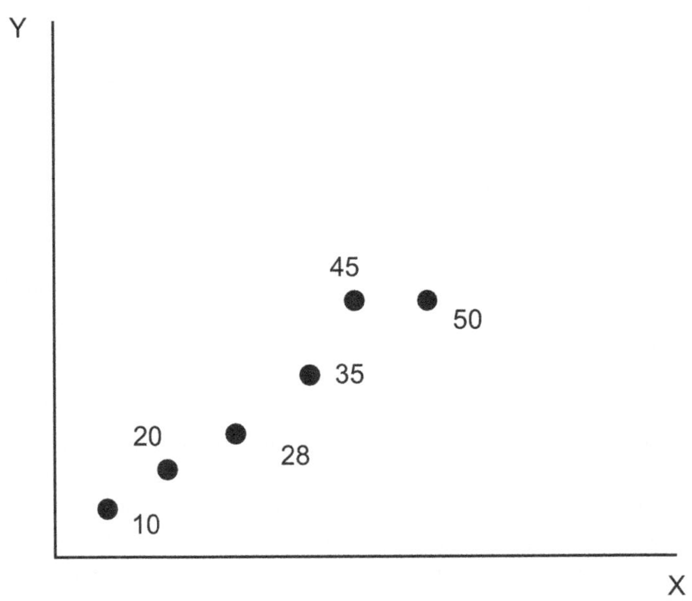

Figure 4.4 Production of output with various factor combinations

As Figure 4.4 shows, the numbers designate the quantity of output yielded at the various points. These quantities can be of any amount, but they must increase as the quantities of X and Y increase, by the nature of production.

With the existence of varying proportions of factors, so that there are alternative factor combinations for each quantity of product, we can draw up *constant product schedules*, and therefore *constant product curves*. If we assume that there are many possible combinations for each possible product, then we may ask the question: suppose, for example, that 1 unit of X and 10 units of Y combine to produce 10 units of product, as in Figure 4.5:

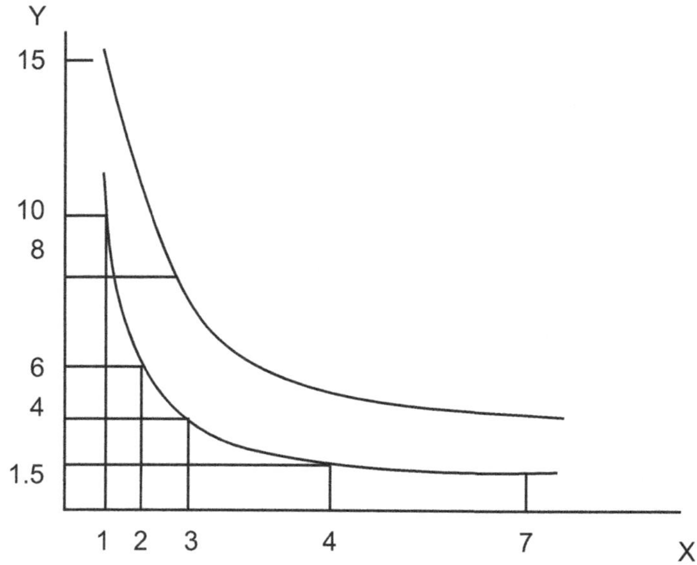

Figure 4.5 Constant product curves with various factor combinations

At this combination (1X; 10Y), there is very little of X and a great deal of Y. Now suppose that X is increased to 2; what will be the loss in Y to compensate and maintain production at 10 units? We cannot know the answer except for the concrete case, but it is clear that since the two factors are imperfect substitutes for each other by their very nature, where the quantity of X is low a slight addition of it will compensate for a big loss in Y to maintain constant production. Let us say that the constant production combination is (2X; 6Y). In the diagram, we may connect the two points for the sake of convenience. Now, what if X is increased to 3 units? Since X has been increased and Y has diminished, it will now take a lesser loss of Y to compensate for an increase of X. Thus, the point (3X; 4Y) might be on the constant product curve. Between the first and second points, the loss of Y was

4 and the gain of X was 1 unit; the ratio of the two is 4/1, or 4. From the second to the third point, Y lost 2 and X gained 1; the ratio was 2. This ratio is the *marginal rate of product substitution* between the factors, or the rate of substitution of X for Y. It is evident that as X increases, this rate *diminishes*. As X increases and Y diminishes, more and more gain of X is needed to substitute for less and less loss of Y. Thus, the succeeding points on the constant product curve above may be (4X; 3Y), (7X; 1.5Y), with marginal rates of substitution at those points 1 and 0.5 respectively.

We have arrived at one constant product curve. At each constant product, it is evident that there will be a similar shape, in that the marginal rate of substitution diminishes throughout. However, it is obvious from the nature of production that the larger product calls forth a larger quantity of both factors at each point. Thus, suppose that we are interested in a constant product curve at 20 units. Suppose X is 1 unit; it is obvious that Y will have to be more than 10 in order to produce these 20 units. What amount this will be we do not know; we only know it will be greater. Let us suppose that the point will be (1X; 15Y). We can now draw in a set of succeeding points, assuming only a diminishing marginal rate of substitution. It is clear that all these points will be above, or to the right of, the corresponding points on the lower constant product line.

Thus, we see that there is a *family* of curves for each constant product. The higher products are above (to the right of) the lower ones. The property of diminishing rates of marginal substitution make these curves tend to be convex to the origin. As the product gets lower and lower, the curves get closer to the origin, finally reaching that point itself at zero product, since zero quantities of factors yields zero product. On the other hand, the curves never cross the X or Y axes. Since both factors are assumed to be necessary ones for the production of the product, and hence the imperfect substitutability of the factors, no increase in the one factor, however great, can compensate for the loss of the whole supply of the other. A common classical example is the case of a wheat farm, where no amount of labor, however great, can produce wheat when there is no land available; on the other hand, no amount of acreage can produce wheat without any labor. The point applies, however, to all types of production.

The point has come when this information can be consolidated. For any process of production using two factors, there are two families of curves: constant outlay curves, and constant product curves. Constant outlay curves hold for all producers who use the two factors, since they depend solely on the market prices of the factors. Constant product curves are estimates by the enterprising producers, and will differ from firm to firm. While the former are regular straight lines determined by the ratio of prices and total outlay in view, the latter are irregularly spaced, their only condition being the diminishing rate of substitution between the factors. The two families of curves will be somewhat as in Figure 4.6:

As we have seen in the text, at any given outlay, the actor will produce at the maximum product. What does this mean in graphic terms? Let us take, as in Figure 4.7 below, a typical constant outlay line, and start at the top.

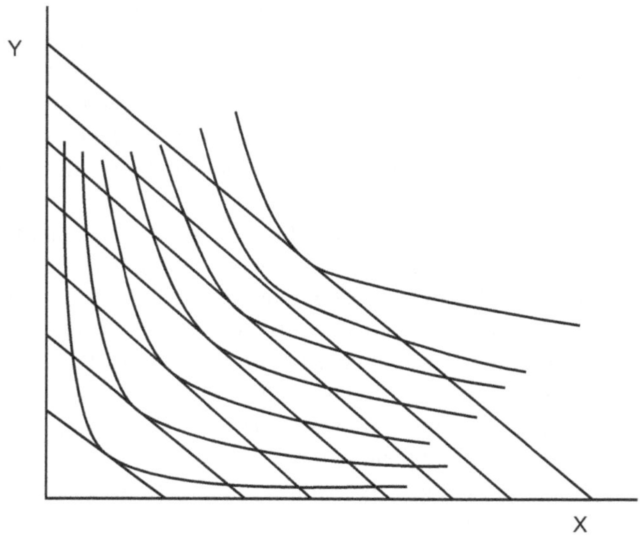

Figure 4.6 Constant outlay and constant product curves

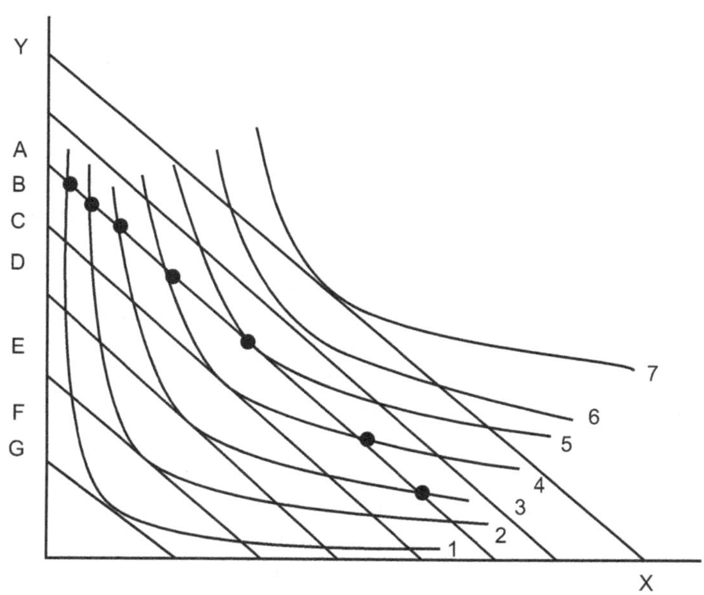

Figure 4.7 Possible production of output with given constant outlay

This diagram has seven constant product curves, marked 1 to 7, in ascending order of the size of the product. As the constant outlay curve begins at the top, it intersects constant product curve 1 at point A. At point A, that combination of factors X and Y yield a total product of order 1. Proceeding further along the constant outlay line, (further in the sense of increasing X and decreasing Y), we intersect point B, at which point X the factors will produce products of size 2. So as we proceed along the constant outlay line, we arrive at higher and higher products – at curves further and further to the right. Finally, we arrive at the point with the highest size product, and the point of production that will be chosen with this outlay. This is point E of size 5, the point of tangency between the constant outlay line and the highest constant product curve obtainable with that outlay. Beyond this point, the constant outlay line again intersects the lower-sized product curves.

For any constant outlay line then, the entrepreneur will strive to act so that his combination of factors will be at a point tangent to the constant product curve. Of course, the entrepreneur in practice does not need to know about such tangencies and curves; he is only concerned with maximizing his output for the given outlay. But we have seen that mathematically this is implied by such maximum output. It must be cautioned that in practice, the constant production curves are a series of dots, of discrete points, rather than continuous lines. A continuous curved line implies that the distance between the points of decision by the actor are infinitely small; actually, this can never be the case – human action of necessity deals with discrete objects and distances. However, in the realistic case, the choice of the maximum product is the closest approximation to such tangency that could be, or should be, achieved.

It is clear that this elaborate analysis of families of curves and tangencies is of no particular aid in this problem; however, it provides analytic tools that will be handy in later analyses of the pricing of factors of production.[38] For one thing, we know geometrically that the marginal rate of product substitution, which is always diminishing, is equal to the *slope* of the constant product curve, when the latter is a continuous curve. At a point such as E, of tangency with the constant outlay line, elementary geometry tells us that the slopes of the curve and the line are equal. The slope of the line equals the marginal rate of outlay substitution, which is constant throughout and equal to the ratio of the factor prices, and therefore, *at the point of tangency, the marginal rate of outlay substitution equals the marginal rate of production substitution.* Under real conditions, this is only an approximation rather than an actual fact, but this proves the assertion in the text that the producer sets his production so that these two marginal rates tend to be equal. And this means, furthermore that, for each producer's decision, *the marginal rate of product substitution between the two factors tends to equal the ratio of their prices.*

This equality is only an approximation, since for the universal case of more or less discrete points, the point of decision will only be the nearest approach to such equality. However, because of the divisibility of money, the constant outlay curve tends to be (although never will be) a *continuous* line, while the more advanced the production structure and the more complex the alternative combinations, the nearer will the constant production schedules approach being continuous curves. The more highly developed the market economy, therefore, the greater will be the tendency to approach equality between the ratio of the prices of factors and the marginal rates of product substitution between them.

At each possible constant outlay line, therefore, the producer will pick his preferred combination of factors at the point of maximum output, or approximate tangency to a constant product curve. The higher the amount of money to be spent, and therefore the higher the constant outlay line, the higher and the further to the right will be the constant product curve, and the various points of tangency. Thus, a typical family of constant product and outlay curves may have points of tangency as seen in Figure 4.8.

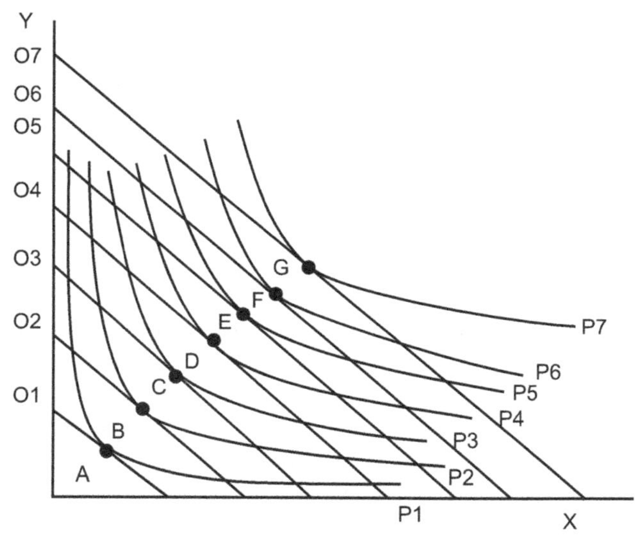

Figure 4.8 Optimal production with various constant outlay and product curves

In this figure, we depict constant product curves, P1, P2, . . . P7, and constant outlay lines, O1, O2, . . . O7. They have points of tangency at A, B, C, D, E, F, and G. The zero point is also a point of tangency, at zero input of factors. The points of tangency enable the producer to determine his *maximum product outlay curve.* For at any given outlay, the tangency points will yield the size of the maximum constant product curve. Thus, O1 will be tangent to P1 at point A. The same is true to every other alternative. Thus, the decision points A, B, C, etc. reveal to the producer: 1) the maximum product for each outlay, and 2) the best combination of factors for this production.

Section 4: the output and investment decision of the producer

We must now return to Jones and his outlay of 1000 ounces. We have already seen that, given an investment of 1000 ounces, Jones will select one combination which will yield him a maximum product. Out of a group of alternative combinations, he will select the best combination. We could diagram this situation as follows:

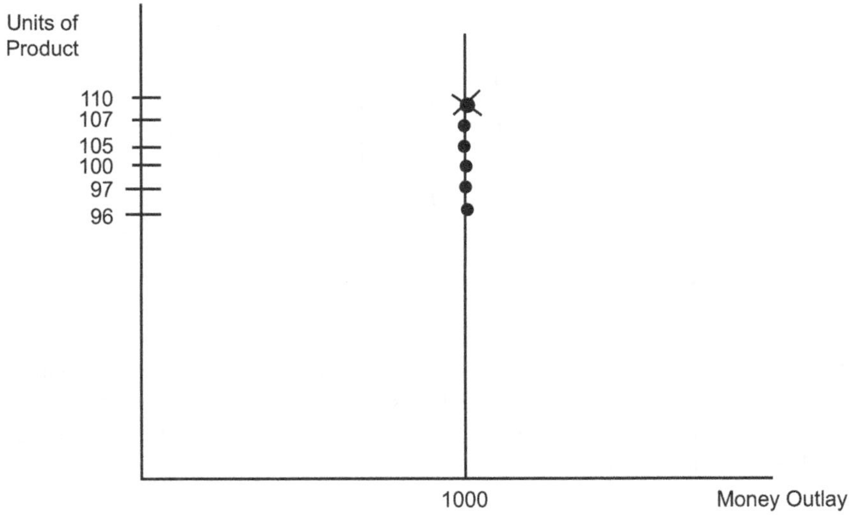

Figure 4.9 Possible production of output with constant money outlay

Figure 4.9 shows that, at an outlay of 1000 ounces of money, different alternative combinations could yield various amounts of product, namely 110, 107, 105, 100, 97, and 96, as listed in Table 4.8 above. The highest production, or the top dot on the line, will be the one that is chosen, and the combination of factors will be picked accordingly. This dot is crossed to represent the product of the combination that will be chosen. The same sort of process will be undertaken regardless of the amount that the producer has to invest. Thus, if he has 990 ounces to invest, he will choose the combination yielding him the maximum product, at 105 units. At each possible investment of money outlay, the producer will choose that factor combination which yields him the maximum product. Thus, the diagram of such a situation will be as follows:

For each straight line, the top crossed dot will be selected. Thus, we see a series of possible vertical straight lines, representing the constant outlay, with units of product on the vertical axis and money outlay on the horizontal axis. Each vertical

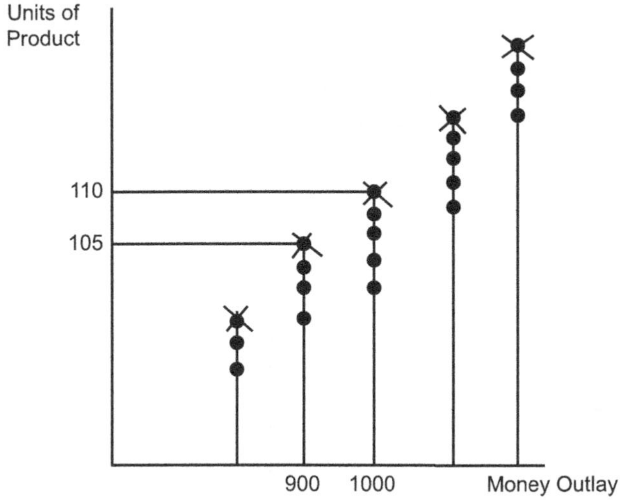

Figure 4.10 Maximum production of output at various money outlays

straight line is a constant outlay line, and the crossed top dot is the maximum product that would be selected in each case. As Figure 4.11 shows, the crossed dots can be joined for convenience to give us a connected line of potential products for each money outlay:

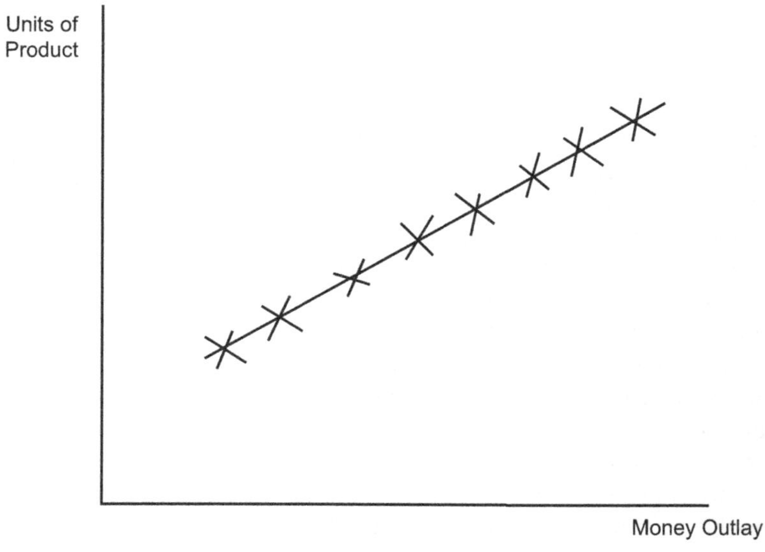

Figure 4.11 Product outlay curve

Each producer will try to determine the various points on this product outlay curve. As we have seen, he estimates the various alternative factor combinations for producing each particular quantity of product, and, using these and the prices of the factors, the producer will be able to judge his constant outlay combinations, and which combination will yield him the maximum product for each outlay. This will give him the series of crossed top dots for each outlay, and yield him the above diagram, which represents the *maximum product schedule* for each outlay.

What can economics say about the shape of this important curve? In the first place, it is obvious that a *greater outlay can never produce a lower maximum product*. We have seen above that the 1000 ounces will yield a maximum product of 110 units. A greater outlay, say 1050 ounces, cannot produce a maximum product of *less* than 110 units. This is obvious from the very nature of production and of factors. At the very least, the 110 units could be produced, even if the excess factors purchased with the other 50 ounces cannot be used. Thus, the maximum product schedule *always* slopes upward or remains horizontal when the money outlay increases. It never slopes downward.

Another characteristic of the maximum product outlay curve is an obvious one: it must pass through the zero point, since no expenditures will obviously result in no production. A typical product outlay curve might therefore look like this:

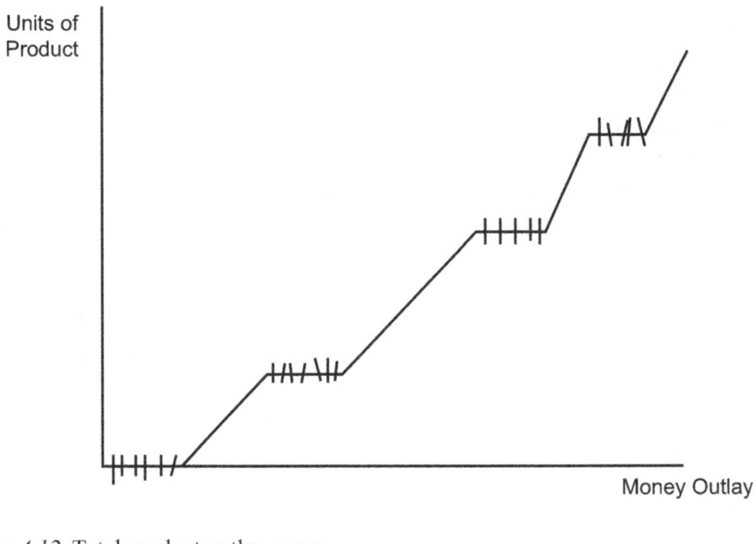

Figure 4.12 Total product outlay curve

We notice that we may conveniently omit the crossed dots from the final connected line. From the line, we may read off the maximum product which would be yielded by the expenditure of any given outlay.

Without discussing at this moment when the curve is likely to be horizontal, it is obvious that no producer knowing the situation will pick any outlay along the horizontal except the cheapest: i.e., the point on the extreme left of each horizontal line. Thus, if 1000 ounces of outlay will produce 110 units maximum and 1050 ounces of outlay will also produce 110 units maximum, it is clear that there will be no hesitation in choosing the 1000 ounces, and not the more expensive outlays. Any other decision would be a pure waste of money by the producer. Therefore, without yet fully answering how much money the producer will decide to invest, we can immediately answer that he will never decide to invest that amount which lies along a horizontal line. Thus, if 1000 ounces will produce 110 units, and all greater expenditures up to 1100 ounces will only produce 110 units (with expenditures of over 1100 ounces yielding more units), we can be sure that Jones will not decide to invest a sum of between 1001 and 1100 ounces. He will either invest more or less. In Figure 4.12 above, we cross the horizontal lines with vertical marks to designate those sums that are ruled out from the producer's decision.

So far, from Figure 4.10 we know two definite points on Jones' maximum product outlay curve: 1000 ounces netting him 110 units of product and therefore 1100 ounces of money revenue; 990 ounces netting him 105 units of product and therefore 1050 units of revenue (selling prices are assumed to be 10 ounces per unit). In the former case, he makes a net money income of 100 ounces, equaling 10% of his outlay; in the latter case, he makes 60 ounces net, equaling about 6% of his outlay. Now, we must directly pursue the question of how much Jones, or any other producer, will decide to invest in any particular line of production, and how much he will decide to produce. It is clear that the determining influences are the expected net income, its amount and its percentage. Their exact nature, however, must wait on a more elaborate explanation of the relation between outlay, product, and revenue, in table and figure.

Before finally analyzing which point on the maximum product outlay curve will be chosen, it is necessary to extend the analysis to remove the restrictive assumption of two factors. What will be the situation with *n* number of factors? This is a vital consideration, since it is very rare to find an actual case where only two factors are used to produce any given product.

If there are *n* number of factors, with market prices assumed to be given, the producer's investment decision turns out to be almost identical with the case of two factors. The situation may not be diagrammed as in the case of two factors, but the greater mathematical difficulties in the description of the case of *n* factors does not by any means signify difficulty for the producer. The producer is, again, confronted with a complex of technological alternatives for producing various amounts of output. Now, the production functions will be combinations of various quantities of factors X, Y, Z, etc. Once again, a constant outlay will enable a certain set of factors to be chosen, in accordance with their market prices. The producer may draw up the list of alternative factor combinations and corresponding outputs, plus a list of factor combinations that can possibly be bought at each given outlay. And, once again, the producer will choose the maximum product combination for each outlay. The fact that there are now many factors does not change the desire of the producer to maximize his product for each possible outlay. The shape of the maximum product curve does not change; it is still true that a greater outlay cannot yield a lower product, and that those greater outlays which will not increase product will not be chosen. It is evident that the analysis based on the maximum product curve is not changed by permitting any number of factors.

What of the interrelationships between the factors and the factor combinations that will be chosen as points on the maximum product curve? Here, it is clear that the situation, with *n* factors, is more complicated. It is, however, essentially the same, and does not materially alter the analysis. It is still true that we can represent the producer as adjusting, and substituting, all of his factors for each other. Each factor is an imperfect substitute for each other factor, the degrees of imperfection varying with the data of each concrete case. There can be no perfect substitutes for different factors, and there are few or no cases of absolute fixed proportions between all factors, so that, within limits, more of one factor can be substituted for less of the others. The marginal rate of substitution *between any two factors* diminishes as one factor increases. The rate of outlay substitution *between any two factors* is equal to the ratio of their prices, and the producer will still tend to approximately equalize the rate of outlay substitution and the rate of product substitution between any two factors. Even if ten factors are involved, if, *for any two factors*, for example, the rate of product substitution is greater than the rate of outlay substitution between them, it will pay the producer to keep substituting, say X for Z, until the rates are approximately equal. For this is equivalent to saying that substituting more X for less Z at constant outlay will yield a greater total product. Conversely, if the rate of product substitution is less than the rate of outlay substitution, it will pay to use less of X and more of Z until the rates are equal.

Therefore, for a case of *n* factors, the producer will always tend to produce at the point where the marginal rate of substitution for any two factors is equal to the ratio of their prices. There is a simultaneous balancing and adjusting in order to find the maximum product for each outlay. It must be emphasized that there is still one maximum product for each outlay, that there is still an array of different products for the alternative combinations at each outlay. Out of this array, the producer selects the maximum product combination; the number of factors involved does not change this.

Now let us turn to the final production decision of the producer who has arrived at his maximum product schedule. How much does he decide to invest and to produce? For convenience, let us take the case of another producer, Smith [*who can invest in a different firm that produces Product P*]. In addition to his maximum product outlay schedule, he estimates his future selling price, and this enables him to estimate his revenue outlay schedule. Thus, assume that his maximum product outlay schedule is as follows (assuming, for convenience, steps of 10 ounces of money outlay):

This product outlay schedule is shown below in Figure 4.13.

Now Smith estimates the future selling price of his product. It is quite possible that, as Smith's prospective product decreases, his selling price will rise. This estimate depends on his idea of the market demand schedule for his individual product.

Table 4.11 Smith's production decisions for Product P

Smith – Product P	
Total money outlay (gold ounces)	*Total maximum product*
0	0
10	0
20	10
30	18
40	28
50	40
60	50
70	55
80	55
90	65
100	70

At this point, we must broaden slightly our application of the concept of monopoly and competitive price. A monopoly price situation will occur *not only* if less produced from a given money investment yields a greater profit, but also if a lower money outlay, and its lower product, yields a greater profit because of the higher selling price. It is clear, however, that this does not materially change our analysis of competitive and monopoly price. In the previous section we assumed a given investment and a lower than maximum product; here, a lower outlay can also yield the same goal of a lower product, and without the waste of the former. This, then, is the actual case. If the demand for the firm's product is inelastic, so that a lower product, thrown as stock on the market, will so raise the price that money revenue is increased, the firm acts as a "monopolist" to cut back production and outlay to the lower figure. Thus, suppose that at a money outlay of 60 ounces, and at a maximum product of 50 units, as in Table 4.11, the price of the product per unit is 2 ounces. The money revenue, then, will be 100 ounces, for a net income of 40 ounces. If the demand schedule for the firm's product is inelastic above this range, then, for example, a sale of 10 units will raise the price to 20 ounces, and a total revenue of 200 ounces. Now, obviously, Smith will not invest 60 ounces, produce 50 units, and then throw 40 of these units away in order to acquire 200 ounces. We assumed this above, because we were dealing with the assumption that money outlay is fixed at a certain amount. Obviously, he will rather choose the minimum money outlay required to produce 10 units, i.e., 20 ounces. There will therefore be no need for him to throw away 40 units, and he will save 40 ounces which he would have needlessly expended.

There is therefore no change in our analysis of the demand curve for the firm, and its relation to the incidence of monopoly price. This curve depends only on the *quantity sold*, and bears no relation to how this quantity is produced. The change in our analysis of the monopolist is that even *he* will choose the maximum product for the money outlay that he spends. Even the monopolist will choose a point on his maximum product outlay schedule, and therefore even he strives to gain further profits producing whatever units he makes as efficiently and as productively as possible. If his demand curve is inelastic, he will simply reduce his money outlay from the amount that he would have invested under a competitive price. The reduction of his outlay will reduce his product to the most profitable amount.

On the other hand, there is no reason to restrict the definition of competitive price to a situation where the amount the firm produces has absolutely no effect on the price. It is clear that a change in the amount a firm produces always *does* change the market stock of the product, and therefore tends to affect the price. It may well be, of course, that, within the relevant range, the action of the firm is not large enough in relation to the product as a whole to change the market price. There is no need, however, to restrict the discussion of competition to this limited case. The only criterion is that the demand curve is not such as to raise revenue for a restriction of output to a price above the competitive one.

The following is a tabulation of Smith's productive situation [*and the firm producing P that he can invest in*], with the above total outlay and total product schedules, plus an *expected selling price* schedule for each quantity produced and sold of P. The selling price declines as the stock increases, but is not such as to yield a monopoly price situation (i.e., an increased total product for the firm does not lower its gross revenue). From these three columns we can deduce three others, which are also presented: *expected total money revenue* (which equals expected selling price times product); *net money income* (which equals money revenue minus money outlay); and *percentage net money income* (which equals net money income as a percentage of money outlay). These three schedules are derived from the primary three:

Table 4.12 Smith's money returns for various money outlays

Total outlay	*Total product*	*Exp. price*	*Exp. revenue*	*Exp. net income*	*Exp. rate of net income %*
(1)	*(2)*	*(3)*	*(4)*	*(5)*	*(6)*
			(= 2 * 3)	(= 4 – 1)	(= 5/1)
0	0		0	0	0
10	0		0	–10	negative
20	10	2	20	0	19
30	18	1.8	22.4	–7.6	negative
40	28	1.7	47.6	7.6	19
50	40	1.6	64	14	28
60	50	1.5	75	15	25
70	55	1.5	83	13	18.5
80	55	1.5	83	3	3.75
90	65	1.4	91	1	1.1
100	70	1.4	98	–2	negative

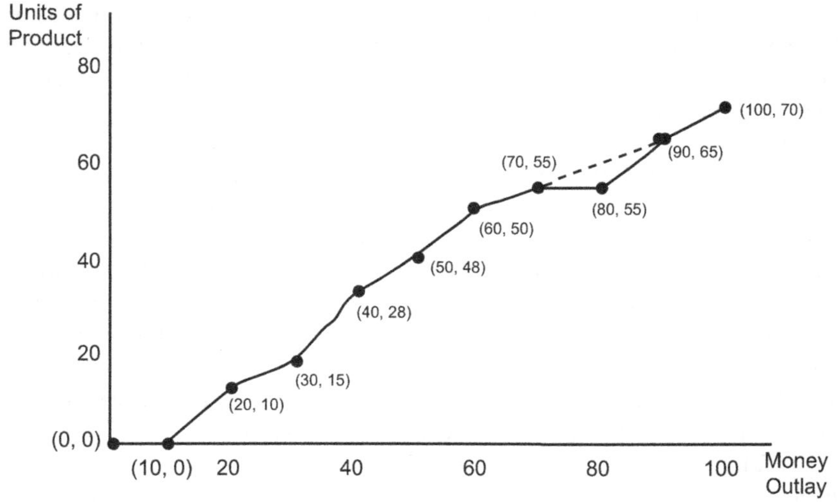

Figure 4.13 Graphical illustration of production of Product P for various money outlays

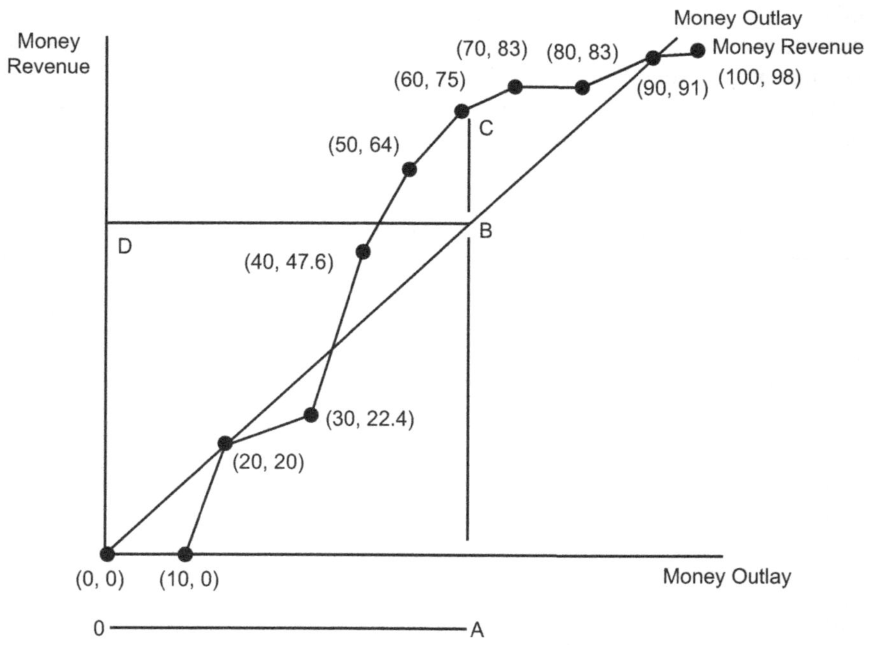

Figure 4.14 Graphical illustration of money revenue and outlay from production of Product P

Figures 4.13 and 4.14 illustrate Table 4.12. In Figure 4.13, total units of product are plotted on the vertical axis, as against corresponding money outlay on the horizontal axis. The figure reveals the amount of maximum total product that could and would be produced at different amounts of monetary outlay. The result is the product outlay curve, which is read vertically. There is a dotted line bypassing the point at the money outlay of 80, because here the product curve is horizontal, and no producer would consider such a waste of his resources as to produce at such a point.

In Figure 4.14, the product schedule is multiplied by the expected selling price at each quantity of product, to yield the expected total revenue for each point of outlay. This yields the total revenue schedule of Column 4. In this figure, money revenue is plotted on the vertical axis, and money outlay on the horizontal axis, the result yielding a *revenue outlay curve*, which expresses the expected revenues for each amount of invested money outlay.

It is clear that there is a direct resemblance between the shape of the revenue and product curves, since the former is derived from the latter. At a 45 degree angle between the two axes, there is a diagonal straight line. Since the units on each axis of Figure 4.14 are exactly the same (money in gold ounces), with the same distances, such a 45 degree line can also (vertically) represent *money outlay* on the diagram. Thus, let us take a money outlay of 60 ounces. This is given by the distance 0A on the horizontal axis. However, if we read vertically upwards from point A, we find that the distance between A and the intersection point B on the *money outlay line* is also precisely 60 ounces. Therefore, AB, and other such vertical distances, may be read as equaling money outlay on the chart.

This device makes figure reading a very easy task. At the outlay of 60 ounces, the money outlay equals AB. What is the money revenue? This can be read off from the revenue curve, and will equal AC, or 75 ounces. This permits a clear portrayal of *net income*, which will be the difference, or the vertical line BC.

Similarly, the expected net income can be read at any desired point. It becomes evident, for example, that there is a *negative* money income at such outlays as 10 ounces, 30 ounces, or 100 ounces.

Such a chart also permits the facile portrayal of the expected *percentage net income*, or *rate of net income*. This will equal the net income divided by the money outlay. On the figure, for example, it will be the ratio of BC divided by AB, or alternatively, BC divided by DB.

Now, armed with this portrayal of the alternatives and their expected consequences, what amount [*of P*] will Smith decide to produce [*in this firm*]? It is obvious that this problem is a central one in the analysis of productive activity on the market, for the question is applicable to all producers, whatever the product or whoever the individual involved.

Smith has a list of alternative courses of action from an investment of 0 to 100 ounces. It is clear that he will not decide on 80 ounces, since this will be a wasteful act with 70 ounces able to produce the same number of units. It is also clear that he will not choose to invest: 10 ounces, 30 ounces, or 90 ounces, since he will suffer monetary loss from such investments. He will not invest 20 ounces, where there would be no income from his investment. Which alternative will he choose of the ones remaining?

Most writers on this important subject have gone astray in their answers to this question. They look at the schedules and simply assume that every producer is interested in "maximum money profits," or, in better terminology, "maximum net income." Almost invariably, they would conclude in Smith's case that Smith would choose a money outlay of 60, and the expected money revenue of 75, since this yields the highest expected net income, i.e., 15 ounces. This is greater than any of the other alternatives. At first sight, this assumption seems plausible. Further analysis, however, reveals the unsoundness of such a simple assumption. It is true that if Smith invests 60 ounces, he expects a return of 75, and a net income of 15. Yet compare this with the alternative of investing 50 ounces and obtaining a net income of 14. In the former case, his *percentage net income* [*or rate of net income*] is 25%, while in the latter case it is greater, 28%. Isn't it plausible that Smith could invest 50 ounces at 28%, and then find a better and more rewarding way of investing the remaining 10 ounces? If we look at the *marginal* rate of net income, it becomes clear that, on the added 10 ounces of outlay, Smith is only making an extra 1 ounce in net income, a percentage net income of only 10% on these last 10 ounces. If, as seems plausible, Smith can find a greater *rate* of net income on these 10 ounces, it is clear that he will only invest 50 ounces in this product, and will invest the other 10 ounces elsewhere.

How many ounces [*in this firm for Product P*], then, will Smith invest? Will he invest 60 ounces to earn a net income of 15, and a rate of net income of 25%; or will he invest 50 ounces to earn a net income of 14, and a rate of 28%?

It is clear from out discussion that, in fact, *there is no precise theory of the determination of the investment in, and output of, the firm*. There is no theory of investment or output of *the firm*, because one firm cannot be considered in isolation from the other firms in the economy. Whether or not Smith will invest 50 ounces or 60 ounces in this firm depends, for example, on whether he will be able to invest the remaining 10 ounces elsewhere to yield more than 1 ounce of net income. The prospective investor considers, in various possible firms, the net returns that he will earn from various amounts of outlay in various possible firms. He must consider which alternative will be more remunerative: to invest 50 ounces here and 10 ounces elsewhere, or 60 ounces here. His marginal rate of return on the last 10 ounces is 10%; if he can earn 15% or 1.5 ounces elsewhere, he will invest them there, and invest only 50 ounces in this firm. Furthermore, the investor might invest *nothing at all* in this firm, for he might be able to earn a 30% return for 60 ounces in some other firm, producing some other product. It is impossible, therefore, to consider a firm in isolation, and attempt to determine how much will be invested in it, or how much it will produce.

Each investor, in a free economy, can range among a myriad of possible enterprises and invest in them. Indeed, by means of the device, to be examined more fully below, of parceling out parts of ownership of a firm's assets to different investors in various *shares*, each individual can invest a few ounces of money in one firm, a few in another, and several in a third, the investors hiring managers to supervise the actual production.[39] In all of his actions, psychic factors being equal, he will attempt to maximize the rate of net income from each unit of money that he invests, thereby maximizing his total net income from his entire investment in all branches. To pursue this approach will lead us to a theory of the savings and investment of the investor, rather than of the output of the firm, and thence to the theory of the savings and investment of all the investors, indeed all the individuals, in the economy. This will be inextricably connected with the problem of *time preference*, which we have already seen in Chapter I to play a determining role in the decision of the individual as to how much he will save and invest compared to the amount he will consume.[40] This will be discussed in a later chapter.[41]

It is evident that, in the pursuit of the maximum possible rates of net return, the investors will invest each sum of money, large of small, in that firm or in those firms where the rate of net return, for each size of money invested, will be at its maximum. Investors will spurn 2% return projects to invest in expected 20% return projects.

At this point, we must make a crucial distinction in our analysis of investment and production – the distinction between the investor or investors considering investment in *new* firms, and those contemplating the extension or continuance of investment in *old* firms. New firms are those which are starting from the beginning. If Smith is a new investor, he will decide as follows: [*with a given 60 ounces to invest*], he will invest 50 ounces so as to produce 40 units [*in this firm for Product P*], and earn an expected 28% net income [*and invest 10 ounces elsewhere to try to earn more than a 10% marginal rate of net income*]. However, if he cannot earn [*more than*] 10%, or 1 ounce, on 10 ounces elsewhere [*in another firm*], he will invest 60 ounces to produce 50 units [*of Product P*], and earn 25% on the investment.

It is clear that there prevails on the market a tendency toward equalization of expected net income rates on *new* firm investments. Suppose that in one firm or product, the rate of net return is expected to be unusually high compared to other investments, say 28%. It is clear that the new investors will flock to invest in this firm, or in competing firms producing the same product. If the data on the market remain the same, then this flood of investments will tend to lower the price of the product, and raise the price of the factors, particularly those specific to that product, until the expected rate of return will be drastically lowered. Furthermore, in unusually unprofitable firms, such as those earning 2%, the *old* investors, given enough time, will allow their capital goods to wear out, and shift their investments to the more profitable investments. Suppose we postulate, then, an *evenly rotating economy*, such that the data never change, i.e., on each day consumer demand, saving and investment, tastes and resources, and technological knowledge, will be the same. *In this case, given enough time, the rate of net return will be equalized in every firm and every branch of production.* This will be an economy of certainty, since there will be no uncertainty of future price, demand, or supply. In this case, the *expected* rate of return will invariably be the realized rate of return, and this will be equalized for every firm and investment. This rate of return is called the *pure rate of interest*. What rate will it be, and how will it be determined, we must leave to further chapters.[42] In the evenly rotating economy, then, every firm will earn the same net return, say 5%. Since there is no uncertainty, every firm will be built and arranged to produce at its optimal level.

[Returning to the individual investor, Smith, in the above example we assumed he was going to invest 60 ounces in one or more firms. But how does Smith choose the amount of money that he is going to invest at all? We have shown above that we cannot simply concentrate on maximum net income from an investment, but must also pay attention to its rate of net income.] Can we then say that Smith will invest that sum which will yield him the largest percentage, or rate of net income? No, we cannot simply make such a plausible statement, either. Suppose, for example, we consider the investment of 40 ounces, yielding a percentage net income of 19%. An additional investment of 10 ounces would yield an additional net income of 14 minus 7.6 ounces, which equals 6.4 ounces [for a rate of net income of 28% on his 50 ounces]. This is a return of 6.4 ounces on an outlay of 10 ounces, a marginal rate of return, or marginal rate of net income, of 64%. Yet, circumstances are conceivable when Smith would not make the additional investment. We must never forget, as we pointed out in Chapter III above,[43] that every individual is always engaged in balancing his various consumption, and his various investment expenditures, and additions or subtractions from his cash balances. Suppose, now, that Smith has a money stock of 200 ounces, which he is in the process of allocating. It is entirely possible that, while he may choose to invest 40 ounces in factors of production yielding him a 19% net income, even so high an additional return of 64% on the next 10 ounces will not induce him to restrict his consumption further. In such a case, Smith prefers present consumption spending with these 10 ounces to the 64% rate of income; therefore, his marginal rate of time preference for these 10 ounces is higher than 64%, and he does not make the investment. His investment in the product will then be 40 ounces and his level of output will be 28, producing an expected revenue of 47.6, a percentage of 19%.

In every case, therefore, the amount of money investment by the producer, and consequently the amount of product made, depends on the interrelationship between the *expected rate of net income* and the individual's *rate of time preference*.

This interrelationship, specifically, is most important in its *marginal* aspects. The reader is referred again to Chapter I, the basic foundation for the later analysis.[44] There we saw how man allocates his stock of goods in accordance with their marginal utility in the various uses.[45] We also saw how man allocates his labor in accordance with the marginal utility of the expected products in the various uses, and with the marginal disutility of the forgone leisure.[46] This is particularly relevant. We recall that each man allocates his labor in units, say hours, to that particular use which provides the greatest value of marginal product on his value scale.

This analysis, in its essence, is applicable to the present problem. Smith is choosing, not between the utility of labor and its product versus leisure forgone, but between the *utility of an expected future net money income*, and between the *disutility of present consumer goods forgone*, by investing in factors of production. Again, his decision in every case is *marginal*, i.e., he deals with divisible units of a good. In this case, he is dealing with units of a money commodity used to purchase factors. He knows, or believes that he knows, the various technological alternatives by means of which certain quantities of factors will yield him certain quantities of product, and from this, he estimates the expected money revenue that will accrue from the sale.

Thus, in Table 4.13 let us consider an expansion of Smith's choices [*for the firm producing Product P*] as shown in Table 4.12 above:

Table 4.13 Smith's money returns for various outlays, continued

Total outlay	*Marginal outlay*	*Exp. net income*	*Exp. marginal net income*	*Exp. rate or marginal net income %*
(1)	*(2)*	*(5)*	*(7)*	*(9)*
				(= 7/8)
		0		
10		–10		
20		0		
30		–7.6		
40	40	7.6	7.6	19
50	10	14	6.4	64
60	10	15	1	10
70	10	13	–2	negative
80	10	3	–10	negative
90	10	1	–2	negative
100	10	–2	–3	negative

Money outlay and *expected net money income* are taken from Table 4.12. The other columns require extended explanation. The purpose of the added columns is to better analyze Smith's final investment decision in production. Column 7 sets forth the *addition* in net money income which will be yielded by an addition to Smith's monetary investment in factors. This is the *marginal net income* expected from his various decisions. However, an investment of 10 ounces will immediately be rejected by Smith; the net income itself is negative. Similarly, an investment of 20 ounces, or 30 ounces, will be rejected for the same reasons. The first possible investment is that of 40 ounces; there is no choice for Smith between 0 and 40. Therefore, the space above that in Column 7 is left blank. Marginal decisions, and their features, refer only to actual choices confronting the actor. The differential in which we are interested is the differential that is significant to the human actor, and not the convenience of algebraic manipulation. Therefore, for example, the marginal net income at an outlay of 40 ounces is *not* the difference between 7.6 and –7.6, equaling 15.2, since there is no possibility that Smith would ever consider an outlay of 30 ounces, yielding a negative return. The *margin* is *not* between 0 and 10, 10 and 20, etc., but between 0 and 40 only. The marginal net income at 40, then, equals 7.6 minus 0, which equals 7.6. From then on, the margin occurs every 10 ounces, for that is the decision unit, so to speak. Smith estimates that the *next* 10 ounces of investment will increase his net income from 7.6 ounces to 14 ounces – giving him a marginal net income by these 10 ounces of 6.4. From 50 to 60, the 10 new ounces only increase the net income from 14 to 15 ounces, a marginal net income of 1 ounce. After this point, the net income declines; therefore, the marginal net income is *negative.* Thus, after 60 ounces, an additional 10 ounces will lower the net income to 13; thus, its marginal net income is *minus 2 ounces.*

Immediately, we have learned something more about Smith's eventual investment production decision. It is obvious that *no one will knowingly invest additional money the marginal net income of which is negative.* Smith will not invest 10 more ounces in order to see his net income dwindle by 2. Therefore, in our example, all points above 60 are eliminated from Smith's final decision. This leaves us with three possible points of decision: 40, 50, and 60 ounces. Now, we may compute the *rate of marginal net income* for each of these amounts. This is equal to the *marginal net income* at each outlay divided by the *marginal outlay* listed in Column 8. The marginal outlay is the *additional* amount of money which each given amount of outlay represents in Smith's decisions. Thus, Smith may either invest nothing or 40 ounces, the next step. His *marginal outlay* for an investment of 40 ounces is *40 ounces.* His marginal outlay at an outlay of 50 ounces is equal to *10 ounces*, or the differential between 50 and 40 – the two successive points of decisions. The marginal outlay at 60 is also *10 ounces.* After that, there is no need to apply the concept, because these decisions have been ruled out. Column 9 lists the *rate of marginal net income*, and this gives the percentage of net income which each additional investment of units of money will earn. At 40, an addition of 40 ounces earns 7.6 ounces net; this is a percentage return of *19%.* At 50, an addition of 10 ounces earns 6.4 more ounces of revenue – a marginal percentage return of *64%.* At 60, the additional 10 ounces earns only one more ounce in revenue – a marginal rate of *10%.*[47]

The alternatives that remain for Smith's consideration are condensed in Table 4.14 below, taken from Tables 4.12 and 4.13:

Table 4.14 Smith's money returns for various outlays, total

Outlay marc.	*Marginal outlay*	*Exp. revenue*	*Exp. net income*	*Exp. marg. income*	*Rate of net income %*	*Rate of net marg. income %*
(1)	*(8)*	*(4)*	*(5)*	*(7)*	*(6)*	*(9)*
0	0	0	0	0	0	0
40	40	47.6	7.6	7.6	19	19
50	10	64	6.4	6.4	28	64
60	10	75	15	1	25	10

To summarize how we obtained these columns: from technological knowledge, Smith could calculate the maximum physical product that could be obtained from each combination of factors, and this with the prices of factors, which we have taken as given, determines the maximum total product schedule for each possible alternative outlay of money investment. Horizontal spaces in the schedule were eliminated, i.e., where the marginal product is zero for each increase in outlay (it can never be negative). For each possible product, Smith estimates the selling price for which he could sell the product, and this times the quantity produced yields him the revenue schedule for each outlay. The net income is then easily calculated, and points where this absolute net money income is expected to be zero or negative are immediately eliminated from consideration. The *rate of net income* is the percentage that the net income bears to the money outlay at each point. *Marginal net income*, then, can be calculated: at each step this is the additional net income earned from the additional dollars invested. *Marginal outlay* can usually be taken at equal steps for each alternative, but this must change when the net income turns out to be zero or negative in certain cases, in which cases the marginal outlay considered by the actor must be greater in order to skip these points. Those points where marginal net income is negative are then eliminated from consideration, since it would be obvious folly to invest additional funds where only losses would be earned. The two key concepts now are the *rate of net income* (which is equal to net income divided by outlay) and the *rate of marginal net income*, which equals marginal net income divided by marginal outlay. These are listed in Columns 6 and 9 respectively.

Before continuing to discuss the decision between the remaining alternatives, we might well consider the question: is there a fixed relationship between the *average rate of net income*, which shows us the percentage return from the total investment, and the *rate of marginal net income*, which gives us the percentage return on each successive dose of monetary investment? The answer is definitively yes; in fact, at any point, the *rate of net income is equal to the weighted average of the rates of marginal net income at that and preceding points*, the weights being the size of the marginal outlay at each point. Thus, at an outlay of 50, the rate of net income is 28. This is equal to the average of the rates of marginal net income at that and preceding points, namely 64 and 19. However, it is not simply 64 plus 19 divided by 2:

$$(64 + 19)/2 = 41.5$$

This would be an *unweighted average* of the two numbers. Each number is multiplied by the *marginal outlay* at that point, and the sums are divided by the sums of the marginal outlays, which is total outlay at the final point. Thus, 19 times 40 plus 64 times 10 is divided by 40 plus 10:

$$((19 * 40) + (64 * 10))/(40 + 10) = 1400/50 = 28$$

Or, at the money outlay of 60, the rate of net income equals 40 times 19, plus 64 times 10, plus 10 times 10, divided by 40 plus 10 plus 10:

$$((40 * 19) + (64 * 10) + (10 * 10))/(40 + 10 + 10) = 1500/60 = 25$$

Furthermore, at the *first* feasible marginal step, whatever it may be (in this case, it is from 0 to 40 ounces), the rate of net income equals the rate of marginal net income, the net income equals the marginal net income, and the total outlay equals the marginal outlay. This is because the starting point is always zero – no investment – and the total of something after the first step is the same as the difference between the step and zero.

Thus, we see that the average rate of return is the weighted average of the preceding marginal rates of return, and that at the first step, the two rates of return are equal. This indicates another important truth: *that the average rate at any point is equal to the marginal rate, if the distance between that point and zero is taken as the unit.* Thus, if Smith is considering the investment of 60 ounces, his expected average rate of net income is equal to the marginal rate of net income, if the "margin" is taken as a unit of 60 ounces. Thus, the decision on an investment of a sum of money is a "marginal" one in two senses: a) in the sense of the last small unit of money and its return, and b) in the sense of the return to a marginal unit taken as the size of the sum itself. Both sizes of marginal chunks are discrete steps, and both are taken into consideration by the actor.[48]

[Now we must return to the important concept of the rate of time preference and integrate our analysis of the rate of net income.] Any man, in deciding upon the allocating of any given sum of money between consumption and investment purposes, estimates the expected yield of net money income to be derived from his investment (modified where necessary by other psychic considerations) and compares it with his minimum required monetary return from that sum of money, taking into consideration his total stock, and his value scale. This minimum rate of return is his rate of time preference: any investment which he expects will yield him a lesser return will not be made. [Thus Smith and his investment decisions in the firm producing Product P, as shown in Table 4.14, are compared with his rate of time preference.] This rate of time preference is set by his relative valuations of present and future satisfaction; it is his "minimum supply price" – the lowest "price" at which he will part with his present money in order to invest in a prospect of a higher income at some time in the future. As an individual allocates more money to investment and less to consumption at any time, his marginal rate of time preference increases, until it finally becomes prohibitively high for any investment. This fact is set by man's necessity to consume in any given present, before making investments for the future. The entire schedule of a man's time preference rate, therefore, increases as the invested outlay increases, finally nearing verticality. [It can be calculated in marginal and average form like net income.] If the rate of net income from the investment outlay is greater than the rate of time preference, he will make the investment; if not, he will abstain from the investment.

The investor Smith, in sum, does not simply try to maximize his expected net money income. He, like every actor in every situation and every choice, tries to *maximize his psychic revenue* and attain a *psychic profit*. He cannot only consider money income from the investment. He must weigh this against his psychic time preference rates. His maximization of psychic revenue, therefore, impels his investing so long as the rate of average and marginal net income exceeds his average and marginal rates of time preference.[49] [*Investment decisions in a firm, then, will always be where the average and marginal rates of net income are greater than or equal to the average and marginal rates of the investor's time preference. More precisely, Smith's investment decision in the firm producing P will be at the last marginal outlay where this occurs. In general, then, investment in a firm will be pushed to the last marginal outlay where expected average and marginal rates of net income are greater than or equal to the average and marginal rates of time preference for the investor. We may call this the Law of Investment Decision.*]

There is an important modification in this analysis of Smith that must be made, before our investigations into his output and investment decisions can be completed. In this example, we have assumed that the investor Smith faces only one alternative: either invest in the given line of production or don't invest at all. In actual life, as we know, the investor has open to him a choice in the investment of money in many lines of production or many firms. [*As explained earlier, the production and investment of a firm cannot be considered in isolation.*] Smith must not only choose whether to invest or to consume (or add to cash balance), he must decide between several alternative lines of production. How then must our law be changed to indicate the determination of his total investment, and of the investment in each line of production? In the first place, it is clear that Smith is primarily interested in maximizing his psychic revenue from the total of the investments in his portfolio. His interest is not in firm A or B or C, but in his income from all of these investments as a whole. Therefore, he weighs his average and marginal rates of time preference against the gross revenue that can be achieved from all of his investments at the given outlay. Thus, at any total outlay, say 120 ounces, he determines what distribution of money among the alternative investments will yield him the maximum total gross revenue, and hence the maximum net income and maximum rate of net income for the given outlay. At each point of outlay, he decided on the distribution that will accord him the maximum gross revenue, and therefore he is able to deduce the maximum average and marginal rates of net income for each outlay. He invests his money up till the largest amount at which the maximum average and marginal rates of net income are larger than his average and marginal rate of time preference, respectively. At this amount, he distributes his outlay among the various enterprises in accordance with the "maximum revenue distribution" at that outlay.

In the final form of the Law of Investment Decision, then, there is not the previous direct and complete link between investment outlay of the individual producer and the output of the individual product as there is when the individual producer invests in only one line of production. It is still true that the actor invests in production – in general up to the last point that his expected average and marginal rates of net income exceed his average and marginal rates of time preference. Since this is true for each man, it is clear that the production *of all goods* in the society at any period is completely determined by these factors. It is *still* true for each individual product that the amount invested is such that the average and marginal net income rates at that point are greater than the time preference rates at that point. In this sense, the law still holds. However, no longer does the investor push his investment *in each particular firm* to the *last* point before his time preference rates outstrip his income rates. He does not do so, because now he wishes to distribute his money outlays among several lines of production, in order to increase his revenue.

We must now return to our original question. How is Smith's, or in general, any investor's outlay in any given line of production, and therefore the output for that particular product, determined? To find the answer, we must look at a hypothetical illustration. Suppose, now, that Smith has to consider not only the product that we have explored in detail above, but also several other lines of production. Alongside the hypothetical money outlays, Smith lists, for each line of production, the expected *net income* from each outlay. Thus, let us say that he decided among firms producing Products P, Q, and R, recalling that our illustration above consisted of Product P. Then we might have the following schedules:

Table 4.15 Smith's money outlays for producing Products P, Q, and R

Net income			
Money outlay	*P*	*Q*	*R*
10	–	2	–
20	–	7	8
30	–	13	7.5
40	7.6	16	9
50	14	18	15
60	15	20	14

The net income schedules in Table 4.15 reveal what net income Smith expects to enjoy when investing a certain outlay in any given line of production. But these schedules permit combination into *one maximum net income* schedule, which will determine the investment distribution that will yield the largest net revenue for each given outlay. Thus, suppose Smith is considering an outlay of 50 ounces. He might invest them all in the firm producing P, in which case his net income will be 14 ounces. If he invests them all in the firm producing Q, his net income will be 18 ounces; in the firm producing R, his net income would be 15 ounces. Clearly, if he can only invest in one firm or in the other, then he will choose firm producing Q. But, since he can distribute his investments, he also considers the various investment combinations adding up to 50 ounces which involve two or more firms. Thus 40 in producing P and 10 in producing Q will yield 7.6 plus 2, a net income of 9.6. Mentally considering the various combinations, it becomes clear that prospectively the best is (30Q plus 20R) which yields a net income of

13 plus 8, or 21 net ounces. At each hypothetical outlay, the investor picks what appears to be that combination that will yield the highest net income. Table 4.16 depicts Smith's *maximum net income* schedule with each money outlay, with the investment distribution in parentheses:

Table 4.16 Maximum net income of Smith for various investment decisions

Money outlay	*Maximum net income*	
10	2	(10 in Q)
20	8	(20 in R)
30	13	(30 in Q)
40	16	(40 in Q)
50	21	(30 in Q; 20 in R)
60	24	(40 in Q; 20 in R)

The best combination for any outlay is that one for which the sum of the net incomes from each line of production is the highest. An equivalent property of this condition is that the weighted average of the rates of net income from each line of production be the highest (where the weights are the money outlay in each line). Thus, take the problem of the best investment of 50 ounces. Fifty ounces all in producing Q would yield 18 ounces of income, or a 36% return. This is higher than an investment of 50 ounces producing P or R. But an investment of 30 ounces in B yields 13 ounces income, or 43%. An investment of 20 ounces in R yields a return of 8 ounces income, or 40%. A weighted average of these two yields by the respective outlays is: 30 times 43, plus 20 times 40, divided by 50. This equals 42%, the weighted average, which also equals the rate of maximum net income (amount of maximum net income divided by money outlay). Thus, the best distribution can be determined from schedules of rates of net income for each of the various outlays in the various lines of production. In this case, the distribution is not confined to producing just Q, even though producing Q is more profitable than either of the others at any given total investment.

As Table 4.17 shows, from the maximum net income schedule, there can be deduced schedules of rates of maximum net income, marginal outlay, marginal maximum net income, rates of marginal maximum net income, etc. Thus:

Table 4.17 Smith's money returns for various investment decisions

Outlay	*Max. net income*	*Rate of max. net income %*	*Marg. outlay*	*Marg. max. net Income*	*Rate of marg. net income %*
(1)	*(2)*	*(2/1)*	*(4)*	*(5)*	*(5/4)*
10	2	20	10	2	20
20	8	40	10	6	60
30	13	43	10	5	50
40	16	40	10	3	30
50	21	42	10	5	50
60	24	40	10	3	30

Smith, or any investor, then proceeds analogously with the case of one product, investing money outlay (in the best distributions) up to the largest amount that his *rate of marginal maximum net income* is greater than [*or equal to*] his *marginal rate of time preference*, and his *average rate of maximum net income* is also greater than [*or equal to*] his *average rate of time preference*. Here again, average rate at any point is equivalent to the marginal rate (of maximum net income) at that point, with the size of the point itself considered as the unit.

We at last come to the end of the tortuous road of analysis of the determination of investor's decisions and of the amount of investment in any one productive firm. An investor will continue to invest rather than not so long as his expected average and marginal rates of return are greater than his average and marginal rates of time preference; and he will make his investment in that productive enterprise or combination of productive enterprises that will yield him the greatest possible net income, or rate of net income, for any hypothetical outlay. If we may eliminate the distinction between average and marginal by varying the size of the marginal chunk, then we may simply say that each unit of money outlay will be spent in the way that promises to yield the actor the greatest utility: in spending on consumer goods, if the rate of time preference for this amount is greater; or in spending on factors of production in that line or lines and in that firm or firm, where the rate of net return promises to be the greatest.

We have thus analyzed the principles according to which a man allocates his stock of money in accordance with expected greatest utility: the allocation of money units between investment in general and present consumption, and the decision between investment in various different firms and lines of production. The quest is for psychic profit, and the course of action that will yield the greatest utility – in the usual case, this line of investment will be the one that is expected to yield the greatest net return from the outlay. Exceptions are cases where other psychic factors, such as particular like, or dislike, for the production process or the product itself, alters the decision from a pure consideration of monetary return. Otherwise, a man invests in those enterprises which he expects will yield the highest rates of return.

We have thus seen what determines the amount of stock of any good that will be produced in any particular period – it will be the amount that the producer had invested in a previous period in order to aim at such production. The amount of previous investment depends on the producer's anticipated net monetary return. It is clear that an increase in anticipated rate of net income in any line of production will tend to increase the investor's outlay in that product, and that on the other hand a decrease in the anticipated return will tend to diminish his investment in that process. If we interpret the concept of "increase in rate of net income" as meaning an increase in the entire rate of net income schedule, so that at each outlay of product, net income is expected to increase, it is obvious that the rate of net income schedule will intersect the investor's time preference rate schedule at a further point, so that an increase in the expected net income schedule will increase the amount of investment outlay in that product, and contrary for the decrease. Furthermore, an increase in expected return for producing P will tend to shift more of the investment outlay to this firm from competing firms Q, R, etc., and the contrary will occur with a decrease in expected revenue.

As a matter of fact, changes in anticipated rate of net income are most likely to take place throughout the entire range of the schedule. The factors that can change the rate of return are: a) expected future selling price, b) the prices of the factors, and c) the producers' production function – the physical efficiency in converting quantities of factors into quantities of product. It is evident that, with factor prices here assumed to be given and known, the producer's anticipations of future income are governed by his anticipations of selling price and of his production function. It is clear that a rise in expected selling price for any good will, *ceteris paribus*, increase the amount of investment outlay in its production; and that an increase in physical productivity for any good will, *ceteris paribus*, increase the amount of investment outlay. Conversely, decreases in expected selling price and/or decreases in physical productivity will, *ceteris paribus*, diminish the investment in that product.

We have learned, therefore, that consumers' goods prices are determined by consumers' demand schedule and by the stock produced and sold; that the sales of produced stock depend on anticipated future price; that the amount of stock produced depends on previous investment in production; that the previous investment in production depends on the net money income that the investor anticipated receiving, and the amount of investment will be up to the last amount at which the anticipated rate of return exceeds the rate of time preference; and that the anticipated rate of return depends on expected future selling price and production technique (given factor prices). In the last analysis, then, consumers' goods prices depend on consumers' demand schedules and general time preferences, producers' anticipations of prices, and productive techniques.

Many questions remain to be answered. Among them is the discussion in Chapter IV on the final supply curve of the producers as compared to the stock on the

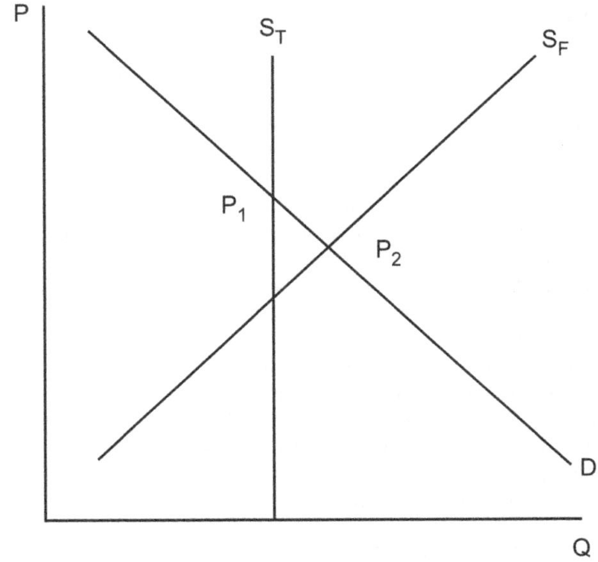

Figure 4.15 Final supply curve of the producer

market.[50] The "final supply curve" is the amount that will be called forth in supply in the future by certain prices. The discussion in Chapter IV implicitly assumed that the present ruling prices would be the ones that would be anticipated in the future. Thus, Figure 4.15:[51]

This implicitly assumes that the present price of P1 is assumed to be the future price, and will call for the equivalent amount on the SF curve, which will tend to lower the final market price to P2. However, we may alter this restriction and make the necessary mental allowances for any anticipated change in price. The main point of the diagram still obtains – that the present market price is not necessarily the "final" one toward which the market forces are tending. The question then remains: what principles determine the "final" equilibrium market prices? Even though this price is never attained in practice, it is important because it is the point (though always shifting) toward which prices tend to move. And a final selling price, given the productive technique, and given factor prices tend to set net entrepreneurial income. On what basis does entrepreneurial net income, the driving force in the money economy, tend to be determined? This problem, along with a discussion of time preference, must be taken up in subsequent chapters.[52]

Notes

* Chapter 4 of this volume is a lightly revised version of a paper published in the *Quarterly Journal of Austrian Economics*, vol. 18, no. 4 (Winter 2015): 456–486.

1 *Editor's endnote*: Rothbard's reference to his earlier presentation of the "final supply curve" is absent from MES. Rothbard's discussion of supply and demand for an already produced stock of goods and his introductory analysis of entrepreneurship and production can be found in Rothbard (1962, 153–161, 249–257). See also (pp. 124–126) Rothbard's further discussion of the final supply curve.

2 *Editor's endnote*: See Rothbard (1962, pp. 187–231).

3 *Editor's endnote*: See Rothbard (1962, pp. 755–874).

4 *Editor's endnote*: See Rothbard (1962, p. 219).

5 "In every case the choice made is, at the moment when made, a present choice. We have no future desires though we may have a present forecast of a future desire. 'Future desires' means desires that will be present at some future time. Present desires are all those desires now being weighed in choice. Present desires may be either desires for present uses or for future uses (either in the same or in different goods). A present desire for future uses is but the anticipation of a future desire, though the two may be of unequal magnitude. It appears therefore that all time-choices are, in the last analysis, reducible to choices between present desires for psychic incomes occurring at different time-periods" Fetter (1915, p. 247). See also Fetter (1915, p. 239).

6 *Editor's endnote*: See Rothbard (1962, p. 220).

7 Fetter (1915, 240).

8 *Editor's endnote*: See Rothbard (1962, pp. 367–451).

9 *Editor's endnote*: See the editor's endnote below on p. 552.

10 *Editor's endnote*: See Rothbard (1962, pp. 13–17).

11 It is, of course, likely that Jones will weigh his decision on the basis of expected returns over a much longer period, say a decade, in which these returns may be considered to take place for a ten year period. We can adjust his calculations to cover any desired time period.

12 See Boulding (1941, pp. 456–457) and Stigler (1946, p. 109ff).

13 Here it must be noted that the constancy of price assumed in Case (a) did not necessarily follow for all possible decisions of Jones. Thus, if he decided not to produce the good at all, the price might well be affected, and be, say, 12 ounces instead of the 10 ounces if he did go into production. But the constancy of price is only assumed for the *relevant range of choice* – in this case between the three different combinations. Case (a) only needed to assume that, between a product of 96 and 110 units, market supply would not be affected enough to change the price.

14 *Editor's endnote*: See Rothbard (1962, pp. 126–130).

15 On competitive price and monopoly price, see Fetter (1915, pp. 77–84, 381–385); Mises (1949, pp. 273–279, 354–376), Mises (1951 [1922], pp. 385–392), Menger (1950 [1871], pp. 207–225) and Wieser (1927 [1914], pp. 204, 211–212).

16 See Brown (1908, pp. 626–629).

17 *Editor's endnote*: Rothbard slightly modifies his definitions of monopoly and competitive price (pp. 110–111).

18 For example, see Chamberlain (1942). Recently, however, Professor Chamberlin has repudiated the implications drawn by his followers that the "pure competition" situation is the ideal; indeed, he implies quite the reverse (Chamberlin, 1950, pp. 85–92).

19 *Editor's endnote*: This later section, whether or not it was intended to be included in the current chapter or in a later one, was not found by the editor in the Rothbard archives. See Rothbard (1962, pp. 677–680) for his mature theory of monopoly gains on the free market. It is important to note that here he no longer uses the competitive-versus-monopoly price distinction.

20 See Ely (1917, pp. 190–191). The famous Blackstone gave almost the same definition, and called monopoly a "license or privilege allowed by the king."

21 The battle of the equal-liberty movement against monopoly has had a long history in England. In 1603, the British courts decided, with respect to one of Queen Elizabeth's numerous grants of privilege: "That it is a monopoly and against the common law. All trades . . . are profitable for the Commonwealth, and therefore the grant to have the sole making of them is against the common law and the benefit and liberty of the subject." In 1624, Parliament declared that "all monopolies are altogether contrary to the laws of this realm and are and shall be void." In the American states, the Declaration of Rights of the Maryland Constitution asserted: "monopolies are odious, contrary to the spirit of a free government and the principles of commerce" Ely (1917, pp. 191–192). See Walker (1911, pp. 483–484).

22 *Editor's endnote*: In this footnote, Rothbard refers the reader to later chapters on the hampered market regarding various monopoly grants. Rothbard originally wrote multiple chapters on the hampered market before the publisher required that he cut down the length of the book and remove controversial parts of the manuscript. Rothbard then had to write a summary chapter of his analysis (Rothbard, 1962, pp. 875–1041). Rothbard's chapters on government intervention were eventually published as Rothbard (2009 [1970]). See Rothbard (1970, pp. 1089–1144) for his analysis of various grants of monopolistic privilege. Rothbard also mentions in this footnote that copyrights and patents would be discussed below: see Rothbard (1962, pp. 745–754) for this analysis.

23 *Editor's endnote*: See Rothbard (1962, pp. 162–169, 176–185).

24 That such was the original definition of monopoly in economics as well as law is demonstrated by the definition of the economist Arthur Latham Perry: "A monopoly, as the derivation of the word implies, is a restriction imposed by a government upon the sale of certain services" (Perry, 1892, p. 190). Still earlier, Adam Smith discussed monopoly in similar terms, and pointed out how monopolists may use the government privileges to restrict sales and raise selling prices: "Such enhancements of the market price may last as long as the regulations of police which give occasion to them" (Smith, 1937 [1776], p. 62).

25 Benham (1941, p. pp. 232–233). On the rapid breakup of even a relatively successful cartel, see Fairchild et al. (1926, pp. 54–55). Also see Molinari (1904, pp. 192–195), Fay (1923, p. 41) and Fay (1912).

26 Menger (1950, pp. 222–225).

27 In many cases, fear of possible outside competition prevents any formation of a cartel, even when other conditions seem favorable. This is known as the influence of *potential competition* on would be cartelists.

28 *Editor's endnote*: See endnote 22.

29 *Editor's endnote*: See Rothbard (1962, pp. 79–94).

30 *Editor's endnote*: See endnote 22.

31 See Tucker (1926, pp. 248–257). For a defense of voluntary combinations from a juristic point of view, see Cooley (1878, pp. 270–271). Also see Flint (1902) and Croly (1909, pp. 359–365) for the economic defenses.

32 Does our discussion imply, as Dorfman (1949, p. 247) has charged, that "whatever is, is right"? We cannot enter into a discussion of the relation of economics to ethics at this point, but we can state briefly that our answer, pertaining to the free market, is a qualified Yes. Specifically, our statement would be: Given the ends on the value scales of individuals, as revealed by their real actions, the maximum satisfaction of those ends for every person is achieved only on the free market. Whether individuals have the "proper" ends or not is another question entirely and cannot be decided by economics.

33 See Stigler (1946, pp. 111–112) and Weiler (1952, p. 147ff).

34 It is obvious that, for each of these combinations, more of both factors will produce at least as much as, and probably more than, the particular product. Thus, if (40X; 100Y) can produce 105 units of product, so can (45X; 105Y). This follows from the nature of scarce goods and scarce factors. The use of the latter combination to produce 105 units, however, would clearly be senseless. The latter, obviously more expensive, combination would either produce more and the surplus thrown away – which would be a ridiculous procedure; or else would produce just as much, in which case the factors would still be wasted and needless money expended. In describing constant outlay combinations, therefore, we assume that those combinations which are obviously more expensive for each product – using *more of both factors* – will be discarded at once. The only question then comes from the partial substitutability of one factor for another.

35 The absurdity of the "technocratic fallacy" here becomes obvious. The technocratic charge is that business conducts "production for profit" instead of "production for use," and that the latter would prevail if engineers were granted dictatorial control over the productive system. It is clear from the discussion that technology cannot solve the production problem, and that therefore "production for (money) profit" *is the only possible method of production* beyond the very primitive level. Technology by itself could neither provide a guide to "maximizing production" nor to determining *what* should be produced. And it is also evident that business on the market takes account of the technological factor as much as is necessarily possible. It should also be clear that production for profit is necessarily production for "use." There is no reason to produce any good except to supply the demand for its use by consumers, whether the consumer is other persons or the producer himself (in the more primitive production situations). All production is for use.

36 *Editor's endnote*: See also (pp. 108–109) Rothbard's analysis when more than two factors are involved.

37 On the vital importance of knowledge of "particular circumstances of time and place" see Hayek (1945, pp. 77–91).

38 *Editor's endnote*: This analysis of factor pricing was planned to be in a later section, however it was never written because Rothbard changed his mind on the usefulness of using this approach. See Newman (2018) for more information.

39 *Editor's endnote*: See Rothbard (1962, pp. 426–435).

40 *Editor's endnote*: See Rothbard (1962, pp. 61–64, 68–70).

41 *Editor's endnote*: See Rothbard (1962, pp. 367–451).

42 *Editor's endnote*: See Rothbard (1962, pp. 367–451).
43 *Editor's endnote*: See Rothbard (1962, p. 220).
44 *Editor's endnote*: See Rothbard (1962, pp. 1–77).
45 *Editor's endnote*: See Rothbard (1962, pp. 21–33).
46 *Editor's endnote*: See Rothbard (1962, pp. 42–47).
47 In Smith's particular case, marginal net income is only negative in the early and later stages. In some cases, there may well be points where the marginal net income is negative *in between* points where it is positive. In such cases, the point of negative marginal income is skipped over, and marginal outlay is assumed to be the difference between the two nearest points of *positive* marginal outlay. Thus, Jones' schedule of outlay and expected net income may be as follows:

Outlay	*Net income*	*Marginal net income*	*Marginal outlay*
10	6	–	–
20	10	4	10
30	8		
40	14	4	20
50	19	5	10

48 This statement will be surprising only to those who have been misled by the use of the differential calculus in economics. In calculus, the steps between points are treated as infinitely small, and therefore the marginal is thought to be the infinitesimal. In that case, "small" sized units will be recognized as approximations to some "ideal" marginal unit, but a "big" unit will not be thought of as marginal. Actually, the size of a marginal unit can be any amount, depending on the decision to be made. There is nothing ideal about infinitesimally small units, and they are not relevant to the real world of human action in any case, since action always deals with discrete steps.
49 *Editor's endnote*: Strictly speaking, it must be greater than *or* equal to. An investor would still invest if the rate of return is equal to the rate of time preference, since his rate of time preference is the *minimum* he would need to earn in order to forgo the present money and invest. In the Evenly Rotating Economy, each investor only earns the interest rate, which is the social rate of time preference.
50 *Editor's endnote*: See endnote 1.
51 *Editor's endnote*: Although not discussed in terms of a "final supply curve," a similar diagram can be found in Rothbard (2008 [1983], p. 27), which is not present in MES.
52 *Editor's endnote*: See Rothbard (1962, pp. 367–451, 509–555).

References

Benham, Frederic. 1941. *Economics*. New York: Pitman Publishing.

Boulding, Kenneth E. 1941. *Economic Analysis*. 1st ed. New York: Harper and Bros.

Brown, Harry Gunnison. 1908. "Competitive and Monopolistic Price-Making." *Quarterly Journal of Economics* 22: 625–639.

Chamberlain, Edward H. 1942. *Theory of Monopolistic Competition*. Cambridge, MA: Harvard University Press.

———. 1950. "Product Heterogeneity and Public Policy." *American Economic Review* 40 (2): 85–92.

Cooley, Thomas McIntyre. March 1878. "Limits to State Control of Private Business." *Princeton Review*, pp. 233–271.

Croly, Herbert. 1909. *The Promise of American Life*. New York: Palgrave Macmillan.

Dorfman, Joseph. 1949. *The Economic Mind in American Civilization*. New York: Viking Press.

Ely, Richard T., T. S. Adams, Max Otto Lorenz, and Allyn Abbott Young. 1917. *Outlines of Economics*. New York: Palgrave Macmillan.
Fairchild, Fred R., Edgar S. Furniss, and Norman S. Buck. 1926. *Elementary Economics*. New York: Palgrave Macmillan.
Fay, Charles Norman. 1912. *Big Business and Government*. New York: Doubleday.
———. 1923. *Too Much Government*. New York: Doubleday.
Fetter, Frank A. 1915. *Economic Principles*. New York: The Century Co.
Flint, Charles R. 1902. "Centralization and Natural Law." *The Independent*, May 1.
Hayek, Friedrich August. 1948 [1945]. "The Use of Knowledge in Society." In *Individualism and Economic Order*. Chicago: University of Chicago Press.
Menger, Carl. 1871. *Principles of Economics*. Glencoe, IL: Free Press, 1950.
Mises, Ludwig von. 1949 [1999]. *Human Action*. Auburn, AL: Ludwig von Mises Institute.
———. 1951. *Socialism*. 2nd ed. New Haven, CT: Yale University Press.
Molinari, Gustave de. 1904. *The Society of Tomorrow*. New York: G. P. Putnam's Sons.
Newman, Patrick. 2018. "From Marshallian Partial Equilibrium to Austrian General Equilibrium: The Evolution of Rothbard's Production Theory." In Matthew McCaffrey, ed., *The Economic Theory of Costs: Foundations and New Directions*. Abingdon, UK: Routledge, pp. 51–71.
Perry, Arthur Latham. 1892. *Political Economy*. 21st ed. New York: Charles Scribner's Sons.
———. 2008 [1983]. *The Mystery of Banking*. Auburn, AL: Ludwig von Mises Institute.
———. 2009 [1962]. *Man, Economy, and State With Power and Market*. Scholar's ed. Auburn, AL: Ludwig von Mises Institute.
Smith, Adam. 1937 [1776]. *The Wealth of Nations*. Ed. Edwin Cannan. New York: Modern Library.
Stigler, George. 1946. *The Theory of Price*. New York: Palgrave Macmillan.
Tucker, Benjamin R. 1926. *Individual Liberty*. New York: Vanguard Press.
Walker, Francis A. 1911. *Political Economy*. New York: Henry Holt and Co.
Weiler, E. T. 1952. *The Economic System*. New York: Palgrave Macmillan.
Wieser, Frederich von. 1914 [1927]. *Social Economics*. London: George Allen and Unwin.

Part 3

Risk, uncertainty, and cost

5 The myth of the risk premium*

Jörg Guido Hülsmann

In economic analysis, the word "cost" is used with two very different meanings. On the one hand, it refers to the subjective value of the most important foregone choice alternative (opportunity cost). On the other hand, it is also used to designate the monetary value of the factors of production that are being consumed in a business venture (production costs). The present chapter deals with costs in the latter sense and with the risk element in the rate of interest in particular.

Most present-day economists consider observable interest rates to be the arithmetic sum of three main components, each of which is held to result from a distinct cause. First, there is a pure or real or risk-free interest rate component, which is typically believed to spring from time preference. Second, there is a risk premium that compensates the investor for market risks. Third, there is a price premium that compensates the investor for losses in the purchasing power of money. If we denominate the observable gross market rate with the letter i, the real or pure interest rate with the letter r, the risk premium with the letter c (as in chance), and the price premium with π, then something like the following equation [1] is supposed to hold:

$$i = r + c + \pi \qquad [1]$$

This equation can then be applied to calculate the risk-free interest rate; with variable i being derived from observation; variable π supposed to be equal to some calculated price-inflation rate; and variable c supposed to be equal to some calculated risk premium, typically a standard deviation around some average value. The equation can also be used to determine the value of risky assets by discounting their future cash flows, etc. Whatever the variant of this approach, such as the capital-asset pricing model, the basic idea is always the same: observable interest rates are held to be the arithmetic sum of different components, each of which can be determined in separation from the others. The basic problem of this conception is that it is disconnected from ordinary supply-and-demand price theory. Human choice and human action either do not enter the picture at all, or they enter the picture under highly contrived assumptions, such as in the capital-asset pricing model.

In the present paper, we present an alternative realist approach to the study of risk, based on Ludwig von Mises's distinction between case probability and class probability. In light of this realist approach, it will appear that the prevailing conception of risk as related to the gross rate of interest is ill-founded. It is wrong to conceive of the gross interest rate as the sum of separate components. A closer analysis reveals that the whole idea of a risk premium within the gross rate of interest is a myth and should be discarded from economic science.

The chapter is organised as follows. In section 1, we present the distinction between case-probable and class-probable judgements. Section 2 contains a realist approach to the analysis of human action under uncertainty. In section 3, we apply this approach to study the impact of risk on the return on capital. In section 4, we discuss the significance of our findings for the theory of costs.

1 Case probability and class probability

Frank Knight (1971 [1921], pp. 11 and 198f) revolutionised the economic analysis of uncertainty, profit, and loss by stressing the crucial difference between two types of uncertainty, namely, quantifiable uncertainty or risk; and unquantifiable uncertainty or, simply, uncertainty. Knight highlighted the crucial fact that risk, strictly speaking, entails no uncertainty at all. It can be anticipated in advance. Entrepreneurs can protect themselves against it through suitable provisions in their balance sheets or by insurance contracts. Risk cannot therefore be the origin of profits and losses. Only uncertainty could be the cause of profits and losses.

Ludwig von Mises (1949) later elaborated on this distinction by stripping it to its logical core. Most notably, Mises dissociated the analysis of probability from the analysis of risk. The theory of probability exclusively concerns *epistemic* questions (the truth of a judgement), while the analysis of risk also concerns *value* judgements (risk is an *undesired* consequence of action). Mises stressed that the Knightian categories of risk and uncertainty were rooted in two completely different types of probability, which shared only one basic characteristic:

> A statement is probable if our knowledge concerning its content is deficient. We do not know everything which would be required for a definite decision between true and not true. But, on the other hand, we do know something about it; we are in a position to say more than simply *non liquet* or *ignoramus*.
>
> (Mises, 1949, p. 107)

However, Mises distinguished class probability from case probability. The former is applied in the natural sciences, while the second is applied in the sciences of human action.

Mises defines class probability as follows:

> We know or assume to know, with regard to the problem concerned, everything about the behavior of a whole class of events or phenomena; but about

> the actual singular events or phenomena we know nothing but that they are elements of this class.
>
> (Mises, 1949, p. 107)

The crucial feature of a class-probable judgement is that the person in question ignores the causal sequence that brings about a concrete event. For example, he ignores *why* this bottle breaks rather than another. He ignores *why* this barn burns rather than another. But he knows from experience that of all the bottles that are filled in that factory, .08% will break on any given day; and that of all the barns in his county .03% will burn down each year. He knows that this concrete bottle is one of the bottles filled in that factory, and he knows that this barn stands in his county. Therefore, even though he is ignorant of the exact causes that will prompt this bottle to break and this barn to burn, he can make a class-probable judgement about all bottles in that factory and about all barns in that county.

Knowledge and ignorance are combined quite differently when it comes to case-probable judgements. This is how Mises defines case probability: "We know, with regard to a particular event, some of the factors which determine its outcome; but there are other determining factors about which we know nothing" (Mises, 1949, p. 110). He immediately adds: "Case probability has nothing in common with class probability but the incompleteness of our knowledge. In every other regard the two are entirely different" (Mises, 1949, p. 110). Indeed, the person who makes a case-probable judgement knows this and that exact causal sequence. For example, he knows that the revenue he will earn with his bakery depends on the number of other bakeries within walking distance. He knows that he can produce computer screens of type X with technique A and also with technique B. He knows that that the tomato output of his farm will be at maximum with 250 sunny days and 80 days of rain. He knows the laws of mathematics, of physics, and of economics.

Knowledge in all these cases is exact and sometimes even universal. But it is deficient in two regards. On the one hand, it is incomplete. The person in question knows the influence that this and that factor will have on his revenue, on his physical output, etc. But there are other factors that also might come into play and about which he knows nothing. On the other hand, when confronted with the choices of other people, he is also ignorant of their future value judgements. That is, he ignores how several factors influencing these judgements will combine in the future.

Consider again the bakery example. Our would-be entrepreneur knows that the revenue of the bakery depends on a multitude of concrete causes, such as the number of other bakeries within walking distance, the number of families with children, the revenue of these families, the effort he puts into merchandising his croissants and breads, the unit prices at which he sells, etc. But he does not know exactly the relative impact of each of these factors on his income. That is, he does not know how much the customers will value a nice presentation and how much their decisions will depend on price. He might have some rough idea about the relative importance of each of these factors in the past. But he cannot extrapolate this knowledge into the future. He needs to speculate or, in Mises's words, he needs to bet on their relative influence in the future (Mises, 1949, pp. 112f).

2 A realist approach to human action under uncertainty

The conventional way to integrate risk into economic analysis is fatally flawed in the very way it conceives of the problem. The implicit assumption is that risk is something 'out there' which can be studied by economists and other scholars, and which sooner or later will also be discovered by all other rational decision-makers. The risk-that-is-out-there can be included in the utility functions of all economic agents and thereby determine demand and supply schedules. However, this conception is untenable because risk (more generally speaking: probability) is an epistemic, not an ontic category. Probable judgements are relevant for economics only to the extent that they are selected by human choice and become manifest in human action.

Subjective value is the filter through which all probably true judgements, and therefore all assessments of risk, have to pass in order to become relevant for human action. And only the judgements that pass through that filter are therefore relevant for economics. Moreover, and most importantly, probable judgements that are considered to be important lead to action. Economic goods that are considered to be important for the realisation of one's projects are being intentionally brought into existence (that is, produced), whereas all factors opposed to that realisation are eliminated as far as possible. Let us explain these considerations in more detail.

A) Subjective value as a filter of relevance

Probability theory makes propositions about *human knowledge* about the world, not about the world as such or about human action in particular. The world as such and the transformation of the world as such are not probable. They are what they are, irrespective of how much human beings know about them. All things that happen in our world are completely determined. They are all subject to the inexorable laws of cause and effect. But human beings can only gain a very partial knowledge of these laws. It is our knowledge about the world that is more or less probable, not the world as such (see Poincaré, 1912, p. 2; Fisher, 1906, p. 266; Mises, 1957, pp. 73f).

Moreover, probability theory as such has no *direct* relevance for economics. Human action is guided by judgements that are subjectively perceived to be probably true. But such judgements of truth are always mediated through value judgements. There is no direct connection between the (probable) truth of any proposition on the one hand, and human action on the other hand. Human beings always and everywhere need to weigh different (and often conflicting) judgements about future states of affairs in order to act.[1]

Economics deals with human action. It deals with the causes and consequences of decision-making in a context of scarcity. It does not concern itself with what the decision-makers *know* about themselves or the world around them. Economists take due account of the fact that the acting persons must have definite ideas about themselves and the world around them. They are not primarily interested in the truth of these ideas. They analyse the (intentional) consequences of true ideas no less than the (unintentional) consequences of wrong ones. But the first step of analysis always consists of adopting the point of view of the acting person. Risk, then, becomes relevant for economics to the extent that it relates to the value judgements of that person. The realist method of analysing risk adopts the point of view of subjective value, not the point of view of any "objective" probabilities to be discovered 'out there.'

The realist approach leads to us to stress two fundamental points that are at odds with the conventional approach. The first is that not all things that are risky (that is, probable and undesirable) from *some* point of view (for example, from the point of view of a scholar) are also relevant from the point of view of the acting person. The second is that the incompleteness of knowledge, which characterises all case-probable judgements, is not risky *per se* and does not necessarily have an impact on the valuation of actions and assets.

From a subjectivist point of view, there is very often no risk associated with the chosen course of action. This is particularly clear in the case of consumer choice. Most of the risks that an external observer might identify in human action simply disappear from the point of view of the protagonist. Smith thinks that drinking beer makes him happy. His mother, the external observer, disagrees. She thinks his beer drinking is risky. But for Smith this is irrelevant. He believes to know that drinking beer makes him happy. It is true that he 'only' believes to know, but for economics this is all that counts. Smith's opinion might be wrong. But from an economic point of view, this would be irrelevant because it would not influence the way Smith values beer relative to money.[2]

Similar considerations can be brought to bear on the problem of incomplete knowledge. The more Smith knows about the multifarious causal connections into which A and B are embedded, the better informed are his value judgements. But more information does not necessarily *alter* his value judgements. He may know only one thing about an economic good and be perfectly happy with this very partial knowledge because, for him, it is the only relevant consideration. For example, in choosing a vacation hotel, Smith might only be interested in the distance between his hotel room and the beach. There are an unlimited number of other circumstances that would also influence his vacation experience. But *what he values* is only the distance between the bed and the beach. We might call him foolish, but if he is honest with himself, then there is no specific risk associated with his choice.[3]

Even if we admit that most consumer decisions are made with more circumspection, the fact remains that very often there is no significant (subjective) risk involved. Consumers' preferences very often depend on a relatively small number of characteristics of the goods that they consider, and they are (or rather, believe to be) perfectly well-informed about these characteristics. If they hesitate, it is not because of the risks associated with the factual assessment, but because of the risks associated with the value judgement they have to make.

The main risk of consumer choices pertains to durable goods. The risk is that one's future valuation will be different from one's present valuation. Future valuations may be different because other factors than the ones that count now will become primordial. For example, in buying an apartment, a young family will not necessarily have a lot of appreciation for single-floor units, whereas a retired couple typically will. Future valuations may change as well because some of the known factors that count will deteriorate. For example, the subjective value of the apartment might sink when very obnoxious neighbours move into the other apartments, etc.

But consumers are typically aware of this problem. Precisely because future conditions might be different from present ones they have an incentive (a) to investigate as much as possible the factors that might influence future conditions, including their own valuations; and (b) *to act strategically in the present*, in such a way as to eliminate as far as possible the influence of factors that are likely to have a negative impact, that is, case-probable risks. Indeed, human action is the most important means through which the probability of desirable influences is increased, and the probability of undesirable influences diminished.[4]

B) The production of success

This strategic approach is likely to be even more pronounced in the case of producers. Brown is an entrepreneur fabricating headphones. The essential purpose of his activity is to gain his living, that is, to earn monetary revenue. He does this through the network of exchanges. He buys factors of production and sells headphones. For him the physical characteristics of the factors that he buys and of the headphones that he sells are only remotely connected to the immediate causes of his success, which are market prices, that is, the conditions of demand and supply.

In assessing market conditions, Brown is very much concerned with the problem of incomplete knowledge, much more so than Smith the consumer. Brown's success depends on the valuations of *other* people. Their valuations are driven by a great number of circumstances, which our producer does not and cannot completely know. Moreover, for Brown the quality of his own knowledge is a crucial factor. Smith might believe that beer drinking makes him happy even if, in fact, it ruins his physical and mental health. Then beer drinking would be the right thing to do from his subjective point of view. Smith would be a "successful consumer." By contrast, for Brown, it would be fatal to use a production technique that impairs the quality of his products as perceived by the customers. He cannot be successful by producing goods and services that are to his own liking. He must meet the demands of the customers. It follows that for entrepreneurs such as Brown there are very strong incentives to fill the voids of his incomplete knowledge of market conditions as far as possible, within the limits of reasonable cost.

Moreover, and crucially, entrepreneurs such as Brown do not so much produce material goods and services as they "produce success." They act strategically, in whatever way is necessary, within the limits of reasonable cost, to bring all factors into play that favour their success, and to eliminate or diminish the influence of all factors that prevent or endanger their success (case-probable risks). They do this most notably by making suitable arrangements for the physical production of the goods and services from which they intend to derive revenue: they must hire the right executives, choose the right location, determine the appropriate amount of capital to be dedicated to this and that venture, etc. But they also try to stimulate all factors that are likely to increase their sales, and to eliminate or reduce the influence of other factors that hamper sales.

The bottom-line is that the very nature of entrepreneurial action is to eliminate the influence of case-probable risks and to bring into play the influence of desired factors. One might say that entrepreneurship tends to reduce the known (case-probable) risks and multiply the known factors of success. However, as we have seen, the risks are not reduced in the sense of a reduction of the stochastic probability of their impact on the overall result; they are reduced in the sense that factors that have a known negative impact will be eliminated. For example, a tomato planter might reduce the risk of insufficient irrigation and insufficient temperature by moving his plantation indoors.

It is clear that not all risks can and will be eliminated. But the known negative influences will tend to be cut back to the extent that marginal cost is still covered by marginal expected revenue. And the presently unknown negative influences are researched as far as possible, within the same constraints of reasonable cost. Let us also notice that there is no one-to-one relation between the incompleteness of knowledge and the value of the activity (or the asset) about which one is ignorant. One may know a lot about an asset, but these bits of information might all point in a negative direction. And, inversely, one might know just a few things about an asset, but these bits of information might make it appear very desirable. Finally, there is no way to value the unknown. Brown might be conscientious of the fact that, despite all his research and business intelligence, there might still be factors around that bear on the success of his endeavour and which he has not considered at all. But he cannot evaluate these factors, precisely because he ignores them. His evaluations can only be based on the factors that he knows to have a positive or a negative impact on his project. He will then rely on the positive factors and try to contain the negative ones as far as possible. That is what production is all about. But he cannot evaluate what he does not know.

3 The mirage of the risk premium

Let us now apply our realist approach to study the question of the risk premium within gross interest rates. Above we stated that the conventional approach is based on the idea that the observable interest rates are an arithmetic sum of different components, each of which can be determined in separation from the others.[5] As far as the component of the risk premium is concerned, this approach involves three related challenges: (1) to define a risk, (2) to measure that risk, and (3) to explain how that risk so measured relates to demand and supply schedules. It is fair to say that there is today no general agreement on how these problems should best be solved.[6] In what follows, we will briefly discuss the most widespread approach, at the heart of which is the capital-asset pricing model, and then contrast it with the realist approach as outlined in the previous section.

A) The risk premium in light of the capital-asset pricing model

The most widespread definition of risk conceives risk as the market risk of an asset, that is, as the standard deviation of its price (respectively as its return) around some average value. This conception goes back at least to Irving Fisher[7] and was developed in more detail after WWII by Markowitz (1952), Sharpe (1964), and others. Sharpe argued that in general equilibrium, all portfolios and, in fact, all individual assets will be perfectly correlated in such a way that there would prevail a linear relationship between their return on the one hand, and their market risk on the other hand. The equilibrium rate of return of each asset (R_i) would be equal to the sum of a risk-free return (R_{RF}) and a compensation for the market risk associated with that asset. Or, in the words of Howells and Bain (2000, p. 45), "the market will price risky assets in such a way that the return on a risky asset will be equal to the risk-free rate of return plus a fraction (or multiple) of the whole market risk premium." This idea is commonly expressed in equations of the sort of equation [2].

$$R_i = R_{RF} + \beta_i \cdot (\mu_M - R_{RF}) \quad [2]$$

The capital-asset pricing model is ingenious because it explains and justifies the standard view, which holds that observable returns on capital are the sum of different components. It responds to all three challenges that we highlighted above. It defines risk, it measures risk, and it explains how risk influences the demand and supply of any asset. Indeed, each market participant would be ready to pay a price for any asset A_i such that its return R_i would correspond to equation [2]. And any current owner of A_i would require to be paid at least that amount.

However, the problems of this approach are numerous and well-known. Let us just mention two very important ones. First, the definition of risk as market risk might be plausible for certain groups of investors, for example, for those with very short-term time horizons or for those who are heavily indebted. It is implausible for all others. Long-term investors are likely to consider market risk a boon rather than a bane.[8] Second, the linear relationship between market risk and return (between the risk premium and the gross interest rate) is premised on the notion that the economy has reached general equilibrium and that all market participants share the same perception of returns and risks. This assumption is highly problematic in that it implies a completely different risk structure than in any real-world market economy. Asset-price fluctuations would be much lower than in the real world, but liquidity risk might possibly be greater. People who agree in their assessments of risks and returns are much less likely to exchange any assets than those who disagree.

Moreover, and most importantly, if the explanation of risk premia concerns an equilibrium world, then at best it could "shed some light" on risk premia as they exist in the real world, in which disequilibrium is permanent and ubiquitous. But what explains the rest? In other words, while the model does *not* explain how case-probable knowledge affects demand and supply schedules in the real world, there can be no doubt that the real world exists and that market participants buy and sell economic goods based on imperfect knowledge. What, then, are the real mechanisms that come into play?

B) A realist perspective on the return on capital assets

Let us start off with the familiar proposition that the return on a capital asset results from the subjective value differences between the asset, on the one hand, and the related future cash flows on the other hand. The present monetary value of a capital asset is, so-to-say, imputed backwards from the expected future cash flows. The present owners of the asset want to sell at some minimum price, which corresponds to a maximum expected return on the capital asset that they forego. Prospective buyers of the same asset want to buy it at some maximum price, which corresponds to a minimum expected return on the monetary capital that they invest. The resulting market price of the asset establishes the going return on capital, that is, the gross interest rate.

Now, it is also well known that this mechanism of backward imputation is a general principle that applies to each single factor that contributes to the final product. This allows us to bring into play our above considerations about case probability and class probability. The knowledge that there is a causal connection between a factor X and the product is case-probable knowledge. There is in the mind of the prospective buyer who invests in X no doubt about that causal connection.[9] In other words, there is no risk associated with acquiring X as far as this basic causal connection is concerned. There *is* a risk pertaining to the subjective evaluation of the monetary value of X's contribution – its marginal value product (MVP_X).[10] For example, the investor might overestimate it relative to another known contributing factor Y. In this case, MVP_X would be too high and MVP_Y too low. The investor also runs a risk because he might ignore the influence of a factor Z, and in this case, too his subjective evaluation of MVP_X would be too high.

However, these risks are irrelevant for the discounting of the MVP of X. Whatever the investor's subjective assessment of MVP_X, he will discount it by the same personal discount rate. If he estimates MVP_X to be relatively high, then the associated $DMVP_X$ will also be relatively high. If he judges MVP_X to be relatively low, then the same follows for $DMVP_X$. In short, whatever the case-probable risks that might come into play, they do not *per se* affect the subject value difference between any factor of production and its contribution to the monetary value of the product. Whatever case-probable risks the investor confronts, they do not show up in a risk premium within the discount rate that the investor uses to assess the present value of future cash flows. Again, this is implied in the very nature of the type of risk that an investor confronts, which is case-probable risk. A risk premium, precisely because it would be included in the discount rate, would compensate him for risks *as far as the causal connection* between a factor X and the monetary value of the product of X is concerned. But in his subjective judgement this connection is not just probable, but known.

The implication of the foregoing considerations is that differences in observable interest rates cannot be explained as compensations for risk. So how can they be explained? In what follows, we argue that they result from different subjective appreciations of available investment opportunities. Different people value different causes differently. Some may think that cause A will entail a rise in the market price of asset X, others might believe that A brings this about only in conjunction with B. Still others might consider that C is the relevant factor, etc. As a consequence, the demand schedule for X will be composed of a continuum of individual demands with very different motivations. If all popular causes are present, the demand will be at its maximum. If C is absent, the demand will be lower, and lower still if B, too, is not given.

Now, from a microeconomic point of view, this might create the impression that the price of X depends on a risk premium. If there are a lot of favourable circumstances, then the risk of owning X seems to be relatively low, and this goes in hand with a relatively high price. And inversely, if there are but a few such favourable circumstances, then the risk of owning X seems to be relatively high, and this goes in hand with a relatively low price. The difference in the two prices can then be interpreted as a "risk premium."

But this interpretation is unwarranted. It is not the case that all market participants evaluate the pros and cons of an asset X in the same way. It is not the case that they share the same view about which negative factors could impact its yield, and how much they might affect its market price. Each of the persons who wishes to own X is motivated by different considerations. There is no agreement between the different contenders. What appears to be a key factor of success in the eyes of one of them is irrelevant in the eyes of the other. They do not agree on the risks involved. Each of them evaluates X in light of the circumstances that he himself, and maybe only himself, considers to be relevant. And each is willing to make a bid for X in light of his personal assessment if and when the relevant circumstances are given.

No entrepreneur gambles with his capital.[11] Each entrepreneur, when he buys an asset, is convinced that this purchase will permit him to preserve and increase his capital. Otherwise, he simply would not buy it. The reason why some are willing to bid a higher price, and others a lower one, for the same asset is that they have different visions of what the relevant investment alternatives are. Suppose Mr. Black is convinced he can make a 10 percent return on that capital by buying the asset X at the current market price. This conviction implies a maximum price he would be willing to pay for the alternative asset Y. Things would be very different for someone with a different vision of his own investment opportunities.

The ordinary difference in price between a 2-year bond and a 5-year bond results from the fact that more people are willing to buy the former at relatively high prices. It does not result from any "discounting" of the 5-year bond. There is in this respect not the least difference between assets that allegedly are subject to a risk premium and the economic goods that are not. Always and everywhere, different goods attract different people who wish to own them at different prices, most notably because they see different alternative results from owning them.

But is it not true that some people discount the price they would otherwise be willing to pay by a risk component? Johnson would pay 100 dollars for a share of XY stock if it were free of risk. But because there are risks associated with it, he is only willing to bid 80 dollars. What is wrong with this representation of the investment process? There is no way of knowing what the price of the share would be if it were risk-free. The share can only be bought as is. It is impossible to compare an actual market price to something that does not exist. Therefore, even if it were true that Johnson fancies himself to be discounting the price with reference to some number that he has made up, or that somebody else has made up for him, this is irrelevant for the economic analysis of what he does. From the economic point of view, there are only two relevant questions. The first is whether Smith is convinced that buying an XY share at this or that price will suit his ends, such as earn a profit, preserve his capital, control the company, etc. The second concerns the available alternatives. If Johnson were not convinced of being successful, then he would be gambling with his capital, not investing it.

4 Risks as costs

The idea that risks are part and parcel of business costs is fundamental for business accounting and reporting. In particular, risk may affect various business costs *indirectly* through the risk component of the internal discount rate. The higher that risk component, the lower is the demand for factors of production, and thus cost expenditure. At the same time, risk may also affect business costs *directly* through the income statement. Firms may create various provisions that enter the annual income statement as business costs. For example, bad-debt provisions can be made for the probable default of debtors and contingent-liability provisions for potential legal costs, etc. All of these provisions enter the annual income statement as business costs. Similarly, in setting up its balance sheet, a firm may estimate the monetary value of its fixed assets by discounting the associated cash flows using an interest rate that may include various risk components. Changes of valuations resulting from changes in the risk component enter the income statement, too, under the rubric of "other comprehensive income," and thereby enter business costs.[12]

From a microeconomic point of view, it is acceptable to think that risks are a "given" part of the firm's environment. However, economic analysis needs to overcome this narrow perspective and explain the ultimate causes of the realities that are given to the immediate experience of any single market participant. This is what Böhm-Bawerk achieved with respect to the general theory of costs of production. He explained how factor prices ultimately result from the prices of their least important products. They are formed by discounting the prices of their products.[13]

As far as risk is concerned, we need to emphasise again that probabilities lead an epistemic existence, not an ontic one; and that risks are subjective elements of human action, not qualities of its objective environment. Provisions for risk are a misnomer. In fact, such provisions are made *after* the investment. They are an *ex post* acknowledgment of an investment error. Errors are without doubt costly; thus it is pertinent to account for them in the income statement as soon as the error is discovered. But errors are not "risky" at all. Risk is by its very nature a quality of *ex ante* judgements about the (imperfectly known) world, not an *ex post* reckoning of what the world is really like.

Similarly, as we have argued, the risk component in the gross interest rate is a sort of optical illusion. Different prices for different assets result from the fact that buyers and sellers appreciate them subjectively. From a microeconomic perspective, the implied differences in yield might be called risk premia. And one might use such premia in computations with an internal interest rate, to distinguish more interesting ventures from less interesting ones. But this does not alter the fact that the idea of a risk premium is an intellectual short-cut. It does not correspond to any real object.

Conclusion

Despite the importance of risk in business accounting and in virtually all other areas of economic life, the economic analysis of risk is not in a satisfactory state. The reason is that economists have too light-heartedly adopted analytical tools forged by mathematicians and statisticians. Most present-day economists consider observable interest rates to be the arithmetic sum of a pure interest rate, a risk premium, and a price premium, each of which can be determined in separation from the others. We have argued that this conception is problematic in that it is disconnected from ordinary demand-and-supply analysis.

As a solution, we present an alternative realist approach to the study of risk, based on Ludwig von Mises's distinction between case probability and class probability, and on the principle of subjective value. This approach leads us to appreciate that, in a free-market setting, known risks that pertain to business tend to be eliminated through entrepreneurial activity. It also leads us to the conclusion that case-probable risks pertaining to business decisions are not reflected in the discounting process *per se*, but rather in the assessment of the marginal value product of factors of production. The implication is that differences in observable interest rates cannot be explained as compensations for risk, but result from different subjective appreciations of available investment opportunities.

Notes

* Chapter 5 of this volume is a reprint of an article published in the *Quarterly Journal of Austrian Economics*, vol. 18, no. 4 (Winter 2015): 487–561.

1 This was recognised early on by Bernoulli, who stressed that "no valid measurement of the value of a risk can be obtained without consideration being given to its *utility*" (Bernoulli, 1954 [1788], p. 24).

2 The economic point of view also makes it irrelevant to consider the (psychological) phenomenon that certain beliefs are strongly held, while others are not. For an economist, strongly-held beliefs are precisely those that are valued more than others. It is not necessary to consider "strength of conviction" as a separate factor.

3 This crucial consideration is prominent in some of the recent literature on "one-reason decision-making." See for example Katsikopoulos and Gigerenzer (2008).
4 We owe this simple, crucial insight to Dr Georges Lane.
5 "The spread between the interest rates on bonds with default risk and default-free bonds, both of the same maturity, called the risk premium, indicates how much additional interest people must earn to be willing to hold that risky bond" (Mishkin, 2013, p. 161). This is also the usual way of presenting the risk premium among Austrian school economists. See Mises (1940, pp. 490–508; 1998 [1949], pp. 543–556) and Rothbard (1993 [1962], p. 497). The latter states "In the real world there is an additional *entrepreneurial (or "risk") component*, which *adds* to the interest rate in particularly risky ventures, and in accordance with the degree of risk" (Rothbard, 1993 [1962], p. 497; emphasis in original).
6 On the intricacies of defining "risk," see Rosa (1998) and Holton (2004).
7 In *The Nature of Capital and Income*, Fisher (1906, p. 279) distinguishes between three types of values: riskless, mathematical, and commercial. He proposes that to obtain the mathematical value of an interest rate, "we simply add to the riskless value the value of the chance of getting more, and subtract that of the chance of getting less" (p. 282).
8 Also, notice that the application of this conception of risk (as a standard deviation) puts the short-term oriented investor at a disadvantage vis-à-vis the long-term investor.
9 That is, unless he gambles, in which case he would by definition not invest (see Mises, 1949, pp. 112f).
10 On the basic mechanisms of the determination of marginal value products (MVPs) and discounted marginal value products (DMVPs), see Rothbard (1993 [1962], pp. 387–409).
11 Again, this is a tautological statement. Somebody who gambles with his savings is by definition not an entrepreneur, but a gambler.
12 Similarly, in French accounting practice, firms may establish provisions for risks and costs such as anticipated law suits (provision pour risques et charges) and provisions for doubtful claims (provisions pour créances douteuses), as well as provisions for exceptional use of fixed assets (provisions exceptionnelles). Firms may assess the value of their fixed assets as the present value of discounted expected future cash flows, based on the CAPM model. The standard procedure is to use a discount rate that results from the addition of three components: a riskless interest rate, a market-risk premium, and a premium for firm-specific risks (Ferdjallah-Cherel, 2014, p. 60).
13 He thereby confirmed the Ricardian insight that the prices of factors were intimately tied up with the price of capital. Ricardo held that factor revenues and capital revenues were caught up in a zero-sum game. The higher the return on capital, the lower must be the aggregate revenue of factors of production, and the other way round. Böhm-Bawerk added nuance to this result by taking account of the time structure of production. In light of his analysis, we can see that there is not necessarily an inverse relationship between the return on capital and aggregate factor income. For example, if, as a consequence of a decrease in the return on capital, the structure of production lengthens, and if the factors are now employed more than before in the higher stages of production (where their prices are discounted more than in the lower stages), then aggregate factor incomes are likely to shrink even though the return on capital diminishes as well. See Böhm-Bawerk (1959 [1921], pp. 377f).

References

Bernoulli, D. 1954 [1788]. "Exposition of a New Theory of the Measurement of Risk." *Econometrica* 22 (1): 23–36.

Böhm-Bawerk, E. von. 1959 [1921]. *Positive Theory of Capital*. South Holland, IL: Libertarian Press.

Ferdjallah-Cherel, E. (ed.). 2014. *Mission d'évaluation: Guide Pratique*. 2nd ed. Paris: Ordre des Experts Comptables.
Fisher, I. 1906. *Nature of Capital and Income*. New York: Palgrave Macmillan.
Holton, G. A. 2004. "Defining Risk." *Financial Analysts Journal* 60 (6): 19–25.
Howells, P., and K. Bain. 2000. *Financial Markets and Institutions*. 3rd ed. New York: Pearson.
Katsikopoulos, K. K., and G. Gigerenzer. 2008. "One-Reason Decision-Making: Modeling Violations of Expected Utility Theory." *Journal of Risk and Uncertainty* 37 (1): 35–56.
Knight, F. H. 1971 [1921]. *Risk, Uncertainty, and Profit*. Chicago: University of Chicago Press.
Markowitz, H. M. March 1952. "Portfolio Selection." *Journal of Finance* 7 (1): 77–91.
Mises, L. von. 1940. *Nationalökonomie*. Geneva: Editions Union.
———. 1985 [1957]. *Theory and History*. Auburn, AL: Mises Institute.
———. 1998 [1949]. *Human Action*. Auburn, AL: Mises Institute.
Mishkin, F. S. 2013. *Money, Banking, and Financial Markets*. 10th ed. New York: Pearson.
Poincaré, H. 1912. *Calcul des probabilités*. 2nd ed. Paris: Gauthier-Villars.
Rosa, E. A. 1998. "Metatheoretical Foundations for Post-Normal Risk." *Journal of Risk Research* 1 (1): 15–44.
Rothbard, M. N. 1993 [1962]. *Man, Economy, and State*. Auburn, AL: Mises Institute.
Sharpe, W. F. 1964. "A Theory of Market Equilibrium Under Conditions of Risk." *Journal of Finance* 19 (3): 425–442.

6 Time and the theory of cost

Jeffrey M. Herbener

Introduction

Although similarities exist between various elements of the Austrian and neoclassical theories of the market economy, on examination they often prove to be superficial, sometimes obscuring significant underlying differences between the two approaches. In other cases, elements of one approach make manifest differences it has with the other. Time is one such element. As Ludwig von Mises wrote:

> Economists often erred in neglecting the element of time. Take for instance the controversy concerning the effects of changes in the quantity of money. Some people were only concerned with its long run effects, i.e., with the final prices and the final state of rest. Others saw only the short-run effects, i.e., the prices of the instant following the change in the data. Both were mistaken and their conclusions were consequently vitiated. Many more examples of the same blunder could be cited.
>
> (Mises, 1998 [1949], p. 247)

This paper contends that the theory of cost is another example of the mistreatment of time in economic analysis. While great strides have been taken in the causal-realist tradition toward integrating time into cost analysis, in particular the recognition of the principle of discounting in determining the prices of factors of production, more insights concerning time have lain dormant. As Murray Rothbard wrote in an assessment of a book by Israel Kirzner,

> The abstention from money is unfortunate but not fatal, but the abstention from time and capital analysis *is*, and this cannot be remedied by an appendix that Kirzner promises us on time. Problems of time, capital, [and] interest must be *infused* into the price analysis.
>
> (Rothbard, 2011, p. 7; emphases in original)

Mises built the conceptual structure of causal-realist economic theory in his magnum opus *Human Action*. In his own treatise on economics, *Man, Economy, and State*, Rothbard developed the analytical apparatus of Misesian economic theory, and through his analytics, wove production theory into the structure contained within *Human Action*. While embracing the device of production curves, however, Rothbard stopped short of adopting the analytics of cost curves. He wrote:

> As an explanation of the pricing of factors and the allocation of output it is obvious that cost curves add nothing new to the discussion in terms of marginal productivity. At best, the two are reversible . . . But, in addition, the shift brings with it many grave deficiencies and errors.
>
> (Rothbard, 2009, pp. 589–590)

Rothbard cited, in particular, the error in neoclassical theory of assuming fixed prices for the factors of production in constructing cost curves from production relationships, while production itself must occur over a definite time period in which factor prices can change. In the Austrian construction, however, such *ceteris paribus* assumptions can be placed within a dynamic analysis in actual time, moment to moment. This technique is used, for example, in constructing a demand curve. The downward-to-the-right shape of the demand curve follows *ceteris paribus*, holding the buyer's preference scale constant and considering the quantity demanded by the buyer at prices both higher and lower than the actual price at which he purchased an actual amount of the good. The position of the demand curve is given only at the moment the buyer makes his purchase, which becomes the relevant moment for economic analysis. As time passes, the demand curve can shift outward or inward as the buyer's preferences and circumstances change. A similar treatment can be given to production decisions and cost curves.

Marginal costs and production decisions

Rothbard accepted the standard account of production relationships (Rothbard, 2009, pp. 453–478). The marginal physical product (MPP) and average physical product (APP) to increasing amounts of a variable factor used in combination with a given set of complementary factors generate ∩-shaped curves because of first increasing and then diminishing returns. An entrepreneur's demand for the variable factor depends on its MPP and the marginal revenue generated by the sale of the increment of output produced by the variable factor in the entrepreneur's line of production or, in short, its marginal revenue product (MRP). The price of the variable factor is determined, in turn, at the point where the demand by all entrepreneurs and supply by all factor owners clear the market for the factor of production. An entrepreneur's production decision in any line of production is made by comparing all factor prices from buying inputs, i.e., costs, with the price of the good from selling output, i.e., revenue.

As noted in the quote above, Rothbard pointed out that the standard short-run cost curves of neoclassical economics add nothing to this argument concerning production decisions.[1] They are merely the reverse of production curves, constructed by monetizing the production curves via multiplication by given factor prices. The ∩-shape of the per-input-unit production curves generates the U-shape of the per-output-unit cost curves. As illustrated in Figure 6.1, the marginal cost (MC) curve is downward-sloping-to-the-right over the range of increasing returns and upward-sloping-to-the-right over the range of decreasing returns. When MC stays below average variable costs (AVC) and then average total costs (ATC), they decline. When MC moves above AVC and then ATC, they rise.

The assumption of given factor prices necessary to generate such a cost structure, however, is untenable in a causal-realist framework, which takes account of actual time. As Rothbard wrote:

> The mathematical bent toward replacing the concepts of cause and effect by mutual determination has contributed to the willingness to engage in circular reasoning.
>
> (2009, p. 455n1)

In a neoclassical model of general equilibrium, all prices are instantaneously determined as the solution of the model's system of equations. The timeless character of the model neatly sidesteps the logical inconsistency, noted by Rothbard in the quote above, of the model's implication that the price of output is a determinate of the prices of inputs (through their MRPs) and that the prices of inputs (through costs of production) are a determinate of the price of output. In the real world, input prices incurred to produce a given output arise before the price for that particular output arises. An entrepreneur's decision to produce output, and concomitant decision to demand inputs, comes before his decision to sell that particular output to buyers who will be demanding it at that later point in time when the sale is offered. Production takes time. Input prices and output prices, therefore, cannot be brought into consistency with each other by assuming they occur synchronously. In the real world, the element that binds input prices now together systematically with output prices in the future is entrepreneurial expectations.

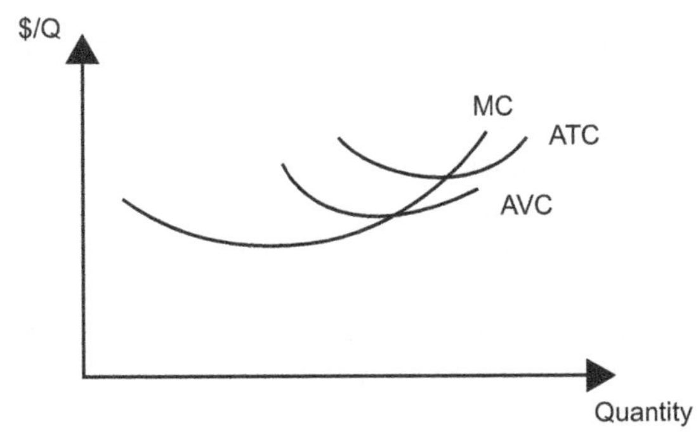

Figure 6.1 Short-run costs of production

Moreover, in the neoclassical model of perfect competition, an entrepreneur considers prices for factors of production given because his decision to alter his demand for inputs has no effect on the overall market demand, and, therefore, on the prices of the factors of production. Whether or not such a condition exists in actual markets, the model omits capitalists who invest in various lines of production by purchasing the assets or claims to assets used in production. In the real world, the prices of the assets owned and used by the entrepreneur will vary as conditions change regardless of what happens to prices for inputs purchased by the entrepreneur. Investors-at-large will increase their bids for such assets when profit arises and reduce their bids for such assets when losses ensue. The consequent change in asset prices will change "fixed costs" and therefore shift the cost structure up and down, even if prices for variable inputs remain constant.

As Rothbard emphasized, profits and losses will be capitalized into the prices of assets specific to an entrepreneur's enterprise. Investors-at-large bring this about by bidding more heavily for assets in lines of production anticipated to be more profitable and bidding less heavily for assets in lines of production anticipated to be less profitable. Ignoring this variability of the prices of capital capacity leads to errors in the analysis of production decisions. Rothbard explains:

> Further, the result of abstention from capital leads to all the crucial errors of the "cost curve" analysis. For example . . . that a firm will invest funds in production up to the point where "marginal revenue" equals "marginal cost."
> (2011, pp. 7–8)

Aside from ignoring the variability of asset prices in calculating "marginal cost," the neoclassical approach errs by assuming that the technical units of the good in the functions underlying marginal revenue and marginal cost are the only relevant units for decision-making by the entrepreneur. As Menger stressed, however, a person who is acting chooses the amount of the good he considers relevant for the action at hand. For economic analysis, the chosen amount of the good is the relevant marginal unit of the good. A consumer who wants to buy enough gasoline to fill the tank in his lawnmower, for example, may purchase 2½ gallons and pay $7.50.

For him, in this action, the unit of gasoline is 2½ gallons and the price to buy that unit is $7.50. The price of gasoline posted on the gas pump of $3/gallon is merely a technical standard chosen by the entrepreneur because consumers and producers consider it convenient. In similar fashion, an entrepreneur chooses the amount of the good to produce and sell along with the myriad of other aspects of producing and selling he chooses. Because it has fundamental importance for his action, the selected amount is the "unit" of the good, not the technical standard. Mises refers to the period of production or what might be called the production run as relevant for assessing the "marginal unit" of the good in production. In considering the profitability of producing and selling the iPhone SE, for example, Apple Inc. may have considered a period of production of several months with a production run of 10 million phones.

In making this decision, the marginal revenue anticipated by the entrepreneurs at Apple must have exceeded the marginal cost they anticipated by an amount sufficient to justify Apple's investment in this line of production. Over the time span of producing and selling the 10 million phones, marginal revenue could vary due to larger or smaller demand than anticipated, and the marginal cost could vary due to higher or lower factor prices than anticipated. Marginal costs are not suffered merely for "variable" or purchased inputs, but also for the prices of "fixed" or owned inputs over the period of production. The existence of markets for all factors of production, separately or in combinations, implies that the opportunity cost of production must include both inputs acquired by an entrepreneur through purchases in the factor markets and inputs retained by an entrepreneur instead being sold in factor markets.

As Rothbard argues:

> [T]here is no one simple, determinate "marginal cost," because, as we have seen . . . there is no one identifiable "short run" period, such as is assumed by current theory. The firm faces a gamut of variable periods of time for the investment and use of factors, and its pricing and output decisions depend on the future period of time which it is considering.
>
> (2009, p. 695)

Figure 6.2 illustrates the analysis suggested by Rothbard. The revenue and cost anticipated for each production-run quantity, and corresponding period of production, are shown as the vertical distances R and C, respectively. The entrepreneur will select the economizing combination of inputs for each level of output production. The marginal costs of production (C_0, C_1, or C_2) vary with each production run (Q_0, Q_1, and Q_2) and include the market prices of all inputs used in production,

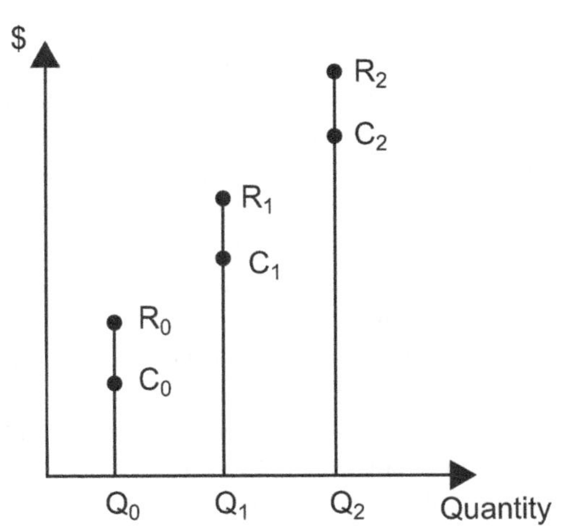

Figure 6.2 Marginal unit of output in production

both those purchased and those owned by the entrepreneur. In some cases, an entrepreneur may choose the same configuration of assets and increase production by purchasing more materials and labor. In other cases, an entrepreneur may choose a different configuration of assets as well as amounts of materials and labor when increasing production. Q_1 may represent the production and sale of 10 million iPhone SEs produced in a factory in China, for example, while Q_0 may represent 4 million iPhones produced in a factory in the United States, and Q_2 may represent 16 million iPhones produced in three different factories in China and Taiwan. Of course, making such changes in production processes takes time, which introduces other considerations for an entrepreneur in selecting an input combination to produce a given amount of output. But as long as all factors of production are saleable, their use by an entrepreneur in his line of production, whether purchased or owned by him, incurs an opportunity cost:

> Some factors are best used in a certain quantity over a certain range of output, while others yield best results over other ranges of output. The result is not a dichotomy into "fixed" and "variable" costs, but a condition of many degrees of variability for the various factors.
>
> (Rothbard, 2009, p. 591)

The analytical apparatus need not, however, be arrested at this step. It is possible to show the implications of the analysis in terms of the technical units of the factors of production instead of merely for the production run as a whole. As noted above, the construction of demand curves makes such a transition. Each buyer of gasoline, for example, has a personal marginal unit of gasoline, i.e., an amount he anticipates will be best suited to the attainment of his end. And yet, demand and supply analysis is conducted in terms of the technical unit, e.g., gallons, in which the price is denominated in the market. The transition is accomplished by conjecturing what must logically happen, given diminishing marginal utility, to the quantity demanded of a good at lower and at higher prices. In similar fashion, it is possible to construct revenue curves and cost curves per-technical-unit as long as the marginal adjustment used as the basis of per-technical-unit revenue and cost computations is the entire production run. For each asset combination chosen by the entrepreneur as best suited for a given production run, a cost curve can be constructed by conjecturing what must logically happen, given increasing and diminishing returns, to per-technical-unit costs at lower and higher levels of production. Given the resulting cost structure, then, corresponding shifts in the cost structure can be implied under various changes in underlying conditions.

In contrast to this causal-realist analysis, the neoclassical treatment of long-run costs displays an array of different production techniques associated with each short-run production function. With input prices given, the production relationships generate a long-run average cost curve (LRAC) that envelops the set of short-run cost curves, as illustrated in Figure 6.3. The U-shape of the long-run cost curves comes from the assumption of initial economies, which pushes down long-run marginal cost (LMC) and eventually diseconomies of scale, which

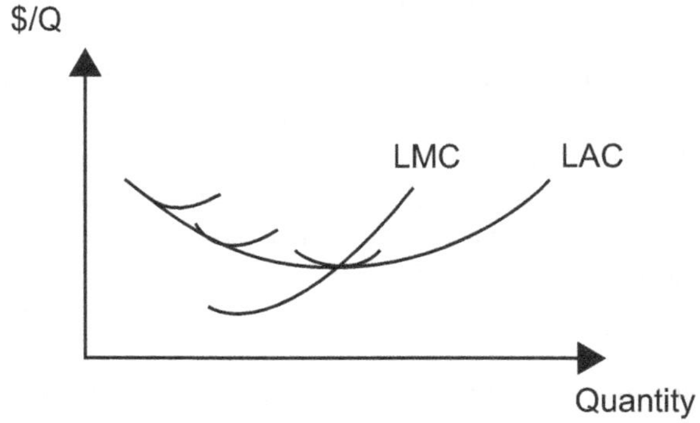

Figure 6.3 Long-run costs of production

pushes up LMC. As with their short-run cost analysis, neoclassical economists can reconcile the assumption of given factor prices across the entire array of production possibilities, capital capacity embodying various technologies and labor and materials, with the further assumption of full, instantaneous adjustment of entrepreneurs to the production technique which renders minimum LRAC. Even if this procedure sidesteps the problem of different prices for the factors of production purchased by entrepreneurs at each level of production for the various production techniques, it cannot account for different prices for assets owned by entrepreneurs across the various production techniques. As illustrated in the corn production example outlined below, a variety of production techniques for a good can coexist as long as the greater physical productivity of more heavily capitalized production techniques is balanced by higher asset prices compared to lower asset prices for production techniques of smaller physical productivity. Such a result depends, in turn, on the existence of a spectrum of specificity of assets across the different production techniques, a condition which is not uncommon in the real economy. For example, older, less physically productive techniques of steel production compete against newly introduced, more physically productive techniques as investors increase demand for the new asset configuration and decrease demand for the old configuration. The value of the superior productivity of the new assets will be capitalized into a higher price of the new asset combination, which will raise the structure of costs of production. And the decreased investor demand for the old, inferior-productivity configuration will lower its capital value, and the lower price for the old asset configuration will lower the cost structure for that configuration.

Time: discounting and costs

Instead of the neoclassical distinction between short-run and long-run costs, which is based solely on the technical circumstances of production, Rothbard suggested two relevant time periods for production analysis: the immediate run and the Evenly Rotating Economy (ERE). As he explains,

> [T]here are in production theory two important and interesting concepts involving periods of time. One is what we may call the "immediate run" – the market prices of commodities and factors on the basis of given stocks and speculative demands and given consumer valuations. The other important concept is that of the "final price," or the long-run equilibrium price, i.e., the price that would be established in the ERE.
>
> (Rothbard, 2009, pp. 590–591)

The question remains: what is the dynamic analysis that links the two together? The immediate-run analysis is depicted in Figure 6.4. At a moment in time, the total stock (TS) of a good possessed by people is given. The price achieves the level at which the total demand (TD) people have to possess the good is satisfied by the total stock of the good. Some people may desire to enlarge their stock, which they do by purchasing some of the good from others who desire to reduce their stock, which they do by selling some of the good. The former persons generate demand for the good and latter persons render supply.

The analysis of demand and supply depicted in Figure 6.5 views market exchange from an equivalent, but different, perspective, as the analysis of total demand and total stock. For a newly produced good, say the iPhone SE, consumers have exchange demand (D) and the entrepreneur has reservation demand or supply (S). The willingness of a consumer to purchase an iPhone SE, or any other good, depends on his anticipation of the realization of the ends to which he will put it and his anticipation of the sacrifice of the best alternative end his purchase entails. Likewise, an entrepreneur's decision to supply or retain a good depends upon his anticipation of the realization of the end attained by selling it and his anticipation of the sacrifice of the best alternative end, which can be categorized as either personal use of the good or sale to another consumer at a later time,

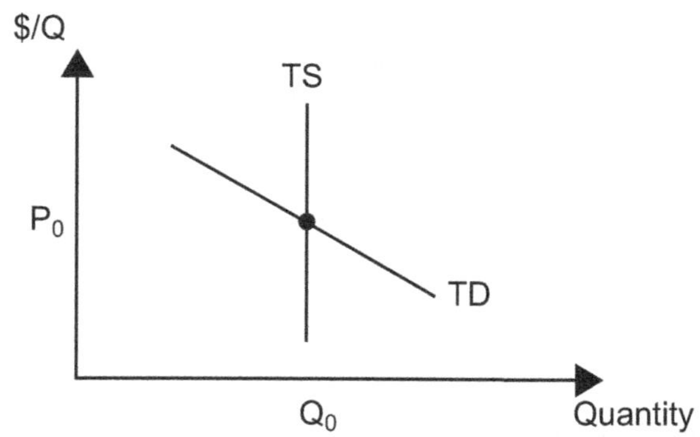

Figure 6.4 Immediate-run price of a good

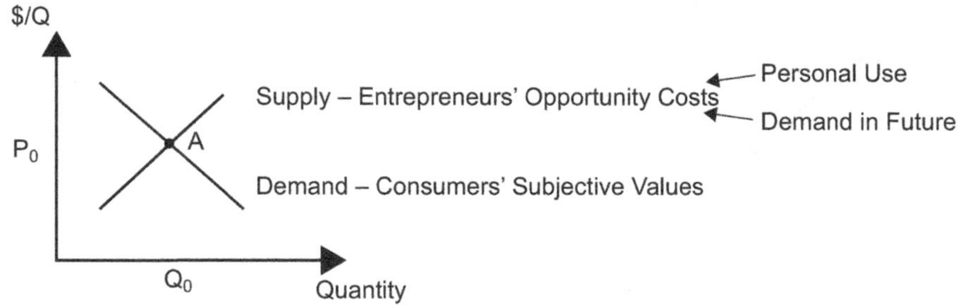

Figure 6.5 Immediate-run price of a good

which his sale now entails. The actual price of a good at any moment is based upon speculation, which provides the link between prices now and prices in the future.

Immediate-run analysis of the price of a factor of production is depicted in Figure 6.6. The actual wage of a labor service, say a tech worker hired by Apple Inc., is also based upon speculation. The worker anticipates the realization of the end attained by selling his labor services and his anticipation of alternatives, categorized as either personal use or sale to another entrepreneur at a later time, which his sale now entails. The entrepreneur anticipates the realization of the end attained by earning the marginal revenue product of the labor service and the anticipation of the sacrifice from attainment of the best ends foregone. Like the actual price of a good, the actual price of a factor of production at any moment is based upon speculation.

Immediate-run analysis highlights the fact that current prices of factors of production do not directly correspond to current prices of goods. The prices of factors of production are bound to prices of goods by speculation, not by the logic of models under the assumption of full, instantaneous adjustments. Moreover, entrepreneurs must pay the costs to acquire or retain factors of production sooner and receive the revenues from selling to customers later. Their demand for factors of production, therefore, will discount the factor's marginal revenue product.

ERE analysis preserves the insights of immediate-run analysis, namely, the time sequence of production and the discounting of payments to factors of production. Although both the neoclassical conception of general equilibrium and the ERE abstract from uncertainty, the neoclassical construct contains neither the time sequence of production nor the discounting of factor payments. As Rothbard puts it:

> In the ERE, of course, all costs and investments will be adjusted, and irrevocably incurred costs for all firms will equal the price of the product minus pure interest return to the capitalist-entrepreneurs, and also, as we shall see,

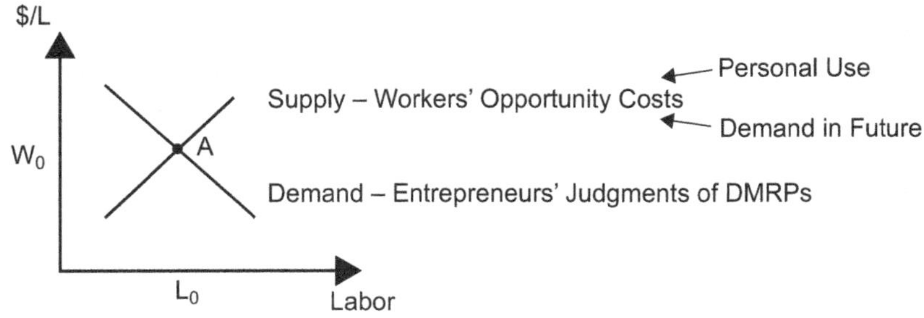

Figure 6.6 Immediate-run price of a factor of production

> minus the return to the "discounted marginal productivity of the owner," a factor which does not enter into the firm's money costs.
>
> (2009, p. 600)

Because entrepreneurs pay DMRPs for factors of production, actual cost structures lie below the cost structures of neoclassical models. Rothbard uses this point to rebut the neoclassical conclusion that an entrepreneur with monopoly power would operate with excess capital capacity. As depicted in Figure 6.7, if the profit maximizing output for an entrepreneur in a monopolistically competitive market is Q_0, then he will not select a cost structure tangent to demand at point A, as the neoclassical model concludes. Instead, he will select the production technique that minimizes average cost at point B. Rothbard maintains that this interest return gap ($P_0 - AC_0$) between the actual cost structure of an enterprise and demand for its product vitiated neoclassical cost-curve analysis. He concludes that,

> Once we bring investment interest return into the picture, we see that the whole elaborate cost-curve structure is totally faulty and should be tossed into the discard.
>
> (Rothbard, 2011, p. 7)

Following Rothbard's lead, however, cost-curve analysis can be reconstructed on solid ground. Doing so sharpens the contrast between causal-realist and neoclassical economic theories and permits further integration of fundamental insights into economic analysis and, therefore, exposes more fully the cause-and-effect relationships of the real economy. To achieve this goal, one need only follow-up on Rothbard's key point that costs adjust to prices of output through changes in demand by capitalist-entrepreneurs. According to Rothbard,

> Costs are not fixed by some Invisible Hand, but are determined precisely by the total force of entrepreneurial demand for factors of production. Basically,

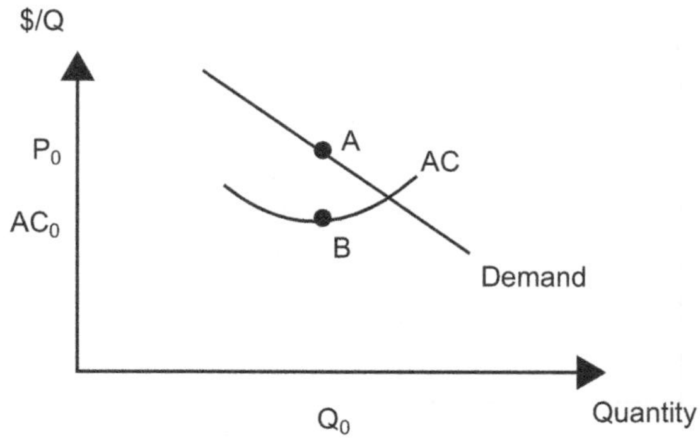

Figure 6.7 Production costs and the interest rate in the ERE

> as Böhm-Bawerk and the Austrians point out, *costs conform to prices*, and not *vice versa*.
>
> (2009, p. 588; emphases in original)

In particular, prices of more-specific factors adjust through capitalization to the price of the good they help produce. Consider the production of a good in the Evenly Rotating Economy in which entrepreneurs have adopted a variety of combinations of factors of production. For example, corn production by an entrepreneur in eastern Nebraska would employ a larger land area and a more capital-intensive process than corn production by an entrepreneur in western Pennsylvania. And yet, in the ERE the price of each bushel of corn is the same as every other bushel, the price of each unit of a less-specific factor of production, like farmer labor or gasoline, is also the same, and the interest rate of return is uniform across the various processes for producing corn. It follows that the prices of more-specific factors of production, like land sites and specialized equipment such as pivoting-irrigation systems used in Nebraska farming, must adjust to make the average cost of production the same across the various production processes. As depicted in Figure 6.8, the average cost curve for production in western Pennsylvania hits its minimum point at an output (Q_1) lower than that for production in eastern Nebraska (Q_2). The greater physical productivity of Nebraska farm land attracts capitalist-entrepreneurs who bid more for such land, generating a higher price for it than corn-growing land in western Pennsylvania. In Rothbard's view,

> [T]he various "costs," i.e., prices of factors, determined by their various DMVPs in alternative uses, are ultimately determined solely by consumers' demand for all uses. It must not be forgotten, furthermore, that changes in demand and selling price will change the prices and incomes of *specialized factors* in the same direction. The "cost curves" so fashionable in current

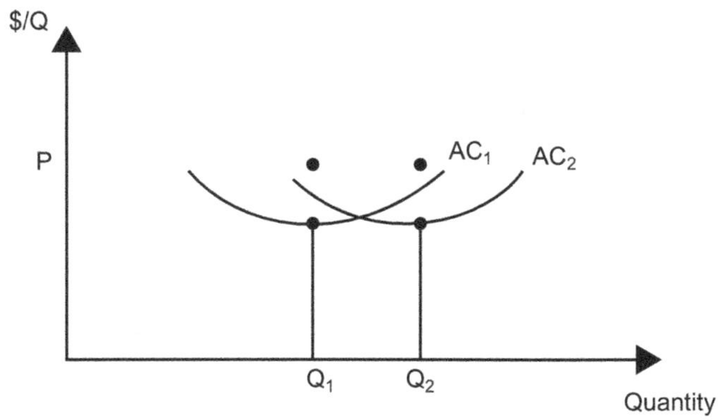

Figure 6.8 Production costs with different techniques in the ERE

> economics assume fixed factor prices, thereby ignoring their variability, even for the single firm.
>
> (2009, p. 589; emphasis in original)

More-specific factors of production will be the locus of capitalization and therefore of shifting cost curves as they adjust to changes in demand for outputs. Then, in turn, as prices rise for the more-specific factors of production, the additional profit from producing them will attract the capitalist-entrepreneurs who are doing so to increase their production, which necessitates increasing demand for the factors of production used to produce them. Greater demand by consumers for corn bread will increase the profit of corn production, which will increase the profit of the production of pivoting-irrigation systems, and so on. The changing pattern of demand will arc across the entire production structure in the economy, bringing with it an economizing reallocation of resources throughout the stages of production. The reallocation ceases when costs have adjusted to revenues in each and every affected line of production.

To illustrate the impact on cost structures of capitalization, consider a final state of rest analysis depicted in Figure 6.9. Starting in an equilibrium in the economy in which the price for the good depicted, say taxi service in NYC, is P_1 and the cost structure is AC_1, suppose demand declines due to the entry of Uber into the market. As a consequence, the price of taxi service declines to P_2, leading capitalist-entrepreneurs to reduce their demands for inputs, which in turn pushes their prices down. The downward adjustment of factor prices will array according to the specificity of the factors. Wages and prices for taxi cabs may not decline at all, but the price of specific assets, such as taxi medallions, will fall significantly. In fact, the prices of specific factors will fall enough to push the cost structure down to the point (AC_2) at which investment in taxi service renders the going interest rate of return, as it did in the original equilibrium. As investors

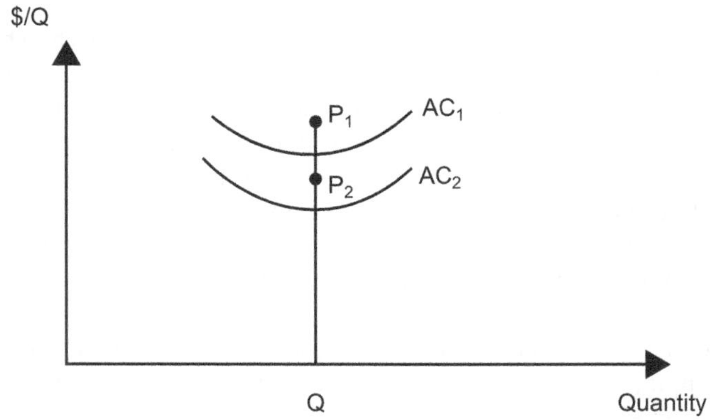

Figure 6.9 Falling demand and cost structure in the FSR

shift demand away from taxi service and into other lines of capital investment, capitalist-entrepreneurs increase the production of capital goods across the capital structure whose prices are rising and reduce the production of capital goods across the capital structure whose prices are falling. Eventually, the economy returns to a new equilibrium in which cost structures have been brought into conformity with the new pattern of prices which was set in motion by the switch of consumer demand away from taxis and toward Uber.

In actual markets, this adjustment process is rarely, if ever, completed, because the underlying causal factors are continuously changing. Mises emphasized that change is bound up with time:

> The notion of change implies the notion of temporal sequence. A rigid eternally immutable universe would be out of time, but it would be dead. The concepts of time and change are inseparably linked together. Action aims at change and is therefore in the temporal order.
>
> (1998 [1949], p. 99)

Change, in turn, implies uncertainty. "Every action refers to an unknown future," Mises wrote, and "It is in this sense always a risky speculation" (Mises, 1998 [1949], p. 106). Rothbard in particular noted the relevance of speculation in the face of uncertainty for prices. In evaluating Kirzner's book, he asked, "General Comment for Book: why has there been no discussion of the important influence of 'speculation' on price determination?" (Rothbard, 2011, p. 18).

The main role of speculation that Rothbard explains in his price theory concerns the adjustment process in the market (Rothbard, 2009, pp. 130–137). Accurate speculation hastens the movement of prices toward market-clearing and makes both demand and supply more sensitive to changes in price. Mises, however, focused on the speculative character of action in the face of uncertainty, and thereby provided the insight essential to incorporating uncertainty into the theory of cost.

It might be helpful to summarize before taking the final step. The general equilibrium analysis of neoclassical economics is timeless. The solution to the system of equations generates prices and quantities traded for all goods and factors of production simultaneously. The array of equilibrium prices and quantities are known to the market participants who act in a manner that brings about those equilibrium prices and quantities. The immediate-run analysis of the Austrians refers to moments of time in actual markets. The prices of outputs and inputs at a moment in time cohere together in a system through speculative anticipations. For example, input prices at the moment are consistent with the output prices anticipated by capitalist-entrepreneurs who will be using inputs to produce output, which they will sell at a later moment in time. The ERE analysis of Austrian economics incorporates the realistic time sequence embedded in immediate-run analysis. Because uncertainty is absent in the ERE, input prices at the moment are consistent with actual output prices that emerge in the future. Unlike the neoclassical analysis, having a realistic time sequence permits the integration of capitalization into cost analysis through the discounting of payments to factors of production.[2] In reality, the passage of time involves not only a time structure or sequence but uncertainty, an element that has not yet been fully integrated into cost analysis, even the Austrian variant. The step necessary to do so is to recognize that entrepreneurial demand for inputs depends on their anticipated DMRPs.

Figure 6.10 depicts contrasting views of the market for a labor service. The far left panel shows the neoclassical equilibrium in which the wage of the labor service conforms to its MRP. The middle panel illustrates the ERE, in which the wage conforms to DMRP. The far right panel, then, adds uncertainty to the time sequence incorporated into the ERE. In the real economy, entrepreneurial demand for labor depends on the anticipated DMRP or ADMRP.

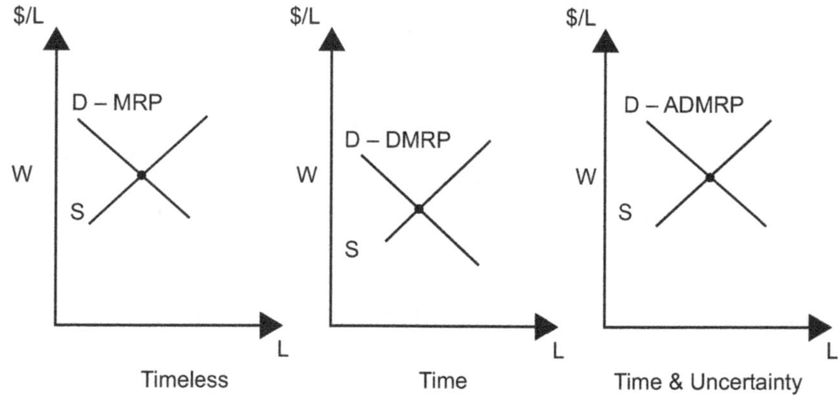

Figure 6.10 Time – sequence and uncertainty

Time: uncertainty and cost

Time implies that entrepreneurs discount factor payments because of the inevitable time sequence of production, i.e., costs occur sooner and revenues occur later, and earn an interest return from production as a consequence. However, time also implies uncertainty and therefore that entrepreneurs base their factor payments on anticipations of the future, and earn profit or suffer losses as a consequence of their superior or inferior foresight, respectively. In Mises's view,

> Attempts to establish cost accounts on an "impartial" basis are doomed to fail. Calculating cost is a mental tool of action, the purposive design to make the best of the available means for an improvement of future conditions. It is necessarily volitional, not factual.
>
> (1998 [1949], pp. 346–347)

Two further implications follow from the fact that "calculating cost is a mental tool of action." First, cost will adjust as the accuracy of entrepreneurial foresight improves. Increasingly accurate foresight by capitalist-entrepreneurs will result in raising (lowering) the capital value of specific assets in profitable (unprofitable) lines of production. Second, the calculation of cost will be personal to each entrepreneur. Those with superior foresight will anticipate the realizable price of factors of production more accurately than entrepreneurs with inferior foresight. Prices of specific assets, in particular, will adjust to the realizable price of output more fully as entrepreneurs with less accurate foresight adjust their anticipation in light of the success of entrepreneurs with superior foresight.

To integrate these insights concerning uncertainty and entrepreneurial anticipations into cost analysis, consider first the immediate-run price analysis. Figure 6.11 depicts the inclusion of anticipations into the demand for and supply of a consumer good. Demand depends upon the anticipated satisfaction the good will help bring about for the consumer compared to the anticipated satisfaction associated with the best alternative foregone. Buyers of the iPhone SE, for example, formulate expectations about its serviceableness in the future as the grounds for their purchases. Likewise, the entrepreneur supplies his good based on his anticipation

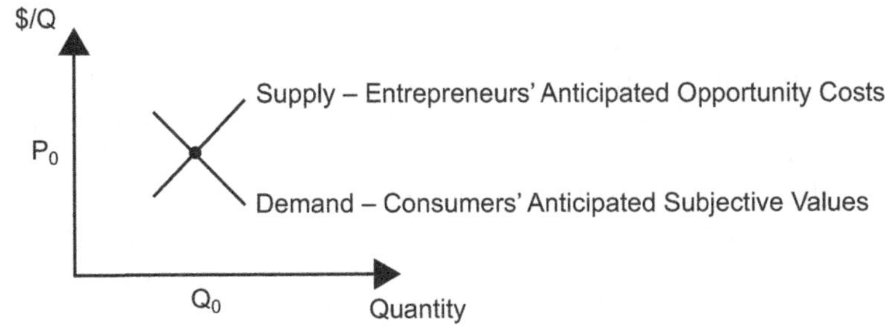

Figure 6.11 Immediate-run price of a good under uncertainty

of satisfaction associated with the revenue received compared to his anticipation of the satisfaction associated with the best alternative foregone. Both sides of the market are speculative and therefore reflect differences in the speculative acumen of various consumers and entrepreneurs.

One important analytical implication of this emphasis on anticipations is a reinforcement of the efficacy of Eugen von Böhm-Bawerk's marginal-pairs analysis of the market price of a good (Böhm-Bawerk, 1959 [1889], pp. 207–247). In the neoclassical analysis, different initial marginal utilities between two traders are based on nothing more than different initial endowments of the traded goods. Once all mutually-advantageous trading has been accomplished, the marginal utility (MU) received by each trader is the same. This conclusion is extended to a market with numerous buyers and sellers. Each buyer continues to purchase additional units of a good until he equates the MU of the last, i.e., least-valued, unit acquired with the price, and each seller disposes of additional units of his endowment of a good until he equates the MU of the last, i.e., least-valued, unit retained with the price. Each buyer, then, is the marginal buyer and each seller is the marginal seller. Böhm-Bawerk's analysis, in contrast, highlights the underlying differences between persons. Supra-marginal buyers enjoy a higher marginal utility, relative to that of a given amount of money, than that received by marginal buyers, even after all trading has occurred. A supra-marginal buyer of the iPhone SE, for example, may have been willing to pay $500 (while unwilling to pay the market price of $400 for a second iPhone), but the marginal buyer is the one willing to pay the smallest premium above the market price of $400. In Böhm-Bawerk's causal-realist conception of the economy, the market does not bring every person into a condition of equal MUs. In addition to the fundamental differences between persons in their preferences that Böhm-Bawerk notes, persons differ fundamentally in the quality of their foresight. Some persons more accurately anticipate the realization of the ends they are striving to achieve via exchange, while other persons anticipate less accurately. Even if this were the only source of fundamental differences among persons, a spectrum of valuation would still emerge. For example, investors trading shares of stock in a company buy and sell on the basis of their divergent foresight in anticipating the stock price in the future. Those possessing superior foresight into the higher (lower) price in the future are able to find sellers (buyers) possessing inferior foresight who are willing to trade with them.

In similar fashion, the demand for and supply of factors of production are speculative. As illustrated in Figure 6.12, an entrepreneur demands a factor based on his anticipation of the MRP that using its services will generate in the future. A worker, and other factor owners, supplies his factor of production based on his anticipation of the value of the income earned by doing so compared to the anticipation of the value of the best alternative uses to which it can be put. As with the spectrum of consumers generating a downward sloping demand curve for a good, the downward sloping demand curve for a factor of production is generated, in part, by the range of foresight among entrepreneurs. Unlike the typical neoclassical model in which a single cost-minimizing method of production exists and is selected by every entrepreneur who produces the product, the causal-realist view

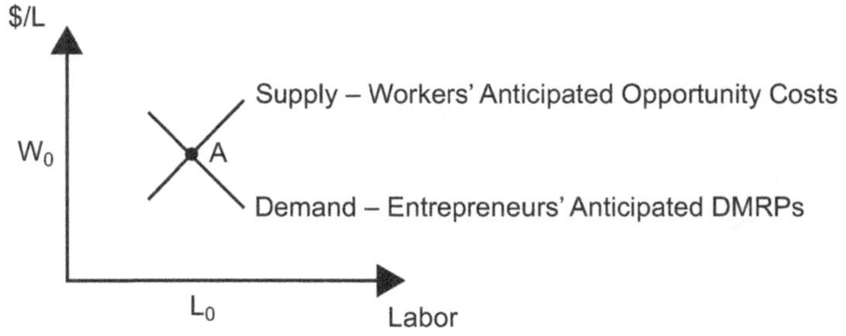

Figure 6.12 Immediate-run price of a factor of production under uncertainty

of the process accepts the underlying differences in the physical productivities among various land sites, among various capital goods, and among various persons. As illustrated in the corn growing example above, in the ERE this condition generates a spectrum of production methods, all of which have the same minimum AC point in equilibrium but otherwise generate different average costs for each level of output. This spectrum of costs is reinforced by the range of foresight among entrepreneurs producing the good and the spectrum of foresight among factor owners supplying the factors of production.

Finally, consider the issue of the dynamic adjustment process in the market. Mises summarized the importance of speculation in this process. He wrote:

> There is nothing automatic or mechanical in the operation of the market. The entrepreneurs, eager to earn profits, appear as bidders at an auction, as it were, in which the owners of the factors of production put up for sale land, capital goods, and labor. The entrepreneurs are eager to outdo one another by bidding higher prices than their rivals. Their offers are limited on the one hand by their anticipation of future prices of the products and on the other by the necessity to snatch the factors of production away from the hands of other entrepreneurs competing with them.
>
> (Mises, 1998 [1949], pp. 332–333)

To illustrate the relevance of integrating anticipations into the adjustment process of the market, consider the exposition in Figure 6.13. Suppose a current production process generates revenue from the price P_0 with the accompanying cost structure that renders AC_0. At the same time a different entrepreneur imagines an alternative production process with anticipated revenues from P_1 and associated costs at AC_1. The profit anticipated in this production process occurs because this entrepreneur anticipates a capital value for the assets associated with the process that is higher than the value of the same assets anticipated by other entrepreneurs. This condition gives room for the entrepreneur with superior foresight to pay lower prices for these assets, incur a lower cost structure, and earn the corresponding profit. When other entrepreneurs come to anticipate the higher realizable value

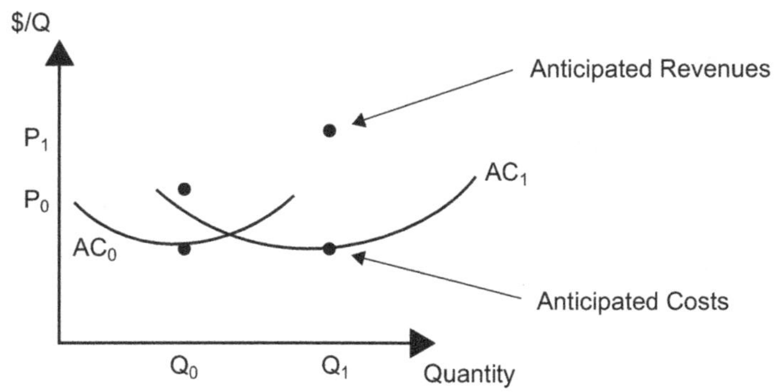

Figure 6.13 Production decisions by entrepreneurs under uncertainty

of the assets, then they too will increase their demand for them and consequently bid up their prices. The higher prices of the more-specific assets will raise the cost structure and eliminate the profit that has been earned by the entrepreneurs with superior foresight. The additional profit is progressively capitalized into the prices of the more-specific assets as more and more capitalist-entrepreneurs awaken to the profitability of the new technique of production and bid more intensely for such assets. The capitalized value of the first-mover advantage is earned by entrepreneurs with superior foresight regardless of the speed of adjustment as the additional profit from increased production is progressively eliminated. The speed and completeness of the adjustment of prices of more-specific assets and the concomitant rise in cost structures depends on the improving accuracy of anticipations by capitalist-entrepreneurs.

As capitalist-entrepreneurs draw resources away from less-valuable and into more-valuable uses in this process, the disproportionately lower prices of more-specific assets, compared to less-specific assets, in the shrinking lines of production and disproportionately higher prices of the more-specific assets, compared to less-specific assets, in the expanding lines of production result in larger losses and profits, respectively, for the production in the more-specific assets in shrinking lines and expanding lines of production. Production is realigned throughout the capital structure in accordance with the adjustment of cost structures conforming to prices for each of the various assets. As with the shifting cost structures in the lines of production that occur first, the speed and completeness of adjustment in shifting cost structures in the other related lines depends on the improving accuracy of entrepreneurial foresight.

Mises also understood the variation across entrepreneurs of the accuracy of their foresight. He wrote:

> [The promoting and speculating entrepreneurs] are people intent upon profiting by taking advantage of difference in prices. Quicker of apprehension and

> farther-sighted than other men, they look around for sources of profit. They buy where and when they deem prices too low, and they sell where and when they deem prices too high.
>
> (Mises, 1998 [1949], p. 325)

The movement of prices of more-specific assets, the corresponding shifting of cost structures, and the resulting earning of capital gains, depend therefore on the spectrum of foresight of the various capitalist-entrepreneurs. For example, the price of lithium mines has risen with the realization of greater demand for lithium as an input in battery production. The capitalist-entrepreneurs with superior foresight purchased lithium mines years ago at lower prices and have been earning profits from lithium production over the last several years. The growing recognition by less-astute entrepreneurs of the realizable price of the lithium mines has led them to invest in these mines also. As more and more entrepreneurs awake to the realizable price of the mines and bid for them as well, the profits of lithium production are capitalized into the price of the mines. Even as the profitability of additional lithium production dwindles from the rising cost structure pushed up by higher prices for lithium mines, the entrepreneurs with superior foresight reap the capital gain of their investment in the mines.

Conclusion

The passage of time has two main implications for production costs, only one of which has been incorporated into the theory of cost in the causal-realist tradition. Production has a time structure as well as a physical structure. The stages of production, from the extraction of natural resources to the construction of higher-stage capital goods down through the construction of lower-stage capital goods and finally the making of consumer goods, are bound together not only by the physical laws relevant to the production techniques adopted in each production process but also by the time sequence of the stages of production. Neoclassical models of general equilibrium incorporate the physical relationships among all of the producer goods and their corresponding consumer goods. Such models conclude that each factor of production commands a price determined by its MRP. The causal-realist theory of cost incorporates the discounting implied by the time sequence of production. Each production process takes time from the payments made to acquire inputs to the receipts received from the sale of outputs. Entrepreneurs will, therefore, discount the MRP of each factor when paying to acquiring its services. Recognition of the interest rate of return as the gap between an entrepreneur's revenue structure and cost structure invalidates some claims of the neoclassical models and leads to insights beyond those gained from such models.

The other implication of the passage of time for production costs is the uncertainty of the future. In making production decisions, an entrepreneur discounts the future revenue to be generated by employing the services of a factor of production, but can only anticipate its MRP and the appropriate discount to apply. Factor prices are, therefore, determined by ADMRPs of entrepreneurs. Being speculative, prices of factors of production and the corresponding cost structures conform to output prices regardless of the technical aspects of production relationships. The speed and accuracy of the process of costs conforming to revenues depends on the spectrum of foresight possessed by various entrepreneurs. Those with superior foresight move earlier into what prove to be profitable lines of production and earn profits which will then be capitalized into the prices of assets more specific to that line of production as the less-astute entrepreneurs follow suit. Even when the adjustment process reaches its climax and no additional profit can be earned from a further expansion of production because cost structures have been pushed up by rising prices for the more-specific assets used, the entrepreneurs with superior foresight will have earned capital gains by buying the more-specific assets earlier in the process than less-astute entrepreneurs. Just as the incorporation of entrepreneurial discounting of factor prices into cost theory has led to advances in understanding the working of the market economy, even deeper understanding awaits from the incorporation of entrepreneurial anticipations into cost theory.

Notes

1 For an example of the development and use of neoclassical cost curves, see Varian (2014).
2 On the importance of discounting in the determination of prices of factors of production, see Block (1990).

References

Block, Walter. 1990. "The DMVP-MVP Controversy: A Note." *Review of Austrian Economics* 4: 199–207.

Böhm-Bawerk, Eugen von. 1959 [1889]. *Positive Theory of Capital*. Trans. George D. Huncke and Hans F. Sennholz. South Holland, IL: Libertarian Press.

Mises, Ludwig von. 1998 [1949]. *Human Action: Scholar's Edition*. Auburn, AL: Ludwig von Mises Institute.

Rothbard, Murray N. 2009. *Man, Economy, and State with Power and Market*. Auburn, AL: Ludwig von Mises Institute.

———. 2011. "Comments on Israel M. Kirzner's MS, *Market Theory and the Price System*." *Libertarian Papers* 3 (25): 7–23.

Varian, Hal. 2014. *Intermediate Microeconomics*. 9th ed. New York: W.W. Norton.

Part 4

Causal-realist price theory

Debate and synthesis

7 Monopsony theory revisited

Xavier Méra

1 Introduction

The core idea of monopsony theory is the possibility of "profits at the expense of wages" (Machlup, 1952, p. 362) or, more generally, profits through an artificial lowering of money costs (expenses). Monopsony has long been a theoretical curiosity in the academic literature, or at least, so it was before the 1990s. To be sure, then as well as now, most microeconomics textbooks included some sections dedicated to monopsony theory, showing how the price and the quantity sold of a good or service – usually labor services – are determined when there is only one buyer. Yet monopsony was seen more as an interesting thought experiment, however impeccably carried out, than as an empirically relevant piece of theorizing (Friedman, 1976, p. 193). The reason is that scholars had difficulty identifying genuine instances of monopsony in the real world.

The situation has changed in the past two decades as a new generation of scholars (Boal and Ransom, 1997; Manning, 2011) has enthusiastically rediscovered and built upon the original insights of Robinson (1933, pp. 211–305). The new thinking holds that mere "frictions" on the labor markets are considered sufficient for "monopsony power" to emerge. Since in this case there is no longer any need for a sole buyer or even a few buyers ("oligopsony") to dominate the market in order for a monopsony price to emerge, the distortions resulting from monopsony, compared to perfect competition, are now taken to be a problem of far higher empirical relevance than they were before.

Obviously monopsony theory has policy implications, such as helping make a case for minimum wage laws, which are otherwise viewed by economists with the utmost suspicion as far as their efficacy in fulfilling the goal of raising wage rates without adverse effects on the labor force is concerned. Unsurprisingly, then, the renewed legitimacy of monopsony theory in the academic field is spilling over to the field of policy-making as well, and no less a group than the White House Council of Economic Advisers has recently released an issue brief relying on the new literature to promote various government interventions in labor markets (Irwin, 2016; Council of Economic Advisers, 2016). Last but not least, if proof was required that monopsony theorizing makes an impact outside the academic world, Blair and Harrison (2010, pp. xiii–14) have shown that since the 1990s antitrust court cases in the US have increasingly dealt with the behavior of buyers.

"The most important idea in the analysis of monopsonistic labor markets," writes Manning (2003, p. 41), is that "the labor supply to an individual firm is increasing in the wage paid so that the labor supply curve facing an individual firm is not infinitely elastic as is assumed in perfect competition." Reading the recent literature, one would not guess that the relevance of this dichotomy between monopsonistic and competitive markets has been challenged. In particular, long-standing criticisms of the underlying imperfect-versus-perfect competition framework from some "Austrian" scholars have generally been overlooked. Yet this is of tremendous importance: if the distinction is artificial, perfect competition cannot serve as a benchmark against which to contrast imperfect competition outcomes – including monopsony prices.

Although older Austrians, such as Böhm-Bawerk (1962, pp. 162–167), and their fellow travelers[1] included room in their price theories for monopsony prices, as a consequence of rejecting the perfect-versus-imperfect competition paradigm, Mises (1949, pp. 380–381, 591–595) and Rothbard (1962, pp. 717–718) ended up almost scrapping the entire idea. To them, monopsony theory essentially belongs within the analysis of socialism (with one and only one possible employer, the State), and believed that even here the concept of a monopsony price did not make sense. This also seems to be the view adopted by contemporary Austrians (Bellante, 2007, Block Barnett, 2009).

However, I want to show here that Mises, Rothbard, and their followers may have gone too far, and that their predecessors were onto something. In other words, there was no need for the perfect-versus-imperfect competition framework to produce a theory of monopsony prices in a market economy, in the same way that Austrians did not need it to endorse a theory of monopoly prices (Mises, 1949, pp. 354–385; Rothbard, 1962, pp. 903–907). Expanding on Méra (2010), which explores the relationship between monopoly prices for products and the prices of their factors of production, I show that the Austrian case against the imperfect-versus-perfect competition framework and Eugen von Böhm-Bawerk's distinctively Austrian law of costs (Böhm-Bawerk, 1930, pp. 223–234) provide the foundations to revisit the issue and build what might be called a theory of "monopoly price-gap," with monopsony prices and monopoly prices arising together out of the same pattern of production in a hampered market economy.

Section 2 is a brief overview of classic and new monopsony literature. Since the Austrian case against their common framework remains largely overlooked, and since it highlights some fundamental principles necessary to our more constructive task, section 3 restates it to show how both the classic and new theories are built on questionable grounds. Section 4 outlines Mises and Rothbard's alternative to the dominant paradigm and how it led them in particular to dismiss monopsony-related concerns. Section 5 questions part of their findings and lays out the foundations of the theory of monopoly price-gap, based on the idea that monopsony and monopoly – defined as grants of privilege in buying and selling (Rothbard, 1962, pp. 665–671) – go hand in hand in the context of production decision-making. Sections 6 and 7 outline this theory for cases where the factors of production involved are specific to one production process and when they are not, respectively. Section 7 stresses in particular that non-specificity does not shield factor owners from downward pressure on their prices, as a consequence of the law of costs, despite mainstream and Austrian claims to the contrary. Finally, the conclusion asks how this recasting of monopsony theory within a larger framework affects the question of its empirical relevance, i.e. the potential pervasiveness of monopoly-monopsony distortions, and provides a non-exhaustive answer.

2 Classic and new monopsony theory

It is common to distinguish between "classic" and "new" monopsony theory (Manning, 2008). Classic monopsony is the typical textbook version. In short, one buyer faces many sellers, so that the quantity supplied to this "monopsonist" is an increasing function of price. This stands in contrast with the perfectly competitive case in which the supply schedule confronting the buyer is perfectly elastic (the corresponding supply curve being perfectly flat) at the market equilibrium price. The buyer is one among many such that any attempt on his part to lower the price would result in the hiring of all units by its competitors at the current price. In other words, the buyer is a "price-maker" in the first case and a "price-taker" in the second.

Since the model typically deals with the market for a factor of production – usually labor factors facing the demand of a profit-maximizing employer – the consequences are as follows: the employer will hire or buy units of the factor until the monetary value of the marginal product of the factor equals its marginal cost. In perfect competition, this means that the employer hires up to the point where the marginal revenue product equals its price. Under less than perfectly competitive conditions, however, marginal cost is above the price for any quantity hired but the smallest, since the price rises for all units hired as the quantity of factors hired grows (except when dealing with the case of price discrimination). Therefore, the profit maximizing point will be reached with a lower amount of factors hired than would have occurred under perfect competition, and there will be a gap between the value of the marginal product and the price of the factor, the marginal revenue product being higher and the price being lower than they would be under perfect competition.

This gap is the extra earning or "profit" per factor hired for the employer that he could not obtain under perfect competition, and also a measure of his "market power." In this setting, a legally mandated minimum price above this monopsony price can conceivably improve the situation of all sellers, as well as improve efficiency in the resource allocation process, as long as it is not set above the market-clearing price. Indeed, if the minimum wage happened to be the exact market-clearing wage, the profit-maximizing quantity of factors hired would be the same as under perfect competition (which usually serves as the benchmark for welfare comparisons).

Classic monopsony also refers to oligopsony, where the market structure is such that a few buyers compete. The theory becomes more complicated because one must take into account the strategic interactions between buyers, since the supply schedules facing each buyer are affected by their competitor's decisions. Nevertheless, the heart of the matter remains that the buyers face less-than-perfectly-elastic supply schedules. In the same way that "monopoly" now often refers to any situation in which a seller has some market power (that is, faces a less-than-perfectly-elastic demand schedule), "monopsony" nowadays often refers to any situation in which a buyer faces a less-than-perfectly-elastic-supply schedule (Manning, 2008), including monopsony in the narrow sense, as well as oligopsony or indeed any other possible configuration within the framework of imperfect (Robinson, 1933) or monopolistic competition (Chamberlin, 1933).

The "new monopsony" literature still concerns imperfect competition, forward sloping supply curves, etc. The main difference with the older literature is, as Manning (2008) puts it, that, "modern theories of monopsony do not generally argue that employer market power over their workers derives from there being a small number of employers. They tend to emphasize the role of frictions in the labour market." It is not surprising then that these authors find more room for monopsonistic distortions in the economy than their predecessors. For as long as workers do not immediately quit a firm *en masse* whenever the employer "cuts wages by one cent" (Manning, 2008), which we can confidently assume never happens, employers have some market power.

Manning (2003, p. 3) merely follows this thread of thought consistently when he asserts that the simple monopsony model is a better first approximation of the situation for any firm than the perfectly competitive model. However, he is a leading author in developing a more sophisticated approach drawing on the "search costs" literature in particular (Manning, 2006), pursuing Burdett and Mortensen's (1998) initial line of thought. In a nutshell, the idea is that looking for a job is a costly endeavor, so that workers do not automatically find it beneficial to switch jobs when a better-paying alternative is available. This leaves room for monopsonistic behavior on the part of employers. As Borjas (2013, p. 192) summarizes it: "In effect, mobility costs help generate an upward-sloping supply curve for a firm."

As a result, a large part of the new monopsony literature is dedicated to estimating the elasticity of supply of various groups of laborers and the extent to which employers actually take advantage of their market power. Manning (2003, 2011) and Ashenfelter, Farber, and Ransom (2010) review most of the relevant papers. In the latter's view, they show that "the allocative problems associated with monopsonistic exploitation are far from trivial" (Ashenfelter, Farber, and Ransom, 2010, p. 209). The new approach has its critics too, of course, such as Kuhn (2004), who finds Manning's (2003) evidence for pervasive monopsony power lacking, especially in the long run.

We do not need to assess this controversy here, however, since what is of interest in the literature for the purpose of this paper is the theoretical framework that the terms of the debate take for granted. To our knowledge, only Bellante (2007, p. 22) has weighed in on the current debate to reject those terms based on Rothbard's case against the perfect-versus-imperfect competition dichotomy.

3 The nirvana fallacy in monopsony theory

It should be clear that the whole point of debating by how much the elasticity of real world supply schedules deviates from perfection, as a proof for the existence and as a measure of monopsony power, must assume that the dichotomy between perfect and imperfect competition is relevant in the first place. The distinction between a monopsony price and a competitive price for factors of production (or for any good), as well as the distinction between a monopoly price and a competitive price for their products, can be relevant only if competitive prices are within the realm of possibility. It must be possible for supply of the schedules individual buyers face (and the demand schedules individual sellers face) to be perfectly elastic, or any discussion contrasting this situation with another one has no relationship to anything real. Can supply schedules (or demand schedules) ever be perfectly elastic?

As Rothbard suggests, it is difficult to see how this could ever be considered a possibility were it not for the habit of thinking of action in terms of infinitely small steps as a consequence of the perceived need to present economics in terms of mathematical models. For it is only in such a case that the decision of any buyer can be considered to be without any impact whatsoever on the total market demand and therefore on the market price. The idea of a perfectly elastic supply schedule precisely assumes that the individual contribution of any buyer to total demand can be neglected, since there are "many" buyers, so that the contribution of each is very small. But the total quantity demanded of the factor on the market at any price is made up of the quantities demanded by each individual buyer. Each one is a contributor, and the individual decision to demand x instead of y units of a factor cannot but affect the total, and therefore the equilibrium price.

In order for the contribution of each to be actually negligible, total demand would have to be infinite: n+x = n only if n equals infinity. But there never can be such a thing as infinite demand. Demand must be limited by the scarcity of whatever is offered in exchange for the good under consideration. It follows that, depending on the specifics of the case, a supply schedule may or may not be very elastic, but it can never be perfectly elastic (Rothbard, 1962, p. 718).

Infinitesimal calculus may be convenient in mathematical modeling, but it cannot have any economic meaning and counterpart in the real world. The problem, as praxeologists such as Mises have argued, is that what we are interested in – action – must occur in terms of discrete steps. After all, altering the state of the world, one way or another, presupposes that the individual actor uses means combined in a definite quantitative relationship which he believes can help achieve some end. However, size-less means can hardly produce anything but size-less results, which for practical purposes means that nothing is produced at all. Only a non-producing producer – a contradiction in terms – can make an infinitesimally small difference, which is to say, no practical difference at all.

Manning is correct then in assuming that supply schedules are normally imperfectly elastic, but not that this is because of the failure of the market to conform to some realistic standard. Since the essential feature of perfect competition is impossible, "deviations" from it, including monopsony and other "imperfections," are not signs of a failure to conform to a normal or superior state of affairs. Welfare comparisons based on this criterion imply a nirvana fallacy (Demsetz, 1969): since such perfection is beyond anybody's reach, the standard of comparison is irrelevant.[2] It follows that equilibrium in no case can be characterized as a situation in which the marginal revenue product and the price of the factor of production are strictly equal. Instead, the marginal revenue product equals the marginal cost of hiring the factor in all cases. And while no one can ever unilaterally decide what the price in a voluntary exchange will be, no one ever is a pure price-taker, either.

In addition, Rothbard (1962, p. 718) also argues that as long as anyone is allowed to enter the market, profit can be arbitraged away, regardless of the degree of elasticity of a supply schedule at any given time. As a result, there is no valid criterion to differentiate monopsony or oligopsony prices from competitive prices in the standard framework. If the idea of market power for a buyer is to be saved, then it must be based on some other framework.

4 Monopsony and monopoly theory without the imperfect/perfect competition dichotomy

Noticeably, Mises and Rothbard's rejection of the imperfect-versus-perfect competition paradigm and the perfect elasticity benchmark did not lead them to reject monopoly price theory. The reason is that they relied on an older view of monopoly prices based on the dichotomy between elastic and inelastic demand schedules above a "competitive" (Mises, 1949, pp. 354–385) or "free-market" price (Rothbard, 1962, pp. 903–907). Rothbard's version of this theory states that if the market demand schedule for a good is inelastic above its free-market price, threats of punishment for entering the field might alter the demand schedules facing the remaining firms from a greater than unitary elastic position to an inelastic position, so that they might restrict their sales, thereby charging a monopoly price, to earn a higher income.[3] Now, we might expect Mises and Rothbard to likewise defend a monopsony price theory which does not rely on the perfect competition benchmark. Yet this is not the case, because the symmetry between imperfect competition in selling and in buying (monopoly and monopsony prices as a consequence of less than perfectly elastic demand and supply schedules faced by sellers and buyers, respectively) is a consequence of the imperfect-versus-perfect competition framework.

Indeed, once we drop this framework and uses the elastic-versus-inelastic demand schedule criterion for monopoly prices, no equivalent criterion appears available on the other side of the monopoly coin, monopsony. Writes Mises,

> Monopoly prices can emerge only from a monopoly of supply. A monopoly of demand does not bring about a market situation different from that under not monopolized demand. The monopolistic buyer – whether he is an individual or a group of individuals acting in concert – cannot reap a specific

> gain corresponding to the monopoly gains of monopolistic sellers. If he restricts demand, he will buy at a lower price. But then the quantity bought will drop too.
>
> (1949, p. 380)

This is certainly not meant to imply that restrictions on buying do not make any difference in the pricing process, or that such restrictions cannot benefit the remaining buyers in any way.[4] Instead, the claim is that there is no analytical criterion allowing for a special category called "monopoly of demand price" or "monopsony price." This is because price and quantity vary in the same direction along a particular supply schedule, so that a lower price is always associated with lower expenses, whereas price and quantity vary in the opposite direction along a demand schedule so that a higher price may be associated with higher or lower expenses depending on the elasticity of demand. The old monopoly price theory relies on this specific feature of a demand schedule, and no equivalent exists when one discusses monopsony. In this sense, there can be no such a thing as a monopsony price. Consequently, there can be no monopsony gain corresponding to the monopoly gain of monopolistic sellers. But the question remains then if a monopsony or oligopsony might take advantage of the exclusion of competitors to push prices downward in order to improve its lot, even if the resulting ratios may not properly be referred to as monopsony prices.[5]

In the case of labor factors, Rothbard, drawing on Mises (1949, pp. 593–595), will have none of this:

> It is often alleged that the buyers of labor – the employers – have some sort of monopoly and earn a monopoly gain, and that therefore there is room for unions to raise wage rates without injuring other laborers. However, such a "monopsony" for the purchase of labor would have to encompass all the entrepreneurs in the society. If it did not, then labor, a nonspecific factor, could move into other firms and other industries.
>
> (Rothbard, 1962, pp. 717–718)

In other words, only socialism with its unique employer could provide the sufficient conditions for lower wage rates.[6] Absent socialism, non-specificity of the factor appears to be what protects its owners from the prospect of monopsonistic pressure when government interventions hamper the bidding of employers. The implication seems to be that, for a market economy, lower prices for the factors of production and the corresponding gains for the buyers are possible, but only when violent threats are made against would-be buyers of the factor – such as when licenses to buy are given to privileged buyers only – and when those factors of production, land factors or capital goods, are specific.

This point is not explicitly stated by Mises or Rothbard, and they make no attempt to systematically analyze pricing under such conditions. Both pay lip service to the limited possibility of lower prices under monopoly of demand conditions under interventionism, but they only deny that this is possible for non-specific factors, without discussing other cases. Their followers on this question do the same (Block Barnett, 2009, p. 80; Bellante, 2007, p. 17). The following analysis both renders explicit what is implicit, in the case of specific factors and, drawing on Méra (2010), reveals that the above conclusion regarding the case of non-specific factors, including labor, is unwarranted, such that monopsonistic pressure on non-specific factor prices can be a widespread phenomenon. In order to better grasp this point, we need first to take a *détour* and establish in broad terms what sort of relationship exists between monopoly and monopsony, if any, once we adopt the praxeological lens of Mises and Rothbard.

5 Monopoly and monopsony: toward a theory of monopoly price-gap

It is useful to introduce here a distinction between a "short run" and a "long run" analysis, or better stated, between an analysis of choice with already-produced goods on the one hand and an analysis of choice regarding production decisions on the other. We begin with the first. This seems all the more relevant given Mises and Rothbard's way of approaching monopoly price theory. Indeed, even though they pay some attention to factor allocation in their analysis of the conditions for the emergence of monopoly prices, it is mainly an afterthought (Méra, 2015, pp. 127–131). Their analysis, as described above, tends to run in terms of already-produced goods, ruling out production costs as a decisive consideration: the basic requirement for a monopoly price to emerge is that demand schedules to remaining sellers are made inelastic above the free-market price (or "competitive" price, for Mises), allowing for the specific monopoly gain Mises alludes to in the above quote. The "monopoly price" here is what Fetter (1915, pp. 80–81) referred to as a "crude monopoly price," the qualifier emphasizing the lack of deliberations about production in this setting (Fetter referred to "monopoly price" in the context of production decision making).

If one contemplates monopsony through the same lens, the following picture emerges. Absent any production decision, the only choice to be dealt with, as far as a buyer is concerned, is the decision of a consumer. The first thing which needs to be stressed is that although it is noticed in the literature that a monopsonist often is a monopolist, this is not the case here. The position of someone as a consumer-monopsonist is unrelated to any monopoly position she might have as a seller. Second, restricting the quantity she buys does not bring about any gain, even if a lower price can thereby be paid. No rationale comes into play that would explain why the buyer would be interested in restricting her exchanges in some way similar to monopoly price theory. If this was advantageous to her, her demand schedule would have been lower in the first place. Therefore, in perhaps a stronger sense than Mises intended in the above quote (1949, p. 380), when one speaks of a demand for consumption goods, "a monopoly of demand does not bring about a market situation different from that under not monopolized demand" (Mises, 1949, p. 380). There is no symmetry beyond the fact that competitors are excluded in both cases: monopoly can bring about monopoly prices, but no monopsony price emerges from a monopsony situation.[7]

So far, Mises's case against the symmetric impact of monopoly and monopsony is unobjectionable, but does it imply that there can never be such a thing as lower factor prices specifically resulting from a monopsonist's choices? Does this mean most economists have taken the wrong track by endorsing one variant or another of monopsony theory, including Mises's predecessor, the master of Austrian price theory, Eugen von Böhm-Bawerk? Is there a fatal flaw in the latter's account of "wage determination under employer's monopoly," for instance? In this discussion, although he does not describe an economy-wide monopoly but rather a cartel of employers in an industry, he nevertheless states that:

> The rate of wages would be fixed according to the general formula applying to a purely selfish monopoly, already mentioned before in another connection: they would be fixed at that point which promises the largest returns, after a careful consideration of all circumstances, and with due regard to the inevitable fact that with changing prices, the amount of goods to be disposed of profitably will change, only that in the case of a buyers' monopoly the results are exactly opposite to that of a sellers' monopoly.
>
> Or stated concretely: the lower is the wage rate fixed by the monopolist, the smaller will be the number of workers available, and from a correspondingly smaller number of workers will the entrepreneurs be able to collect that increased return which might accrue from pushing the wage scale down below the value of the product of the marginal laborer . . . in fact, this value might even increase through a reduction in the output, which would cause a rise in the price of the finished goods.
>
> (Böhm-Bawerk, 1962, p. 165)[8]

This situation is different from the one the consumer-monopolist finds herself in, however, since Böhm-Bawerk deals with capitalist-entrepreneurs hiring factors of production. This is the realm of production decisions, more specifically, the production decisions of those who invest their money in a productive process. In their capacity as capitalist-entrepreneurs, they act as buyers and sellers, sequentially, with or without physically transforming what they have bought in the meantime. They buy in order to sell and earn a net income based on a hoped-for price differential. This has profound implications for the issue at hand, implications that neither Böhm-Bawerk nor Mises and Rothbard appear to have completely drawn: monopsony implies a different market situation when buyers are producers, although the corresponding gain might not be said to be specific to the buyers' position as monopsonists only.

Indeed, the first implication to be stressed is that, whether a threat of infringing upon the property rights of some would-be capitalist-entrepreneurs is made in their capacity as sellers (granting a monopoly privilege to other capitalist-entrepreneurs) or in their capacity as buyers (granting a monopsony privilege), or both, a restriction on one is a *de facto* restriction on the other (Wieser, 1927, p. 219; Méra, 2010, p. 55). This is because buying and selling are parts of the same production plan, so if someone is barred from entering the market as a producer-seller, he will not be able compete on the market for the required factors of production (at least, not for that particular use), and *vice versa*.[9]

If it is often noticed that a monopoly is a monopsony or a monopsony is a monopoly, this is rarely considered a necessity. And it is true that, with an exclusive grant of monopoly privilege on the sale of a good, one may be its sole seller while still one among many buyers of its non-specific factors of production. However, even in this case competition is hampered on the factors' markets since no competitor is allowed to hire them for the production of the monopolized good. With an exclusive grant of monopsony privilege, one may be the sole buyer of a factor of production while still one among many sellers of a good it helps to produce, provided this factor is not indispensable to its production. Yet even in this case competition is hampered in the product market, because competitors are not allowed to produce the product using this factor.

The only way the capitalist's positions as a buyer and as a seller could be considered as independent from each other is by introducing the perfect competition hypothesis in one market or the other. Then we could claim that the exclusion of some competitors from the perfectly competitive market has a negligible impact on the price (as long as there are still many participants competing, that is). A capitalist could then be a price taker in one market and a price maker in the other. Yet we have already ruled out perfect competition as a point of reference. Outside perfect competition, then, the forced exclusion of some competitors will make a difference, albeit a very small one in the above case. No one's position in the product market is independent from one's position in the factors' markets. The impact of hampering competition in one market must reverberate throughout the others. In the large sense of being shielded from the competition of some other capitalists, a privileged capitalist is both a monopolist and a monopsonist.

Second, when viewed in this light, it is immediately plausible that monopsony-monopoly is a market situation in which prices are affected in both product markets and factor markets, or at least product markets and divisible factor markets. All that seems really necessary for such an outcome to emerge is that monopoly-monopsony hampers the arbitrage process otherwise occurring across the whole social structure of production in all its dimensions in such a way that the price-gap between products and factors cannot be reduced to the height determined by time preferences.[10]

Before examining in more detail the required conditions for such a result, let us at this stage emphasize that this situation is simply another aspect of the process described by Böhm-Bawerk in the above quote, and that it contradicts Mises and Rothbard's idea that no downward pressure on wages exerted by a cartel of employers can ever succeed in establishing a permanently lower wage rate for some workers. On the other hand, when realizing that product prices will rise when capitalists-monopsonists "fix" a lower wage rate, Böhm-Bawerk hints at, but nevertheless seems to miss, the idea that monopoly and monopsony go hand in hand for capitalists. As a consequence, he sees these situations as symmetric but unnecessarily intertwined, and suggests there can be a specific gain for a buyer's monopoly and a specific gain for a seller's monopoly. Yet if monopolistic grants of privilege to capitalists grant both kinds of monopoly to them as sellers of their products and as buyers of the required factors – no matter how the restriction was nominally introduced – that is, if monopoly and monopsony are two sides of the same coin, then there is no specific gain to each. There is no specific gain for the monopsonist corresponding to the gain of a monopolist in the same sense that there is no separate interest revenue for a capitalist as a buyer of factors' services and as a seller of their products. The capitalist-monopolist benefits from a specific monopoly price-gap accounting for a specific gain.

Now, if it is problematic even to speak of a gain associated with the capitalist as a buyer only – since the alterations of factor and product prices accounting for it are certainly not independent – a special emphasis on factor prices is required when reassessing monopsony theory and its features. In order to explain the conditions under which the monopoly price-gap can arise, and also the contribution of lower factor prices to such an outcome, it is convenient to begin with the simpler case involving factors of production specific to their industry.

6 The monopoly price-gap with specific factors of production

Under (general) equilibrium in the free market, i.e. when all expectations errors have been avoided and no privilege in buying or selling exists (free competition), all profits and losses have been arbitraged away so that the remaining gap between the average expense on factors of production and the price of the product remunerates the capitalist *qua* capitalist (with what Mises calls the "originary interest rate").[11] For any remaining firm, any attempt to increase net income would be self-defeating as long as preferences, resources, and all the determinants of this equilibrium position remain the same. Expansion would be such that gross income would fall while expenses would rise, or, that gross income would rise at a slower pace than expenses. On the other hand, if a firm tries to increase net revenue by buying and selling less, it would fail because its income would fall at a higher pace than its expenses. Gross income would fall and not rise, because the demand schedule of the firm for its product must be elastic above the equilibrium price (otherwise the initial situation would not be properly characterized as general equilibrium) and it would fall at a higher pace than expenses (for the same reason). In other words, and the demand schedule that each firm faces for its product must be elastic enough in the voisinage of their equilibrium prices that no other choice would bring about a higher net income for the firm owners.

Therefore a grant of monopoly-monopsony privilege can increase the gap if and insofar as the forced exclusion of competitors decreases the elasticity of the demand schedule for the product and/or the elasticity of the supply schedules of the factors in the relevant ranges (above the free-market equilibrium price of the product and below the free-market equilibrium prices of the factors). The net incomes of the remaining firms are maximized through contraction in this branch (compared to the free-market level of activity). In this market situation, a monopoly-price gap emerges and the corresponding monopoly gain under the new equilibrium position cannot be arbitraged away.

Let us assume that a grant of monopolistic privilege has been conferred upon some firms in the chocolate industry (as sellers of chocolate).[12] The more exclusive the grant is, the less elastic the demand schedule becomes to each remaining firm, the more drastic the contraction, and the higher the new product price will be. If only one seller is authorized, it faces the whole market demand schedule, which is necessarily less elastic than the demand schedules all the competing firms would have faced under less restrictive conditions. As a consequence, the net income-maximizing quantities of output and of factors hired are bound to be lower than they would otherwise be.

Four remarks are in order at this stage. First, and directly relevant to our central concern about monopsony theory: if it is true, as explained above, that there can be no such thing as a perfectly elastic factor supply schedule, the monopoly price-gap is partially accounted for by lower factor prices. Clearly, lower production requires fewer units of at least one divisible factor, a market situation under which no upward pressure on its price can be felt (Méra, 2010, pp. 57–59), and contraction can then be implemented by "moving along" the supply schedule to a position where the price is lower (with lower quantities bringing about a higher price for the product).

Second, how low the price is depends on the reservation demand of the factor owners. With a specific factor, the only alternative consists in being employed by another of the remaining employers, if there are any, or in being unemployed. If the monopoly grant is exclusive to one firm, this firm is the sole buyer of the services of the factor. It faces the market supply schedule of the factor, which must be less elastic than any supply schedule any one firm faces under less restrictive conditions. The more exclusive the grant is, the more drastic the contraction and the fall in the specific factor prices are. It is not simply that prices must fall because there is never such a thing as a perfectly elastic supply schedule that faces buyers. It is that hampering competition results in those supply schedules to each remaining buyer becoming less elastic, which must then account for a part of the monopoly price-gap. This must be the case if it is true, as argued above, that the situation of capitalists as buyers is not independent from their role as sellers, such that hampering competition in the chocolate market *de facto* hampers competition in its specific factor markets.[13]

Third, this does not mean that a grant of privilege makes no difference, whether it is a monopoly grant on the sale of chocolate or a monopsony grant on the purchase of one or several of its specific factors. In the second case, it could be that other ways to produce the same chocolate product are known that do not require the use of this specific factor. We would then expect the elasticity of the demand schedule for chocolate faced by any remaining sellers to be altered less relative to the elasticity of the supply schedules of this factor that they face as buyers. As a consequence, the monopoly price-gap would arise more as a consequence of a fall in the specific factors' prices than as a consequence of a rise in the product price, while both would nevertheless occur.

Fourth, to the extent that a lowered factor price is related to a change in the elasticity of the supply schedules faced by the remaining buyers, one may refer to the resulting price as a "monopsony price." Recall that Mises rules out the concept of a monopsony price or "monopoly of demand" price because no equivalent to the inelasticity of demand criterion for monopoly prices exists in monopsony. However, this inelasticity criterion turns out not to be decisive once we shift focus away from "crude monopoly price" theory and toward an analysis of the requirements for the emergence of a mere "monopoly price" in the context of production decisions. Indeed, as Méra (2015, pp. 130–131) argues, Mises (1998, p. 7) implicitly admits this when he allows himself to discuss the emergence of monopoly prices in relation to production expenses by devising an instance of monopoly price reached through a move along an elastic demand schedule (with the move being profit-enhancing since the example is devised in such a way that the fall in expenses is higher than the fall in gross income). And as Rothbard (1970, p. 44) claimed – contradicting his previous presentations of the theory – the relevant circumstance for a monopoly price to arise is that a demand schedule facing a firm is made "sufficiently less elastic" through the forced exclusion of competitors, not necessarily that it is made inelastic. If it is legitimate to refer to such an outcome as a monopoly price, it is certainly legitimate to refer to its counterpart in the factor markets and its corresponding outcomes as a monopsony price.[14]

Semantics aside, the most important result is that a monopoly price-gap can emerge with higher product prices and lower specific factor prices, specifically as a result of a monopolist's choice to contract its activity in order to take advantage of demand and supply schedules made less elastic through the threats of fines, taxes, imprisonment, and other coercive methods.

7 The monopoly price-gap: non-specific factors and the law of costs

What difference do non-specific factors make? Is it true that non-specificity shields them, and especially the labor factors among them, from monopsonistic pressure? Or, as in the framework of the monopoly price-gap theory above, could it be that only increases of product prices (as well as decreases of specific factor prices) account for the price-gap and monopoly gain?

First, in regard to labor, the sense in which Rothbard speaks of it as non-specific, when he claims that only an all-encompassing monopsony could extract a gain from it, does not appear to be a strict one. He must be alluding to "labor-in-general" (Rothbard, 1962, pp. 572–575) as a class of factors. Otherwise, the universal monopsony clause would hardly be required. Strictly speaking, a non-specific factor performs a task which can be used in several production processes (Rothbard, 1962, p. 39), but is nevertheless "homogeneous in its supply" (Rothbard, 1962, p. 562). This is certainly true of many tasks that laborers are able to perform. But labor-in-general is non-specific in the larger sense that each person is able to perform various labor tasks. It would be more accurate to say, then, if one sticks to the strict definition, that a person normally can embody several labor factors and that she can switch from being a supplier of one to a supplier of another. The reason it is important to keep this in mind is that there will be a different marginal revenue product schedule for each task, and the next most remunerative task an employee will be able to perform may pay far less than the current one. Furthermore, this particular factor they embody may be specific to the process they participate in. As a consequence, privileged employers (monopolists-monopsonists) may be in a position to pay a lower than free-market wage rate without such workers fleeing *en masse* to another field, although the lower limit below which workers will quit is higher than if they could not perform other labor tasks.[15]

What about a genuinely non-specific factor, be it a labor factor, a land factor, or a capital good? Rothbard claims, following Mises, that a non-specific factor will simply go elsewhere if the employer attempts to push its price below the free-market level. One problem, however, is that Rothbard's point proves too much. If it really followed from the non-specificity of a factor that a monopsony could not lower factor prices, would it not follow too from the marketability of money that no monopoly price of the sort Rothbard envisages can emerge from a monopoly of supply? After all, one could say that the buyers' money "can move elsewhere" when the monopolist tries to charge a monopoly price, especially given that money is the non-specific asset *par excellence*, by definition. Yet the theory of monopoly price, as understood by Rothbard and others, implies that such non-specificity does not prevent monopoly pricing.

This tension suggests that there is something wrong about Rothbard's view, but it does not pinpoint what the issue is exactly. The essential weakness in the thesis of the necessity of socialism to lower non-specific factor prices should be clear, however. This thesis invites the question: for what price could non-specific factors move into other firms and industries under partial monopsony? The claim suggests that the prices the factor owners can charge elsewhere are a given, "independent variable" that has nothing to do with the pattern of monopolistic action under examination. And yet the well-known insights about the price relationship between substitute goods (Rothbard, 1962, pp. 280–288), combined with the distinctively Austrian "law of costs," imply that this is not the case.

Böhm-Bawerk (1930, pp. 223–234) developed the view that costs, in the sense of money expenses, are ultimately determined by consumers' preferences so that the determination of relative prices has to be entirely driven by consumers in the market. In the absence of obstacles, arbitrage aligns the prices of the products with their costs throughout the economy: this is the common knowledge shared by classical and pre-classical economists. But where do the costs come from? For Böhm-Bawerk as well as later Austrians, there is no such thing as a "natural price" derived from a somewhat exogenous cost of production. Capitalists who want to keep operations going in whatever industry must advance payment to factor owners at prices high enough that they do not go elsewhere. The price the factor owners can obtain elsewhere reflects the bids of other capitalists. And the most that each capitalist can profitably pay in a particular stage of a process is determined by what the capitalists at the next stage are ready to pay, which is in turn determined ultimately by what consumers are ready to pay for the final product of these factors in this branch. Capitalists everywhere compete for the use of these factors and the whole arbitrage process then determines costs of production as imputed backward from consumption goods prices, not the other way around. Hence, the height of the bids for factors of production anywhere at the beginning of a stage depends on the expected income from the sale of their products received at the end of the stage, which is ultimately determined by consumer choices.

What is missing when Rothbard tells us that non-specific factors can simply go elsewhere when a monopsonist attempts to bid down their prices is the following insight: since a grant of monopoly-monopsony may distort the pattern of spending on various products[16] beyond the one produced by the monopolist, the upper limit on the capitalists' bids for the factors of production "elsewhere" may be a different price than it would be absent the grant.

Indeed, what happens on the side of the buyers of a product when a monopolist produces and sells less than he could have if he had been happy to earn a "normal" income only? Let us assume first that the demand schedule above the free-market price is inelastic, for even though this is not a necessary condition for such a decision to pay off, it certainly cannot hurt. In such a case, the pattern of spending by the firm's clients is altered in such a way that they are going to spend more on the product they have to pay a monopoly price for and less on other products than they would have otherwise. This means that their demand schedules for those other goods are lower. Therefore, their prices tend to be lower and capitalist-entrepreneurs have fewer reasons to invest there than they would have had otherwise. In other words, the marginal revenue product schedules of the factors employed there were lower than otherwise. Now, if a factor used in the production of the product charged a monopoly price is also used in one or several of those sectors, its lower marginal revenue product schedules there affected its reservation demand here, in the first process (Méra, 2010, pp. 59–64). What it can earn "elsewhere" can be negatively influenced by the monopolistic pattern of action occurring here, via the spending shift of the final buyers of its products.

Insofar as there exists a tendency for the factors to command a lower price elsewhere because of these shifts, their reservation demand here is affected. Their supply schedule here becomes even less elastic below the free market price, with more room for a monopolistic-monopsonistic contraction and the establishment of a monopsony price than otherwise, reflecting the formation of a larger phenomenon, a monopoly price-gap. The fact that under monopoly-monopsony here they can earn less than they otherwise could here and elsewhere are two sides of the same pattern of action originating in the monopolistic grant. The less specific such a factor is, the higher the likelihood it will be in use in a branch where its marginal revenue product schedule must be lower because of the aforementioned shifts. This is why the non-specificity of a factor does not automatically shield its owners from the adverse effects of monopolistic-monopsonistic pressure. Depending on the direction of shifts in product spending, it can actually expose the owners to such effects.

On the other hand, what if the demand schedule for the good a monopolist produces remains elastic above the free-market price? A monopoly price then results in lower spending on the product (the monopolist, if successful, will correctly anticipate that this lower income is more than compensated by lower expenses). This means that the demand schedules for other goods are higher. Therefore, their prices tend to be higher and capitalist-entrepreneurs were justified in investing more there than they would have otherwise, which implies the marginal revenue product schedules of the factors used there are higher. If a factor used in the production of the product charged a monopoly price is also used in some or all of those sectors, its higher marginal revenue product schedules there affected its reservation demand here. This is a factor in the increase of the elasticity of its supply schedule to the monopsonist-monopolist, although the exclusion of competitors inherent in this monopsony position has the opposite effect.

This means is there is less room for a monopoly price-gap in such a case, although we cannot rule out this possibility, since the elasticity of the demand schedule for the monopolized product could still have decreased relative to the elasticity of the supply schedules of its factors of production in the relevant ranges. And there is even less room for the establishment of a monopsony price for the factor (a price which would be lower as a consequence of employers taking advantage of an absolute decrease of the elasticity of its supply schedule), although it remains possible. Here, non-specificity is a mitigating or even a shielding influence, but whether it is neutral or whether it increases monopolistic-monopsonistic pressure on the factors' prices depends on the direction of the shifts in spending on the products and on what goods those factors help produce.[17]

8 Conclusion

The possibility of lower non-specific factor prices as a consequence of grants of monopolistic privileges, deduced from Böhm-Bawerk's law of costs and the law of substitutes, suggests an anomaly in the history of economic thought that this paper was intended to identify and correct. The anomaly is that the authors who did not follow Böhm-Bawerk's lead in some important matters have insisted there exists significant room for monopsony distortions in the economy, while the authors who placed Böhm-Bawerk on a pedestal tend to dismiss concerns about monopsony, even when it is conceived as a manifestation of interventionism. This is an anomaly insofar as the first group tended to emanate from the Marshallian partial equilibrium tradition (Robinson), which naturally lead to taking factor prices outside a particular branch of production as given, while the second endorsed an insight that could have led them to think of those factor prices as dependent upon actions within that same branch. In other words, taking Böhm-Bawerk's law of costs seriously could have led them to realize that there is more room for monopsony distortions in a market economy than a Marshallian approach suggests. And yet, by and large, the opposite occurred.

If monopsony theorists, and especially the new wave of scholars among them, have been able to advance monopsony theory as empirically relevant, it is because they took a completely different approach. Pure and perfect competition is used as a benchmark status for welfare comparisons, so any deviation from it originating from any source can be considered an issue in need of corrective action. A less-than-perfectly-elastic supply schedule for a factor of production, for instance, can be taken as a manifestation of an employer's market power and a sign of inefficient resource allocation.

What has been argued above is that this way of conceiving of the issue is a dead end, in that it compares real world situations with an impossible ideal, so that mainstream monopsony theory, old and new, lacks a realistic criterion to distinguish between monopsony and its absence, i.e. between monopsony prices and competitive prices. This is the application to monopsony of the fundamental Austrian criticism of the perfect-versus-imperfect competition paradigm, which lies at the heart of mainstream monopsony theories. On the other hand, this paper has also challenged the Austrian view that any monopsony theory should therefore be considered at best of small empirical relevance and at worst as an absurd piece of theorizing.

On the contrary, once we endorse a causal-realist outlook in the Mises-Rothbard tradition – the view that human action occurs in discrete steps, that the supply schedules of factors of production must always be less than perfectly elastic, and that they can be made less elastic as a result of coercion – we naturally arrive at an Austrian theory of a monopoly price-gap, with monopoly and monopsony prices as two features of the same phenomenon. A monopoly price-gap and a corresponding monopoly gain can emerge when the everyday arbitrage activities of capitalist-entrepreneurs throughout society's structure of production are hampered in such a way that the demand schedules for products and the supply schedules of their factors of production are made less elastic as a consequence of coercion.

The possibilities of such distortions are more widespread in a market economy than Mises and Rothbard's writings on monopoly price theory suggest, for two reasons. First, the requirement they put forward for the formation of a monopoly price – demand schedules for products made inelastic – is valid only in the context of decisions over an already-produced stock of a good. In the realm of production decisions, there is no need for demand schedules to become inelastic for contraction to pay. This is because maximizing gross income is not the relevant consideration. Expenses are compared with gross incomes, so that an expected falling gross income is an insufficient reason not to contract activity. Contraction and its outcome – lower factor prices and higher product prices – can therefore be a more widespread phenomenon than the inelasticity-of-demand-based theory suggests. Second, non-specificity of the factors of production does not necessarily protect their owners from monopolistic-monopsonistic pressure, since the amount they can earn outside of the monopolized branch of industry can be negatively affected as an indirect consequence of that very same grant.

Finally, if coercion-induced changes in the elasticity of demand schedules for products and supply schedules for their factors are the decisive requirements for monopsony prices and a monopoly price-gap to emerge, it immediately follows that the removal of those grants allows wage rates and the marginal revenue product of labor factors to be as close as possible at any given time. A thorough analysis of minimum wage legislation is beyond the scope of this paper. Yet while such price controls can conceivably mitigate the impact of monopoly-monopsony on factor prices – if they are not set above and remain below (prone to change) market-clearing prices – their lack of flexibility and adaptability to various factor market and situational changes render them rather inadequate, as compared with the simple abolition of those polices.

Notes

1 See, for example, von Wieser (1927, pp. 218–220), Clark (1915, p. 76), and Davenport (1913, pp. 481–482).

2 Applying this insight to Manning's approach, which explains less-than-perfect elasticity through search costs, we only need to realize that there is no possible world in which they can disappear. Search costs exist because no one is omniscient. If we argue that welfare losses result from this lack of omniscience, we might as well claim that having to pay any price at all for anything entails tremendous welfare losses as compared with the state of eternal bliss prevailing in the absence of scarcity.

3 See Rothbard (1962, pp. 661–704) for the justification of his thesis that only aggressive violence or the threat thereof implies a market situation that is distinguishable from a "competitive" market environment.

4 As Mises (1949; p. 380) adds: "In the same way in which governments restrict competition in order to improve the position of privileged sellers, they can also restrict competition for the benefit of privileged buyers. Again and again governments have put an embargo on the export of certain commodities. Thus by excluding foreign buyers they have aimed at lowering the domestic price. But such a lower price is not a counterpart of monopoly prices."

5 To be sure, a monopsonist can take advantage of the exclusion of its competitors in the sense that any buyer, given a market supply schedule, is better off when the market demand schedule and equilibrium price are lower. But the gain here is not specific to its situation as a monopsonist. By the same token, the monopolist can benefit from the exclusion of competitors in the sense that any seller, given a market demand schedule, is better off when the market supply schedule is lower and the equilibrium price consequently higher. But this is not specific to its situation as a monopolist, and occurs regardless of the elasticity of the demand schedule.

6 Even here, speaking of a monopsony price is problematic because in socialism, there are no such things as market prices, be they competitive, monopolistic, or monopsonistic.

7 Again, it is true that the equilibrium price will be lower as a consequence of the exclusion of competing would-be buyers. But the gain involved is not specifically a monopsonistic gain. In fact, far from aiding in somehow restricting demand, a simple supply and demand analysis shows that the monopsonist buys higher quantities than it would have bought if its competitors were not excluded.

8 To avoid any misunderstanding, at the time Böhm-Bawerk was writing, the word "monopsony" was not yet in use. Economists were only speaking of a "monopoly of demand," hence the expression "monopolist" here, not to be confused with the monopolist as a seller.

9 One could then wonder if it makes any sense to speak of "monopoly" and "monopsony" instead simply using "monopoly" for all related examples. However, in the structure of production, not everyone can be both a buyer and a seller in his capacity as a producer, and not everyone can be a capitalist. Some will have to be sellers of original factor services since production processes must use some original factors of production (land and labor). As a consequence, it still makes sense to maintain the distinction between buyers' monopolies and sellers' monopolies because some people can only be granted a monopoly of supply. The symmetry is with the situation of a consumer-monopsonist who cannot be a monopolist. They have one thing in common, which is that they cannot be both monopolists and monopsonists, while capitalists are both insofar as at least some of their would-be competitors are forcefully excluded from the relevant markets.

10 Or whatever cause actually results in a "normal" price-gap. See Mises (1949, pp. 521–533) for the view that such an "originary" interest rate is determined by time preferences.

11 Because error is an ever-present possibility in the realm of human action (Rothbard, 1962, p. 7), there is no reason that equilibrium, especially general equilibrium, must occur. The assumption is made only as a way to analytically disentangle various sources of discrepancies in the rates of return we can observe in an actual market economy.

12 The assumption is that one or several sellers have been given a license to sell chocolate, so that no one else is allowed to. This is an explicit monopoly grant. However, it should be clear that any other regulation which, in effect, drives competitors out of the market is not fundamentally different.

13 Incidentally, this means that the standard distinction between the case in which labor allocation and pricing is affected by monopsony (Borjas, 2013, pp. 187–194) and the case in which it is affected by monopoly in the market for the product (Borjas, 2013, pp. 194–197) does not hold in our framework.

14 It follows that, for the analysis of production decisions, the Mises-Rothbard-inspired theory of monopoly price-gap, with monopoly and monopsony prices as its symmetric components, is actually more similar to the mainstream one than Mises and Rothbard's explicit discussions of monopoly prices and monopsony would have seemed to imply, with the important difference that these discussions have no room for a perfect competition benchmark.

15 In this respect, one would expect that the possibility of lowered wages under monopsony-monopoly pressure would mostly concern very specific, highly qualified jobs, as Block and Barnett (2009, pp. 73–74) claim.

16 As Rothbard (1962, p. 905) puts it, "the consumers are only fully responsible for their demand curve on the free market; and only this demand curve can be fully treated as an expression of their voluntary choice."

17 In this paper I essentially focus on factor prices and production in a branch where a monopoly-monopsony grant exists to explain how a monopoly price gap can arise. Other industries are dealt with only insofar as the grant indirectly affects the marginal revenue product schedules of the same factors there, leaving more or less room for a monopoly price gap (and therefore a monopsony price) in the first. However, other indirect consequences in the pricing process are to be expected and can be felt virtually anywhere in the economy. For a more complete analysis, see Méra (2010). In short, grants of monopoly-monopsony privileges to capitalists imply a prevailing tendency for lower land and labor prices and aggregate income than under free competition – even though some of them may command higher prices – the overall distribution of incomes being altered to the disadvantage of those classes of factors. In addition, overall output is reduced insofar as some units of those factors leave production altogether in the face of declining prices for their services, while the allocation of the remaining units is distorted to the detriment of the bulk of consumers.

References

Ashenfelter, Orley C., Henry Farber, and Michael R. Ransom. 2010. "Labor Market Monopsony." *Journal of Labor Economics* 28 (2): 203–210.

Bellante, Don. 2007. "The Non Sequitur in the Revival of Monopsony Theory." *Quarterly Journal of Austrian Economics* 10 (2): 15–24.

Blair, Roger D., and Jeffrey L. Harrison. 2010. *Monopsony in Law and Economics*. Cambridge: Cambridge University Press.

Block, Walter E., and William Barnett. 2009. "Monopsony Theory." *American Review of Political Economy* 7 (1/2): 67–109.

Boal, William M., and Michael R. Ransom. 1930. *The Positive Theory of Capital*. Trans. William Smart. New York: G. E. Stechert & Co.

———. 1997. "Monopsony in the Labor Market." *Journal of Economic Literature* 35 (1): 86–112.

Böhm-Bawerk, Eugen von. 1962. "Control of Economic Law?" In *Shorter Classics of Eugen von Böhm-Bawerk, Vol. 1*. South Holland, IL: Libertarian Press, pp. 139–199.

Borjas, George. 2013. *Labor Economics*. 6th ed. New York: McGraw-Hill Education.

Burdett, Kenneth, and Dale T. Mortensen. 1998. "Wage Differentials, Employer Size, and Unemployment." *International Economic Review* 39 (2): 257–273.

Chamberlin, Edward. 1933. *The Theory of Monopolistic Competition*. Cambridge, MA: Harvard University Press.

Clark, John B. 1915. *Essential of Economic Theory*. New York: Palgrave MacMillan.

Council of Economic Advisers. 2016. "Labor Market Monopsony: Trends, Consequences, and Policy Responses." White House Issue Brief, October 2016. https://obamawhitehouse.archives.gov/sites/default/files/page/files/20161025_monopsony_labor_mrkt_cea.pdf.

Davenport, Herbert J. 1913. *The Economics of Enterprise*. New York: Palgrave Macmillan.

Demsetz, Harold. 1969. "Information and Efficiency: Another Viewpoint." *Journal of Law & Economics* 12 (1): 1–22.

Fetter, Frank A. 1915. *Economic Principles*. New York: The Century Co.

Friedman, Milton. 1976. *Price Theory*. Chicago: Aldine Publishing Company.

Irwin, Neil. 2016. "A New Movement in Liberal Economics That Could Shape Hillary Clinton's Agenda." *The New York Times*, November 4. www.nytimes.com/2016/11/06/upshot/monopsony-liberal-economics-policy-hillary-clintons-agenda.html?smid=fb-share&_r=1.

Kuhn, Peter. 2004. "Is Monopsony the Right Way to Model Labor Markets? A Review of Alan Manning's Monopsony in Motion." *International Journal of the Economics of Business* 11 (3): 369–378.

Machlup, Fritz. 1952. The Political Economy of Monopoly: Business, Labor, and Government Policies. Baltimore: The John Hopkins Press.

Manning, Alan. 2003. *Monopsony in Motion: Imperfect Competition in Labor Markets*. Princeton, NJ: Princeton University Press.

———. 2006. "A Generalised Model of Monopsony." *The Economic Journal* 116 (508): 84–100.

———. 2008. "Monopsony." In *The New Palgrave Dictionary of Economics*, Second Edition, eds. Steven N. Durlauf and Lawrence E. Blume. Palgrave Macmillan. doi:10.1057/9780230226203.1136

———. 2011. "Imperfect Competition in the Labor Market." In David Card and Orley Ashenfelter, eds., *Handbook of Labor Economics*, Vol. 4B. Amsterdam: Elsevier, pp. 973–1041.

Méra, Xavier. 2010. "Factor Prices Under Monopoly." *Quarterly Journal of Austrian Economics* 13 (1): 48–70.

———. 2015. "A Note on the Limits to Monopoly Pricing." In *The Next Generation of Austrian Economics: Essays in Honor of Joseph T. Salerno*, eds. Per Bylund and David Howden. Auburn, AL: Mises Institute, pp. 123–136.

Mises, Ludwig von. 1998. "Monopoly Prices." *Quarterly Journal of Austrian Economics* 1 (2): 1–28.

———. 1998 [1949]. *Human Action: A Treatise on Economics*. Scholar' ed. Auburn, AL: Ludwig von Mises Institute.

Robinson, Joan. 1969 [1933]. *The Economics of Imperfect Competition*. 2nd ed. New York: Macmillan St Martin's Press.

Rothbard, Murray N. 1993 [1962]. *Man, Economy, and State: A Treatise on Economic Principles*. Auburn, AL: Ludwig von Mises Institute.

———. 2006 [1970]. *Power and Market: Government and the Economy*. Auburn, AL: Ludwig von Mises Institute.

Wieser, Friedrich von. 1927. *Social Economics*. Trans. A. Ford Hinrichs. New York: Adelphi Company.

8 Costs and pricing

An Austro-Post-Keynesian synthesis?

Mateusz Machaj

Post-Keynesian challenges to neoclassical marginalism

The fundamental feature of neoclassical price theory is the U-shaped average cost curve and its twin curve, the U-shaped marginal cost curve. Firms and producers seem to automatically respond to the existing marginal revenue curve crossing the marginal cost curve at a certain point. The "optimal" choice for the individual firm may be established under the famous MR=MC equation. The reason why the company does not boost production further is the disappearance of falling marginal cost, and also of average cost. As costs start to rise, the L-shaped curve reaches its lowest point and becomes the U-shaped curve, which stops the firm from expanding further. The boundary is set and the firm loses previously beneficial economics of scale, which turn into diseconomies of scale (Eiteman, 1947, p. 911).

A further feature mainstream price theory is revealed in the mostly arbitrary distinction between long- and short-run production. Fixed costs are not really relevant for immediate price formation, since they have already been covered. The marginal cost curve crossing the marginal revenue curve seems to allow for the highest possible profit (or lowest possible loss). Often this point is presented using mathematical language, where derivatives allow for local maxima in accordance with graphical presentations. In the short run, only variable costs matter. Apparently, fixed costs seem to be at the same time sunk costs, borne in the past and with no relevance for current decision making.

Another side feature of this approach is its treatment of prices as parameters resulting from the interaction of other underlying factors. In the choice of various theoretical frameworks, prices (which always respond to changing conditions) can either be central in the decision making process, or be more like end results of the market process. Despite their recognized importance, however, prices are seen in the neoclassical framework as almost completely passive final outcomes. In other words, prices are determinate rather than determinates. One questionable consequence of this view is the high flexibility of prices – which no doubt exists in some markets, but is not a universal phenomenon. Prices are not perfectly flexibly or adjustable once surrounding factors change. As a result, it is suggested in the Post-Keynesian literature that economic theory could start with a division into flex-price markets as opposed to fix-price markets, which also makes for a distinction between markets corresponding to the traditional theory and markets corresponding to other approaches (Kenyon, 1978, p. 43).

The core of the challenge to the above version of marginalism comes from various empirical studies related to assessments of business and management practices. These studies show that managers working in different industries do not act according to marginal principles. Naturally, in and of itself this may be a completely irrelevant argument, because the responses of the people polled in these studies may not be accurate. Just as people may deny the influence of gravity, so it may be with the case of accurately articulating the influence of marginal thinking on economic decisions. Denial may be an equivocal quibble about some unknown factor, or it may be unclearly and imprecisely defined by the questionnaire, yet contribute significantly to the results. Nevertheless, detailed inquiries into business practices and the workings of price setting are actually instructive for seeing how prices work from the perspective of a single enterprise (on cost studies, see Lee, 1986, pp. 411–421). An individual company appears not to obey neoclassical principles because its actual curves, based on real data, are shaped a certain way, rather than because of free-floating beliefs expressed in a vacuum. In many of the firms that were questioned, the curves were not in a typical marginal U-shaped style (Eiteman and Guthrie, 1952, p. 837).

The central observation of these studies is that prices are "administered" by firms. They are "fixed" in their business plans based on the costs incurred in production. This is not to say, though, that companies are acting in a "monopolistic" manner in the neoclassical sense. Rather, the whole neoclassical notion of monopoly and monopolization loses its value and becomes of marginal importance (Hall and Hitch, 1939, pp. 30–31). What matters in business calculations are average total costs, which include, besides variable costs, fixed costs that do not vary with the amount of product created. Firms apply a markup over those total costs (Fabiani et al., 2006, p. 41). In the neoclassical approach, the marginal cost curve dictates the decision of how much to produce and which price to set, whereas fixed costs play no part in the marginal cost curve.[1]

Yet the reality of pricing seems to run against the practice of ignoring fixed costs. In practice, marginal costs – costs incurred because of increased output – are not the decisive element. This is not because entrepreneurs do not know what "marginal cost" means, but because they price their products based on the relevant factors of production. Various empirical surveys confirm that total costs are considered in pricing, but not variable costs, and therefore the whole notion of marginal cost seems to be disconnected from the pricing process (Shim and Sudit, 1995, pp. 37–38).

How does pricing happen? A firm starts off with an accounting calculation of the necessary expenses to produce a product, say, running shoes. The variable costs are measured (leather, rubber, etc.), but also costs which must be covered no matter what the level of production is. These costs come to be known as fixed because they do not vary with output. Next, assuming a particular level of production, average cost is assessed, say at 50 dollars per pair of shoes at current capacity. On top of this there is an additional markup to be earned by the company, for example, an overhead of 100% percent, so that the shoes are sold at 100 dollars per pair. Fifty dollars of this is a money surplus that stays within the company in return for adding something productive to the market (organizing the factors, allocating them through the passage of time, etc.). As an aside, there are some differences between Post-Keynesian approaches to pricing, especially involving the concepts of: mark-up pricing, full-cost pricing, normal-cost pricing, historic normal-cost pricing and target return pricing. Yet as Lavoie argues (2014, p. 157), there are no substantial differences between these five variants. All rely on the idea that companies are focused on their total (not marginal) costs of production. The variances come from dissimilarities in the accounting definitions used in business calculations, which from an economic standpoint are of no importance.

The notion of cost-based pricing should not be confused with a deterministic classical doctrine in which prices are thought to be formed almost automatically based on the past costs of production (actually, we should be careful about assessing the classical school this way – it simply did not go into these issues beyond the general intuitive level). Even though costs are part of business projects, prices are not simply cost determined. There is no mechanical transmission of costs into prices. Rather, they are "strategically" determined in the decision process of the company, which is cost-focused in managing allocations and price setting (Shapiro and Sawyer, 2003, pp. 355–356).[2]

One of the main points of the Post-Keynesian critique of neoclassicism is to emphasize the fact that prices are not constantly readjusting, and that sellers of final goods adjust inventories first and prices second (Eiteman, 1947, pp. 916–917). Once goods are purchased in higher quantities, the decision is made to increase inventories and prepare additional stocks to offer to consumers. In the case of decreased demand for products, unsold inventories will pile up, and fewer goods will be ordered by the seller. If this state of affairs continues, prices will also adjust. Prices can fall to clear the inventories, and the same is true of goods ordered from producers. Both costs and prices will eventually adjust, with specific lags along the way. The typical business practice is to periodically review prices, and after such a review (which is not done on an everyday basis, but only rarely), sometimes adjust them (Melmies, 2010, pp. 450–453). Reviews and readjustments can be spread throughout a whole year, but some empirical studies suggest that the adjustments are concentrated around one month, such as January, in which most of the contract reassessments are done (see e.g. Martins, 2005, p. 25).

Firms in general are not operating at what we might call "full capacity." They make decisions alongside generally downward-sloping average cost curves, and marginal costs that are roughly constant in the spectrum of decisions. There is always room for reserved extra capacity in case inventory adjustments must be triggered. The main argument for rejecting the typical U-shaped neoclassical MC = MR analysis is the observation that firms do not operate in the face of rising marginal costs (Lavoie, 2014, pp. 147, 150).

Post-Keynesians argue that prices are fixed, though it would be more accurate to say that prices are expected to be fixed for a chosen amount of time at some future date. We may slightly clarify this approach by pointing out that producers undertaking an investment process need not assume that current prices will prevail under future circumstances. They do not even have to assume that particular cost levels will stay the same. The vital point is to keep the business plan in sight – or actually, to use a much better expression, to keep the business canvas in sight (Blank 2013). A business plan is a fixed and equilibrated approach to decision making. It assumes prior knowledge of a particular product with known average costs of production and revenues at particular turnover levels. In practice, business plans are never executed, however. The reality of uncertainty quickly verifies the plan, and the efficiency of the market allows for adjustments to take place. Sellers adjust both products and monetary prices. Instead of talking about business plans, it is much better then to talk about the business canvas and the ability of the enterprise to respond properly both to consumer preferences about the product (its functioning included) and the monetary surroundings of the firm: the costs and prices of competition.

A neoclassical response?

Neoclassical economists are well aware of Post-Keynesian criticism. Their general response is to claim that there is no inherent conflict between how businesses function and how economic theory describes the tendencies of market activity. In other words, it is always possible to use the supply and demand framework. The Post-Keynesian argument is that if customers decrease purchases at the same time, firms will probably increase inventories. There is nothing in the supply and demand framework to prevent us from agreeing with this point, which can be explained either as a form of reservation demand or as a consciously chosen optimal market surplus. Also, the long-run change can be shown through supply and demand curves that change their shapes and elasticities in order to conform to the environment.

Supply and demand schedules are one way to conceptualize parties' preferences about potential trades and bargains. There is nothing specifically neoclassical about this. Things become a little more problematic once we try to answer the MC=MR challenge. If firms appear to price their products based on average costs of production, can the scheme of marginal costs and revenues be defended at all? It appears so, but the argument may be somewhat surprising – the neoclassical defense is that the marginalist description leads to the exact same results as the ones presented in the markup pricing approach. In order to arrive at these results various redefinitions are necessary. Langlois makes a point persuasively while developing a marginalist model with inventories included:

> The model developed below [in Langlois's paper] transforms the neoclassical vision of the firm to integrate the holding of inventory as a strategic response of the manufacturing firm. This approach relies on the assumption that consumers respond to the availability of commodities, and firms hold inventory to endow their output with this characteristic. Thus production and pricing decisions will take explicit account of a firm's desired or target level of inventory. The model developed in this paper is descriptive of the particular level

> that a firm could choose for target inventory, but it does not make explicit the dynamic process of adjustment of production and price that must take place to maintain inventory at its target level. The hypothesis presented and empirically tested in what follows is that the level of target inventory is chosen together with its selling price so that profit is maximized over the time it will take to sell the inventory. The firm achieves this goal by maximizing profit *per unit of time*, optimization which generates a formula for optimal markup over the *average cost* of goods in inventory, where average cost is the average production cost of the goods themselves. Thus, by transforming the neoclassical vision of the firm to integrate inventory, direct cost pricing is predicted using marginalist terms.
>
> (Langlois, 1989, pp. 129–130; emphases in original)

A counterargument could begin with Occam's Razor – if the end result of the revised approach is the same, why take a longer route? Besides, as Langlois explains, the model excludes the explicit elements of the adjustment process, the heart of everyday market adaptation. However, we will not judge here whether it is possible to defend the neoclassical position. Instead, we turn to the Austrian perspective on the problem.

An Austrian take on markup pricing

Even though the Post-Keynesian criticism may create potential problems for the neoclassical version of marginalism, this need not be the case with respect to Austrian theory, which at times is poles apart from neoclassical analysis. Actually, in some cases the Post-Keynesian contribution to price theory strengthens Austrian arguments about the market process, especially in those aspects where Post-Keynesians are anti-neoclassical.

A) Out of equilibrium

First, consider the question market equilibration and stabilizing tendencies. Post-Keynesians argue that markets do not clear in the neoclassical sense: prices are not constantly responding to changing supply and demand conditions (or actually, as neoclassicals would say, within the framework supply and demand curves have specific elasticities). Perfect market-clearing equilibrium would be the case with consistent movements towards equilibrium in the non-monetary sense, where valuations of consumer preferences are almost perfectly imputed back onto the factors of production. Two forces working from opposite sides of the market – subjective utility and physical limitations on supply (marginal rates of substitution and marginal rates of transformation) – would create constantly shifting prices as adjustable parameters. With all the data frozen, a final equilibrium could be reached (whatever that means).

Since the data change all the time, the various adjustments performed by non-omniscient humans are imperfect. Completely flexible prices could still miss the target, which under uncertain conditions may generate more chaos than more stability. We could never be sure that automatic and instantaneous adjustments happened in the proper direction and did not result in the piling up of mistakes on mistakes. The rational method for market participants is to create optimal price stickiness and price rigidity with rational idle capacity (Salerno, 2010, pp. 192–193). For every market the variable of elasticity is unique and is only discovered as the process goes on. In case of a stock market, prices are very flexible. In case of retail markets, prices are more fixed and the appropriate responses are revealed over longer periods of time, since the immediate "clearing" of the market – that is, emptying the shelf – may be a poor economizing decision. The discovery procedure of competition also allows us to find the proper price elasticity.

All this relates to the concept of the plain state of rest – a moment when market transactions cease and people are no longer interested in trading. This concept of equilibration was developed by Mises (1966, p. 245). In no sense should this point be seen as either a full equilibrium or a final state of rest with complete adjustment of costs to prices. There is no imaginary construct involved. "Plain state" means that under current circumstances there is simply no consensus between the trading parties that an exchange should take place. Either the market is closed, or there are no more customers willing to purchase the product at the current price. In order to attract more customers, the price would have to fall. This is not guaranteed, though: the only potential buyers and sellers interested in trading were dissatisfied with the price and believed it to be either too high or too low at its previous point. Hence, the preferences of sellers who decide not to boost sales further by lowering their prices fit well with the notion of a temporary plain state of rest (Mises, 1966, p. 246).

To relate the notion of "rest" to the above discussion: marginalist neoclassicals seem to talk about the final state of rest – when future prices are in full accordance with the costs existing throughout all industries, including interest payments. Post-Keynesian reservations are the result of a plain state of rest perspective. In the immediate run, in everyday transactions, sellers make inventory adjustments based on their capacities and their business canvas. As decisions become more incorrect, further mistakes are capitalized into the project. The adjustment toward a (never attainable) final state of rest is a constant process that includes temporary optimal lags. Therefore, despite the fact that changing supply and demand conditions do not produce equilibrium prices as conventionally defined, economic reasoning can rely on the realistic momentary equilibrium of the plain state of rest for analyzing the pricing process.

B) Execution of economic calculation

A second point, related to the first, has to do with the economic calculation debate. Mises's challenge was centered on the concept of a common denominator properly employed in order to rationally assess production projects (Mises, 1990). This occurs ex ante, when speculative business decisions are made, and ex post, when profits and losses are capitalized into the current market value of capital.

Mises's critique focuses on the lack of a properly functioning price system in which appraisements are at the heart of economic decision making (Salerno, 1990, p. 44). Post-Keynesian descriptions of how prices are formed, instituted, and "fixed" by firms are stories about the important role these organizations play in setting monetary values. The "administration" of prices in relation to their costs of production and overall market demand is an essential part of the market process. It is subjected to entrepreneurial decision making, with each entrepreneur constantly trying to hit the "right" prices with sufficient markups; this requires active judgment as opposed to passive alertness (McCaffrey, 2015). Prices in themselves are not automatically produced by underlying conditions. They are "set" by competing entrepreneurs, and further subjected to critical consumer judgment and to the competitive pressures of rivals. The inclusion of the costs of production in business calculations is actually the inclusion of the whole social appraisement process involving other competitive bidders and other possible ways of employing the factors.[3] Part of the empirical research on pricing by managers actually confirms this view: managers give reasons for not raising prices that include fear of competition and a preference for higher turnover (Machlup, 1946, p. 545).

While discussing the impossibility of socialism, Mises nowhere attempts to argue that the main problem with market socialism is the insufficient speed of price adjustments because of changing supply and demand conditions (as argued by Hayek, 1940, p. 135). Rather, the crucial argument for Mises is about the lack of competitive appraisement due to the abolition of financial and managerial markets. Markets cannot be "played," not because prices adjust over a long time (Mises, 1966, pp. 706–709), but because under central ownership there is no true competition among entrepreneurial assessments of resources. Competitive planning – actually, competitive canvasing – is substituted for bureaucratic planning. Part of this story may have something to do with optimal price rigidity and price adjustments based on entrepreneurial expectations, but this is never more than part of the story. Competition is also not homogenous. New ways of producing things do not appear uniformly in the market and affect all firms to the same extent. There is much heterogeneity in markets, both in the ability to reduce costs and in the field of product diversity. The point is further strengthened by the Post-Keynesian reference to the "Schumpeterian" type of competition (Lavoie, 2014, p. 127).

Prices are not phenomena straightforwardly reducible to other underlying and determining factors, for example, physical factors (Huerta de Soto, 2010, pp. 206–207). Surpluses and shortages are not simply calculated by measuring physical quantities being added to a pile, or that are removed from one. Instead, they are assessed in comparison to already-existing prices and estimations of the prices that could have been formed if the market was not centrally controlled. Therefore, price-setting and price-formation on the part of entrepreneurs are the driving forces of the markets. They have to be placed within the scope of economic reasoning, and cannot be reduced to alternative other forms of imputation, for example, "value imputation" or imputation based on physical characteristics (Herbener, 1996).

Another theme similar to questions of equilibration relates to the problem of price coordination as opposed to plan coordination. As Salerno argues, market developments should be seen in the spirit of W. H. Hutt's analysis, which emphasizes price coordination (Salerno, 2010, p. 182). In contrast, plan coordination is a concept mainly developed in the Walrasian tradition, where the data themselves equilibrate the market. Price coordination, however, emphasizes the entrepreneur's role, in that this view does not see prices as intermediate steps toward an equilibrium fully reducible to other variables (such as utility, scarcity, etc.). This approach to prices inherently leads to Lange's perspective, in which prices are pure parameters equalizing and balancing out other, more relevant and fundamental elements (Lange, 1956, p. 89). However, contrary to this view, prices are themselves fundamentals, and are not reducible to anything less than human creativity and entrepreneurship.

Waters articulates the problem this way:

> Suppose that we define an essential element in any firm called "entrepreneurship." This cannot be bought on the market, but is a specialised and personal attribute of each individual in the community. A firm exists when an individual employs his entrepreneurial ability. But since the amount of entrepreneurial ability possessed by a man is an attribute specific to him, the production function will vary from one person to another.
>
> (Walters, 1963, p. 4)

In other words, as Post-Keynesians argue, prices are not set by "invisible forces" or fictitious omniscient auctioneers (Lavoie, 2014, p. 156; Melmies, 2010, p. 455). Frederic Lee, one of the most prominent Post-Keynesians, uses the concept of "sequential acts of production," which firms use to finance plans for growth and expansion. Part of these plans has to do with coordinating prices and avoiding complete elasticity, which would complicate things (Lavoie, 2016, pp. 3–4). In Lee's words, "competition is pervasive but not pernicious or destructive" (Lee, 2011, p. 18). Entrepreneurs do not equate marginal costs and revenues, at least, not unless we allow for a sufficient amount of redefinition and restatement in order to make these terms conform to reality.

C) The imputation process

A third point involves tracing the challenges of the imputation process. The central but broad idea behind marginal economics is that prices are determined by marginal utilities of goods. During the development of marginal economics it has sometimes been argued that people often pay prices for goods that are even lower than their marginal utilities would suggest (indicating a consumer surplus). In this view, marginalism works perfectly in the case of closed markets with no supply responses (such as markets for rare paintings, an example that was mentioned already in the work of David Ricardo). Yet once the analysis shifts to markets for reproducible goods, prices can fall below the limits set by marginal utility.

Demand becomes less decisive and important, and becomes only a limiting final factor.

Examples can be given for various goods. Take the hypothetical case of blue shirts, demand for which is much higher than for green shirts. Despite significant differences in demand, the prices of these two goods can generally be assumed to be the same. Adjustments mostly occur on the inventories side – there are more blue shirts in the warehouse, because higher consumer demand is expected. According to the overall market marginal utilities, the price of blue shirts could be higher (as higher marginal utility of shirts indicates that people would be inclined to pay a higher price than for green shirts).[4] Instead, sellers adjust the quantity available, not prices. In the standard case they could increase the prices of blue shirts, but if they do so they also create a profit opportunity for other sellers to step in and sell blue shirts for a lower price. Rivals can compete with entrepreneurs who raise prices precisely because costs are low enough to be comparable with green shirts. Hence, costs bring prices down to their levels. The same story can be told about sports jerseys and other types of products with similar price labels but significant differences in demand (we abstract here from branding that could independently increase market value).

The Post-Keynesian story seems to fit well in these examples. Yet do these cases prove that there are limitations to the marginalist approach? No, at least, not in light of Böhm-Bawerk's analysis of the law of costs and marginal utility (Böhm-Bawerk, 1962; Böhm-Bawerk, 2002). Marginal utility is a broad concept applicable to a wide variety of the products in the market. The basic examples of marginal utility suggest that a loss of the first unit does not entail the loss of the highest goal in the preference ranking. It simply means that the last unit must be used for that purpose, so that only the least important goal is lost. We "reproduce" a lost unit by reallocating the least valuable unit to the most valuable goal. As Böhm-Bawerk brilliantly demonstrated, the same applies to cases of reproducible goods. Once we lose a unit of some final good, we do not necessarily lose the particular utility currently attached to it. We simply reallocate other units – in the case of reproducible goods, we employ complementary factors of production to recreate the lost utility.

According to Böhm-Bawerk, the law of costs is actually an idea about marginal utility in disguise. In the shirts example, for instance, it does not matter that demand (and marginal utility) for blue shirts is higher relative to green shirts. What matters are the marginal utilities of other goods and services that would have to be given up in order to reproduce blue shirts. And since green and blue shirts require basically the same sacrifice, virtually the same marginal utility would have to be lost. If we lose the last-produced blue shirt, we only have to give up the production of the last green shirt and switch green dye for blue (just as when we lose the most important blue shirt we only have to use the marginal shirt as the first). Therefore we have a perfect explanation of why the costs of both shirts are the same – in the end, their marginal utilities of reproduction are the same.

It may be sensibly argued that Böhm-Bawerk's work anticipates some elements of the Post-Keynesian critique of neoclassicism. He elegantly demonstrated the connection between final prices and the costs of production expended during production. From the perspective of an individual producer, it may seem that sellers practice cost-based pricing. Yet at the same time, this fact in no way validates the broad marginalist point that costs themselves result from other potential investment avenues that could be undertaken. Once we look at the economy as a whole, we see price-based costing despite the fact that firms attempt to engage in cost-based pricing. A markup is simply another price for a productive service performed by a firm. Its value depends on the usefulness of organizing production subjected to the diminishing marginal utility. After all, markup levels depend on the quality of entrepreneurship and the amount of competition in the sector – important and valuable factors of production.

D) The relevance of fixed costs

A fourth point has to do with the appraisement process permeating all the factors of production, even the ones already devoted to production processes. So-called fixed costs do not automatically fall outside business calculations simply because they were already covered in the past. Fixed costs are not a synonym for sunk costs (Wang and Yang, 2001). They matter just as much as marginal costs. If only additional marginal costs mattered for pricing, then in most circumstances sellers would give away most goods they possess for free, since giving away existing supplies does not generate any costs (and the materials have already been paid for in the past, just as in the case of fixed costs!). The reason sellers never do this is that they know or expect that their goods will be more highly valued. They economize the goods they have by increasing their reservation demand, because they expect future values to increase beyond their momentary current levels. That is why their calculations include fixed costs also. Only parts of these costs covered are sunk and cannot be recovered. These are labeled as money wasted, and their current prices represent capitalized losses. Only once this occurs do costs already paid become irrelevant for current pricing.

Consequently, as long as there is potential economic value in existing, already-paid fixed costs, they are part of the pricing process (Machaj, 2013, p. 487). Potential economic value exists as long as there are valuable opportunities for factor employments. For example, an already-rented place of work is a fixed cost, since it does not vary with output. Yet it is not a loss simply because it was paid for in the past (simply put, it is not a sunk cost because it was covered in the past). If work is canceled the cost, or at least parts of it, can be recovered, say, by using the place for some other purpose (as a consumer good or by re-renting). Remember Böhm-Bawerk's law of costs. If the place can be rented by someone else, then it has an alternate utility. In order to justify not using it in its alternative capacity, the chosen use has to generate sufficient employment value. In this way the fixed costs of renting are part of normal everyday business calculations, even if the costs have already been paid. The past is definitely not irrelevant, so long as it does continue to play a role in value formation.

Mises does not mention the concepts of marginal revenue and marginal cost while discussing the basic functions of profits and losses (Mises, 1966, pp. 289–294). Instead, he focuses on total costs and total revenues from production. Yet at one point he does adopt the neoclassical view:

> If the entrepreneur is still free with regard to the project in question, because *he has not yet made any inconvertible investments for its realization*, it is average costs that count for him. But if he has already a vested interest in the line of business concerned, he sees things from the angle of additional costs to be expended. He who already owns a not fully utilized production aggregate *does not take into account average cost of production but marginal cost*. Without regard to the amount already expended for inconvertible investments he is merely interested in the question whether or not the proceeds from the sale of an additional quantity of products will exceed the additional cost incurred by their production.
>
> (Mises, 1966, p. 434; emphases added)

Mises appears to have fallen into the confusion that fixed costs (and past costs) are always sunk costs. Nevertheless, as we have shown above, past and committed costs are not yet what Mises calls in this paragraph *inconvertible investments*, at least, not until the losses are realized and capitalized. While making a decision about future output, entrepreneurs surely include the values of previously purchased capital equipment as long as there is potential value in them. This also includes past fixed costs, since they can be reallocated and economic value could be extracted from of them in one way or another.[5]

Conclusion

Post-Keynesian teachings on price formation are quite relevant for empirical descriptions of entrepreneurial choices. As we have seen, Post-Keynesians raise challenges to existing neoclassical versions of marginalism. At the same time, these criticisms do not pose a threat to the Austrian version of marginalism; rather, they strengthen some Austrian arguments about price formation, especially in regard to concepts such as coordination, calculation, and price setting. The Austrian version of marginalism can easily be enhanced by the real-world business practice of markup pricing. This practice neither undermines the backwards imputation of value nor changes the Böhm-Bawerkian notion of the law of costs working as an implication of marginal utility in disguise. Additionally, the concept of markup pricing enriches calculation arguments and the entrepreneurial approach to the theory of pricing.

Notes

1 Actually, fixed costs may be included in the marginal cost curve, but only at the beginning, that is, when moving from zero output to minimal production.
2 See also Herbener (2018).
3 Interestingly, Post-Keynesians also emphasize the process nature of the market, although from a somewhat different perspective than Austrians. For example, "Competition in classical economic thought from Adam Smith to Karl Marx is thus a process, not an

end-state. As reflected in investment and growth policies, competition involves the process by which resources are allocated – and, ultimately, income distributed – between social classes over time rather than just their allocation among individuals at a point in time. This emphasis reflects the preoccupation of the classical economists (particularly Ricardo and Marx) with the concept of capital and the process of capital accumulation" (Kenyon, 1978, pp. 44–45).

4 This would be the case if the supplies of both types of shirts were fixed and nonadjustable by the producers.

5 As Mises (somewhat) confirms in a discussion of fixed capital in the accounting books: "What is alone decisive is whether, after covering all current operating costs and after paying interest on the circulating capital, there is still so much left over from the gross revenue that something more can be reaped than an adequate return on the value which, after discontinuation of the enterprise, *the fixed capital would have in view of the possibility of using it for other production* (occasionally this will be only the scrap value of the machines and bricks). In that case the continuation of the enterprise is more profitable than its discontinuation. If the fixed capital has a higher book value than corresponds to its present and probable future earning capacity, then the book value must be lowered to that extent" (2003, p. 245, emphasis added). While discussing "inconvertible capital" Mises surely did not mean "all past capital," but only capital that was malinvested. The above quote confirms that fixed costs are part of investment (and pricing) considerations. They cannot be brushed aside in favor of a narrow focus on marginal costs.

References

Blank, Steven. 2013. "Why the Lean Start-Up Changes Everything." *Harvard Business Review*, May 2013 Issue, pp. 63–72.

Böhm-Bawerk, Eugen. 1962. "The Ultimate Standard of Value." In *Shorter Classics of Eugen von Böhm-Bawerk*. South Holland, IL: Libertarian Press.

———. 2002. "Value, Cost, and Marginal Utility." *Quarterly Journal of Austrian Economics* 5 (3): 37–79.

Eiteman, Wilford J. 1947. "Factors Determining the Location of the Least Cost Point." *American Economic Review* 37 (5): 910–918.

Eiteman, Wilford J., and Glenn E. Guthrie. 1952. "The Shape of the Average Cost Curve." *American Economic Review* 42 (5): 832–838.

Fabiani, Silvia, Martine Druant, Ignacio Hernando, Claudia Kwapil, Bettina Landau, Claire Loupias, Fernando Martins, Thomas Matha, Roberto Sabbatini, Harald Stahl, and Ad Stokman. 2006. "What Firms' Surveys Tell Us About Price-Setting Behavior in the Euro Area." MPRA Paper No. 808.

Hall, R. L., and C. J. Hitch. 1939. "Price Theory and Business Behaviour." *Oxford Economic Papers* 2: 12–45.

Hayek, Friedrich August. 1940. "Socialist Calculation: The Competitive 'Solution.'" *Economica* 7 (26): 125–149.

Herbener, Jeffrey. 1996. "Calculation and the Question of Arithmetic." *Review of Austrian Economics* 9 (1): 151–162.

———. 2018. "Time and the Theory of Cost." In Matthew McCaffrey, ed., *The Economic Theory of Costs: Foundations and New Directions*. Abingdon, UK: Routledge, pp. 147–166.

Huerta de Soto, Jesus. 2010. *Socialism, Economic Calculation and Entrepreneurship*. Cheltenham, UK: Edward Elgar.

Kenyon, Peter. 1978. "Pricing in Post-Keynesian Economics." *Challenge* 21 (3): 43–48.

Lange, Oskar. 1956. *On the Economic Theory of Socialism*. New York: McGraw-Hill.
Langlois, Catherine. 1989. "Markup Pricing Versus Marginalism: A Controversy Revisited." *Journal of Post Keynesian Economics* 12 (1): 127–151.
Lavoie, Marc. 2014. *Post-Keynesian Economics: New Foundations*. Cheltenham, UK: Edward Elgar.
———. 2016. "Frederic Lee and Post-Keynesian Pricing Theory." *Review of Political Economy* 28 (2): 169–186.
Lee, Fred. 1986. "Post Keynesian View of Average Direct Costs: A Critical Evaluation of the Theory and the Empirical Evidence." *Journal of Post Keynesian Economics* 8 (3): 400–424.
———. 2011. "Old Controversy Revisited: Pricing, Market Structure, and Competition." MPRA Working Paper.
Machaj, Mateusz. 2013. "Sunk Costs and Contestable Markets." *Quarterly Journal of Austrian Economics* 16 (4): 479–502.
Machlup, Fritz. 1946. "Marginal Analysis and Empirical Research." *American Economic Review* 36 (4): 519–554.
Martins, Fernando. 2005. "The Price Setting Behaviour of Portuguese Firms: Evidence From Survey Data." European Central Bank Working Papers Series no. 562.
McCaffrey, Matthew. 2015. "Economic Policy and Entrepreneurship: Alertness or Judgment?" In P. Bylund and D. Howden, eds., *The Next Generation of Austrian Economics: Essays in Honor of Joseph T. Salerno*. Auburn, AL: Ludwig von Mises Institute, pp. 183–199.
Melmies, Jordan. 2010. "New Keynesians Versus Post Keynesians on the Theory of Prices." *Journal of Post Keynesian Economics* 32 (3): 445–466.
Mises, Ludwig. 1966. *Human Action. A Treatise on Economics*. Chicago: Yale University Press.
———. 1990. *Economic Calculation in the Socialist Commonwealth*. Auburn, AL: Ludwig von Mises Institute.
———. 2003. *Epistemological Problems of Economics*. Auburn, AL: Ludwig von Mises Institute.
Salerno, Joseph. 1990. "Ludwig von Mises as Social Rationalist." *Review of Austrian Economics* 4: 26–54.
———. 2010. "The Concept of Coordination in Austrian Macroeconomics." In *Money, Sound and Unsound*. Auburn, AL: Ludwig von Mises Institute, pp. 181–197.
Shapiro, Nina, and Malcolm Sawyer. 2003. "Post Keynesian Price Theory." *Journal of Post Keynesian Economics* 25 (3): 355–365.
Shim, Eunsup, and Ephraim Sudit. 1995. "How Manufacturers Price Products." *Management Accounting* 76 (8): 37–39.
Walters, A. A. 1963. "Production and Cost Functions: An Econometric Survey." *Econometrica* 31 (1/2): 1–66.
Wang, Henry X., and Bill Z. Yang. 2001. "Fixed and Sunk Costs Revisited." *Journal of Economic Education* 32 (2): 178–185.

Part 5

Economic organization, entrepreneurship, and the firm

9 Austrian economics and transaction cost economics

Notes on a doubtful compatibility

Mihai-Vladimir Topan

Introduction

The transaction cost economics paradigm was born, in our opinion, as a byproduct of the perfect competition revolution.[1] When a highly abstract – and unrealistic – picture of the economic process occupies the central place in the toolbox of economic analysis, it is no wonder that every now and then a reverse tendency toward reconnecting real-world phenomena and processes makes itself felt. It is a rather obvious feature of the transaction costs paradigm that it depends, both in its content and implications, on the background of the functioning of the price mechanism (Coase, 1937). Coase himself considered the perfect competition conceptualization of the price mechanism to be a valid starting point of analysis. Even though he considers it to be incomplete, his goal is to perfect the model using the scalpel of transaction costs rather than to replace it entirely. This seems to avoid the main problem, however, because if something more (or rather, something else) than transaction costs has been lost on the road from the real market process to the Neverland of perfect competition and general equilibrium, then restoring transaction costs to the system amounts to little more than hoping to rescue a paralytic by providing him with a cane.

In what follows, we ask a few fundamental questions concerning the transaction costs paradigm, its validity, internal consistency, and degree of compatibility with Austrian economics. If the impression is that we have undertaken a critique – even a harsh one, here and there – we will not consider that our intentions have been misconstrued or misunderstood. Transaction costs economics has acquired much fame and many followers, has been directly and positively sanctioned through the Nobel Prizes of Ronald H. Coase (1991) and Oliver E. Williamson (2009), and informs a great deal of research in various fields within economics, including theories of the firm (and economic organization generally), property rights, institutions and contracts, the economic analysis of law, etc. Especially given this prominence, an effort to set the record straight is in order. Obvious forgeries do not pose a danger to a genuine art market, but rather skillful fakes. Likewise, the most dangerous heresies are not the ones evidently at odds with orthodoxy, but those which differ only slightly – but decisively – from it.

We open the discussion on Coase and transaction cost economics by briefly discussing three fundamental issues which we believe shed important general light on the nature of this paradigm: the production-exchange (markets versus firms) dialectic, the nature of transactions, and the nature of transaction costs. We then attempt to show that the transaction costs perspective raises more problems than it solves in both fields where Coase put it to work: the problem of social cost and property rights, and the theory of the firm and economic organization. We end by suggesting that the concept has at most a heuristic validity, namely, in analyses where the meanings of "transacting" and "transaction costs" are unproblematic.

A false dialectic: production versus exchange

One of the most important economic legacies left by Coase is a strong dialectic opposing production and exchange:

> Outside the firm, price movements direct production, which is co-ordinated through a series of exchange transactions on the market. Within a firm, these market transactions are eliminated and in place of the complicated market structure with exchange transactions is substituted the entrepreneur-co-ordinator, who directs production.[2] It is clear that these are alternative methods of co-ordinating production.
>
> (Coase, 1937, p. 388)

While this dichotomy is analytically useful in the limited context of a Crusoe model in order to properly understand the two fundamental concepts of production and exchange, in a complex economy based on the extended division of labor and the use of money it does not hold. It has nevertheless – inadequately in our opinion – morphed into the so-called make or buy problem. Otherwise stated, this problem contrasts "in-house production versus acquisition on the market," or firms versus markets, or management versus transactions, or "markets versus hierarchies." Austrian economics, especially in the Misesian tradition, is well-equipped to handle these problems.

Ludwig von Mises was probably the first economist to understand the fact that a complex economy based on the extended division of labor is impossible without private property, exchange, and money (Mises, 1920, 1951 [1922]; Salerno, 1990, p. 49). His contribution has been retained as part of the famous socialist calculation debate, in which he argued that in the absence of monetary prices for the factors of production (i.e. the situation that obtains as a consequence of the abolition of private property over the means of production), socialism is impossible as a viable economic system. There is, under socialism, no method for calculating whether a certain (centrally planned) allocation of resources is – retrospectively or prospectively – more profitable or economic than others. Nevertheless, this Misesian impossibility theorem actually consists of three overlapping impossibility theorems: (1) the impossibility of a socialist (extended or complex) economy; (2) the impossibility of a complex barter economy, even if based on private (dispersed) property;[3] and (3) the impossibility for the isolated individual to economically manage (construct, maintain, and expand) a large structure of heterogeneous resources held in the form of undispersed private property.[4]

One important implication of these theorems is that in the unhampered, modern, complex market economy, production and exchange cannot be meaningfully disentangled or separated: neither theoretically, nor operationally. Production in the market economy involves exchanges, and exchanges involve or presuppose production, albeit in various degrees. A business firm consists in the actions of the entrepreneurs who own and run it, employing means to achieve certain ends, buying inputs to produce goods and services for actual and potential customers, and selling them. Business activity consists of numerous actions, some of which involve (interpersonal) exchanges, and some of which do not. And the actions considered to be part "of the firm" are constantly judged in terms of monetary calculation using market prices. Moreover, whatever seemingly happens "inside firms" that cannot in any way be related to the rest of the market via monetary calculation of costs, receipts, profits, or losses, is economically irrelevant.

Thus, the firm is part and parcel of the market (Mathews, 1998). What happens in the firm, happens in the market, and for any firm, what happens "inside" it, or – at least as importantly – "inside" other firms, is at the same time something that happens "in (or on) the market."[5] It is not, as Coase says, that the firm "replaces" or "supersedes" the market; rather, the firm is the other side of the market, or the market seen not only from the point of view of its main product/outcome (the structure of prices), but more broadly in term of its structure and components.[6] In the end, what would a market without firms be like?[7]

We belabor the above in order to shed light on the starting point of Coase's 1937 analysis. He intends first to establish a sharp dichotomy between "the price mechanism" and "the firm." Thus, he accepts and treats as valid the idea that the price system "works itself" ("Itself"? To who or what exactly does this term refer?) and can allocate resources quite well – an implication being that the sphere of this misty "price mechanism" contains no firms.[8] Finally, he raises the question of why there are firms if this is the case. All this is intended to suggest that there must be some "cost of using the price mechanism" that the firm could avoid or economize. Thus, the transaction cost paradigm is open for business. If this procedure is contested, namely if we do not concede that the price system works itself without firms, then a more realistic – and fruitful – question can be raised: in what way are firms involved in, or necessary for, the explanation of the functioning of the price system itself? Pursuing this route means explaining the firm as a constitutive part of the market. And transaction costs (as defined by Coase) can play no part in this story.

To sum up, this false production-exchange dichotomy can be shown to be inadequate within the framework of Austrian economics by pointing to two theoretical results. First, categorially, there is no fundamental difference between production and exchange. Praxeologically, as Mises would say, any human action has the structure of an exchange – autistic exchange or interpersonal (direct or indirect) exchange – involving the giving up of a certain state of affairs in favor of another that is expected to be more satisfactory. Both Mises and Rothbard speaks of "action as an exchange" (Rothbard, 2009, p. 70; Mises, 2008, p. 97). Thus, the general category of costs, understood as opportunity costs of the actions undertaken by human agents, cannot *theoretically* be split into two categories – production costs and exchange (or transactions) costs. They are simply part of the same general category of cost with no substantive difference to set them apart.[9] Second, human action in complex modern economies is dependent on (dispersed) private property, market exchanges, and monetary prices, all of which constitute the preconditions for economic calculation. Any calculated action in this context is exchange-dependent (even indirect or monetary exchange). Thus, no "outside the market" sphere is available to make economically meaningful choices. This is valid for factors of production in particular. Let us now move on to the transaction and transaction cost concepts themselves.

What are "transactions" and "transaction costs"?

Ronald Coase never clearly defined or conceptualized the idea of a "transaction." At first glance, the "transaction" of which transaction costs economics speaks is the same thing as interpersonal exchange. Nevertheless, closer inspection reveals a more peculiar use of the concept. In passages such as "a firm will tend to expand until the costs of *organizing an extra transaction within the firm* become equal to the costs of carrying out the same transaction by means of an exchange on the open market" (Coase, 1937, p. 395; emphasis added), or "[as] more *transactions are organized by an entrepreneur*, it would appear that the transactions would tend to be either different in kind or in different places" (Coase, 1937, p. 397; emphasis added), it becomes clear that the transactions Coase speaks of are not only interpersonal exchanges. They might appear in this form outside the firm, but inside it they are simply operations or actions performed by the entrepreneur or by someone under him at his request. We are confronted here with an almost technological view of transactions, or at least a hybrid view – here economical, there technological. Transactions are somehow objective bits of action or operations or tasks that could be done inside or outside the firm.[10] Later, this becomes explicit in the work of Williamson. In a fragment titled "The Technology of Transacting" he adopts

> Commons' proposal that the transaction be made the basic unit of analysis . . . attention is focused on economizing efforts that attend the organization of transactions – where a transaction occurs when a good or service is transferred across a technologically separable interface. One stage of activity terminates and another begins.
>
> (Williamson, 1996, p. 58)

This non-catallactic view of "transacting" renders the name of the paradigm itself ("transaction cost economics") a misnomer from the perspective of the traditional, economic view of exchange. This is even truer from the point of view of Austrian economics. It opens up a technological, objectivist, mechanical, "real"-cost view of the economic system which is impossible to treat in terms of human action.

As for the transaction costs concept, it was not coined as such by Coase in the "The Nature of the Firm." There, the specific idea is rendered as "the costs of using the price mechanism" (Coase, 1937, p. 390; at page 391 he uses interchangeably "costs" with "disadvantages" of "using the price mechanism"). Or, sometimes more succinctly, the idea is expressed in terms of "marketing costs." Coase also subsequently provides enumerative definitions of transaction costs:

> In order to carry out a market transaction it is necessary to discover who it is that one wishes to deal with, to inform people that one wishes to deal and on what terms, to conduct negotiations leading up to a bargain, to draw up the contract, to undertake the inspection needed to make sure that the terms of the contract are being observed, and so on.
>
> (1960, p. 7)

Alternatively, he accepts the crystallization provided by Dahlman, for whom transaction costs are "search and information costs, bargaining and decision costs, [and] policing and enforcement costs" (Coase, 1988, p. 6). Gradually, the established view of transaction costs has come to analogize them with frictions in mechanics:

> In mechanical systems we look for frictions: do the gears mesh, are the parts lubricated, is there needless slippage or other loss of energy? The economic counterpart of friction is transaction cost: for that subset of transactions where it is important to elicit cooperation, do the parties to exchange operate harmoniously, or are there frequent misunderstandings and conflicts that lead to delays, breakdowns, and other malfunctions? Transaction cost analysis entails an examination of the comparative costs of planning, adapting, and monitoring task completion under alternative governance structures.
>
> (Williamson, 1996, p. 58)

From a seemingly specific and narrow category, transaction costs become generalized. Thus, later interpreters and commentators are left with the task of figuring out for themselves what to consider "transactions" and/or "transaction costs." In fact, almost anything can be interpreted as a transaction cost: asymmetric information, incomplete contracts, bounded rationality, opportunism and shirking, team organization, frequency of interaction, asset specificity, bargaining and searching, contract enforcement, administration or management, monitoring and inspecting, etc.

At this point, it is useful to recapitulate Mises's view on mechanical metaphors and their value in economics:

> The economist is often prone to look to mechanics as a model for his own work. Instead of treating the problems posed by his science with the means appropriate to them, he fetches a metaphor from mechanics, which he puts in place of a solution. In this way the idea arose that the laws of catallactics hold true only ideally, i.e. on the assumption that men act in a vacuum, as it were. But, of course, in life everything happens quite differently. In life there

> are "frictional resistances" of all kinds, which are responsible for the fact that the outcome of our action is different from what the laws would lead one to expect. From the very outset no way was seen in which these resistances could be exactly measured or, indeed, fully comprehended even qualitatively. So one had to resign oneself to admitting that economics has but slight value both for the cognition of the relationships of our life in society and for actual practice. And, of course, all those who rejected economic science for political and related reasons – all the etatists, the socialists, and the interventionists – joyfully agreed . . . Once the distinction between economic and noneconomic action is abandoned, it is not difficult to see that in all cases of "resistance" what was involved is the concrete data of economizing, which the theory comprehends fully.
>
> (Mises, 2003[1933], p. 172)

The risk of such a comprehensive view of transaction costs is that it is vulnerable to reductions to the absurd. For instance, Hülsmann (2004, p. 49) identifies "nutrition costs" as a friction in the economic system on which the economist's attention might be focused, and on the basis of which he could explain the nature of all sorts of instruments designed to facilitate economies in terms of nutrition costs.

Lastly, at this point, one must ask: what does the "zero transaction costs world" really mean? We propose thinking of it in two forms: a strong version and a weak version. The strong version of the zero transaction costs world is one devoid of any "friction," where everything works smoothly, un-problematically, even instantly. In Coase's own words, "where there are no costs of making transactions, it costs nothing to speed them up, so that eternity can be experienced in a split second" (Coase, 1988, p. 15). Insisting upon using this version of the theory is not likely to bring any useful results.

On the other hand, if we try to construct the weaker version of the zero transaction costs world, in which we try to abstract only from the categories that Coase explicitly includes in the transaction costs category (searching and information, bargaining and deciding, policing and enforcing), we may obtain more interesting results. Thus, we argue below that property rights can also be proven necessary in the zero-transaction world – given the weak interpretation – and that, therefore, transaction costs are not as essential for understanding property rights as Coase and his followers suggest. Likewise, if rationales for the existence of firms can be squared with the (weak) zero-transaction costs assumption, then the paradigm also fails to be important for the theory of the firm. This will be shown below.

Undermining property rights while explaining and defending them

Coase's later works (1959, 1960) raise the problem of the best (most socially productive or least socially costly) allocation of resources at the social level. In his view, transaction costs seem to be just the right theoretical instrument to shed light on the matter. Starting from the puzzling question of what is to be done in those situations where the actions of a business firm have harmful effects on others, Coase departs from the traditional (Pigovian) manner of looking at things in terms of an externality that must be internalized. Instead of judging the matter in terms of aggressor and victim, where, for instance, smoke from a factory reaching neighboring properties is either stopped, or moved, or fined, or taxed, for Coase, the problem should be seen more as "reciprocal" in nature, like a clash of equally valid concerns. The problem, in Coase's opinion, is not "who is right," but rather, "how to avoid the more serious harm," or the greater social cost:

> The question is commonly thought of as one in which A inflicts harm on B and what has to be decided is: how should we restrain A? But this is wrong. We are dealing with a problem of a reciprocal nature. To avoid harm to B would inflict harm on A. The real question that has to be decided is: should A be allowed to harm B or should B be allowed to harm A? The problem is to avoid the more serious harm.
>
> (Coase, 1960, p. 1)

Thus, taking the example of the cattle that stray into neighboring crops, Coase frames the problem as one of social choice. If the cattle are allowed to destroy the crops, there is more meat and fewer crops. If they are not allowed, there will be less meat and more crops. This imposes a social choice of meat versus crops, a choice that presupposes that "we know the value of what is obtained as well as the value of what is sacrificed to obtain it" (Coase, 1960, p. 2). The so-called Coase Theorem is then brought to bear on the discussion. With zero transaction costs, it does not matter what the initial allocation of property rights is (as long as there is one), for the final allocation of resources will be the same (the strong version of the theorem). Or, even if it is not the same, it will maximize the value of production (the weaker version of the theorem).[11] Thus, in the world of zero transaction costs the free interaction of people on the market, whatever the initial allocation of property rights, always maximizes wealth.

However, if transaction costs are positive, or high, the free interaction of people on the market, given a certain initial allocation of property rights, does not automatically maximize production. Institutions other than the free market are required if wealth is to be maximized. As Hülsmann (2004) observes, these institutions might be firms, or governmental institutions like courts and legislation. If the ideal is to approximate – with the help of transaction cost-economizing institutional instruments – as closely as possible the outcomes of a zero transaction cost world, then it follows that the role of these institutions is precisely (and sometimes it just seems to be so positively) to put resources in the hands of those who would maximize production if there were no costs of transacting.

This perspective raises a number of important problems. First, in judging interpersonally whether meat is more important "socially" than crops, Coase adopts an objectivist perspective, or at least one based on an objective theory of value. The value of what is lost and the value of what is gained in such cases can be compared and balanced against one another only if they are the same in the eyes of all parties (the two parties involved and any outside observers). James Buchanan points this out:

> It is unfortunate that Coase presented his argument (through the examples) largely in terms of presumably objectively-measurable and independently-determined harm and benefit relationships. In his formulation, these relationships become *identical* in the perception of all parties to any potential exchange of rights. Hence, the unique "efficient" (benefit maximizing or loss minimizing) allocation of resources exists and becomes determinate conceptually to any external observer. The efficacy of free exchange of rights in attaining the objectively-determined "efficient" outcome becomes subject to testing by observation. The exchange process, in this perspective, is itself evaluated in terms of criteria applied to the outcomes that the process is observed to produce. There are values inherent in allocations that exist quite independently of the means through which these allocations are generated.
>
> (Buchanan, 1999 [1984], pp. 262–263; emphasis in original)

Austrian critics of Coase (Block, 1977; Rothbard, 1982; North, 1992, 2002) have also argued this point forcefully, emphasizing the subjectivity of costs and, especially, indicating possible psychic or non-monetary income or benefits which cannot be taken into account by third parties, including courts (and that thus would be unjustifiably excluded from social welfare). Nevertheless, we feel that these criticisms have not sufficiently exploited the monetary aspects of the discussion.

If we adopt the weak version of the zero-transaction cost economy described above, which aims at a modicum of relevance for the real world, it can be shown that the initial allocation of property rights matters even in this world. Bearing in mind all the above considerations, if zero transaction costs were interpreted to mean not that the parties will instantly and effortlessly reach an agreement (which is tautological: parties get along in a zero transaction costs world because zero transaction costs would mean precisely that parties get along), but only that they will instantly find out whether their views and judgments concerning certain resources coincide or are compatible,[12] then a situation is conceivable in which, with zero transaction costs, one person would use a resource one way, and another person, another way. Thus, given the *different judgments* and the subsequent *mutually exclusive uses* for a certain piece of property, the initial allocation of property rights over the said resource becomes essential. Crucially, transaction costs play no part. Differences in judgments between persons in our scenario are not necessarily confined strictly to non-monetary considerations. The differences may contain the whole range of elements – monetary, non-monetary; short-term, long-term; personal, social, etc.

The special character of monetary entries into acting man's economic calculations prevents us from even setting up the tables and numbers by means of which the Coase theorem is usually discussed. A reminder from Mises is in order here:

> But the exchange ratios which we have to deal with are permanently fluctuating. There is nothing constant and invariable in them. They defy any

> attempt to measure them. They are not facts in the sense in which a physicist calls the establishment of the weight of a quantity of copper a fact. They are historical events expressive of what happened once at a definite instant and under definite circumstances. The same numerical exchange ratios may appear again, but it is by no means certain whether this will really happen and, if it happens, the question is open whether this identical result was the outcome of preservation of the same circumstances or of a return to them rather than the outcome of the interplay of a very different constellation of price-determining factors. Numbers applied by acting man in economic calculation do not refer to quantities measured to but to exchange ratios as they are expected – on the basis of understanding – to be realized on the markets of the future to which alone all acting is directed and which alone counts for acting man.
>
> (2008, p. 211)

Again, if the above is true, then it is not surprising to find that Mises is absolutely skeptical concerning "social costs or benefits":

> The height of conceptual confusion is reached when one tries to bring calculation to bear upon the problem of what is called the "social maximization of profit." Here the connection with the individual's calculation of profitability is intentionally abandoned in order to go beyond the "individualistic" and "atomistic" and arrive at "social" findings. And again one fails to see and will not see that the system of calculation is inseparably connected with the individual's calculation of profitability.
>
> (2003[1933], p. 169)

But if we reach such a conclusion, then it means the essential element for explaining property rights and related institutions is once again the scarcity of resources and the impossibility for two agents, or two wills, to make use of the same resource for mutually exclusive purposes. As we have explained in the discussion above, transaction costs play no necessary role in this story (though in one case or another, they could even be the most important issue).

Transaction cost-based explanations of the firm: neither necessary, nor sufficient

Let us now turn to the transaction cost-based theory of the firm. Given the elusiveness of "transactions" and "transaction costs," it is not surprising that firm activity very often relates to them. But the claim of transaction cost economics – especially of Coase – is not a weak one, of the "there are certain connections between transaction costs and firms" sort. Rather, it is a strong thesis: transaction costs themselves and the need to economize on them fundamentally *explain* the firm, revealing its *nature*, or essence. The implication is that the phenomenon cannot otherwise be understood. "It was the avoidance of carrying out transactions through the market that could explain the existence of the firm in which the allocation of factors came about as a result of administrative decisions (and I thought it did)" (Coase, 1992, p. 715). Or:

> What I think will be considered in the future to have been the most important contribution of this article is the explicit introduction of transaction costs into economic analysis. I argued in *The Nature of the Firm* that the existence of transaction costs leads to the emergence of firms.
>
> (Coase, 1992, p. 716)

We will argue in the next few pages that there is no such thing as a valid or coherent transaction cost-based theory of the firm.

The discussion is important because the field has grown enormously following the contributions of Oliver Williamson. Explanations of the multinational, or transnational, or international firm have also been coined, in part or in full, in terms of transaction costs (Hymer, 1990[1968]; Hennart, 1977; Teece, 1985). In hindsight, we can look back at these efforts with feelings similar to those suggested by C. S. Lewis in *The Screwtape Letters*, in which he mocked the academic habit of asking irrelevant or inconsequential questions. In fact, any question at all can be asked, other than the one that matters: whether or not a theory is true. In the present case, almost the whole transaction costs research program has ended up asking whether this or that explanation is one in terms of transaction costs, and if so what specific type thereof, whether transaction cost explanations were coined earlier or later, and so on. The only question that is not asked anymore is whether the transaction costs theory of the firm makes sense, or otherwise said, if it is true. Let us now proceed to give a few reasons why the Coasean transaction-based theory of the firm is problematic.

Serfdom and the firm

In a neglected footnote of his 1937 article, Coase makes a surprising statement:

> It is the essence of serfdom that the price mechanism is not allowed to operate. Therefore, there has to be direction from some organizer. When, however, serfdom passed, the price mechanism was allowed to operate. It was not until machinery drew workers into one locality that it paid to supersede the price mechanism and the firm again emerged.
>
> (Coase, 1988, p. 46)

For Coase, the relations inside a firm are somewhat ambiguous. Even though sometimes the idea is that they must be completely voluntary and contractual (albeit of a special contractual nature), quite often the same relations are presented as equivalent to relations of power or authority. The serfdom reference is a case in point, as is the example of the master-servant relation. Moreover, all the explicit identifications of planning in the firm with planning at the national level (e.g. "a firm, that little planned society"; Coase, 1992, p. 716) fall into the same category.

Coase does not have a theory of property rights and therefore cannot properly set or identify the boundaries of the market economy. He therefore ends up searching (and often finding) the firm ambiguously on both sides of that frontier. As Bylund rightly points out, the context of the socialist calculation debate and Coase's early socialist leanings make themselves felt in these claims (Bylund, 2014).

If the avoidance of costs of using the price mechanism is, in a strong sense, realized only in non-voluntary settings (e.g. slavery, serfdom, socialism), then what Coase has obtained is not a transaction costs-based theory of the firm, but a transaction cost-based theory of these aggressive or coercive institutions. The voluntary cooperation-based business firm, which cannot so strongly supersede the price mechanism – if it can at all – remains unexplained. Moreover, even if both phenomena are explained in terms of transaction costs, it still remains for Coase to provide us with a theory of the regular, non-coercive, business firm. One might also suspect at this point that the supersession of the price mechanism, far from being the moment of birth of the firm, is rather the marker of its death.[13]

The same problem can be found in the works of Williamson, whose view evolves from a market-versus-hierarchy dichotomy to the idea of a spectrum of governance, as suggested in both *The Economic Institutions of Capitalism* (Williamson, 1985) and *Mechanisms of Governance* (Williamson, 1996). Yet even in the latter theory Williamson includes in the spectrum of governance everything from spot contracts to hybrid ones, to firms, and finally, to legislation and bureaus (his term for the state sector).[14] All of these are explainable in terms of transaction costs economies. Yet if this is correct, what explains the business firm in particular? We are of the opinion that no adequate answer has been provided.

Apart from the ethical problems involved, the difference between voluntary and non-voluntary structures is that in voluntary ones (e.g. regular business firms) all parties involved participate through the specific contracts and prices they negotiate. Through this process they create what Mises calls the "intellectual division of labor," which makes possible the formation, maintenance, and constant revolution of the structure of monetary prices on the market. That is why all the components of the firm and all the participants in it are unavoidably connected via monetary calculation to the market environment outside the firm. The firm does not supersede this market, but rather is a part of it. Serfs or slaves, on the other hand, are not connected to the price mechanism as they cannot negotiate the terms of their employment, and therefore do not participate in the abovementioned intellectual division of labor. Their masters exercise authority or command over them. But the position of the employee in the firm puts him at the disposition of the managers or bosses no more than a plumber, or a dentist, is at the disposition of his clients.[15]

Transaction costs prove too much

Another reason for considering that a transaction cost explanation of the firm has not actually been provided by Coase is the fact that he (and also Williamson) gradually developed what might be called transaction cost imperialism. Not only firms, but the market itself, along with money and all the institutions of capitalism, are in fact instruments of transaction cost economies:

> Markets are institutions that exist to facilitate exchange, that is, they exist in order to reduce the cost of carrying out exchange transactions. In an economic theory which assumes that transaction costs are nonexistent, markets have no function to perform.
>
> (Coase, 1988, p. 7)[16]

> In fact, a large part of what we think of as economic activity is designed to accomplish what high transaction costs would otherwise prevent or to reduce transaction costs.
>
> (Coase, 1992, p. 716)

> I know of only one part of economics in which transaction costs have been used to explain a major feature of the economic system, and that relates to the evolution and use of money . . . The benefits brought about by the use of money consist of a reduction in transaction costs.
>
> (Coase, 1992, p. 716)

Coase suggests that the effects of transaction costs are "pervasive in the economy." The problem is that if transaction costs explain everything, they end up explaining nothing.

Firms in the zero-transaction cost world

As in the previous section, we will end by pointing out the important possibility of the existence of firms in a zero transaction costs world. If this world is not simply tautologically interpreted to mean that any two parties taken together will have the same view or judgments concerning all relevant aspects concerning the immediate or more remote future, then firms make sense. Various potential business partners in a firm – entrepreneurs – might discover (effortlessly, or instantly, as imposed by the exigency of zero transaction costs; once more, the weak version) that their business plans and judgments are irreconcilable. Thus, the only possible path consists of establishing different firms. Either both partners establish firms, or one of them does while the other refrains. Thus, if we corroborate this insight with the praxeological analysis of entrepreneurship as specific business project uncertainty-bearing, which can implicitly manifest itself only by means of firms, we have arrived at a severe verdict concerning the importance of transaction costs for the theory of the firm: they are neither a necessary nor a sufficient condition for the existence of business units.

The missed opportunity for a better explanation of the firm

Ironically enough, Coase provided what, from the point of view of Austrian economics, could be an adequate theory of the firm. Thus, he claims that "[a] firm, therefore, consists of the system of relationships which comes into existence when the direction of resources is dependent on an entrepreneur" (Coase, 1937, p. 393). Of course, the resemblance with the Austrian theory of entrepreneurship is only superficial. For Coase, entrepreneurship is nothing more than another factor of production, namely, management or administration, and he even strives to take this factor out of the normal functioning of the market and instead point to its similarities to socialist central planning. Here, again, we join Per Bylund's interpretation of Coase, which views his discussion of the nature of the firm in the context of the socialist calculation debate, in particular the search for arguments in favor of the possibility of rational central planning (Bylund, 2014). Coase even touched on the Knightian view in which entrepreneurship is functionally tied to uncertainty, much as in Mises's theory. Sadly, Coase dismissively collapsed the complex problem of uncertainty into one of "mode of payment":

> The question of uncertainty is one often considered to be very relevant to the study of the equilibrium of the firm. It seems improbable that a firm would emerge without the existence of uncertainty. But those, for instance, Professor Knight, who make the *mode of payment* the distinguishing mark of the firm – fixed incomes being guaranteed to some of those engaged in production by a person who takes the residual, and fluctuating, income – would appear to be introducing a point which is irrelevant to the problem we are considering. One entrepreneur may sell his services to another for a certain sum of money, while the payment to his employees may be mainly or wholly a share in profits.
>
> (Coase, 1937, p. 392)

We should point out immediately that this dismissal of the uncertainty view is obviously inadequate. First of all, the idea that an entrepreneur (who must bear the uncertainty of a business unit) could "sell" entrepreneurship does not hold. Either he sells the whole business and stops being an entrepreneur at all (the buyer now assuming this role); or he simply offers some consultancy services or advice to another entrepreneur, in which case he remains an entrepreneur in his firm, while the consultancy client remains the true (and sole) entrepreneur in the consulted firm. Moreover, the key to this issue is not so much the idea of the fixity or variability of the income share (the "mode of payment") as it is the incidence of losses if they occur. Thus, even if an entrepreneur pays his employees with variable sums ("shares in profit"), the crux of the matter is whether they also participate in losses. If not, the mode of payment or the type of wages they receive remains irrelevant, and does not make them entrepreneurs. But if the correct way to pinpoint the role of uncertainty in business is to discover who bears the losses rather than who receives income by means of a variable "mode of payment," the uncertainty theory of entrepreneurship and the firm has not been adequately criticized. Moreover, such a theory can be laid out with no reference whatsoever to transaction costs.[17]

A petitio principii?

We end this section with an observation by Harold Demsetz, who – after getting very close to wondering whether Coase simply rediscovered the concept of cost (see note 8) – locates another delicate spot in transaction cost-based theories of the firm. Namely, if the idea of a "transaction" or "transactions" presupposes that previously we have dealt adequately with the possible agents who engage in them, then "transactions" require definitions in which the firm concept is already involved. Thus, the firm is a more fundamental concept than a transaction, and is presupposed by it. Explaining firms in terms of transactions, therefore, amounts to getting stuck in a *petitio principia*:

> One person phones another and directs him to purchase specific assets by certain time if they can be acquired for less than a stipulated price. Is this activity transacting or managing? . . . Since the call might be from an owner/manager of a firm to his employee in the purchasing department or from a customer/investor to the brokerage house whose services he purchases, it is hard to know whether we are dealing with a transaction or management cost until we *already know* whether we are discussing a firm or a market . . . The inherent difficulty is that the same organizing activities often characterize exchange *and* management.
>
> (Demsetz, 1988, p. 149; emphasis in original)

Conclusion: at most a heuristic success

As a theoretical concept, we believe "transaction costs" remain elusive, while transaction cost economics is a chameleonic instrument which raises more questions than it solves. In situations where transaction costs can be meaningfully particularized – as what Mises, echoing Weber, called ideal types – reasoning in terms of transaction costs is possible and can yield relevant results. Thus, if in a certain context, "transaction costs" are unambiguously interpreted to mean "bargaining costs," then any solution that implies, other things equal, a reduction in those costs, is beneficial. If, for instance, in an internally divided village the priest makes the effort to convince all the villagers to participate in a certain project (building a school, rebuilding the destroyed house of a widow, etc.) and succeeds, we cannot say this justifies developing a transaction cost-based theoretical explanation of priesthood.

As for Austrian economics and possible cross-fertilizations with transaction cost economics, we believe these raise more problems than they solve. Based on the praxeological paradigm, which looks at economic phenomena in terms of human action, takes entrepreneurship (seen mainly in terms of uncertainty-bearing by property-owning capitalist-entrepreneurs who undertake specific investment projects) as its core, being subjectivist and employing the all-important concept of economic calculation for understanding the major aspects of the complex modern monetary economy based on the extended social division of labor, Austrian economics can handle adequately on its own terms whatever puzzles or conundrums the transaction cost paradigms raises. On the other hand, the occasions for imports from the latter are as many occasions for error. For, in the end, is there such a thing as a "cost of using the price mechanism"? Perhaps the question is meaningless from the point of view of economics.

Notes

1 For a study of the impact of perfect competition theory on economics in general, see Machovec (1995).
2 Coase includes the following footnote at this point: "In the rest of this paper I shall use the term entrepreneur to refer to the person or persons who, in a competitive system, take the place of the price mechanism in the direction of resources."
3 Even though traces of the idea are present, for instance, in *The Theory of Money and Credit* (1912) and *Epistemological Problems of Economics* (1933), it is in *Human Action* (1949) that Mises speaks explicitly of "the barter fiction," harshly criticizing the idea that the phenomena of the market economy (mainly the formation of prices) can all be explained in terms of direct exchange, with the subsequent addition of monetary aspects reflecting only minor complications that do not alter the discussion in a fundamental way. For the important implications of the barter fiction and its corollary, "neutral money," see Salerno (2016).
4 Options (1) and (3) are included by Mises under the heading of "the autistic economy" (Mises, 2008, p. 244).
5 Thus, properly understood, the "make or buy" decision is not a Coasean one of market versus firm, but a more complex choice between one mixed alternative (involving some exchanges and some other operations) and another (involving different operations and different exchanges). The decision of a firm to buy a piece of furniture instead of making it "in house" does not involve a more enhanced use of the market and a less intensive use of management or non-interpersonal exchange operations. It means that some combination of transactions and operations (buying the factors of production needed to build the furniture and then handling both them and the furniture) is replaced by another combination of transactions and operations (buying ready-made furniture and handling it). "Make or buy" is actually more akin to a choice between "(make plus buy) 1" and "(make plus buy) 2," both options being made comparable only by the possibility of monetary calculation.
6 For the view that Coase, and Williamson after him, did not mean to create a strong firm-market dichotomy, see Klein (2010), p. 188 and the following discussion.
7 Even if someone were to claim that in a market without firms only individuals would trade and engage in productive activities, in our opinion, the correct framing of the situation is not "here is the market without firms," but "here is a market with exclusively unipersonal firms." Then, a possible puzzle of the Coase type would be: why are there multi-person firms and not exclusively unipersonal ones?
8 This is echoed by Oliver Williamson in his well-known saying, "in the beginning there were markets." The idea of the "market without firms" (or we could say, with a Misesian twist, "the imaginary construction of the firm-less market") has to a certain extent been entertained by authors in the Austrian tradition, such as (most recently) Per Bylund. See his *The Theory of Production. A New Theory of the Firm* (2016).
9 Harold Demsetz is close to deriving such a conclusion when – in his attempt to rigorously make sense of the alternative implied in Coase's reasoning in terms of the combined bargaining and management costs of both firms and markets – he asks,

somewhat puzzled: "Have we come to the point of saying that firms are used when they are cheaper, all costs considered, but not when markets are cheaper?" (Demsetz, 1988, p. 147).

10 Thus, a little later in his article Coase writes: "[at] the margin, the costs of organizing within the firm will be equal either to the costs of organizing in another firm or to the cost involved in leaving the transaction to be 'organized' by the price mechanism" (Coase, 1937, p. 404). Thus, not only do we have "transactions in the firm"; we have "organization outside the firm," on the market. In what sense do firms/entrepreneurs *supersede* the market, then?

11 We do not offer any numerical examples here, as these have been more adequately dealt with in Block (1977) and Rothbard (1982).

12 In terms of the Dahlman enumeration, for instance: the parties would almost instantly find each other and all relevant information about them; they could instantly bargain and decide (we resist the temptation to equate costless bargaining with successful costless bargaining; costless bargaining can occur only for the parties who bargain to discover their preferences are incompatible). Should an agreement be reached, the parties could very easily or quickly police and enforce the contract. As stated above, we want to avoid the tautological stipulation of the zero transaction costs economy as a world in which parties instantaneously agree on everything. Perhaps some elements of humanity, individuality, subjectivity, and entrepreneurship can be retained. In this respect, our weak version of the zero transaction cost economy must be understood as differing from perfect foresight, certainty, and even the Misesian Evenly Rotating Economy.

13 This is the way we believe Rothbard's discussion of the limits that economic calculation imposes on firm size is to be interpreted. This argument is anything but Coasean in spirit. Where the firm begins for Coase, for Rothbard it actually ends: "The difference between the State and the private case is that our economic laws debar people from ever establishing such a system in a free-market society. Far lesser evils prevent entrepreneurs from establishing even islands of incalculability, let alone infinitely compounding such errors by eliminating calculability altogether" (Rothbard, 2009, p. 615).

14 By 1960, Coase also mentions governments, or "super-firms . . . of a very special kind," besides firms, as transaction cost reduction devices (Coase, 1960, p. 9).

15 Given this discussion, we think that Klein's interpretation – that Coase and Williamson should be read not as opposing the firm to the market, but rather the *taxis* to the *cosmos* – is a bit too charitable (Klein, 2010, p. 190).

16 In a sense, what has just been said is a piece of mental gymnastics: if the use of the price mechanism is costly and firms are meant precisely to avoid these costs, saying that markets exist to reduce transaction costs is tantamount to saying that they exist to reduce their own costs! The only way out of this problem is to consider that the price mechanism is something abstract, independent from the market. Using this mechanism is costly in an absolute sense. A first step toward reducing its cost is through markets; another is through firms; and a final one through governments. This could make sense only with the crudest objective theory of value. Bylund (2014) argues that Coase has in mind allocations of resources that would be identical, irrespective of where they would finally be undertaken (markets, firms, governments, etc.). He only posits that the option chosen must include economies in terms of transaction costs. This approach, once again, has a very objectivistic flavor. It could also explain the puzzling fact that Coase rarely, if ever, speaks of *profits*, the true compass of economic activity (not costs as such, of whatever type!).

17 It is also somewhat ironic that Coase undertakes this analysis of Knight's views in order to show that the latter, focusing on a seemingly *ad hoc* mode of payment, cannot "give a reason why the price mechanism should be superseded" (Coase, 1937, p. 401), and therefore has not, presumably, succeeded in establishing the need for the firm. Again, this suggests the market-firm dichotomy Coase has in mind, but which is stipulated or simply postulated more than proved. This whole discussion should speak in favor of Knight, who provides a rationale for the firm based on uncertainty-bearing

entrepreneurship and which, in addition, is fully integrated in the market and in the orbit of the price system.

References

Block, Walter. 1977. "Coase and Demsetz on Private Property Rights." *Journal of Libertarian Studies* 1 (2): 111–115.

Buchanan, James. 1999 [1984]. "Rights, Efficiency, and Exchange: The Irrelevance of Transactions Cost." In *The Logical Foundations of Constitutional Liberty*, Collected Works of James M. Buchanan, Vol. I. Indianapolis, IN: Liberty Fund, pp. 260–277.

Bylund, Per L. 2014. "Ronald Coase's "Nature of the Firm" and the Argument for Economic Planning." *Journal of the History of Economic Thought* 36 (3): 305–329.

———. 2016. *The Problem of Production: A New Theory of the Firm*. London: Routledge.

Coase, Ronald H. 1937. "The Nature of the Firm." *Economica* 4 (16): 386–405.

———. 1959. "The Federal Communications Commission." *Journal of Law and Economics* 56 (4): 879–915.

———. 1960. "The Problem of Social Cost." *Journal of Law and Economics* 3: 1–44.

———. 1988. *The Firm, the Market and the Law*. Chicago: University of Chicago Press.

———. 1992. "The Institutional Structure of Production." *American Economic Review* 82 (4): 713–719.

Demsetz, Harold. 1988. "The Theory of the Firm Revisited." *Journal of Law, Economics, and Organization* 4 (1): 141–161.

Foss, Nicolai J., and Klein, Peter G. 2012. *Organizing Entrepreneurial Judgment: A New Approach to the Firm*. Cambridge: Cambridge University Press.

Hennart, Jean-François. 1977. *A Theory of Foreign Direct Investment*. PhD thesis. https://pure.uvt.nl/portal/files/749290/THEORYOF.PDF.

Hülsmann, J. G. 2004. "The A Priori Foundations of Property Economics." *Quarterly Journal of Austrian Economics* 7 (4): 41–68.

Hymer, Stephen H. 1990 [1968]. "The Large Multinational 'Corporation.'" In Mark Casson, ed., *Multinational Corporations*. Hants: Edward Elgar, pp. 6–31.

Klein, Peter G. 2010. The Capitalist and the Entrepreneur: Essays on Organization and Markets. Auburn, AL: Ludwig von Mises Institute.

Machovec, Frank. 1995. Perfect Competition and the Transformation of Economics. London: Routledge.

Mathews, Don. 1998. "Management vs. the Market: An Exaggerated Distinction." *Quarterly Journal of Austrian Economics* 1 (3): 41–46.

Mises, Ludwig von. 1951 [1922]. *Socialism: An Economic and Sociological Analysis*. New Haven, NJ: Yale University Press.

———. 1990 [1920]. *Economic Calculation in the Socialist Commonwealth*. Auburn, AL: Ludwig von Mises Institute.

———. 2003 [1933]. *Epistemological Problems of Economics*. 3rd ed. Auburn, AL: Ludwig von Mises Institute.

———. 2008. *Human Action: A Treatise on Economics*. Scholar's ed. Auburn, AL: Ludwig von Mises Institute.

North, Gary. 1992. *The Coase Theorem: A Study in Economic Epistemology*. Institute for Christian Economics.

———. 2002. "Undermining Property Rights: Coase and Becker." *Journal of Libertarian Studies* 16 (4): 75–100.

Rothbard, Murray N. 1982. "Law, Property Rights and Air Pollution." *Cato Journal* 2 (1): 55–99.

———. 2009. *Man, Economy, and State With Power and Market*. Scholar's ed. Auburn, AL: Ludwig von Mises Institute.

Salerno, Joseph T. 1990. "Postscript: Why a Socialist Economy Is 'Impossible'." In *Economic Calculation in the Socialist Commonwealth*. Auburn, AL: The Ludwig von Mises Institute.

———. 2016. "The Development of the Neutral Money Concept: The Austrian School Further Dehomogenized." January 30, 2016. SSRN. https://ssrn.com/abstract=2738140 or http://dx.doi.org/10.2139/ssrn.2738140.

Teece, David J. 1985. "Multinational Enterprise, Internal Governance, and Industrial Organization." American Economic Review: Papers and Proceedings of the Ninety-Seventh Annual Meeting of the American Economic Association 75 (2): 233–238.

Topan, Mihai Vladimir. 2013. *Întreprizătorul în firma internațională. O teoretizare în tradiția Școlii Austriece* (The Entrepreneur in the International Firm: A Theorization in the Austrian School Tradition). Editura ASE, Bucharest.

———. 2017. "A Walk Outside the Extent of the Market: A Review of Per Bylund's '*The Problem of Production: A New Theory of the Firm.*'" Unpublished Manuscript.

Williamson, Oliver E. 1985. *The Economic Institutions of Capitalism: Firms, Markets, Relational Contracting*. New York: The Free Press.

———. 1996. *The Mechanisms of Governance*. New York: Oxford University Press.

10 Management is what's wrong with socialism

Cost at the expense of value

Per L. Bylund

After Ludwig von Mises published his essay on economic calculation and the impossibility of planning in a socialist economy (Mises, [1920] 1935), economists engaged with and debated his ideas for nearly three decades. The socialist calculation debate, as it is often referred to, was "one of the most significant controversies in modern economics" (Blaug, 1997, p. 557). It was also a controversy in which Austrian economists played a significant role, both as instigators and as consistent defenders of the market process perspective in economics. Ultimately, however, the Austrians were not victorious; instead, many of the assumptions and views held by their opponents have been integrated into the formal models of modern mathematical economics.

Austrians stick to their guns, however, and claim their argument remains the better one. In fact, there is an argument to be made that the opponents of Mises and the other Austrians failed to understand their arguments. Rather than viewing economic calculation as an issue of computing power, or of the difficulty of collecting and aggregating dispersed information, and consequently the limited ability of the state to *set* prices, as for instance the market socialists asserted (e.g. Taylor, 1929; Lange, 1936, 1937), Austrians maintain that calculation is about the *basis* for prices and calculable action (Salerno, 1990a). What matters for Austrians are real market prices, which reflect anticipations of actual consumer valuations and thereby approximate social opportunity cost as it applies to the real, temporal, and dynamic market as a value-creating discovery process (Hayek, 1978).

In a recent critique of Mises's argument, Andy Denis (2015) attempts not to rebut but to reassess his argument on its own terms. Denis accepts Mises's conclusion that there can be no rational basis for prices in an economy with centralized ownership and control of the means of production. However, Denis argues, there is nothing in Mises's argument to support his conclusion that private property is a necessary institutional framework for a functioning economy. The institution of private property is a sufficient but *not a necessary* criterion for proper market prices to emerge, which leaves room for a solution on Mises's own terms without private property through what Denis calls "several control" – a single owner (the state) with dispersed control. Under such a system, the economy would have one principal but a myriad of agents acting independently, and would therefore act in the same way as modern-day corporate capitalism with its passive owners (shareholders) and active management (Berle and Means, 1932). Despite having common ownership through the state, Denis's system would function like a market and determine real market prices through individual competing producers' bids for the factors.

While Denis's approach is clever, I maintain that it offers no real challenge to Mises's argument. Instead, I argue that Denis makes the same fundamental mistake as other critics of Mises's argument, as well as of the economic positions found in the Austrian tradition more generally. This mistake, which I elaborate on in this chapter, is to focus on – and indeed even theorize from the point of view of – cost, and therefore from the perspective of a closed or, at a minimum, a non-expanding economic system. While cost is an important – if not the most important – aspect of effective management and of efforts to improve business processes and profitability, as well as a core concept in economic theorizing, my claim is that it is nevertheless of secondary importance for market-creating – and therefore market-*shaping* – action: entrepreneurship.

My argument suggests that the proper way of understanding the Misesian argument, and therefore why a socialist economy is truly impossible and not simply a computational difficulty or a practical obstacle, is to focus on the value-creating nature of entrepreneurship and, consequently, how the function of entrepreneurship treats cost. I will show that cost is of secondary importance in a free market, whereas in a planned economy it is and must be the main, if not the only, variable considered. In what follows, I discuss the characteristics of entrepreneurial decision-making, contrast entrepreneurship and management, and note the difference between open-endedness and closed-endedness in coordinating economic activity. I argue, in line with Mises ([1949] 1998; cf. Salerno, 1990a), that the only possible outcomes for an economic system are growth or decline, and that these follow directly from the prevailing "driving force" of the market: entrepreneurship or management.

Entrepreneurial decision-making

There are many definitions of entrepreneurship, but a common theme is the undertaking of uncertain endeavors with the potential to create value in the market (Cantillon, [1755] 2010; Knight, [1921] 1985). As such, entrepreneurs coordinate efforts that aim to exploit a specific situation that they imagine can (or will) emerge at some point in the future. Entrepreneurial decision-making is consequently directed toward the creation of a specific value, often in the form of a new product or service for which they believe there will be sufficient market demand. What is notable about entrepreneurship is that neither the state of supply nor of demand in that aimed-for situation can be known in the decision-making present, and therefore both are uncertain but – or so the entrepreneur believes – imaginable with some degree of plausibility.

When deciding to pursue an opportunity, the entrepreneur is ignorant of how the undertakings of other entrepreneurs, as well as other factors endogenous to the market and purely exogenous effects, may influence the imagined market situation. Therefore, the entrepreneur cannot know that he will be able to sell what is hoped or planned. In fact, the imagined opportunity may turn out to be exploited by other entrepreneurs while "our" entrepreneur is still procuring, coordinating, and combining the means of production. It may also be the case that the imagined opportunity is undermined by other and seemingly unrelated innovations in the market that change consumer behavior or affect their preference rankings in other ways. Furthermore, consumers' real interest in the offered product will be affected by fashions, fads, and temporary hype, as well as their choice to consume or save the money on hand, and thus alter their time preferences.

Nevertheless, the entrepreneur aims for this situation because he estimates that the value of the product or service to consumers will be high enough to warrant a selling price that makes the undertaking worthwhile for him. The actual price at which the good can be offered is not ultimately chosen or set by the entrepreneur, but is ultimately determined by consumers' subjective expectation-based valuation of the good in question as compared to other goods (Menger, [1871] 2007; Mises, [1949] 1998, pp. 328–329). The entrepreneur must speculate about what he will be able to charge for the anticipated good. Indeed, to be successful the entrepreneur must estimate a revenue-maximizing price – a price that is not too high, but that the market (that is, consumers) will bear. This price offers the best chance of succeeding in the undertaking, since it combines a price level that leaves enough consumer surplus to attract customers in sufficient numbers to make the opportunity worthwhile to the entrepreneur.

After estimating the revenue potential of his opportunity, and therefore its potential "value," the entrepreneur next chooses how best to exploit it. In other words, he chooses a cost structure for production that offers sufficient flexibility and scalability for the nascent enterprise to make the entrepreneur and any investors comfortable with the chances of success. This choice is limited by the estimated selling price but guided by the available market prices of the factors of production, which in a market – through entrepreneurial bidding – tend to approximate the social opportunity cost of the available varieties of the means of production. There is in this situation no way for the entrepreneur to "maximize" the outcome with precision, as his calculations are based on many unknown and uncertain variables, the exact values of which are at best imaginable and thus subject to the entrepreneur's business judgment (Knight, [1921] 1985). Indeed, it is even unknown ex ante which variables should be considered important in the undertaking and therefore identified and assessed using the entrepreneur's judgment.[1] The entrepreneur can only rely on existing factor market prices for guidance in his choice of cost structure, which, along with his own revenue estimates, allow him to calculate the profitability of each alternative.

It should be clear from the brief overview above that entrepreneurial decision-making is in many ways better described as an art than an exact science. The potential profitability of the different alternatives is subject to approximations and conjectures that are ultimately based on the entrepreneur's judgment; any calculations are therefore not exact but only estimates. The best information available to the entrepreneur in estimating the value of alternative courses of action is found in the cost of each, since prices are available in the market.

Value as a basis for factor prices

Without market prices for the factors of production, the entrepreneur is blind regarding the tradeoffs between different uses of productive resources and how they contribute to consumer value. Whereas the entrepreneur must carry out the task of comparing different cost structures in order for his intended product to be offered to consumers, he is unable to compare the social value of different types of goods and services potentially offered in the market by entrepreneurs collectively. Part of the reason is the dispersed, fragmented, and tacit knowledge of "the particular circumstances of time and place" (Hayek, 1945, p. 521), which requires decentralized decision-making or, at a minimum, decentralized collection of data for aggregation. Yet another part relates to the entrepreneur's specific personal expertise and thus, his inability to comprehend the needs and possibilities available in the market. These possibilities are better understood – and will in fact be revealed and discovered by individual entrepreneurs – as an "intellectual division of labor" among entrepreneurs pursuing profit as they understand it, a division that allows their appraisements to be assessed through the working of the competitive market process (Mises, [1920] 1935, p. 102; Salerno, 1990b, p. 54). The social opportunity cost of different courses of action becomes available to the entrepreneur through this process, but would be unavailable without factor markets to determine estimates in the form of prices of the means of production.

These prices emerge from entrepreneurs bidding for resources they need to complete their planned production projects. As each of the individual entrepreneurs has only one or a set of very few specific value targets he is aiming for, each can estimate, using economic calculation, the cost burden that their specific undertakings can support without generating losses. Calculations are still uncertain, as they are based on the entrepreneur's "guesstimates," based at least in part on tacit information in the form of experiential knowledge, impressions, and beliefs about how the market will progress in the future. The expected revenue of a project provides some guidance as to what may be the maximum cost possible while still generating sufficient profits, and present prices provide important information about factors' relative uses. These present prices result from other entrepreneurs' actions, which in turn were taken based on those entrepreneurs' *previous* anticipations of future exchange ratios (Mises, [1949] 1998, p. 211), and therefore reflect the market's approximated opportunity costs. These prices are taken as inputs by budding entrepreneurs and are an "auxiliary for entrepreneurial understanding of the future course of prices," but because they are historic they are also "by no means indispensable" for economic calculation (Salerno, 1990a, p. 44).

As the bidding process is always ongoing, prices are subject to change as entrepreneurs revise their judgments or exit, and new entrepreneurs enter to place bids based on their estimates. Each entrant entrepreneur, with a specific project in mind, seeks to exploit his anticipated future exchange ratios, and he thus chooses the cost structure most promising for the planned endeavor – and as a result, bids for those resources. The entrepreneur's bids are limited by the revenue he expects to receive from the output of the new production process, adjusted for his profit requirement and compensation for felt uncertainty in the estimates he devised. It follows that if the market prices he needs to pay to acquire the necessary resources are too high, or are expected to rise to a level that would make the project relatively unprofitable, the entrepreneur will abandon it. If present prices are high but the entrepreneur expects profitability nevertheless, he will bid for the resources he subjectively considers undervalued. He will also steer his bidding toward those resources that he considers most undervalued, from the point of view of the production project he is pursuing, and will therefore bid up their prices.

The result of this behavior by numerous entrepreneurs is a dynamic pricing mechanism of the means of production where determined prices in the present reflect entrepreneurs' joint anticipations of the value that each resource can contribute to creating final consumption goods. Entrepreneurs thus cooperate to "discover" the cost of their value-creating production plans.

What has been discussed in this section is not novel and does not differ from Mises's original calculation argument (Mises, [1920] 1935), which relies on decentralized bidding by future-oriented profit-seeking entrepreneurs looking for the least-cost means that will take them toward their preferred imagined product. As entrepreneurs outbid each other to secure necessary resources, prices are determined at levels where those entrepreneurs who pursue the, relatively speaking, most highly valued production projects, combined with relative certainty about their value, will be able to outbid those with undertakings perceived as lower-value or higher-uncertainty. In this sense, the individual entrepreneur's " 'cost' of factors is largely determined by forces outside himself and his own sales" (Rothbard, [1962] 2004, p. 356). For our purposes, it is sufficient to note that the market prices of the means of production that any one entrepreneur faces in his aims to produce are ultimately their valuations in projects pursued by *other* entrepreneurs. In other words, value precedes and determines cost in the individual production process and, more generally, the market prices of factors. Time cannot therefore be excluded from the analysis of production but, as Jeffrey Herbener (2018) shows in Chapter 6, is vital to it.

What matters for entrepreneurs, and consequently for the entrepreneurially driven market process, is not therefore cost minimization as it is generally understood, but a leveraging of already-pursued value-generating production projects to create even greater value for consumers. Factor prices determine which production projects are undertaken in the market overall, but are leveraged by entrepreneurs in those endeavors – the cost is chosen after the value of a project has already been estimated. In fact, it can be argued that entrepreneurs are not even able to decide how to minimize or "cut" costs at this stage. They can only choose a cost structure for their production undertaking that, based on their expectations of future prices and, to the degree they find it useful, using information of present prices in the factor markets, appears as sufficiently profitable to make the whole endeavor worth their while. The entrepreneur's choice involves appraising expected profitability – and leveraging costs to create new value.

Entrepreneurship versus management

The discussion in the previous section suggests that the role of entrepreneurship is to bear the uncertainty of imagined production projects and, by acting on them and thus bidding for resources in factor markets, entrepreneurs individually and collectively contribute to – if not *constitute* – the market mechanism for determining the prices of the means of production. Entrepreneurs do this through their efforts to establish supply functions in the market, which are intended to create new value for consumers and thereby improve the productivity and value-creating ability of the overall market process. As a result, by finding more effective uses for scarce resources the market process in aggregate progresses toward producing ever more value. Factor markets produce a tradeoff between different value-creating projects by making factors available only to those entrepreneurs who imagine they will create greater value for consumers – and who are relatively confident in this estimation.

As noted by Schumpeter ([1911] 1934), innovative entrepreneurs do not only produce new goods but also find new and better ways to produce goods already offered in the market. They also imagine and establish new types of organization that are more effective in production and thereby further contribute to the market's overall value creation. As also noted by Schumpeter ([1911] 1934, p. 66), these innovations are often introduced to the market through forming new firms. There is good reason for this, because, as I argue elsewhere (Bylund, 2016; see also Bylund, 2015), the economic function of firms is to establish more intensively specialized production than is currently supported by the market through exchange contracts. In other words, the economic function of the firm is to provide entrepreneurs with an effective means to implement innovations that cannot be implemented using market means. The firm is how entrepreneurs create and establish a new supply function in the market; it is how entrepreneurs leverage the costs of factors procured in the market to generate "above-normal" profits.

This conception of the economic firm suggests that entrepreneurship, as I have discussed it here, is more than simple arbitrage (Kirzner, 1973). Arbitrage, after all, can take place without a firm, and, indeed, it can be a proper means to minimize costs in an already-established production process. Yet this is not how we have examined entrepreneurship above, where we instead treated the entrepreneur as the bearer of uncertainty in creating a new supply function that he imagines is "superior." The entrepreneurial function is here one that provides value creation relative to other types of production that already exist in the market.

Seeing entrepreneurship this way reveals that it is the true driving force of the market (Mises, [1949] 2008) in that it not only pushes the boundaries of the market's present production capabilities, but also changes and refines its capital structure and thus the production apparatus that constitutes the economic "organism."

It is then indeed the case, as Lachmann ([1956] 1978, p. 13) noted, that "capital combinations, and with them the capital structure, will be ever changing, will be dissolved and re-formed" and that it is "[i]n this activity we find the real function of the entrepreneur." This "real function" is not purely responsive to exogenous events and therefore equilibrating within the market's already existing boundaries, but is imaginative and innovative in finding out how to leverage resources already used in valuable ways to produce even *more* value. Entrepreneurship, from this perspective, contributes to and improves the market's overall value creation, creates economic growth, and, through establishing innovative supply functions in new firms, increases the extent of the market (Bylund, 2016; cf. Smith, [1776] 1976).

This creative function is different from the management function that runs the already-established firm's supply function. When a new supply function has been established and the entrepreneur therefore has implemented his imagined production process and confirmed that it satisfies real consumer wants, the subsequent phase is not (in fact, it cannot be) intended to create new value but rather to exploit the value already created and thus "maximize" the effectiveness of the entrepreneur's new supply function. This is achieved by minimizing the costs of production and thereby attempting to maintain the profitability of the firm at an above-normal level. The objective of management, following the entrepreneur's act of creation, is therefore to improve productivity within the supply function to increase profitability and, furthermore, to extend the venture's profitable life cycle. Management is thus tasked by the uncertainty-bearing entrepreneur, who owns and has established the new supply function, with maximizing the function by reducing input use and waste to push the cost per unit down and to use this increased effectiveness to exploit the slope of the demand curve.[2] In other words, the manager is employed to increase margins and reduce prices, which can attract customers in larger numbers.

When the management function assumes decision-making power, the value created for consumers is neither new nor uncertain, but revealed through actual sales in the market. The new value was already created as the entrepreneur established the supply function and bore the related uncertainty. The role of the manager, following and acting on behalf of the entrepreneur, is to maintain this function. As a consequence, the proper focus of the profit-seeking endeavor shifts from new value creation to cost minimization. The value produced using the existing supply function can only marginally be increased by tweaking the product to make it more usable, refine its design, and perhaps reposition it in the eyes of consumers, but the potential for cost-cutting and streamlining the production process offers great possibilities for increasing profitability. Indeed, the creation of a new supply function is the task of entrepreneurship and not of management. What matters to us here are not the exact actions taken by management, but the idea that the management function differs from the entrepreneurial function in a fundamental way: whereas the entrepreneur bears the uncertainty of an undertaking aiming to create new future value, illustrated by the creation of a new supply function in a new firm, the manager takes this supply function as a starting point and seeks to maximize the effectiveness by which this value is created. In contrast to the entrepreneur, management holds value-creation relatively constant, but varies and attempts to reduce the cost side in order to increase profitability.

This observation is instructive for understanding the Austrian view of the market process and therefore the Misesian argument that economic calculation is impossible under socialism. With a single owner of society's resources, there can be no entrepreneurship as discussed above: there is no uncertainty-bearing under the threat of loss because loss is not personal, and there is also no individual benefit from profiting. In other words, there is no intellectual division of labor within value creation, which makes calculation impossible, which in turn makes entrepreneurial value creation impossible. As a result, the extent of a socialist economy does not – and indeed *cannot* – expand, as there is no value creation through the creation of new supply functions in competition with other imagined and already-existing ventures: there is only management of existing production structures and the resources allocated between projects already underway.

This conclusion applies not only to the market socialist critique of Mises's argument but also to Denis's (2015) more recent challenge in which several control replaces private property. Under several control of public property there will indeed be a factor market determining prices for the means of production as assigned leaders of society's production units place bids for resources to use in their respective processes. These bids are, as Denis points out, real market bids placed by decision-makers in a decentralized production structure; the managers of production units do not simply "play market as children play war, railroad, or school," as Mises ([1949] 2008, p. 703) put it, just like managers of corporations do not play market. Nevertheless, this factor market will be severely crippled because it remains unaffected by value-creating entrepreneurship: the economy's capital structure will not be "ever changing . . . dissolved and re-formed" (Lachmann, [1956] 1978, p. 13), but will instead remain structurally the same. What changes are made to the capital structure are at best changes in response to changing consumer preferences and exogenous influences in order to adjust the existing production processes. Managers may even act as arbitrageurs as they shift their bids to cheaper inputs to be used in their processes, and thus respond to changing market data. As a result, their combined efforts are reallocated between production processes (cf. Kirzner, 1973). Yet new supply functions that disrupt the market and discover previously unknown demands are different: they require new uncertainty-bearing and are consequently entrepreneurial. Indeed, the ultimate decision to shift a firm's capital to creation of a new supply function entails the withdrawal of capital from its existing use and the subsequent investment in the new endeavor, which requires ownership (Hülsmann, 1997; Machaj, 2007; Bylund and Manish, forthcoming).

The conclusion is that a common basis for critiques of Mises's argument against socialism is the perception of a market economy as shaped primarily through the *management* function and therefore characterized by cost minimization within the existing capital structure. In contrast, Mises and the Austrians view the market as an open-ended process driven by the *entrepreneurship* function characterized by new value creation that disrupts the existing structure as well as the extent of the market. In other words, the solutions offered to the problem Mises raised are based on different assumptions about the very nature of the economy.

The management function is impotent with respect to reshaping an economy's capital structure and production apparatus, because it is limited to adjustments to, and within, already established supply functions. This influences factor prices as the manager of a venture bids on and shifts between alternate resources, but factor prices determined only by managers cannot reflect potential new production, as this is the function of entrepreneurship, which requires bearing uncertainty through the ownership of invested property. Managers act within the boundaries of the supply functions created by entrepreneurs, and they therefore cannot produce an economy characterized by growth through value creation.

Importantly, the argument formulated above is applicable to more general problems than the socialist economy, because the distinction between the entrepreneurship function as value-creating and the management function as cost-focused is universal and should apply to all cases of similar structure: where economic action relates to the coordination of efforts without open-ended creation and thus is limited to varying the inputs used in production, the undertaking is limited to management and therefore cannot produce increasing value.

This argument is also stronger, because where value creation is the focus, what matters to decision-makers and actors is the relative creation of value – not the cost involved to carry out the action. Indeed, we briefly noted above that cost should be of little concern – and only of secondary import – if the expected outcome is of greater value. Cost, in fact, is only a means toward producing that value and is therefore always chosen *as a function of the value potential* of the project. In contrast, where cost is the primary concern the struggle is to keep existing value from falling. This is, as I shall now illustrate, a battle that cannot be won.

How cost destroys value

Although their functions are distinct, management and entrepreneurship tend to co-exist in the real market. Private businesses aim both for sustained and increasing profitability through process improvements and cost minimization (management) and create new value by investing funds in novel supply functions (entrepreneurship). Whereas the management function follows and replaces the entrepreneurship function when the supply function passes the market test, managers are commonly used at least in part as a means for further entrepreneurship aiming to improve the venture's position in the competitive market. Businesses that survive over longer periods of time generally engage in repeated new product development and invest large amounts in research and development: they stay in business by reinventing themselves. The original supply function established through forming the firm may therefore come to be replaced, and sometimes combined with or augmented by, a new supply function of greater anticipated value as a result of successful entrepreneurship efforts "internally" – that is, within the *legal* firm's boundaries (cf. Jensen and Meckling, 1976, pp. 310–311).

Such legal firms can increase and extend profitability by continually assessing their situation and entering new markets. They repeatedly consider their options and thereby establish an internal value tradeoff between possible supply functions. Existing functions are rejected (the invested capital withdrawn) when they no longer contribute sufficiently relative to the potential value to the firm's bottom line of new (entrepreneurial) supply functions under consideration (new investments). Yet whereas shifting from one opportunity to another is a task that may be delegated to employed managers, it is still the owner of the capital in the firm who is the ultimate decision-maker: he is the one to suffer loss from bad investments and thus bears the uncertainty, and necessarily has the veto right through ownership.

The case is clearer when considering *economic* firms, which are defined by and limited to their unique production undertakings (Bylund, 2016). They do not attempt to recreate production and enter new markets through entrepreneurship, which would generate a new firm; this means they rely on the value created in the original supply function throughout the firm's life cycle. By thereby holding the firm's value creation relatively constant,[3] they are fully dependent on the management function of cost minimization. In other words, the possibility of increasing and sustaining profitability is limited to *reducing cost*. Consequently, the profitability of the undertaking can increase or be sustained only for as long as the market situation does not radically change in such a way that it undermines the organization's position and thus its ability to satisfy demand in a valuable way. During a period of relative market stability, achieved profitability depends on the firm's ability to extend or entice new demand and thereby expand the possibility of selling the good in greater quantities.

Cost minimization efforts initially allow the firm to improve on and exploit the full potential of the entrepreneur's implemented innovation. This is done by implementing tweaks for increased effectiveness and reduced resource use in production, streamlining the production processes, and considering other materials available at lower prices in the market. Technologically speaking, the supply function may be improved both by increasing the quality of the product and reducing waste. Economically, production is shifted to utilize relatively lower-cost resources while the value produced changes minimally as consumers are not offered a different product but "more of the same" – yet perhaps offered at a lower price to sell greater quantities.

To illustrate, consider a firm producing a certain product that has value to consumers and is thus demanded in the market. The firm does not engage in entrepreneurship and therefore neither attempts to replace the product with a new one or to develop products with which to enter new markets. We thus hold the supply function constant for this firm, by which is meant the original function remains intact but in revised and perhaps improved form, to illustrate the effects of market action based on management only. This allows us to work through the logic and determine how generally applicable the thesis drafted above is, without resorting to the specific conditions under which public sector services that are not held to profitability requirements or competitive service offerings in the open market operate. The manager within this firm is consequently tasked with increasing and sustaining the firm's profitability, but is not allowed to act entrepreneurially by abandoning the supply function or shifting the firm's production efforts into new markets. The invested capital, in other words, remains in the original supply function.

As should be evident from the discussion above, holding the supply function constant does not entail fixed output volumes, which the manager can adjust as needed, but only a fixed *kind* of output. For instance, a producer of light bulbs continues to produce light bulbs, but the quantity produced, the materials used for inputs, and the factors used to aid production are variable. In other words, we are speaking about running the business, not creating a new one. The example considered here begins as the newly created supply function (for the new good, light bulbs) has passed the market test (that is, sufficient quantities were sold at cost-covering prices), which means there is sufficient demand to support the business, at least for the moment. This is why the task of management is to increase and sustain profits, which can be accomplished by cutting costs in production, tweaking the end product, or varying the selling price to effectuate changes in sales volume that could better exploit the market situation.

Cost-cutting can be accomplished by shifting production to favor inputs that are offered at relatively cheaper prices in factor markets, the knowledge of which may be limited by, for example, transaction costs (Coase, 1937).[4] This amounts to what Farrell (1957) refers to as price efficiency, or of "choosing an optimal set of inputs" (Farrell, 1957, p. 259), and requires that the manager is responsive to changes in prices. Within the firm's production process, the manager can improve its technical efficiency (Farrell, 1957) or the effectiveness of the already-established production process by reducing waste and lead times, and consequently increasing overall resource utilization. Both of these activities suggest reduction in cost per unit, which contributes to the increased profitability of the firm.

The product can also be refined in its functionality, features, and quality, particularly as the firm learns about its customers' specific wants and can therefore better target those most highly valued. As the product is tweaked to better fit the real wants of consumers, the selling price may be increased, at least in the short term. Yet whereas a "better" product is potentially demanded in greater quantities, increasing sales generally includes reducing the selling price.

More importantly, and applicable in the longer term, the firm can exploit the shape of the demand curve to maximize revenues. This can be done by adopting techniques for implementing different forms of price discrimination that allow the firm to capture a greater part of the value produced and thus replace some consumer surplus with producer surplus. However, the possibility of using such techniques diminishes with the efficiency of the market, leaving the firm to lower prices in response to competitive pressures and as demand is satiated. For instance, a lower price point can increase the firm's sales and therefore, assuming elastic demand, its revenues by increasing the overall quantity demanded and, in a competitive situation, its market share. Depending on the firm's specific cost structure, increased sales can contribute to higher profits or sustain profitability over a longer time period.

Management needs to consider cost-cutting, product improvement, and lower prices to maximize performance, and the firm will consequently experience falling relative prices for input *and* output. Whereas lower selling prices increase volume and thus allow the firm to exploit the full extent of the former, at some point the firm will no longer be able to reduce input prices at the same rate as the reduction necessary in output prices to increase sales. Indeed, cutting prices as a seller is easier than reducing prices as a buyer. With the actions of entrepreneurs in the market where the firm operates, factor prices will be bid up as more valuable production is pursued, which allows them to assume more highly-priced cost structures, thereby pushing the firm's cost of inputs up, while the relative value of the firm's product diminishes.

It follows that without the addition of value-creative entrepreneurship, cost minimization is an effective strategy only for a limited time period. At some point, in order to further cut prices with the intent to increase sales, the manager will be forced to consider a reduction in input or production costs that could also reduce the market value of the product offered. This decision should be made whenever the expected effect is a net contribution to the firm's bottom line, which suggests that any given supply function will tend to produce *lesser value* to consumers over time (but at lower cost).

The benchmark for consumers considering purchasing a product is the opportunity cost of that decision and, consequently, the most highly valued opportunities that are foregone by making the purchase. If the firm we are analyzing acts in a competitive market with new entrants or where other incumbent firms engage in entrepreneurship, the opportunity cost will tend to increase, perhaps rapidly. Indeed, consumers' relative costs of buying the firm's product will increase by the value increase in alternative opportunities in the market *plus* the value decrease in the cost-reduced product that the firm offers. This suggests consumers will tend to abandon the only-management firm's product as they can obtain higher value elsewhere.

If the firm acts in an economy where entrepreneurship is not common or expected (or perhaps not even permitted), the period during which the firm can sustain profitability should be comparatively much longer. The opportunity cost of consumers will not increase as a result of value creation, which suggests the value of competing goods (new and old) does not increase (opportunity costs may not increase), and the relative value of the good in question will therefore not be undermined. If the absolute value of the product offered by the firm would remain the same, which is unlikely for more than a short period of time, its relative value should increase as the value of other products diminish with cost-cutting efforts. However, the absolute value of "our" firm's product will also diminish as management attempts to increase and sustain profitability, and thus prolong the life cycle, by minimizing production costs. The firm's profitability may then be sustained as long as the absolute value of its product is higher and the rate of reduction in value does not exceed that of products offered by other firms.

Implications for socialist calculation

The above discussions have implications for arguments on both sides of the socialist calculation debate. I showed that the Austrian conception of the market process is one of consistent (but nevertheless fluctuating) economic progression by means of entrepreneurial value creation. This invalidates all relevant critiques to date that assume an economy with unchanging or static boundaries. More importantly, I also showed that the assumption that challengers of Mises's argument make about the state of the market must be false: the alternative to a progressing economy, in which the extent of the market expands through innovative entrepreneurship (Bylund, 2016), is not a fixed-pie economy but a retrogressive, value-destructive process.

This observation is not based on a very strict interpretation of socialism (which has been a source of criticism of Mises, [1920] 1935), but is an implication of the economic state of affairs that obtains where management is the predominant force on resource allocation. Mises suggests a similar argument when stating that "the crucial and only problem of socialism, is a purely economic problem, and as such refers merely to means and not to ultimate ends" (Mises, [1949] 2008, p. 693).[5] This is indeed what management, limited to within-system adjustments, does, and it does so in stark contrast to entrepreneurship's value creation. Coase (1988, p. 8) noted the relevance of this connection when speculating that the planning of Soviet Russia was "essentially the same puzzle" as the planning undertaken by managers within firms. The major difference, to Coase, is that a market has many "islands of socialist planning" (Bylund, 2014).

But the greater difference between a market and non-market economy is, as we established above, entrepreneurship. Within the firm, the manager is but the "junior partner" of the entrepreneur (Mises, [1949] 2008, p. 301) whose task is to minimize costs and increase profitability in the given supply function created by the entrepreneur. While managers act as bidders in the market for the means of production, their effect on the market system is solely allocative *between already-existing supply functions*. Both the means and the ends are given, though potentially variable in order to increase overall effectiveness and profitability. Prices determined through managerial bidding are thus based only on supply functions that already exist, without influence by entrepreneurship through value creation in new supply functions.

In contrast to managers, innovative entrepreneurs act beyond the boundaries of the market (Schumpeter, [1911] 1934; Bylund, 2016) to create new value. The result of their actions is the expansion of the extent of the market and thus the progression of the economic system overall toward an increased ability to satisfy consumer wants. Entrepreneurship as a market function thereby brings about some of the uncertainty that individual entrepreneurs necessarily bear when undertaking productive endeavors, because the market data that are available for economic decision-making are constantly changed and challenged by entrepreneurial action.

In other words, the issue of economic calculation is not one of how to maximize resource allocation and usage within a fixed system, but one of calculation within *changing* boundaries where the scope and extent of economic action are either expanding (market system) or contracting (non-market system). In an expanding market economy the anticipated value created by entrepreneurial undertaking takes precedence over the cost necessary to realize it. Cost is ultimately an implication of the true choice variable: value creation. Cost is thus a lower bound for value creation efforts as the prices determined in factor markets approximate social opportunity costs. This lower bound is consistently pushed upward as factor market prices reflect anticipated value creation, thereby pressuring entrepreneurs to create even more value. But there is no upper bound for value creation other than that imposed by the imagination of entrepreneurs and consumers, and consequently, entrepreneurs try to find the best way to leverage cost.

In a contracting economy, in contrast, the aim of decision-makers is management: to minimize cost in order to sustain profitability for an already established supply function that generates a product of fixed or falling market value. The question in this scenario is whether decision-makers can be guided by prices, and whether their combined bids for resources in the factor markets can determine prices that approximate their social opportunity costs. In an outright socialist economy, as Mises showed, there are no proper prices and producers are therefore blind as to where they can contribute to consumer welfare. In our model of the management economy, which is not a full-scale socialist economy but simply an economy lacking entrepreneurship (that is, with no new entrepreneurial entry), factor prices are relevant for decision-making in everyday tasks but unimportant for long-term welfare. Bids for resources are not intended to create new value, which requires new supply functions, but to extend the life cycles of already-established supply functions. Thus, factor prices may here approximate the social opportunity cost of resources in existing production,[6] but this is of little use to decision-makers in firms as the economy is neither progressing nor stable but in fact retrogressing and contracting. Without entrepreneurship and the creation of new supply functions, the market will be unable to respond to new and previously-unaddressed demand of any sort – it can only address changes to the extent they relate to existing types of production. The economy should therefore at any point in time be at its maximum in terms of value creation; the only possible development is a reduction in total value produced, either through managerial failure or shifting demand.

Both entrepreneurial and managerial economies are characterized by change and thus uncertainty, which means the solutions offered to the calculation problem cannot be limited to a fixed-boundary system. The question that Mises posed is whether calculation is possible in the non-progressing economy, which we now understand is necessarily a *contracting* economy. In a socialist contracting economy, Mises found economic calculation to be impossible; our analysis above suggests that in a non-socialist economy that lacks entrepreneurship economic calculation may be possible, but that it is meaningless because it applies purely to the management of existing types of production and is not directed toward the overall satisfaction of consumer wants.

Concluding remarks

This chapter attempts to reformulate and extend Mises's original argument that calculation is impossible in a socialist economy. We found that without entrepreneurship, even in a setting where economic action is taken to earn profits and decision-making is decentralized, the economy tends to contract rather than expand. In an economy where the "driving force" is economic management rather than entrepreneurship, value will not only not be created but will be actively destroyed. In contrast, a market with entrepreneurship as its driving force is distinguished by its progression in terms of new value creation. There appears to be no middle ground.

This conclusion follows from the distinction between two economic functions, both of which may be necessary for a properly functioning market: management and entrepreneurship. Socialist economies are characterized by management but no entrepreneurship, hierarchically structured production, and a central plan; market economies rely on both innovative entrepreneurship to increase the extent of the market and management to improve already-established production processes cooperating in a process of creative destruction. Both systems grapple with uncertainty, but there is an important difference between them: uncertainty-bearing in a progressing system of entrepreneurship is offensive and focused on value creation, whereas uncertainty-bearing in a contracting economic order is limited to management of existing production and is thus defensive and preoccupied with minimizing cost.

For a market order under entrepreneurship, the role of cost is to set a lower bound to value creating endeavors and thus force some (the least successful) entrepreneurs to exit. This lower bound is pushed ever higher as entrepreneurs challenge the status quo by attempting to create new and even greater value, and thus undermine the rationale for existing production. Entrepreneurs engender the market economy's process of "creative destruction," as Schumpeter ([1942] 1950, pp. 81–86) noted. In a pure management system, in contrast, the value created through existing production processes constitutes an *upper* bound, and the chief struggle is therefore to maintain this level of satisfaction if at all possible. In short, economic theorists siding with socialist ideals tend to assume socialism is not only possible, but that it can be automatically achieved. Our conclusions are not so optimistic.

Notes

1 Knight's concept of entrepreneurial judgment, which is different from Kirzner's entrepreneurial alertness (High, 1982), is further analyzed in Foss and Klein (2012) and McMullen (2015).

2 I am of course using the concept of the demand curve figuratively.

3 Value creation is limited to the already-established supply function and variations thereof, which exclude creation of new value. Firms can improve their production process as well as their product offerings, but cannot innovate new products or shift production to novel capital structures.
4 For an elaboration of the relevance of Coase's theory of transaction costs and management, see, for example, Bylund (2014).
5 This point is made even clearer by Salerno, who summarizes Mises's view of the problem of socialism as "the problem purely of Robbinsian maximizing, of deciding how *given* means are to be allocated in light of a *given* structure of ends" (Salerno, 1990a, p. 46; emphasis in original). In other words, it is a problem of economic actions taken during the maintenance phase of an existing production structure (or, within the firm, an existing supply function).
6 Factor prices may reflect future prices as well, but as the expectations of managers relate only to "business as usual," or to failure, the only options without new entrepreneurship, it is unclear what guidance for action such prices can provide.

References

Berle, A. A., and G. C. Means. 1932. *The Modern Corporation and Private Property*. New Brunswick, NJ: Transaction Publishers.

Blaug, M. 1997. *Economic Theory in Retrospect*. Cambridge: Cambridge University Press.

Bylund, P. L. 2014. "Ronald Coase's 'Nature of the Firm' and the Argument for Economic Planning." *Journal of the History of Economic Thought* 36 (3): 305–329.

———. 2015. "Explaining Firm Emergence: Specialization, Transaction Costs, and the Integration Process." *Managerial and Decision Economics* 36 (4): 221–238.

———. 2016. The Problem of Production: A New Theory of the Firm. Abingdon: Routledge.

Bylund, P. L., and G. P. Manish (forthcoming). "Private Property and Economic Calculation: A Reply to Andy Denis." *Review of Political Economy*.

Cantillon, R. 2010 [1755]. *An Essay on Economic Theory*. Trans. C. Saucier. Auburn, AL: Ludwig von Mises Institute.

Coase, Ronald H. 1937. "The Nature of the Firm." *Economica* 4 (16): 386–405.

———. 1988. "The Nature of the Firm: Origin." *Journal of Law, Economics & Organization* 4 (1): 3–17.

Denis, A. 2015. "Economic Calculation: Private Property or Several Control." *Review of Political Economy* 27 (4): 606–623.

Farrell, M. J. 1957. "The Measurement of Productive Efficiency." *Journal of the Royal Statistical Society* 120 (3): 253–290.

Foss, N. J., and P. G. Klein. 2012. *Organizing Entrepreneurial Judgment: A New Approach to the Firm*. Cambridge: Cambridge University Press.

Hayek, F. A. 1945. "The Use of Knowledge in Society." *American Economic Review* 35 (4): 519–530.

Hayek, F. A. V. 1978. "Competition as a Discovery Process." In *New Studies in Philosophy, Politics, Economics, and the History of Ideas*. Chicago: University of Chicago Press, pp. 179–190.

Herbener, J. M. 2018. "Time and the Theory of Cost." In Matthew McCaffrey, ed., *The Economic Theory of Costs: Foundations and New Directions*. Abingdon, UK: Routledge, pp. 147–166.

High, J. 1982. "Alertness and Judgment: Comment on Kirzner." In I. M. Kirzner, ed., *Method, Process, and Austrian Economics: Essays in Honor of Ludwig Von Mises*. Lexington: D.C. Heath, pp. 161–168.

Hülsmann, J. G. 1997. "Knowledge, Judgment, and the Use of Property." *Review of Austrian Economics* 10 (1): 23–48.

Jensen, M. C., and W. H. Meckling. 1976. "Theory of the Firm: Managerial Behavior, Agency Costs and Ownership Structure." *Journal of Financial Economics* 3 (4): 305–360.

Kirzner, I. M. 1973. *Competition and Entrepreneurship*. Chicago: University of Chicago Press.

Knight, F. H. 1985 [1921]. *Risk, Uncertainty and Profit*. Chicago: University of Chicago Press.

Lachmann, L. M. 1978 [1956]. *Capital and Its Structure*. Kansas City, MO: Sheed Andrews and McMeel.

Lange, O. 1936. "On the Economic Theory of Socialism: Part One." *Review of Economic Studies* 4 (1): 53–71.

———. 1937. "On the Economic Theory of Socialism: Part Two." *Review of Economic Studies* 4 (2): 123–142.

Machaj, M. 2007. "Market Socialism and the Property Problem: Different Perspective of the Socialist Calculation Debate." *Quarterly Journal of Austrian Economics* 10 (4): 257–280.

McMullen, J. S. 2015. "Entrepreneurial Judgment as Empathic Accuracy: A Sequential Decision-Making Approach to Entrepreneurial Action." *Journal of Institutional Economics* 11 (3): 651–681.

Menger, C. 2007 [1871]. *Principles of Economics*. Trans. J. Dingwall and B. F. Hoselitz. Auburn, AL: Ludwig von Mises Institute.

Mises, L. V. 1935 [1920]. "Economic Calculation in the Socialist Commonwealth." In Friedrich August Hayek, ed., *Collectivist Economic Planning*. London: George Routledge & Sons, pp. 87–130.

———. 1998 [1949]. *Human Action: A Treatise on Economics*. Scholar's ed. Auburn, AL: Ludwig von Mises Institute.

Rothbard, M. N. 2004 [1962]. *Man, Economy, and State with Power and Market*. Scholar's ed. Auburn, AL: Ludwig von Mises Institute.

Salerno, J. T. 1990a. "Ludwig Von Mises as Social Rationalist." *Review of Austrian Economics* 4 (1): 26–54.

———. 1990b. "Postscript: Why a Socialism Economy Is 'Impossible'." In L. V. Mises, ed., *Economic Calculation in the Socialist Commonwealth*. Auburn, AL: Ludwig von Mises Institute, pp. 49–69.

Schumpeter, J. A. 1934 [1911]. The Theory of Economic Development: An Inquiry Into Profits, Capital, Credit, Interest, and the Business Cycle. Cambridge, MA: Harvard University Press.

———. 1950 [1942]. *Capitalism, Socialism, and Democracy*. 3rd ed. New York: Harper & Row Publishers.

Smith, A. 1976 [1776]. *An Inquiry Into the Nature and Causes of the Wealth of Nations*. Chicago: University of Chicago Press.

Taylor, F. M. 1929. "The Guidance of Production in a Socialist State." *American Economic Review* 19 (1): 1–8.

11 Economic calculation and the limits of social entrepreneurship

Matthew McCaffrey

Introduction

Ludwig von Mises's theory of economic calculation is a strong contender for the title of greatest contribution to twentieth-century economics. Mises's writings revolutionized economic thinking in at least two ways: first, they explained the indispensable role calculation plays in the market process, and second, they demonstrated the impossibility of calculation under a system of socialist central planning. Socialist organization inevitably fails because it lacks the necessary means to appraise the costs and benefits of any planned allocation of resources. Without this basis for decision making, socialism descends into "planned chaos," leading inevitably to economic and social destruction.

Mises's contributions to the economic analysis of socialism are widely acknowledged. However, the fact is sometimes overlooked that his work on calculation offers much more than a critique: it is also a positive theory of the market economy. In other words, it is a comprehensive account of the process by which individual exchanges produce a vast and complex system of market prices that are continuously responsible for the rational allocation of scarce resources in society. Furthermore, his theory "provides the rationale for the price system, purely free markets, the security of private property against all encroachments, and sound money" (Salerno, 1993, p. 69). Economic calculation is thus inextricably linked with the most essential social institutions. More specifically, it is an indispensable tool for entrepreneurial decision making, which Mises called the "driving force" of the market and of economic progress. The price system allows profit-seeking entrepreneurs to assess the costs and benefits of their production decisions, and thus to make good use of society's scarce resources. Moreover, calculation establishes the boundaries of profit-seeking firms and places limits on their horizontal and vertical integration and use of bureaucracy (Klein, 1996).

However, economic calculation is also a useful and necessary framework for analyzing a wide range of organizations that fall outside strictly for-profit enterprise or socialist central planning. These include organizations in the voluntary market economy that are not founded with a primary goal of earning monetary profits, such as charities, cooperatives, trusts, mutual societies, social enterprises, and other forms of economic activity that might be considered "not-for-profit."

Understanding calculation – or the lack thereof – within these organizations is vital for evaluating their true costs and benefits, the role they play in the economy, and their ultimate impact on society. Mises's theory thus holds enormous potential for economists hoping to expand their analysis to non-traditional areas of inquiry. In fact, some scholars argue that "Mises's concept of economic calculation . . . belongs at the forefront of . . . research into the nature and design of organizations" (Klein, 1996, p. 4).

This chapter focuses specifically on the role of economic calculation in "social entrepreneurship." Social enterprises are business organizations that are not motivated by the desire to generate monetary profits for traditional shareholders. Instead, the profits of social enterprise are used to solve "social" problems, often by addressing the same kinds of needs as charitable organizations. Social enterprises are special, however, because they support their missions through successful commercial ventures rather than through donations. This type of business is increasingly prevalent around the world, and in its many variations is the subject of much entrepreneurship and management research. However, little work has been done to integrate the social entrepreneurship literature with the economic approach to cost and benefit, i.e. the theory of economic calculation. Yet this is a vital task for economics, which already contributes influential ideas to entrepreneurship research. Applying the theory of calculation outside traditional market entrepreneurship is a natural extension of previous work, and is even crucial if emerging research fields in entrepreneurship are to be grounded in sound economic ideas.

The following chapter takes a first step in this direction by integrating the theory of economic calculation with some current research on social entrepreneurship. I first explain the meaning of social action in economics and in entrepreneurship studies, and use the contrast between disciplines to highlight the distinctive domain of social entrepreneurship. I then discuss the profit motive in traditional and in social enterprises, and clarify its influence on entrepreneurial decision making. This leads finally to a discussion of calculation within social enterprises. I explore two different models of social entrepreneurship, and explain the role of calculation in each. I argue that the price system plays an indispensable role in placing boundaries on the size and scope of social enterprises. I conclude with a discussion of directions for future research.

The economic foundations of social entrepreneurship

Mises demonstrated that the defining characteristic of the market process is entrepreneurial action using economic calculation in terms of money prices (Mises, 1990a, 1998). Given the overarching importance of his theory, it is no surprise that calculation is relevant for research in social entrepreneurship as well as for its more traditional profit-focused counterpart. However, although calculation is indispensable to a functioning economy, it does not play the same role in all organizations, and there are many institutions in which the extent of calculation is ambiguous or undefined. This is especially true of *social enterprises*, which employ a number of non-traditional business methods and objectives that are difficult to analyze using conventional economic tools. Defining the "social" aspects of social enterprise – and explaining how social entrepreneurship is distinct from "mundane" market entrepreneurship – is particularly challenging (Zahra et al., 2009). The purpose of the present section, then, is to explain the economic basis of social action by showing that pro-social behavior is at the root of both mundane and social entrepreneurship.[1]

As the name implies, the significance of social entrepreneurship lies in its "social" meaning. Understanding how social enterprises work therefore requires explaining their uniquely social facets. However, explaining these implications and what they mean in practice for the economic structure of social enterprises is difficult. Social entrepreneurship is variously and sometimes vaguely defined, and its use in social science can be inconsistent with its legal meaning or with the ways it is understood by many real-world social entrepreneurs (Agafonow, 2015).

The first step toward addressing this problem is to unpack the economic assumptions of social enterprise. Typically, the key economic difference between mundane entrepreneurship and social entrepreneurship is said to lie in their respective ends: in general, social enterprises are defined as "mission-driven," while ordinary enterprises are profit-driven (Dees, 2001; Abu-Saifan, 2012). However, this distinction is inaccurate for two reasons, both of which make it difficult to draw a simple line between the two types of entrepreneurship: first, profit-seeking entrepreneurship is always to some extent social, and second, social entrepreneurship is always to some extent profit-seeking (Austin, Stevenson, and Wei-Skillern, 2006). The following two subsections explore each of these claims in turn and lay the foundation for a discussion of economic calculation in social entrepreneurship. I explain that social entrepreneurship is a subset of a larger social process that occurs through the division of labor. Furthermore, the pursuit of monetary profit is necessary for social enterprises to attain their goals.

Social action and social entrepreneurship

Human beings act socially when they cooperate and collaborate. In fact, mutual understanding between individuals is the basis of economic and social order (Mises, 1998, pp. 143–145). Social bonds emerge when individuals begin to understand the inherent advantages of concerted action over isolated or violent actions, especially the idea that violence precludes or destroys social bonds. Specifically, society is founded on the joint recognition by individuals of a vital economic truth: concerted action is more productive than isolated action (Mises, 1998, pp. 157–160). Cooperation is an acknowledgement of the universal benefits of the *division of labor*, which Mises describes as "the ultimate social phenomenon" (Mises, 1998, p. 157). In his view, action is "social" to the extent it fosters cooperation and thereby encourages specialization and the division of labor.

One vital implication of this approach is that the entire market economy is a profoundly social process of mutual want satisfaction. It is comprised of many individual exchanges that each contribute to the formation of the prevailing structure of money prices. Economic affairs are organized by the price system, which reflects from moment to moment the value of goods and services in society (Salerno, 1990a; Salerno, 2018). Profit-seeking entrepreneurs use prices to estimate the future value of the factors of production and to compare the costs and benefits of different available combinations of these factors (Salerno, 1990b). Based on their appraisals, they make judgments about how best to allocate scarce resources among innumerable competing uses (Foss and Klein, 2012, 2015). Good judgments yield profits and increased market shares; poor judgments yield losses and, eventually, bankruptcy. Competition thus functions as a selection mechanism that eliminates any entrepreneurs who fail to satisfy consumers, or who do so at too high a cost.

This entrepreneurial process of appraising the future value of factors of production using money prices is the essence of the market economy. In the absence of this social appraisement process – for example, in a socialist economy in which there are no factor markets and hence no factor prices – entrepreneurs are left without the ability to compare the costs and benefits of alternative production plans. The result is the systematic waste and destruction of resources by central planning committees and the collapse of the economy's capital structure. Ironically, socialism is in this sense inherently *anti*-social in that it eliminates economic calculation and ultimately undermines the division of labor and human cooperation. The inevitable outcome of socialist central planning is social disintegration.

Conversely, the entrepreneurial process underlying the market economy is thoroughly social in that it embodies the cooperation of many individuals working for mutual benefit within the division of labor. This notion of social action is more inclusive than those typically used in entrepreneurship studies; most importantly, it includes a range of profit-seeking actions and business organizations that are not typically described as social and that do not possess specific social goals. However, focusing on collaboration and specialization reveals that even mundane businesses motivated mainly by the desire to generate profit for shareholders are deeply social. It is therefore inaccurate to contrast social with non-social enterprises as such; as far as the market is concerned, "there is no such thing as 'non-social' entrepreneurship" (Seelos and Mair, 2005, p. 243).

The question for economists, then, is not *if* entrepreneurship is social, but *how* it is (Tan, Williams, and Tan, 2005). Profit-driven enterprise is only one of many different kinds of cooperative action that are compatible with the division of labor. Social entrepreneurship is another. Social enterprises are typically defined as business organizations that do not narrowly pursue monetary profit and returns for shareholders, but instead aim to provide solutions to "social" problems (Harding, 2004; Martin and Osberg, 2007). Social problems are in turn defined as basic human needs that are unmet by prevailing market and political institutions (Seelos and Mair, 2005). In practice, social entrepreneurs use business ventures to directly and indirectly transform disadvantaged or marginalized communities, especially those affected by low levels of education and high levels of poverty, unemployment, homelessness, or even injustice (Alvord, Brown, and Letts, 2004; Martin and Osberg, 2007; Abu-Saifan, 2012). The positive outcomes created by social organizations are referred to as "social value" (Seelos and Mair, 2005; Haugh, 2006; Peredo and McLean, 2006; Dacin, Dacin, and Matear, 2010). Social value

> can emerge in the ways the products or services of the venture function; the ways they are distributed and delivered; the advocacy approach of the venture; the ways the venture accumulates and deploys financial, human, and other resources; or the ways the venture's networks or partnerships are configured.
>
> (Bloom, 2012, p. 73)

The key element in this approach is that social enterprises are fundamentally business organizations. That is, they aspire to be independent of charitable and governmental support (Dees, 1998). Ideally, they earn revenue through the sale of goods and services just as ordinary businesses do, rather than relying on donations or public funds (Emerson and Twersky, 1996). Like traditional entrepreneurs, social entrepreneurs use judgment to allocate scarce resources in the face of uncertainty (Mort, Weerawardena, and Carnegie, 2003; Peredo and McLean, 2006; Foss and Klein, 2012).[2]

Focusing on the business at the heart of social enterprise avoids confusion about the scope of social ventures by concentrating on a specific kind of economic organization. This approach is not always standard practice in the literature, however. For example, early empirical work on social enterprises defined them essentially as innovative organizations outside the for-profit and governmental sectors (Leadbeater, 1997). As a result, previous research includes a wide range of organizations under the label of "social entrepreneurship," including institutions that span or blur the lines between business, charity, and government (Leadbeater, 1997; Dees, 2001; Thompson, 2002). These hybrid organizations and cross-sector collaborations are worth studying, but they are not the main subject of this chapter, which focuses on social enterprise as it has come to be understood in more recent research, as a distinct form of business venture. Of course, real-world social enterprises can seek out non-market sources of revenue or make strategic alliances with governmental organizations or NGOs. Yet when social entrepreneurs choose to rely on donations or public funds rather than earning revenue through trade, they change the economic structure of their ventures, thereby creating organizations that require different kinds of analysis. Importantly though, the theory developed in this chapter can also contribute to the study of these organizations.

The profit motive and social entrepreneurship

The profit motive is a key assumption in contemporary economic theory. It is especially important for the theory of the firm, which usually takes the profit-maximizing business as a starting point. It is also frequently invoked in definitions of market and social entrepreneurship. Yet like many concepts in economics that are taken for granted, the idea of the profit motive deserves closer attention. The reason is simple: contrary to its name, "the" profit motive does not refer to a static, homogeneous incentive that confronts all entrepreneurs in the same way. Instead, it reflects a dynamic, diverse range of human purposes that may or may not exist for particular entrepreneurs. Given that social entrepreneurship is often thought to avoid traditional profit-seeking, it is important to ask whether profit motives actually play a necessary role in all business organizations. In this subsection, I explain how a realistic, inclusive theory of profit motives reveals that profit-seeking in a non-trivial sense does influence the decision making process of social enterprises.

All action – defined as purposeful behavior – aims at the achievement of an end. Ends are valuable because of their perceived ability to provide benefits to actors. The benefits of action are weighed against the costs, i.e. opportunity costs, and individuals choose the alternative that yields the greatest perceived net benefit (Newman, 2018). However, benefits and costs are personal and subjective. They can only be understood as a kind of feeling or psychological state that individuals experience. When this feeling is positive enough to inspire action – when benefits are greater than costs – an actor receives "psychic income" (Fetter, 1915, pp. 26–29). This surplus of psychic benefit over psychic cost is known as "psychic profit" (Mises, 1949, p. 287; Rothbard, 2009, pp. 71–72). The pursuit of psychic profit is a universal feature of human action: every action aims at bringing about conditions that are more desirable from the point of view of the actor. Psychic profit is present even when individuals act charitably out of loving care for others (McCaffrey, 2015b).[3]

The idea of psychic profit carries important implications for social ventures. If all action involves the pursuit of psychic profit, then it is inaccurate to classify certain kinds of action as for-profit and others as not-for-profit (Mair and Marti, 2006). Likewise, all organizations embody the actions and values of the people who direct them, and in this sense there are no such things as completely not-for-profit organizations. Even the directors of charities attempt to use them to improve conditions from their own points of view. What is needed, then, is a more specific way to distinguish between different profit motives. Profit in the universal, psychic sense is not the only kind of profit that entrepreneurs pursue, and it is not the only kind that can be used to explain the boundaries of social enterprise.

Economics and entrepreneurship research do not usually refer to psychic profit. Instead, they focus on the pursuit of *monetary profit* by entrepreneurs, which is a major criterion used to distinguish the domain of social entrepreneurship. Unlike psychic profit, individuals only pursue monetary profit under certain conditions. This point has led to some confusion in economics and management research. Specifically, in order to explain entrepreneurial motivation economists have sometimes appealed to the concept of an "economic man" interested only in the selfish maximization of monetary income (Mises, 1998, p. 241, 2003, pp. 191–192; Rothbard, 2009, p. 217n15). Unfortunately, the use of such unrealistic assumptions has led entrepreneurship researchers to believe that economics is simply a method for studying selfish or materialistic behavior (Kirzner, 2011). In this view, economics has nothing to offer research into "non-economic" or "social" motivations such as those found in social enterprises.

However, the concept of economic man (and related models) is unrealistic and provides a misleading picture of the true scope of economic analysis. The subjective theory of value that underlies modern economics reveals that human ends are more complex and varied than textbook analysis implies. In fact, the subjective theory of value accounts for all possible human motivations. It therefore undermines the claim that economics can only focus on monetary profit or other narrow goals. As a result, "[Economics] must not restrict its investigations to those modes of action which in mundane speech are called 'economic' actions, but must deal also with actions which are in a loose manner of speech called 'uneconomic'" (Mises, 1998, p. 235).

Of course, it could be argued that the prospect of money income has historically been an important motivation for entrepreneurs. This is likely true, yet "While the profit motive [i.e. income-earning] might be 'a central engine' of entrepreneurship, it does not preclude other motivations" (Mair and Marti, 2006, p. 38). There is nothing to imply that the pursuit of greater personal income is necessarily related to entrepreneurs' decision making process. This point is made in both theoretical and empirical literature. For example, in his much-cited work on "creative destruction," Joseph Schumpeter argued that entrepreneurs are driven more by the desire to create than by narrow considerations of income (Schumpeter, 1942). And, more recently, a growing body of research has argued that real-world entrepreneurs are motivated by a variety of psychological and economic factors, which include but are not limited to the desire for income and wealth (Shane, Locke, and Collins, 2003).

Yet, although it is not universal, monetary profit is relevant in many real-world situations. Money's role as a general medium of exchange gives it a special significance for individuals who participate in the division of labor. In a monetary economy, money makes up one side of every exchange, and must be used whenever goods and services are purchased. Indirect exchange allows consumers to purchase consumer goods that would not otherwise be available. Therefore, in order to increase their welfare through consumption, individuals must also increase their money incomes. It can even be argued that "in the money economy, other things being equal, [all actors] will attempt to attain the highest possible money income" (Rothbard, 2009, p. 213). This rule holds true for both individuals and firms under these conditions. More importantly, it sometimes holds true even for individuals who wish to spend their incomes on charitable or "social" causes. For example, giving alms and buying food for the homeless each require income to donate or to spend on consumer goods (actions that yield psychic profit to the giver). Anyone who wishes to give more, thereby creating social value, must acquire more income. Other things equal, each individual and organization in a monetary economy is bound to pursue money income in order to obtain psychic profit. This applies to pro-social organizations just as it does to mundane businesses.

The profit motive is a constraint on entrepreneurs' *decisions* rather than their *values*. As Mises argues,

> the entrepreneur is actuated by the profit motive. This enjoins upon him the urge to prefer the most economical solution, i.e. that solution which avoids employing factors of production whose employment would impair the satisfaction of the more intensely felt wants of the consumers.
>
> (1998, pp. 300–301)

The price system serves as a guide for entrepreneurs navigating the uncertainty of the marketplace. Yet no matter how entrepreneurs ultimately decide to spend their profits, it is clear that they will attempt to earn as much profit as possible, because in a monetary economy larger profits enable greater spending on consumer goods, even when these are used for social purposes.

Yet there are important exceptions to the above rule, as we shall see. We have assumed thus far that "other psychic ends are neutral," and that individuals are primarily able to increase their welfare by purchasing consumer goods (Rothbard, 2009, p. 441). These assumptions provide the basis for the initial discussion of economic calculation in the following section, in which social entrepreneurs are said to maximize monetary profits. However, they are relaxed in a later discussion of social entrepreneurship in cases where other psychic ends come into play that conflict with the pursuit of money profits.

Economic calculation and social entrepreneurship

We are now ready to examine the economic organization of social enterprises and determine the role economic calculation plays within them. Social enterprises face essentially the same key decisions as mundane businesses: "just what activities ought to be undertaken? What investments should be made? Which product lines expanded and which ones contracted?" (Klein, 1996, p. 12). In other words, what goods and services should social enterprises produce, and how should they produce them? These fundamental questions are answered through the process of economic calculation. And although some researchers do not realize it, many studies of social entrepreneurship are also searching for these answers, and for something akin to calculation. For example, Thompson (2002, p. 427) observes that, "Strong leadership and good management of socially entrepreneurial initiatives is important. There is always an opportunity cost for the resources being utilised. Achievement below that which could be achieved is a lost opportunity, an unmet need." That is, social entrepreneurs need to know the value of the alternative uses of scarce resources. Likewise, other scholars ask:

> Which "social needs" should have priority? Without an overarching objective, it is impossible to decide whether using resources to help the homeless in Paris creates as much social value as feeding hungry children in Kabul.

> Unless we set boundaries to the scope of SE [Social Entrepreneurship], it may be impossible to define the unique characteristics that differentiate it from traditional or business entrepreneurship.
>
> (Seelos and Mair, 2005, p. 244)

Calculation explains both the comparative costs and the boundaries of social entrepreneurship. Explaining just how it works requires discussing one more aspect of the profit motive: the question of entrepreneurs' income and spending. In common speech, the term "profit motive" refers to two separate questions: first, do entrepreneurs use monetary profits as the test of their success or failure? Second, how do entrepreneurs spend any profits they have earned? The answers to these questions define the major kinds of organizations that entrepreneurs create: mundane, social, political, and charitable. The different possible combinations of income/spending and organizational method are listed in Table 11.1.[4]

We have already seen that psychic profit is a universal feature of action, but that money profit only motivates individuals under certain conditions. There are, of course, organizations that do not use the profit-and-loss test as a guide for their activities. Charities are one example. They refuse to compete commercially because they view profit-seeking as inappropriate or immoral. This refusal precludes the guidance of the price system and economic calculation, which do not place the same limits on charities as they do on businesses. Unlike businesses, charities are not responsible to shareholders expecting to receive a return on their investments. Instead, they spend their income according to bureaucratic rules laid down by their directors (Mises, 1944, pp. 47–48; 1998, pp. 307, 721–722). The donors to the organization are the true consumers of the charity's services (Rothbard, 2011, pp. 453–454). A second example is government or political entrepreneurship, which is also bureaucratic and lacks access to economic calculation (Mises, 1944; McCaffrey and Salerno, 2011). Government organizations are different from charities, however, in that they are not directed toward genuinely social goals, but rather the goals of political decision makers (Salerno, 1993; McCaffrey, 2011).

Table 11.1 Types of entrepreneurship by income and organizational method

		Organizational method	
		Money profits & economic calculation	**No monetary profits & no economic calculation**
Income & spending	**Income retained by owner/shareholders**	Mundane entrepreneurship	Political entrepreneurship
	Income spent on social goals/stakeholders	Social entrepreneurship	Charitable entrepreneurship

Returning to the first question posed above: in general, the pursuit of monetary profits goes hand-in-hand with economic calculation and the profit-and-loss test. This is obvious in mundane entrepreneurship, but is less clear for social entrepreneurship. I argue below that social enterprises, as business organizations, cannot ignore the price system when making their production decisions. This leads to the second question posed above: the problem of how entrepreneurs use their profits. All forms of enterprise must maintain their capital, and all businesses have the option of investing profits back into the organization in order to increase production (Mises, 1990b, p. 269). In this sense there is no difference between mundane and social enterprise. However, conventional entrepreneurs make an additional choice between reinvesting profits and either retaining them (in an individual-owned firm) or paying them out to shareholders as dividends (in a joint-stock company). These options do not exist for social enterprises because their economic and sometimes legal organization prohibits retaining profit as income, requiring it instead to be spent creating social value. Social enterprises thus provide a combination of method and spending that results in a form of organization different from mundane entrepreneurship, charity, and government.

We now arrive at a key point in the argument: the question of whether social entrepreneurs engage in economic calculation. Based on the above discussions, I argue that they do. Given that social enterprises are business organizations that use their own scarce resources to serve consumers in the marketplace, and given that they earn profits or losses according to their ability to do so, it follows naturally that in order to survive they can and must engage in economic calculation. The special missions that define social enterprises do not negate their ability to engage in economic calculation, because calculation does not require that entrepreneurs use profits to increase their personal income or wealth. What matters is that entrepreneurs subject their firms to the discipline of the market when making their production decisions. Any organization that hopes to succeed based on successful production and exchange must submit to the price system. Calculation then reveals whether a firm's social mission is compatible with a rational allocation of resources.

Entrepreneurs are not necessarily motivated by the selfish pursuit of profit. Nevertheless, it is important that their decisions, whatever they might be, are not artificially restricted by the institutional environment. Calculation is an institutional process that rests on the security of private property and the division of labor. Among other things, this implies that strong property rights and freedom from expropriation are necessary for entrepreneurs to calculate effectively (Salerno, 1993; Machaj, 2007; McCaffrey, 2015a). Yet these institutional requirements do not imply that entrepreneurs are only concerned with increasing their personal incomes, or that they cannot be concerned with solving social problems. Rather, the issue is that entrepreneurs must be able to use profits in ways that allow them to reach the highest points on their individual value scales. Ultimately, entrepreneurs' specific motivations are less important than their freedom to pursue them.

Economic calculation and the limits of the social enterprise firm

A previous section argued that pro-social goals are compatible with economic calculation. Yet their relationship consists of more than simple compatibility: pursuing such goals actually *requires* social entrepreneurs to focus on earning profits and avoiding losses. Nevertheless, the question remains how economic calculation specifically affects the structure of social enterprises. The present section shows that for social ventures to compete they must use the price system to appraise the costs and benefits of their production decisions. Furthermore, economic calculation through the price system acts as a limit on the size and scope of social enterprises, which cannot survive without external markets to guide them.

Economic calculation in complementary social enterprises

So far this chapter has described social enterprise in general terms. I now provide a more detailed analysis by examining two different types of social organizations. The first and simpler case involves *complementary social enterprises*. These are social ventures in which business activities are completely separate from the enterprise's social mission (Fowler, 2000). The most common examples are social businesses that donate the entirety of their profits to causes such as charitable organizations. These charities may or may not also be owned and operated by the social enterprise: what matters for this discussion is that the social cause does not directly influence the decisions of the business. Instead, it receives operating income to the extent that the business is successful at earning profits. In this case, how do entrepreneurs make their production decisions?

For an enterprise to remain profitable, entrepreneurs must accurately price their inputs and correctly estimate the value of their outputs. Complementary social enterprises approach this problem in much the same way as conventional businesses: even though social enterprises are organized around distinct goals, consumers still determine their viability. In other words, if social entrepreneurs are subject to the profit and loss test in competitive markets, they must allow consumer satisfaction to guide their decisions. Funding a social cause requires resources, and social entrepreneurs will therefore attempt to maximize monetary profits. This is a necessary implication of the market process, and does not undermine the missions of complementary social enterprises:

> To buy in the cheapest market and to sell in the dearest market is, other things being equal, not conduct which would presuppose any special assumptions concerning the actor's motives and morality. It is merely the necessary offshoot of any action under the conditions of market exchange.
>
> (Mises, 1998, p. 241)

Social entrepreneurs strive to accurately appraise the future prices of the factors of production and to purchase them, in the present, at prices that are lower than the selling prices of the goods they will eventually produce. Competition between social enterprises, and between social enterprises and ordinary businesses, will still be strong.[5] Their success depends ultimately on consumers, who assign value to goods based on the psychic benefits they expect to receive from them. In social enterprises, the value of consumer goods has two general sources: the benefit these goods provide through use (direct consumption) and the benefit provided by the knowledge that buying helps to advance a valuable social mission (indirect consumption). These benefits are not mutually exclusive, and often exist side by side. For example, consider a social enterprise restaurant that sells sandwiches and donates the profits to the homeless. Consumers might value the sandwiches for their particular characteristics (e.g. their taste) or for their social significance (e.g. the feeling of contributing to a worthy cause), or for some combination of the two. These different sources of value determine how consumers define the good being sold, i.e. the ends it serves. They therefore also influence the pricing of social goods and explain how consumers ultimately determine the prices of the productive factors used by social enterprises.

In order to determine whether production is profitable, entrepreneurs use the price system to make judgments about future consumer values. Yet production takes time, and entrepreneurs can err in their appraisals. As a result, there is always an element of uncertainty in the pricing process (Herbener, 2018). In the case of social enterprise, there is a special uncertainty involving the two sources of value of social goods. Entrepreneurs must anticipate whether the value attached to direct and indirect consumption will be sufficient to justify charging market prices for their outputs. If not, the value of the productive factors in the enterprise will fall and the entrepreneur will earn losses.

Charities and competitive social enterprises are obliged to buy or rent factors at prevailing market prices (Rothbard, 2011, pp. 454–455). If entrepreneurs cannot afford to pay these prices because consumers do not sufficiently value their products, the factors will be bid away to other more productive uses and their enterprises will eventually close. On the other hand, if entrepreneurs correctly appraise factor prices in light of future consumer demand, they can maintain and increase the value of the capital invested. Factors of production are priced competitively according to their discounted marginal productivity, which is imputed to them by consumers through the price system. Whether an enterprise is productive enough to be profitable is ultimately determined by consumers.

Complementary enterprises charge market prices for their products, prices that result from the interaction of the two sources of value mentioned above. Importantly, it makes a difference which one dominates in the minds of consumers. If the social mission is not a source of value for consumers, social entrepreneurs will have to compete for patronage based solely on their ability to produce valuable products for direct consumption. In this case the visibility of the social mission shrinks or even vanishes in the minds of customers. However, social entrepreneurs whose missions are considered valuable in their own right may be able to charge a premium for their products. If so, social goods take on a different kind of goods-character (to use Menger's term) than products that do not serve social ends. They become similar to branded goods that may be physically similar to lower-priced goods available on the market, but are different in the eyes of consumers because they serve different ends.

Entrepreneurs know that they must price their inputs and outputs competitively. Yet to do so they must have recourse to economic calculation. They must be able to estimate the opportunity cost of each factor employed in production, and this means external markets for each factor must exist that can be used to establish its implicit price (Rothbard, 2009, pp. 606–611). Once an external price is available, the economic calculation of profit and loss becomes feasible. If, however, there is no external price, an "island of noncalculable chaos" appears (Rothbard, 2009, pp. 613–614). The firm becomes unable to accurately appraise a part of its business, and as a result its overall performance suffers. All mundane firms avoid this situation wherever possible in order to minimize losses. Consequently, they never produce to the extent that no external price remains for their factors.

This result explains why it is impossible for One Big Firm to control all production in the economy: it would suffer from the same calculation problem as a socialist system. Importantly, it also means that no economy could ever consist entirely of *producers' cooperatives*, because such organizations would also be unable to separate the prices paid for different factor contributions (Rothbard, 2009, pp. 608–609). Likewise, no social enterprise can grow so large that it becomes the "unique producer and user of [a] capital good" (Klein, 1996, p. 16), or else its business division would be unable to successfully allocate resources and generate income. Its performance would suffer, and eventually funding for the social mission would disappear. Economic calculation thus places an upper bound on the size of both social enterprises and conventional firms.

Importantly, social enterprises may have a harder time finding external prices more than some conventional businesses do. The reason is that many social enterprises rely on innovative business models that do not have counterparts among traditional enterprises. In particular, social ventures employ unique and previously unpriced factors of production, especially labor (Dacin, Dacin, and Matear, 2010). That is, they are more prone to calculation errors to the extent that they allocate resources without the price system to guide them. As Klein observes, "innovation carries with its benefits the cost of more severe internal distortions" (1996, p. 17n16). The most reliable cost estimates come from mundane businesses because these organizations strive the most to appraise prices correctly. Social enterprises are therefore most efficient in sectors where ordinary entrepreneurs have established a well-developed network of prices that they can use to estimate their own implicit costs. However, it is not always possible to find such a network in practice because some social business customers find it difficult to pay even the minimum required prices (Mair and Marti, 2006). As a result, social enterprises often exist on the boundaries of economic calculation. Frank Fetter remarked that entrepreneurs take "the more exposed frontier of risk" (Fetter, 1915, p. 347). Along similar lines, we might say that social entrepreneurs take the more exposed frontier of economic calculation.[6]

We conclude that successful complementary social enterprises will adapt their behavior to the same standards used by conventional businesses. That is, they will encourage efficient production and avoid waste as much as possible. A more difficult question involves exactly how effective their social investments are without prices to guide them. When the business is independent from the social mission, the latter is effectively reduced to a charity. In turn, the lack of external prices for goods and services means that charities will suffer from problems relating to the inefficient use of physical and human resources. Only when the social mission is more closely connected with the business venture do charities begin to overcome these organizational problems. External social enterprises are the most straightforward examples of social entrepreneurship at work. Consequently, they provide the clearest picture of the role of economic calculation in social ventures. However, they are also simple organizations that are ultimately quite similar to conventional firms. Relaxing some of our previous assumptions about them will allow us to account for more complex forms of social entrepreneurship, as demonstrated in the next section.

Economic calculation in integrated social enterprises

There are many ways that the business and social aspects of an enterprise can be connected. This section examines the case of *integrated social enterprise*, wherein the business venture and the social mission overlap. Unlike complementary ventures, integrated social enterprises are not set up primarily to fund other organizations. Instead, they advance their social missions directly through the operations of their businesses (Fowler, 2000). Typically, this involves social firms adopting organizational forms or special business methods that are used as bases for entrepreneurial decision making. Consider again the example of the sandwich producer. An integrated social enterprise might maintain the same general business while also specifying that at least 25% of the company's workforce be homeless persons. It thus serves consumers through its ordinary business, but also provides special consumption benefits to any workers it employs who would not otherwise be able to find employment (or who could not find it at the same wage rate). As mentioned above, besides their specific social elements, such ventures are run like typical businesses.[7]

In this scenario, we can no longer hold equal other values besides profit-seeking. In this case, social value creation through business operates directly and indirectly. As a result, the assumption of monetary profit-maximizing no longer applies. Instead, integrated social enterprises attempt to reconcile different and possibly conflicting objectives sometimes referred to as the "double bottom-line" (Emerson and Twersky, 1996, p. 12). I argue that this conflict represents a trade-off between efficient decision making and *gift-giving*.

To the extent that they insist on making unprofitable decisions, entrepreneurs step outside the sphere of economic calculation: they strategically choose certain divisions in their businesses that are not subject to the profit and loss test.

Lacking this guide, some divisions will tend to produce inefficiently. In conventional business, poor performance encourages entrepreneurs to scale back failing departments and increase production in more profitable lines; in social enterprise, however, keeping an inefficient division alive is often a key requirement of the core mission. Social entrepreneurs have no choice but to subsidize failing divisions using the profits from more successful ones. This is consistent with empirical research showing that social enterprises tend to sacrifice monetary profits in order to expand consumption among their target groups (Agafonow, 2015). It is also consistent with the idea that all people, including social entrepreneurs, constantly try to maximize psychic profit, but not necessarily monetary profit (Mises, 1949, p. 287; Rothbard, 2009, pp. 71–72).

In the restaurant example, suppose one of the homeless workers earns wages greater than his discounted marginal productivity.[8] In a conventional business, the worker's wages will be bid down. However, what if the entrepreneur is committed to keeping the worker employed? One consequence is that any wage the employee receives above his marginal productivity is actually a gift from the entrepreneur that is subtracted from the value of some other part of the business. The source of the gift may be the entrepreneur's profits, the capital of the enterprise, the land of the enterprise, or the wages of other employees if they are willing to forego part of their potential earnings, as in the case of volunteers for a charitable cause.[9] The gift reduces the profitability of the organization, but maximizes the social entrepreneur's psychic profit (Rothbard, 2011, pp. 455–456). Naturally, entrepreneurs can avoid monetary losses by convincing consumers to pay higher prices for social goods in order to compensate for what would otherwise be artificially high wages.

It is not always easy in practice to separate factor payments from gifts. As Mises explains,

> The boundaries between buying goods and services needed and giving alms are sometimes difficult to discern. He who buys at a charity sale usually combines a purchase with a donation for a charitable purpose . . . Man in acting is a unity. The businessman who owns the whole firm may sometimes efface the boundaries between business and charity. If he wants to relieve a distressed friend, delicacy of feeling may prompt him to resort to a procedure which spares the latter the embarrassment of living on alms. He gives the friend a job in his office although he does not need his help or could hire an equivalent helper at a lower salary. Then the salary granted appears formally as a part of business outlays. In fact it is the spending of a fraction of the businessman's income. It is, from a correct point of view, consumption and not an expenditure designed to increase the firm's profit.
>
> (Mises, 1998, p. 242)

Once again, economic calculation acts as a boundary on social entrepreneurs' choices. The greater the number of decisions that entrepreneurs make outside the sphere of economic calculation, the more inefficient their businesses will become.

In the most extreme case, every decision is treated as social, and there is no scope for economic calculation at all. Essentially, the social enterprise becomes a conventional charity. We can infer from this that if entrepreneurs want to effectively deliver on their promises to alleviate social problems, they will strive wherever possible to use the price system so as to limit inefficiencies as much as possible. They can then focus their attention on a small number of non-calculable decisions that deliver the bulk of the social value generated by the enterprise. But the overarching problem is that integrated social enterprises cannot expand their social missions to the point that prices for all factors of production disappear.

The above discussions focused on two specific types of social enterprise organization. However, real-world social businesses are not limited only to these forms: there is a wide range of combinations of goals that social entrepreneurs might choose. Furthermore, social organizations can change in response to internal and external stimuli. Uncertainty and complexity thus make social organizations difficult to describe in terms of universal principles. Yet despite this fact, we can still use economic theory to draw some general conclusions about social enterprises.

First, there is a spectrum of involvement between the business and social aspects of social enterprises (Dees, 1998; Thompson, 2002; Tan, Williams, and Tan, 2005; Peredo and McLean, 2006). The distinct role of the business, and of economic calculation, becomes clearer the more the two sides are separated. Conversely, the greater the number of factors of production that entrepreneurs hold outside the pricing process, the smaller the scope for economic calculation, effective resource allocation, and ultimately, delivery of social value. As a result, social organizations that want to pursue their goals in the most effective way will use the price system wherever possible.

This argument also applies to the increasing number of profit-seeking firms that include social elements in their business models without fundamentally altering their objective of delivering profits to shareholders. For example, Corporate Social Responsibility (CSR) guidelines offer firms the chance to contribute to social causes outside their typical business operations.[10] These self-imposed rules can help to increase business through generating publicity, but they also involve firms making gifts to specific producers. For example, in order to support a developing economy or encourage the ethical sourcing of products, a firm can buy from a supplier at prices higher than could be obtained elsewhere. Or it could commit to donating a small percentage of its profits to charity, thus making a gift out of what might otherwise have been entrepreneurial income. In any case, if CSR or similar guidelines crowd out the price system, the scope for efficient decision making is reduced.

Second, social enterprises are influenced in many ways by government regulation and monopoly privileges. The more the system of government intervention expands – especially government's role as a major financier of social organizations – the more economic calculation is hampered and distorted. It remains an open question, though, exactly how these distortions will affect social enterprises. Does intervention encourage artificial growth in the number or size of social ventures? Or does it have the opposite effect by monopolizing traditional industries and excluding new, alternative kinds of firms? Furthermore, what is the major cause of entrepreneurs' interest in alternative forms of economic organization? Is social enterprise, as sometimes argued in the literature, a response to market failures? Or is it a response to public policy failures that create and institutionalize the kind of marginalized groups that social enterprises seek to help, or who might be likely to found a social enterprise? A full analysis of the relationship between social enterprises and government intervention is beyond the scope of this paper. However, the arguments made above lay the foundation for answering these and other questions.

Conclusion

The theory presented in this chapter addresses important problems in both economics and entrepreneurship research. From an economic perspective, it offers a novel way to explain the organization of social enterprises, which have until now been studied mostly by the management disciplines. Economics provides wide-ranging theories of social interaction, value, calculation, profit, and pricing that can be used to rigorously define the domain of social entrepreneurship. Applying these theories expands the scope of economic reasoning and can provide a realistic account of many types of economic organization in the voluntary and public sectors. Doing so improves our understanding of these sectors while reinforcing the universality – or limitations – of several essential principles of economics. It also undermines the criticism that economics is unconcerned with or unable to explain behaviors and organizations that fall outside the sphere of profit-maximization (McCaffrey, 2015c).

The economic approach outlined above also helps to resolve some of the most controversial questions in social entrepreneurship research (e.g. Austin, Stevenson, and Wei-Skillern, 2006). For example, the idea of economic calculation explains the tension between two general theories of social enterprise: those focusing on profit-maximization and those that emphasize avoiding mission drift (Agafonow, 2015). As explained in this chapter, this tension actually reflects the boundary between economic calculation and non-calculation. Prices and gifts play an endless game of tug-of-war in social enterprise. If one side wins, social businesses end up behaving like traditional firms or voluntary sector organizations.

The question of how to measure the efficacy of social enterprises is also ubiquitous in the literature (Dees, 2001; Zahra et al., 2009; Dacin, Dacin, and Matear, 2010). Fortunately, economic calculation provides a basis for estimating the true social value of social enterprises, which is demonstrated from moment to moment through the actions of consumers and the reactions of entrepreneurs and the price system (Salerno, 1993, pp. 52–53). Of course, calculation cannot be used to estimate every possible conception of value, but it can at least be used to ensure that social businesses support their social missions in the most effective ways, for example by supporting "sustainable" practices. This is a noteworthy advance, because resources are often stretched thin in social organizations, which urgently seek to minimize waste.

Social entrepreneurship is only one of many innovative forms of economic organization to emerge in the last few decades. Its increasing presence in commercial society makes it an important area of study for economists, who have sometimes limited their research to more traditional forms of business. However, this chapter has shown that economic theory is well-suited to the study of social organizations, which present a valuable opportunity for economists to improve their ideas and extend them to related fields like management studies. At the same time, economic arguments can also serve to encourage entrepreneurship researchers to return to their roots in the social sciences.

Notes

1 Cf. Klein (2008) for an overview of the "mundane" economic theorizing of the causal-realist tradition.
2 Cf. Zahra et al. (2009) and Dacin, Dacin, and Matear (2010) for surveys of different definitions of social entrepreneurship. Although the term is often used loosely and inconsistently, the general approach taken in this chapter is consistent with many current definitions. Furthermore, as I explain, by relaxing some assumptions and expanding the scope of economic analysis, it can be applied to many more.
3 As Mises explains: "Even an action directly aiming at the improvement of other people's conditions is selfish [in the sense of pursuing psychic profit]. The actor considers it as more satisfactory for himself to make other people eat than to eat himself. His uneasiness is caused by the awareness of the fact that other people are in want" (Mises, 1998, p. 243).
4 This chapter uses the term "entrepreneurship" in a broader sense than some economic literature, to refer to judgmental decision making about the use of scarce, heterogeneous resources under conditions of uncertainty (Foss and Klein, 2012). Such decisions take place in many different contexts, as illustrated in Table 11.1. However, it can be argued that true entrepreneurship is inextricable from economic calculation, and that terms such as "political entrepreneurship" or "charitable entrepreneurship" are therefore contradictory. However, this approach does not alter the underlying arguments made in this chapter, which could be rephrased without changing any of the conclusions about economic calculation in social enterprises.
5 Kirzner (2011) imagines a scenario where all businesses in the economy are essentially complementary social enterprises. He concludes that such a situation would produce the same "ruthless" competition as an economy filled with "selfish" entrepreneurs.
6 This fact explains why social enterprise is sometimes less attractive to prospective entrepreneurs than conventional business: social enterprises are more prone to failure due to calculation problems, and this danger is not necessarily offset by the prospect of increased returns.
7 In practice, social enterprises often include more than one social element in their business models. However, this fact does not alter the arguments in this section, which are valid even if there are several "islands of noncalculable chaos" within a social firm. This case of multiple social elements actually helps emphasize the importance of external prices for limiting the size and quantity of the islands.
8 Throughout, I assume that the lack of calculation leads to losses. It is possible, though, that wages set by a social entrepreneur happen to be equal to the worker's marginal productivity. Yet if this were the case, there would be no need for a special rule about hiring particular kinds of employees: entrepreneurs could simply hire those workers who are expected to be the most productive. Presumably, such rules exist because

social entrepreneurs recognize that their target employees will be relatively inefficient. Furthermore, coincidences in labor pricing are unlikely to occur systematically: labor markets tend to be efficient precisely because entrepreneurs can use trial and error via the price system to guide their negotiations with workers. If this process is not used by social ventures, there is no reason to think wages will tend toward marginal productivity.

9 Cf. the discussions of psychic and monetary income in labor markets in Rothbard (2009, pp. 575, 629–630).

10 Baron (2007) actually defines social entrepreneurship as the willingness to found a CSR firm at a loss.

References

Abu-Saifan, S. 2012. "Social Entrepreneurship: Definitions and Boundaries." *Technology Innovation Management Review* 2 (2): 22–27.

Agafonow, A. 2015. "Value Creation, Value Capture, and Value Devolution: Where Do Social Enterprises Stand?" *Administration & Society* 47 (8): 1038–1060.

Alvord, S. H., L. D. Brown, and Christine W. Letts. 2004. "Social Entrepreneurship and Societal Transformation an Exploratory Study." *Journal of Applied Behavioral Science* 40 (3): 260–282.

Austin, J., H. Stevenson, and J. Wei-Skillern. 2006. "Social and Commercial Entrepreneurship: Same, Different, or Both?" *Entrepreneurship Theory and Practice* 30 (1): 1–22.

Baron, D. P. 2007. "Corporate Social Responsibility and Social Entrepreneurship." *Journal of Economics & Management Strategy* 16 (3): 683–717.

Bloom, P. N. 2012. "Introduction to the Special Section on Social Entrepreneurship." *Journal of Public Policy &* Marketing 31 (1): 73–74.

Dacin, P. A., M. T. Dacin, and M. Matear. 2010. "Social Entrepreneurship: Why We Don't Need a New Theory and How We Move Forward From Here." *Academy of Management Perspectives* 24 (3): 37–57.

Dees, J. G. 1998. "Enterprising Nonprofits." *Harvard Business Review* 76: 54–67.

———. 2001. "The Meaning of 'Social Entrepreneurship.'" *Center for the Advancement of Social Entrepreneurship*. https://centers.fuqua.duke.edu/case/knowledge_items/the-meaning-of-social-entrepreneurship.

Emerson, Jed, and Fay Twersky (eds.). 1996. *New Social Entrepreneurs: The Success, Challenge and Lessons of Non-Profit Enterprise Creation*. San Francisco: The Roberts Foundation.

Fetter, F. A. 1915. *Economic Principles*. New York: The Century Co.

Foss, N. J., and P. G. Klein. 2012. *Organizing Entrepreneurial Judgment: A New Approach to the Firm*. Cambridge: Cambridge University Press.

Foss, N. J., and P. G. Klein. 2015. "Introduction to a Forum on the Judgment-Based Approach to Entrepreneurship: Accomplishments, Challenges, New Directions." *Journal of Institutional Economics* 11 (3): 585–599.

Fowler, A. 2000. "NGDOs as a Moment in History: Beyond Aid to Social Entrepreneurship or Civic Innovation?" *Third World Quarterly* 21 (4): 637–654.

Harding, R., 2004. "Social Enterprise: The New Economic Engine?" *Business Strategy Review* 15 (4): 39–43.

Haugh, H. 2006. "Social Enterprise: Beyond Economic Outcomes and Individual Returns." In J. Mair, J. Robinson, and K. Hockerts, eds., *Social Entrepreneurship*. Basingstoke, UK: Palgrave Macmillan, pp. 180–205.

Herbener, J. M. 2018. "Time and the Theory of Cost." In Matthew McCaffrey, ed., *The Economic Theory of Costs: Foundations and New Directions*. Abingdon, UK: Routledge, pp. 147–166.

Kirzner, I. 2011. "The Economics of Greed or the Economics of Purpose." *The Annual Proceedings of the Wealth and Well Being of Nations* 3: 17–29.

Klein, P.G. 2008. "The Mundane Economics of the Austrian School." *Quarterly Journal of Austrian Economics* 11 (3 and 4): 165–187.

———. "Economic Calculation and the Limits of Organization." *Review of Austrian Economics* 9 (2): 3–28.

Leadbeater, C. 1997. The Rise of the Social Entrepreneur. London: Demos.

McCaffrey, M. 2011. "On Government Investment and Consumption." *New Perspectives on Political Economy* 7 (2): 163–176.

———. 2015a. "Economic Policy and Entrepreneurship: Alertness or Judgment?" In P. Bylund and D. Howden, eds., *The Next Generation of Austrian Economics: Essays in Honor of Joseph T. Salerno*. Auburn, AL: Ludwig von Mises Institute.

———. 2015b. "What's Love Got to Do With It? Action, Exchange, and Gifts in Economic Theory." *Quarterly Journal of Austrian Economics* 18 (2): 210–221.

———. 2015c. "Review of 'Austrian Theory and Economic Organization: Reaching Beyond Free Market Boundaries'." *Quarterly Journal of Austrian Economics* 18 (3): 368–379.

McCaffrey, M. and J. T. Salerno. 2011. "A Theory of Political Entrepreneurship." *Modern Economy* 2 (4): 552–560.

Machaj, M. 2007. "Market Socialism and the Property Problem: Different Perspective of the Socialist Calculation Debate." *Quarterly Journal of Austrian Economics* 10 (4): 257–280.

Mair, J. and I. Marti. 2006. "Social Entrepreneurship Research: A Source of Explanation, Prediction, and Delight." *Journal of World Business* 41 (1): 36–44.

Martin, R. L., and S. Osberg. 2007. "Social Enterprise: The Case for Definition." *Stanford Social Innovation Review* 5 (2): 28–39.

Mises, L. von. 1944. *Bureaucracy*. New Haven, CT: Yale University Press.

———. 1990a. *Economic Calculation in the Socialist Commonwealth*. Auburn, AL: Ludwig von Mises Institute.

———. 1990b. "Observations on the Cooperative Movement." In *Money, Method, and the Market Process: Essays by Ludwig von Mises*. Norwell, MA: Kluwer, pp. 238–279.

———. 1998 [1949]. *Human Action: Scholar's Edition*. Auburn, AL: Ludwig von Mises Institute.

———. 2003. *Epistemological Problems of Economics*. 3rd ed. Auburn, AL: Ludwig von Mises Institute.

Mort, G. S., J. Weerawardena, and K. Carnegie. 2003. "Social Entrepreneurship: Towards Conceptualisation." *International Journal of Nonprofit and Voluntary Sector Marketing* 8 (1): 76–88.

Newman, J. 2018. "Contemporary Debates on Opportunity Cost Theory and Pedagogy." In Matthew McCaffrey, ed., *The Economic Theory of Costs: Foundations and New Directions*. Abingdon, UK: Routledge, pp. 11–26.

Peredo, A. M., and M. McLean. 2006. "Social Entrepreneurship: A Critical Review of the Concept." *Journal of World Business* 41 (1): 56–65.

Rothbard, M. N. 2009. *Man, Economy, and State with Power and Market*. Auburn, AL: Ludwig von Mises Institute.

———. 2011. "The Myth of Neutral Taxation." In *Economic Controversies*. Auburn, AL: Ludwig von Mises Institute, pp. 449–501.

Salerno, J. T. 1990a. "Ludwig von Mises as Social Rationalist." *Review of Austrian Economics* 4 (1): 26–54.

———. 1990b. "Postscript: Why a Socialist Economy is 'Impossible'." In *Economic Calculation in the Socialist Commonwealth*. Auburn, AL: The Ludwig von Mises Institute.

———. 1993. "Mises and Hayek Dehomogenized." *Review of Austrian Economics* 6 (2): 113–146.

———. 2018. "The 'Income Effect' in Causal-Realist Price Theory." In *The Economic Theory of Costs: Foundation and New Directions*. Ed. Matthew McCaffrey. Abingdon, UK: Routledge, pp. 27–48.

Schumpeter, J. A. 1942. *Capitalism, Socialism, and Democracy*. New York: Harper and Brothers Publishers.

Seelos, C. and J. Mair. 2005. "Social Entrepreneurship: Creating New Business Models to Serve the Poor." *Business Horizons* 48 (3): 241–246.

Shane, S., E. A. Locke, and C. J. Collins. 2003. "Entrepreneurial Motivation." *Human Resource Management Review* 13 (2): 257–279.

Tan, W. L., J. Williams, and T. M. Tan. 2005. "Defining the 'Social' in 'Social Entrepreneurship': Altruism and Entrepreneurship." *International Entrepreneurship and Management Journal* 1 (3): 353–365.

Thompson, J. L. 2002. "The World of the Social Entrepreneur." *International Journal of Public Sector Management* 15 (5): 412–431.

Zahra, S. A., E. Gedajlovic, D. O. Neubaum, and J. M. Shulman. 2009. "A Typology of Social Entrepreneurs: Motives, Search Processes and Ethical Challenges." *Journal of Business Venturing* 24 (5): 519–532.

Index

ADMRP *see* anticipated discounted marginal revenue products
aggregation 228
Alford, R. F. G. 43n6
anticipated discounted marginal revenue products (ADMRP) 160, 165
Arce, Daniel 18
Ashenfelter, Orley C. 172
Austrian school 2, 23, 53, 145n5
Austro-Wicksellian theory 46n31, 54

backward-bending labor supply curve 4, 37–43, 46n30
Baron, D. P. 261n10
barter 95, 208, 221n3
Belante, Don 172
Benham, Frederic 86–87
Bernoulli, D. 144
Blair, Roger D. 169
Blaug, Mark, 69n2
Block, Walter 166n2, 187n15, 222n11
Böhm-Bawerk, Eugen von 2–3, 6, 31, 43n2, 44n14, 51, 54, 63, 143, 145n13, 157, 162, 170, 177, 178, 182, 184, 186n8, 199–200, 201
Boyes, William J. 24n6
brands 85, 86, 199, 255
Braun, Eduard 13, 23; *Finance Behind the Veil of Money* 20, 22
Buchanan, James 30, 39, 46n31, 214; *Cost and Choice* 7; *L.S.E. Essays on Cost* 7
Buridan ass problem 22, 25n17
business plan 192, 194, 218
Bylund, Per L. 6, 217, 219, 222n16

capital-asset pricing model 133, 140–141
capital assets 133, 140; realist approach on return 141–143
capitalism 16, 180, 182–183, 187n9, 187n17, 218, 225
capitalist-entrepreneurs 5, 30, 32, 52, 53, 57, 59, 62, 63, 75, 150, 155, 156, 157–158, 159, 160, 161, 164, 165, 177–179, 183, 184, 185, 220; capitalist-entrepreneur and optimal level of investment in a firm 64–69;
Caplan, B. 38, 43, 46nn28–29
cartel action 89–90
case probability and class probability 134–136, 144
causal-realist theory 2, 4–5, 6, 7, 11–13, 16, 17, 18, 22, 23, 23n4, 43n2, 44n14, 45n21, 45n26, 51, 147–148, 149, 152, 156, 162–163, 165, 185; Menger 3; *see also* costs and pricing; income effect" in causal-realist price theory; monopsony
ceteris paribus 28, 29, 35, 36, 40, 125, 148
Chamberlain, Edward H. 127
Chiang, Eric 24n8
Chicago school 30, 52, 69n1
Clark, John Bates 2, 43n2, 62
Coase, Ronald 5, 69n1, 207–208, 209, 212–214, 215–219, 220, 221n2, 221nn5–6, 221n9, 222n10, 222nn13–17, 237, 240n4; "The Nature of the Firm" 210–211, 216, 219
Coke, Lord 84
comparative advantage 7, 13
competitive-monopoly price distinction 53, 68; perfect-imperfect competition 55–60
competitive prices 5, 53, 55, 56, 57, 65, 74, 95, 111, 174, 176; monopoly 56, 83–90, 110, 127n15, 127n17, 173, 185
constant outlay 54, 74, 108, 109; combinations 91–92, 94, 107; curves *60*, 97–99, *98*, 101, *102*, 104; line 103, 104, 105–106; schedule 96
constant product 93; combinations 92, 94, 95, 100, 128n34; curves *100*, 100–101,

102, 103, 104; schedules 74, 95, 100, 104; substitution 54, 74
cost-curve analysis 52, 156
cost-cutting 231, 235, 236
costs and pricing 191–201; Austrian take on markup pricing 195–201; execution of economic calculation 196–198; imputation process 198–200; out of equilibrium 195–196; Post-Keynesian challenges to neoclassical marginalism 191–194; relevance of fixed costs 200–201
cost structure 149, 150, 152, 153, 156, 158, 159, *159*, 163, 164, 165, 166, 227, 228, 229, 236

Dacin, M. T. 260n2
Dacin, P. A. 260n2
Dahlman, 211, 222n12
Davenport, Herbert J. 2, 43, 43n2, 45n19
demand curve: causal influence of output prices 60–63; downward-sloping 56, 57, 59; individual *40*; individual scale of values 30–31; "instantaneous" 28, 35–36; Marshallian 28; neoclassical controversy 28–30, 57, 60; purchasing power of money 34
Demsetz, Harold 220, 221n9
Denis, Andy 225–226, 232
DMRP *see* discounted marginal revenue products
discounted marginal revenue products (DMRP) 5, 62–63, 156, 160, 182; *see also* anticipated discounted marginal revenue products
Dorfman, Joseph 128n32

economic calculation 5–6, 30, 32, 59, 210, 214–215, 220, 222n13, 225, 228, 232, 237–238, 243–260, 260n4; complementary social enterprises 253–256; entrepreneurship 244–250; execution 196–198; integrated social enterprises 256–259; limits of social enterprise firm 253–259; marginal costs 198; socialism 237–238; social entrepreneurship 244–250
equal-liberty movement 127n21
Ekelund, R. B. 43nn4–6
entrepreneurship: cost of production 24n15; decision making 226–228; economic calculation 244–250; neo-classical 150, 156; uncertainty 6, 59, *164*, 218, 219, 222n17, 229, 230, 231, 232, 233, 237, 247, 250, 260n4; versus management 230–233; *see also* capitalist-entrepreneurs; social entrepreneurship
ERE *see* Evenly Rotating Economy
Evenly Rotating Economy (ERE) 62, 63, 66, 67–68, 115, 116, 129n49, 154, 155, 157, *157*, *158*, *160*, 163, 222n12
ex ante nature of valuations 12, 20, 24n16, 35, 45nn23–24, 144, 196
ex post 22, 24n13, 24n16, 144

Farber, Henry 172
Farrell, M. J. 235
Ferraro, Paul J. 11, 15–16
Fetter, Frank A. 2, 43, 43n2, 54, 55, 76, 126n5, 176, 255; pure-time preference 51
final supply curve 75, 125, *125*, 126, 126n1
Fisher, Irving 43n3, 140; *The Nature of capital and Income* 145n7
forgone opportunities 12, 15, 24n14
Friedman, Milton 28–30, 32, 43nn6–7, 52; "The Marshallian Demand Curve" 28; positivism 17

Giffen Paradox 27, 43n7, 44n8
Gonzalez, R. 27, 38
gross revenue 32, 78–79, *79*, 80, *82*, 83, 111, 121, 202n5

Harrison, Jeffrey L. 169
Hayek, Friedrich August 44n15, 51, 52, 59, 197
Herbener, Jeffrey M. 6, 24n10, 24n15, 229
Hershey Chocolate Company 59
Hicks, John R. 27, 28, 30, 32, 38, 39, 41, 43, 43n5, 44n8, 46nn29–30
Hirschleifer, David 69n8
Howden, David 22, 24n13
Hülsmann, Jörg Guido 4, 212, 213

immediate-run analysis 154, 155, 160, 161
immediate-run price 154, *155*, *156*, 161, 163
imperfect competition 53, 68, 69n6, 69n11, 83, 172, 173, 174; competitive-monopoly price 55–60; perfect-versus-170, 172, 174, 185
imperfect substitutability of factors 92–93, 101

"income effect" in causal-realist price theory 27–43; backward-bending labor supply curve 4, 37–43, 46n30; *ceteris paribus* 28, 29, 35, 36, 40, 125, 148; illusion 35–36; individual scale of values and demand curve 30–31; money income or money stock 32–33; neoclassical controversy over demand curve 28–30; purchasing power of money and demand curve 34; substitution effect 4, 27, 28, 36–37, 38, 39, 61
infinitesimal calculus 129n48, 173
infinity 58, 173
"instantaneous" demand curve 28, 35–36
isoquant-isocost framework 53, 61, 63, 68, 73

Jevons, William Stanley 2, 44n14
Journal of Economic Education 11, 16

Keen, Steve 69n9
Kirzner, L. M. 44n11, 55, 59, 69nn10–11, 147, 159, 239n1, 260n5
Klein, Peter G. 53, 222n15, 239n1, 255, 260n1
Knight, Frank 38, 41, 46n30, 52, 62, 134, 219, 222n17, 239n1
Krugman, Paul 14, 23

labor supply curve 4, 46n29, 46n31, 170; backward-bending 37–43; individual 39
Lachmann, Ludwig 59, 231
Lange, Oskar 198
Langlois, Catherine 194–195
Lavoie, Marc 193
law of costs 63, 170, 171, 199, 201; non-specific factors 181–84
Law of Investment Decision 67, 74, 121
Lee, Frederic 198
Lewis, C. S.: *The Screwtape Letters* 216
long-run average cost curve (LRAC) 152, 153
long-run change 194
long-run costs 1, 152, 153, *153*
long-run demand curve 63
long-run equilibrium price 154
long-run marginal cost (LMC) 152–153
Ludwig von Mises Institute 52

Machaj, Mateusz 5
Mankiw, N. Gregory 13, 14
Manning, Alan 169, 170, 172, 173, 186n2
Marget, Arthur 44n13, 45n22
marginal costs 5, 53, 61, 139, 171, 174, 193, 194, 200–201, 202n5; curve 191, 192, 201n1; entrepreneurs 198; and production decisions 148–153
marginal net income 117–120, 121, 122, 129n47
marginal rate of production substitution 93, 101, 103
marginal revenue product (MRP) 62, 63, 148, 149, 155, 160, 162, 165, 172, 174, 183, 184, 186, 187n17
marginal unit of output in production *151*
marginal utility 2, 3, 27, 28, 29, 30, 31, 33, 34, 35, 36, 37, 38, 39, 40, 41, 42, 43, 46n30, 54, 76, 116, 162, 198, 199, 201; diminishing 152, 200
marginal pairs 31, 54, 162
market supply 44n13, 53, 57, 58, 75, 78, 79, 127n13, 180, 186n5
Markowitz, H. M. 140
Marshall, Alfred 2, 29, 41, 43n3, 43n6, 46n32, 52, 62
Marshallian demand curve 28
Marshallian partial equilibrium 4, 52, 53, 55, 56, 57, 64, 66, 68, 69n2, 184
Maryland Constitution 127n21
Mason, Will E. 43n3
Matear, M. 260n2
maximum physical output 78, 82
McCaffrey, Matthew 6, 23n4
McGraw, Hill 69n13
Menger, Carl 2, 3, 6, 27, 43n2, 44n14, 51, 55, 150, 254
Méra, Xavier 5, 57, 170, 176, 181
Mises, Ludwig von 43, 69n3, 69n10, 225, 233; acting man 23n4; "action as an exchange" 209, 260n3; "the autistic economy" 221n4; barter 208, 221n3; calculation argument 229; capital 44nn15–16; capitalism and socialism 16; case probability and class probability 134, 135, 136, 144; catallactics 44n10; causal-realist price theory 43n2, 185; competition 59, 186n4; costs and pricing 197; "costs are equal to the value attached" 23n2; difference between entrepreneurs and managers 6; economic calculation 5–6, 196, 225, 226, 232, 237, 238, 239, 243–244; entrepreneurs 164–165, 219; *Epistemological Problems of Economics* 221n3; equilibration 196; Evenly

Rotating Economy 222n12; exchange ratios 214–215; factor payments and gifts 257; fixed capital 202n5; *Human Action* 27, 53–55, 73, 147–148, 221n3; human action 23n1; ideal types 220; imperfect/perfect competition dichotomy 174; impossibility theorem 208; income effect 38; "intellectual division of labor" 217; labor factors 175; marginal revenue 200–201; market socialism 197, 221n8, 237, 238; mechanical metaphors 211–212; money assets 33; monopoly price-gap 176–177, 185, 187n14; monoposony 177, 178, 181, 187n14; non-specific factor 182; "originary interest rate" 179, 187n10; perfect and imperfect competition 69n11, 170, 174; praxeology 45n26, 54, 173, 176, 209; prices and income distinction 33; pricing process 31; probability analysis 134; production run 150; production theory 51, 69n3; pure time preference theory 51; regression theorem 45n17; restricted competition 186n4; "social costs or benefits" 215; social entrepreneurship 244, 245, 250; socialism 240n5; speculation 163; substitution effect 23n4, 45n26; supply and demand curve 44n9; *The Theory of Money and Credit* 221n3; time 147–148, 159, 161; value scales 31

money income 28, 29, 32–34, 35, 42, 43n6, 65, 76, 94, 95, 249; negative 113; net 108, 111, 116, 117, 119, 120, 121, 125

monopoly price 53, 54, 55, 56, 57, 59, 65, 68, 69n7, 74, 110, 111, 127n15, 173, 174, 175, 186n4; competitive prices 83–90; gap 5, 170, 176–184, 185, 186, 187n14, 187n17; *see also* competitive-monopoly price; competitive-versus-monopoly price

money returns: Jones *77*; net 77; Smith *111*, *117*, *118*, *123*

Monopolistic Competition Revolution 55

monopoly 176–179; definition 84–86; nirvana fallacy 173–174; price-gap with non-specific factors and the law of costs 181–184; price-gap with specific factors of production 179–181; theory without imperfect/perfect competition dichotomy 174–176; *see also* competitive-monopoly price distinction; ; competitive-versus-monopoly price

monopoly competitive prices 56, 83–90, 110, 127n15, 127n17, 173, 185

monopsony theory 5, 169–186, 186n6, 186n8, 187n9, 187nn13–15, 187n17; classic and new theory 171–172; monopoly 176–179; monopoly price-gap with non-specific factors and the law of costs 181–184; monopoly price-gap with specific factors of production 179–181; monopoly theory without imperfect/perfect competition dichotomy 174–176; nirvana fallacy 173–174

Mortensen, Dale T. 172

Murphy, Robert P. 14, 23

neoclassical economics 28, 43n3, 59, 64, 147, 149, 162: competitive-monopoly price distinction 55, 56; cost curves 166n1; demand curve 28–29, 57, 60; disequilibrium 67; entrepreneurs 150, 156; equilibrium 160, 165, 195; fixed prices 148; income effect 43; interest 64; Knightian input price theory 62; long-run costs 152; marginalism 150, 162, 191–194, 195, 196; MRP 62; paradigm 53; Post-Keynesian challenges 191–195, 199, 201; price theory 27; producer 64; rational choice models 18; short-run cost 148, 153; single "industries" 88; time 153, 155; utility functions 13

net income 32, 65, 74, 108, 113–126, *122*, *123*, 129n47, 177, 179, 180; rate of 113, 114, 115, 116, 119–120, 121, 124–125

Newman, Jonathan 3

Newman, Patrick 4, 73, 75

nirvana fallacy 173–174

non-specific factors 176, 178, 181–184

Nordhaus, W. D. 20, 22

Occam's Razor 195

O'Donnell, Rod 18–19

offer curve 41, 46n32

opportunity-cost doctrine 20, 21, 22

opportunity cost theory 11–23; Braun follows Reisman 22–23; causal-realist theory 11–13; critical views in Austrian literature 20–23; critics 18–19; definition 11–15; Ferraro and Taylor spark debate 15–16; mainstream confusion 15–20; Parkin's "reexamination" 16–18; production tradeoffs 19–20; textbook examples 13–15

"originary interest rate" 179, 187n10

Parkin, Michael 16–19, 24n11
Patinkin, D. 45n21
perfect-versus-imperfect competition 170, 172, 174, 185
period of production 76–77, 150, 151
Perry, Arthur Latham 127n24
Pigou, A. C. 38, 41, 46n30
point of tangency 103, 104
Post-Keynesian theories 5, 196, 197, 198, 199, 201, 201n3; Austro- 191–195
praxeology 23n4, 45n26, 51, 173, 176, 209, 218, 228
price assumption 58, 69n5
production coefficients 69n12, 74, 91
productions costs 133, 165, 176, 195, 236; constant output *93*; ERE *157*, *158*
production function 69n1, 74, 78, 90, 91, 95, 99, 108, 125, 152, 198
production tradeoffs 13, 14, 16; opportunity costs 19–20, 23
profit motive 6, 244, 247–250, 251
profits and losses 66, 134, 150, 179, 196, 200
psychic: benefits 254; considerations 120; cost 248; ends 250; factors 77, 115, 124; income 34, 95, 126n5, 214, 248, 261n9; nonmonetary matters 95; profit 13, 25, 121, 124, 248, 249, 251, 257, 260n3; revenue 121; time preference rates 121
purchasing power of money 28–29, 32, 34, 36, 43nn5–6, 45nn18–19, 45n21, 133

Quarterly Journal of Austrian Economics 20, 22

Rajsic, P. 46n29
Ransom, Michael R. 172
rate of outlay substitution 91, 92, 96, 97, 98, 103, 109
reciprocal demand 41, *41*, 46n32
regression theorem 45n17
Reisman, George 13, 23, 24n12, 24n14; *Capitalism* 20–22
restriction of production 57, 83, 86
Ricardo, David 145n13, 198, 201n3
risk premium 4, 133–144, 145n5, 145n12; capital-asset pricing model 140–141; case probability and class probability 134–136; filter of relevance 136–138; mirage 139–143; production of success 138–139; realist approach on return on capital assets 141–143; realist approach to human action under uncertainty 136–139; risks as costs 143–144
Ritenour, Shawn 14–15, 23
Robbins, Lionel 2, 38–39, 40, 41, 42, 43, 43n2, 46nn30–31
Rothbard, Murray 5, 22, 23n2, 27, 46n2851–69, 69nn3–4, 69n9, 73–126; "action as an exchange" 209; aggressive violence 186n2; capitalist-entrepreneur and optimal level of investment in a firm 64–68; causal-realist price theory 43n2, 45n26, 149, 185; Coasean framework 69n1; competitive price and monopoly price 83–90; competitive-monopoly price and perfect-imperfect competition 55–60; cost curve 150; " 'Cost' is simply the utility of the next best alternative" 23n2; costs 156–157; demand curve 69n12, 187n16; demand for a firm's product 75–83; economic calculation 222n13; elastic demand curve 69n11; entrepreneurship 145n5, 151, 156; equilibrium 187n11; ERE 155; *ex ante* nature of valuations 12, 20, 24n16, 35, 45nn23–24, 144, 196; factor demand curve and causal influence of output prices 60–63; factor ratios 69n12; final supply curve 75, 125, 125–126, 126n1, 129n51; fixed prices 148; historical overview 53–55; imperfect/perfect competition dichotomy 174; income effect 43; income taxation 27, 38, 42; individual's value scale 44n11; labor factors 175; *Man, Economy, and State* 4, 33–34, 36, 38, 42, 51, 52, 54, 73–126, 147–148; marginal unit of output in production *151*; monopoly 69n7, 127n17, 127n19, 127n22, 175, 176, 181, 185, 187n14; monopsony 170, 172, 173, 174, 176, 177; nirvana fallacy 173–174; non-specific factor 182, 183; opportunity cost 152; ordinal value-scale approach 46n29; output and investment decision of producer 105–126; perfect-versus-imperfect competition paradigm 170; producer's activity 73–126; product and outlay schedules of the firm 90–104; product and outlay schedules of the firm-mathematical analysis 96–104; production function 69n1, 74, 78, 90, 91, 95, 99, 108, 125, 152, 198; production relationships 148; production theory 51–69, 148; profits and losses 150; short-run cost curves 148; speculation 159; time 147, 149,

153–154; "Toward a Reconstruction of Utility and Welfare Economics" 24n5; wages 178

Salerno, Joseph T. 3, 4, 198, 240n5
Salin, P. 38
Samuelson, Paul A. 20, 22
Smith, Adam 127n24
social enterprises 243–256; integrated 256–259; limits of firm 253–259; uncertainty 254, 258
social entrepreneurship 6; decision making 226–228; definition 260n2, 261n10; economic calculation 244, 250–252; economic foundations 244–250; profit motive 247–250; social action 245–247; versus management 230–233
socialism 225–239; calculation 237–238; cost destroys value 233–236; entrepreneurial decision-making 226–228; entrepreneurship versus management 230–233; value as basis for factor prices 228–230
socialist calculation 237–238
Stigler, George 52, 54, 58, 62, 63, 69n12
Stone, Daniel 18, 24n11
subjective value 2, 3, 14, 16, 30, 133, 136, 141, 144; filter of relevance 136–138
substitution effect 4, 27, 28, 36–37, 38, 39, 61, *61*

Taylor, Laura O. 11, 15–16
"technocratic fallacy" 128n35
technology 6, 14, 55, 90–95, 99, 108, 115, 117, 119, 128n35, 153, 210, 234
theory of investment 64, 67, 75, 114
theory of value 2, 45n24, 213, 222n16, 249
Thompson, Henry 46n32
Thompson, John L. 250
time 147–166; discounting and costs 153–160; marginal costs and production decisions 148–153; uncertainty and cost 161–165
Topan, Mihai-Vladimir 5
trademarks 85
transaction cost economics 12, 207–221; Coase and relationships 218–219; definition of "transactions" and "transaction costs" 210–212; Demsetz observation 220; false dialectic 208–210; firm 215–216; imperialism 217–218; property rights 212–215; serfdom and the firm 216–217; zero-transaction cost world 218
true value specification 11, 17–18
Tucker, Benjamin R. 90

uncertainty 13, 238, 239; business plan 194; change 159; entrepreneurs 6, 59, *164*, 218, 219, 222n17, 229, 230, 231, 232, 233, 237, 247, 250, 260n4; equilibrium 63, 155, 219, 220; future price 115, 160; immediate-run price, *163*; owner of the capital 234; price system 250, 254; rate of return 66, 116; realist approach to human action 134, 136–139; risk 4–5; social enterprise 254, 258; speculation 159–160; time 160, *160*, *161*, 161–165

value: basis for factor prices 228–230; cost destroys 233–236
value creation 230, 231, 232, 233, 234, 236, 237, 238, 239, 239n3
value scales 3, 4, 12, 14, 23n2, 27, 31, 32, 33, 35, 36, 42, 43, 44n11, 77, 89, 116, 120, 128n32, 252; ordinal 28, 38, 46n29; subjective 30; unitary 34, 37
value specification 11, 16–18
Volker Fund 53

Walras, Léon 2, 27, 52, 62, 69n2, 198
Weiler, Emanuel T. 54, 61, 69n12
Wells, Robin 14, 23n3
White House Council of Economic Advisers 169
Wicksteed, Philip 2, 40, 43, 43n2, 44nn11–12, 44n14, 45n19, 45n25, 46n31, 51
Williamson, Oliver E. 207, 216, 221n6, 221n8, 222n15; *The Economic Institutions of Capitalism* 217; Mechanisms of Governance 217; "The Technology of Transacting" 210–211

Yeager, Leland 28, 30, 43n4, 44n8